*Newest ed 5/2004*

# BOSTON &
# NEW ENGLAND

FODOR'S TRAVEL PUBLICATIONS
NEW YORK • TORONTO • LONDON • SYDNEY • AUCKLAND

Published in the United States by Fodor's Travel
Publications.
Published in the United Kingdom by AA Publishing.

Fodor's is a registered trademark of Random House, Inc.

ISBN 0-679-00702-4
ISSN 1095-4554
Fourth Edition

**Fodor's Exploring Boston & New England**

Authors: **Tim Locke and Sue Gordon**
Additional material: **Sean Connolly**
Cartography: **The Automobile Association**
Cover design: **Tigist Getachew, Fabrizio La Rocca**
Front cover top photograph: **The Automobile Association**
Front cover silhouette: **Peter Guttman**

Printed and bound in Italy by Printer Trento srl.
10 9 8 7 6 5 4 3 2 1

# How to use this book

## ORGANIZATION

### New England Is, New England Was
Discusses aspects of life and culture in contemporary New England and explores significant periods in the region's history.

### A–Z
Breaks down the region into state chapters, and covers places to visit, including walks and drives. Within this section fall the Focus On articles, which consider a variety of subjects in greater detail.

### Travel Facts
Contains the strictly practical information vital for a successful trip.

### Accommodations & Restaurants
Lists recommended establishments throughout New England, giving a brief summary of their attractions.

## ABOUT THE RATINGS
Most places described in this book have been given a separate rating:

▶▶▶    Do not miss

▶▶    Highly recommended

▶    Worth seeing

## MAP REFERENCES
To make the location of a particular place easier to find, every main entry in this book is given a map reference to the right of its name. This includes a number, followed by a letter, followed by another number, such as 139D2. The first number (139) indicates the page on which the map can be found. The letter (D) and the second number (2) pinpoint the square in which the main entry is located. The maps on the inside front cover and inside back cover are referred to as IFC and IBC, respectively.

## ADMISSION CHARGES
Standard admission charges are categorized in this book as follows:

| Inexpensive | Under $5 |
| Moderate | $5–10 |
| Expensive | $10 or over |

# Contents

How to use this book  4

Contents pages  5–7

My New England  8

**NEW ENGLAND IS**  9–26
  A regional view  10–11
  Architecture  12–13
  The economy  14–15
  Shopping  16–17
  The fall  18–19
  Cuisine  20–21
  Academia  22–23

A musical tradition  24–25
Film and drama  26

**NEW ENGLAND WAS**  27–47
  Natives and explorers  28–29
  Friction and dissent  30–31
  The Revolution  32–33
  Seafaring  34–35
  The new industrialists  36–37
  Immigrants  38–39
  Early tourism  40–41
  Top politicians  42–43
  The art scene  44–45
  Writers and thinkers  46–47

6

## A–Z

**Boston** 48–85
  Introduction 50–51
  Getting around 52–53
  Events 54
  Boston A to Z 66–73
  Cambridge 74–75
  **Focus On**
  Paul Revere 55
  The pulse of Boston 56–57
  The Boston Symphony Orchestra 79
  Sports 81
  **Walks**
  The Freedom Trail: Part I 58–59
  The Freedom Trail: Part II 60–61
  Back Bay 62–63
  Beacon Hill 64–65
  Harvard and Cambridge highlights
    76–77

**Connecticut** 86–107
  **Focus On**
  The New England village 100

**Drive**
  The Litchfield Hills 98–99

**Maine** 108–137
  **Focus On**
  Lobster fishing 116
  Native Americans today 124–125
  Outdoor recreation 132–133
  **Drive**
  Acadia's Park Loop Road 114–115

**Massachusetts** 138–187
  **Focus On**
  The Shakers 148–149
  Norman Rockwell 150
  Lighthouses 153
  Coastal wildlife 164–165
  Emily Dickinson 176
  The Pilgrim Fathers 180–181
  The Salem witches 183

**New Hampshire** 188–209
  **Focus On**
  Christmas and First Night 194

Forest wildlife 200–201
Robert Frost 209
**Drive**
The White Mountains 206–227

**Rhode Island** 210–221

**Vermont** 222–243
**Focus On**
Winter sports 228–229
Vermont specialties 234
Folk art and crafts 238–239
**Drive**
Southern Vermont 240–241

**New England for children**
244–246

**TRAVEL FACTS** 247–266
Arriving 248–249
Essentials 250–253
Getting around 254–259
Communications 260–261
Emergencies 262–263
Other information 264–265
Tourist offices 266

**ACCOMMODATIONS &
RESTAURANTS** 267–283

**Index** 284–288

**Picture credits** 288

**Maps and plans**
New England: states and three-star
sights IFC and IBC
Boston 48–49
Boston subway 52

Cambridge 74
Connecticut 86–87
New Haven 102
Maine 108
Acadia National Park 112
Penobscot Bay 129
Massachusetts 138–139
Cape Cod and the Islands 156–157
Lexington and Concord 168–169
Plymouth 177
Salem 184
New Hampshire 188
The White Mountains 204
Rhode Island 210
Newport 214
Providence 219
Vermont 222

**Tim Locke has
traveled widely in
Europe, the U.S.A., and
the Far East.** In his
native Britain he has
written several books
on walking, as well as
guidebooks to scenic
regions of England. He
is the author of *Fodor's
Exploring Britain* and
contributed to
*Germany* and *Thailand*
in the same series.

**Sue Gordon** is the
author of *CityPack
Boston* and *Explore
Britain's Villages,* and
has contributed to
several walks books,
including *Walking
Britain's Rivers and
Canals* and *Country
Walks and Scenic
Drives.* Tim and Sue
are also guidebook
editors.

# My New England

Those six little states that are crammed into the northeastern corner of the map of the U.S.A. must be one of the
most written-up and talked-about areas of the world.
They represent much of a great nation's historical and
cultural emergence, the roots of modern America.

To me they are a never-ending source of discovery.
The quintessential aspects of New England's character—
its village greens, its delightful architectural variety, its
covered bridges, its wooded hills, to name but a few—
stay in the memory of all visitors.

But the more I see of the region, the more I realize how
much there is yet to explore. Boston is a great city of
many facets: follow the red line of the Freedom Trail and
in a few hours you have a remarkable cross-section of its
history. Yet the city harbors many lesser-known gems
too—my favorites include the Athenaeum (which Sue
Gordon urged me to visit), with its bookish tranquillity,
the surreal stained-glass Mapparium, with its extraordinary echo, and the gas-lit backstreets of Beacon Hill.

History and heritage are celebrated with flair at the
great museums at Mystic, Plymouth, Sturbridge,
Shelburne, Strawbery Banke, and elsewhere. Yet equally
memorable are some of the more modest parcels of a
well-preserved past: among those that spring to mind are
the idiosyncratic Paper House near Rockport and Mount
Washington's little steam train.

The natural scene is blessed with delightfully distinct
seasons. The fall foliage presents a truly spectacular
show, while the winter snows again transform the scene
magically. I savor impressions of the view on a summer
dawn from Mount Cadillac in Acadia National Park,
looking along the indented coast of Maine and across the
vast inland forests and folded hills. And of basking in a
hot outdoor tub in an inn in Stowe, Vermont, with
snowflakes falling gently on me in the dark, after a day's
cross-country skiing in the birchwoods. Meanwhile, the
events calendar is busy with country fairs, bean
cookouts, maple sugaring, historical reenactments, and
more—encouraging a return visit at any time of year.

I find New England gives a warm welcome second to
none. It is a friend for life.
**Tim Locke**

# New England Is

*The states of Massachusetts, Connecticut, Rhode Island, New Hampshire, Vermont, and Maine constitute New England. Although relatively small in area, this is the cultural and historic cradle of the nation. There are qualities that characterize the region as a whole, but there are also subtle differences within it.*

**THE ELEMENTS** The clichés have their own element of truth: against a blue sky, the wood steeple of a church stands high over a village green fringed with neat, white clapboard houses. Back roads wind over covered bridges and through seemingly endless forests that in the fall burst into brilliant hues of russet, gold, and crimson. Bright orange pumpkins lie stacked in mounds by wood barns and on farm stands. Lighthouses look out over the ocean from shores of rock and sand. Fishing boats unload the daily catch, and lobster and clam chowder appear on virtually every menu.

New England is a region of firsts, in industrialization and historical events. It has been the seedbed of intellectual and political thought for three centuries. It has magnificent art collections in museums, colleges, and universities. New England has produced—and continues to produce—many great names in music, art, and literature.

New England has a small-scale quality that is an integral part of its charm, and has been described as "America with the volume turned down." Many of the region's inhabitants greatly value their

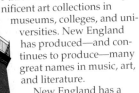

*Point Judith Light, Rhode Island*

*A white steeple framed by autumn foliage: quintessential New England at Sugar Hill, New Hampshire*

lifestyle and are fiercely proud of their history and roots. The Yankee mentality—formed by a keen work ethic, frugality, shrewdness, and a serious, conservative outlook—is deeply ingrained.

**EARLY DAYS** The great ice masses that once covered this land have left their mark. Glaciers sculpted the mountains and valleys, and created a deeply indented coastline. The landscape was scoured, and the bedrock and boulder-strewn earth proved infertile for the first farmers. On this soil the first European settlers established themselves, primarily along the coast and the rivers. The Pilgrim Fathers arrived from England aboard the *Mayflower* in 1620. More than a century later, in 1775, the first shots

10

of the American Revolution at Lexington and Concord signaled the end of British colonial rule.

As settlers moved westward over the continent, New England's farmlands were gradually abandoned, and the trees, once cleared by the farmers, reestablished themselves. Today, some 80 percent of New England is forested, and much of Vermont, New Hampshire, and inland Maine is also hilly or mountainous and sparsely settled.

**VISITING THE REGION** Boston is by far the largest city, and one that every visitor to the region should see. The Freedom Trail wends an intricate route past the city's historic sites. This is a city of superb museums, excitingly contrasting neighborhoods, and striking architecture. Visitors without a car can find plenty of rewarding excursions by public transportation.

New England's thick tree cover can mean that sweeping panoramic views are hard to come by, at least from a car. For the most spectacular views, however, you can take high-level walks in the White Mountains or Acadia National Park, or explore the coast by boat. Outdoor pursuits in the hills and mountains of northern New England are well developed and include winter sports, water sports, hiking, and fishing. The region's southern states— Massachusetts, Rhode Island, and

Connecticut—are more densely populated and have more historic sights.

The long and complex seaboard has a lasting appeal, with the sandy beaches of Cape Cod, the islands, and southern Maine among the most popular. There are many opportunities for cruises and sailing, and a number of museums commemorate New England's maritime heritage, including the vanished whaling industry. Today, whale-watching cruises are big business, and no visitor should miss the chance to join an exhilarating tour to the feeding grounds of the humpback whales.

New England's charms change with the seasons. Spring brings freshness and greenery. In summer, delicious Atlantic breezes make the coast a pleasant retreat from the heat, while fall's foliage is deservedly famous. Winters are harsh but bring photogenic snowfalls and a Christmas-card look as sports enthusiasts put on their skis.

*With so much of the area heavily forested, clapboard is widespread*

11

*Explore New England and you experience a range of building styles from early Colonial through to postmodernism. White clapboard is an integral feature of New England's charm and is a dominant theme outside the major cities; observe closely and you should be able to identify stylistic variations.*

12

**EARLY COLONIAL** The early English colonists brought with them a tradition of building in wood and, as hardwoods were plentiful in New England, the timber-framed house became—and remains—universal. The frames were covered with cedar shingles or clapboards, which were painted in a variety of colors. Built with steep roofs, as they had been back home to help the rain run off, the earliest Colonial houses had an overhanging upper story, central chimney, and small, irregular casement windows. The steeper the roof, the older the house. Quite commonly, a lean-to was added at the back under one sloping roof, the outline giving rise to the term "saltbox." Few of the very earliest houses survive, although Paul Revere's House in Boston and the House of Seven Gables in Salem, Massachusetts, date from the late 1600s.

*Colonial: the Mission House (1739) at Stockbridge, Massachusetts*

**GEORGIAN** The classical Palladian style that was introduced to Britain from Italy reached eastern New England in the 18th century. The handsome houses in this style, many built by wealthy maritime traders, are recognizable by their strict symmetry. Still in clapboard, they typically have a hipped roof, a central door that is sometimes pilastered, and equally spaced sash windows; Portsmouth, New Hampshire (see pages 202–203), has a number of Palladian-style residences. Many modern clapboard houses are still built in this manner.

**FEDERAL** After Independence, Charles Bulfinch (see panel on page 72) introduced the neoclassical Adamesque style, known as Federal, with public buildings such as the State House in Boston and, notably, his Beacon Hill development of genteel, redbrick homes for the elite (see pages 64–65). These stand proudly foursquare, lightly detailed, with a shallow, sometimes balustraded, hipped roof, an imposing porch, and a fan-shaped window over the door. Inside, rooms may be oval, circular, or polygonal, with cornices and fireplaces decorated with garlands and urns of flowers. Salem, Massachusetts, and Providence, Rhode Island, have some of the finest examples of the Federal style.

**VICTORIAN** After the mid-1820s the design of public, academic, and domestic building became more diversified, reflecting European influences. Boston's Quincy Market is an example of the Greek Revival style, featuring the columns and pediments of ancient Greek temples. The Gothic Revival style is easily recognized by

*Above: a Second Empire house in Kennebunk, ME*
*Right: the Federal-style Goodwin Mansion, Strawbery Banke, NH*

its steeply pitched gables, turrets, and intricately carved bargeboards. Italianate buildings (from 1840) include Victoria Mansion in Portland (see page 134). A variety of historical and decorative elements such as mansard roofs and ironwork balconies characterize the Second Empire style (from 1860), Parisian buildings being a major source of inspiration. The Queen Anne style owes little to the English Queen Anne period but is characterized by contrasts of texture—often shingle and clapboard laid out decoratively—as well as of color and form; tall chimneys and round verandas are typical hall-marks. The Renaissance Revival style of the 1880s and 1890s, used for some public buildings such as the Boston Public Library, is also termed "Beaux Arts." The architect of Boston's Trinity Church gave his name to the uniquely American Richardson Romanesque style, notable for its heavy stonework with chunky columns and arches. Many Victorian styles are represented in Newport's fabulously ornate man-sions. Boston's Back Bay, one of history's most splendid pieces of urban planning, also makes a won-derful sampler of Victorian architecture, with bow-fronted rowhouses of various styles (see pages 62–63).

*A Cape Cod vignette: painted clapboard, screen door, and wreath*

**MODERN** By far the most exciting contemporary architecture in New England is to be found in Boston and Cambridge. The leading architects are international: I.M. Pei, responsible for the city's 1970s rejuvenation scheme, and the Bauhaus architect Walter Gropius.

Two houses by great 20th-century architects that are open to visitors are the Gropius House in Lincoln, Massachusetts (see page 170), and Frank Lloyd Wright's Zimmerman House in Manchester, New Hampshire (see page 198).

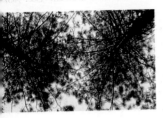

*After the demise of its maritime trade and then its textile industry, the region is now one of the country's main centers of technology. Tourism is of major importance, and, although agriculture and fishing are of somewhat diminishing significance, the pulp and paper trade is a high-growth area.*

*Farming meets tourism: orchards and cider mills welcome visitors*

## INSURANCE, INDUSTRY, EDUCATION, AND RESEARCH

Hartford, Connecticut, is the "Insurance City." The business started in the 19th century, in the heyday of New England's shipping trade, and today some of the country's largest insurance companies have their headquarters here.

The academic institutions of New England make a significant contribution to the economy, partly by generating business locally, but chiefly through the research and development work on which the region's electronics and communications industries depend. Connecticut has acquired the nickname of the "Gadget State," but the manufacture of electronic components and machinery is also the economic mainstay of Rhode Island, Massachusetts (particularly along Route 128), and the southern part of New Hampshire.

**TOURISM** The wealthy of the Northeast recognized New England's potential as a summer playground at the end of the 19th century. Today, with the continuing popularity of snow sports, the region attracts as many visitors in winter as in summer to its mountain and coastal areas. In addition to these natural assets (and not forgetting the glory of the region's autumn foliage), the tourist industry can draw on a particularly fine maritime heritage. Tourism is New England's second largest industry, after health care.

> ❑ Pulp and paper mills at Rumford and Jay in Maine manufacture 1,500 tons of paper daily for books, magazines, catalogues, and business stationery, with those at Bucksport and Madawaska following not far behind. ❑

**THE LUMBER TRADE** A visitor to the northern areas of New England cannot fail to be impressed by the extent of the tree cover—some 80 percent in New Hampshire and Vermont, and 90 percent in Maine. It should come as no surprise that these forests make a substantial impact on the region's economy, to the tune of some $6 billion a year, although in Maine, for instance, less than 3 percent of the total forested area is actually

I Have Visited
COLD HOLLOW
CIDER MILL
...erbury Center
...mont 056...

**14**

harvested. Maine is the second largest paper-producing state (after Wisconsin) in the U.S.A., making around 4 million tons of paper per annum. The building trade and furniture makers also make significant use of what is a relatively new natural resource, for only a century ago most of the region's timber was cleared for farmland. Today, both environmentalists and the trade are anxious to ensure that this rapidly expanding industry is managed well.

**FARMING, FISHING, AND QUARRYING** Vermont is traditionally associated with dairy farming, and this is still an important part of the state economy, albeit a declining one. The state also specializes in turkeys.

Rhode Island is known for the breed of hen named Rhode

*There are about 2,400 dairy farms in Vermont, each with an average of 70 cows*

Island Red. Immense quantities of potatoes are grown in northern Maine, the third largest crop in the country after Idaho and Washington. Other crops include tobacco in the Connecticut River Valley, blueberries in Maine, and cranberries near Plymouth, Massachusetts, and on Cape Cod and the nearby islands.

The fishing industry is in decline. There is foreign competition in the Atlantic fishing grounds, and stocks of cod and haddock have been depleted, but fishing is still vital in ports such as Gloucester and Cape Ann in Massachusetts, and in the many lobstering ports along the coast of Maine.

New Hampshire, the "Granite State," has many granite quarries. Vermont's Green Mountains are also quarried for granite, at Barre (see page 226), and for marble, at Proctor (see page 235).

*Lobstering in Maine alone brings in over $70 million a year*

15

*For anyone who considers shopping one of life's pleasures, New England has to be paradise. It is particularly famed for its antiques and crafts, for the local produce sold at farm stands and in country stores, and for its factory outlets.*

For a taste of everything New England has to offer, shopaholics need to visit a factory outlet, an antiques shop or fair, a crafts gallery or show, a village store, a farm shop, and some of the one-of-a-kind shops that proliferate throughout the region. Museum shops often make good browsing territory; for example, Mystic Seaport's bookstore has a huge range of maritime titles as well as the museum's own CDs of sea shanties. Then there is always the shopping mall: in Boston, try the

*The outlet store (above, one of dozens in Freeport, Maine) and the village store (right) offer two very different shopping experiences. Every visitor should try them both at least once*

Prudential Center and Copley Place or, for a really grand one, Chestnut Hill. (For more on shopping in Boston, see pages 82–83.)

**FACTORY OUTLETS** Love it or loathe it, outlet shopping is one of New England's big draws. All manner of merchandise—clothing, household goods, and gifts—is offered at these manufacturers' and distributors' outlets, either at wholesale prices or at discounts varying from 25 to 80 percent. Bargains include older lines

being sold off as well as other items made specifically for the outlets; many places have quarterly sales for which it is worth timing a visit precisely. Well-known brand names to be found include L.L. Bean (the famous mail-order clothing company), Liz Claiborne, Calvin Klein, Benetton, Black & Decker, Van Heusen, Polo/Ralph Lauren, Levi, Nautica, Samsonite—the list is endless. The outlet capitals of New England are Kittery and Freeport (also the home of L.L. Bean) in Maine (see also panel on page 128); Fall River in southern Massachusetts; and North Conway—also known as Mount Washington Valley— in New Hampshire (particularly popular because New Hampshire has no sales tax). Worcester Common, Massachusetts, has 90 stores, all together and under cover at the heart of the city, with direct Peter Pan buses (see page 259) from Boston reducing the journey time

*Bargain hunters in Boston's downtown area make for Filene's Basement, where goods are reduced according to how long they have been on display*

considerably. There are also scores of smaller complexes in many other towns throughout the region.

**ANTIQUES** Although some visitors come to New England simply for the outlets, others come purely for the antiques-hunting. Cape Cod, the Berkshires, much of Vermont, and Newport, Rhode Island, have particular concentrations of antiques shops, but it is hard to go anywhere without coming across an emporium of some sort, whether it trades in rusty farm tools or exquisite European furniture. The best bargains may be in flea markets and antiques shows (listed locally), but

---

❏ New England's most famous country store is in Weston, Vermont, where artifacts from the past jostle for space with Vermont Common Crackers, penny candy, and much more. For a mail-order catalogue, tel: 802/824–3184. ❏

---

❏ For a full list of crafts outlets, including shows, see official state guides and local listings. The League of New Hampshire Craftsmen (205 North Main Street, Concord, NH 03301), the Maine Crafts Association (15 Walton Street, Portland, ME 04103), and the Vermont Crafts Council (P.O. Box 938, Montpelier, VT 05601) publish touring guides to studios, shops, fairs, and galleries. ❏

---

you need to know what you are doing. The biggest shows are held in May, July, and September in Brimfield, Massachusetts.

**CRAFTS** Visitors to New England can buy examples of traditional and contemporary crafts at a broad range of prices in shops and galleries. At any time, in any area, you will also be able to find a craft fair within easy distance. The Annual League of New Hampshire Craftsmen Fair, the oldest in the nation, is held in the second week of August at Newbury in New Hampshire. Some fairs are restricted to "juried" designers who have been judged to meet the highest of standards. These standards are reflected in the prices, but the quality is outstanding. Excellent crafts can be found all over New England, but it is in Vermont that arts and crafts are particularly important. The Vermont State Craft Center at Frog Hollow has retail galleries in Burlington, Middlebury, and Manchester, and there are dozens of other outlets throughout the state.

17

*In the northeast states, the weather conditions and the variety of broad-leaved trees combine perfectly to produce a sensational display of autumn color. During September and October, virtually the whole of New England is given over to the fall.*

*The red maple brings the first hint of color to the hillsides*

❏ In September and October, call Foliage Hotlines for a free events calendar, a foliage guide, and regularly updated reports. Connecticut: 800/282–6863. Maine: 888/624–6345 or 800/533–9595. Massachusetts: 800/227–6277. New Hampshire: 800/258–3608 or 800/262–6660. Rhode Island: 401/222–2601 or 800/556–2484. Vermont: 802/828–3239. Or you can visit the official website: www.leafpeepers.com. ❏

Vast areas of New England are forested, and where, over the years, loggers have felled the evergreen softwoods, hardwoods have grown in their place, creating a full palette of autumn colors. Like the richest of oriental carpets, the vivid reds of the red maple, sugar maple, sweetgum, blackgum, sassafras, red oak, and scarlet oak interweave with the deep reddish purples of the sumacs and dogwoods, the golden yellows of the hickories, trembling aspen, and birches, and the rich bronzes and browns of beech and the other oaks.

**THE CAUSE OF THE COLOR** When the Great Bear was hunted down in the heavens, so goes the Native American legend, his blood dripped onto the forests, turning some of the leaves red, while the fat that spattered out of the hunters' cooking pot turned others yellow. A more scientific explanation has to do with the food-making process that goes on in leaves. The cells in which this takes place contain pigments, notably chlorophyll, which makes leaves green. Leaves also contain carotenoids that give them a yellow color, masked during spring and summer by the larger amount of green. When the days get shorter and the nights cooler, food-making slows down, the green goes as the chlorophyll breaks up, and yellows come to the fore. Similarly, when temperatures at night drop below 45°F, sugar made during the day is trapped, forming the pigment anthocyanin, responsible, for example, for the fire engine-red color of the swamp or red maple.

No one can predict exactly when the leaf change will come, how long

the season will be, or how bright the color. The most brilliant foliage occurs when warm, sunny days are followed by cool nights. The season (about three weeks) starts in the northwest around mid-September.

**SEEING THE SHOW** Every state has a list of fall foliage attractions for enthusiasts, known locally as "leaf-peepers" (see box opposite). Roads such as the Kancamagus Highway in New Hampshire's White Mountains (see Drive on pages 206–207) and the Mohawk Trail in western

❏ "No pen can describe the turning of the leaves—the insur-rection of the tree people against the waning year. A little maple began it, flaming blood-red of a sudden where he stood against the dark green of a pine-belt. Next morning there was an answering signal from the swamp where the sumacs grow. Three days later, the hill-sides as far as the eye could range were afire, and the roads paved, with crimson and gold."
– Rudyard Kipling, *Leaves from a Winter Notebook*, 1900. ❏

Massachusetts can get very busy, and you may be better off on the back roads (see Drives on pages 98–99 and 240–241).

In Vermont, you can combine leaf-peeping with craft shows and antiques fairs, taking in some covered bridges on the way. In Maine, family outings can include visits to lighthouses and fishing villages, craft festivals and antiques fairs, farm stands and bean suppers. In New Hampshire, the Isles of Shoals Steamship Company runs cruises out of Portsmouth for a view from the sea, while the Lakes Region offers cruises where the reflections of the trees in the water provide a double dose of color. The Massachusetts fall foliage guide suggests hot-air balloon trips and areas that are ideal for boat or canoe excursions. In Connecticut, cruises go down the prettiest part of the Connecticut River.

*The gold of the sugar maple, most prominent around mid-October*

*Lobster may be the undisputed king, but seafood does not end there. And while New England is the home of maple syrup, there are many more treats for the sweet-toothed to enjoy. Orchard fruits and farm produce are of the very best.*

Traditionally, New England farmers were set up for the day with a hearty breakfast of eggs with ham. Nowadays many inns and bed-and-breakfast establishments produce similarly filling fare—typically cornmeal pancakes with maple syrup, fish cakes, and cornbread—as well as more elaborate concoctions such as puréed fruits atop waffles with sausages, or eggs with poached scallops and tarragon. In season, edible flowers sometimes put in an appearance. Later in the day, depending on the season, there may be an outdoor cookout, an ice-cream social, a clambake (see box), or a bean supper.

Baked beans, a favorite at church suppers, were invented by thrifty early colonists. Prepared in molasses, Boston baked beans, however, may be less easy to find in a restaurant than Boston cream pie, which is actually a custard-filled sponge cake covered in chocolate. Desserts tend to be very sweet and wicked. Indian pudding is a traditional recipe, a light, spicy dessert made with cornmeal and molasses. Pumpkin pie, another favorite, was also learned from the Native Americans. A more recent New England specialty is Ben & Jerry's ice cream (see pages 232 and 234).

*A blue lobster, a rare sight*

❑ The clambake is a New England tradition, an outdoor event for at least 30 or 40 people. Traditionally, a deep hole is dug in wet sand, and clams, lobsters, potatoes, corn, sausages, and chicken are steamed in it over hot rocks and covered with seaweed (or, nowadays, canvas). ❑

**SEAFOOD** Imagine a lobster 5 feet long, as they were reported to be back in colonial times, and you can understand why the Pilgrim Fathers, setting eyes on *Homarus americanus* for the first time, thought it had been sent by the Devil. Seeing the Native Americans catching the beasts, however, and feeling pangs of hunger as they waited for their first crops to take root, the early colonists soon recognized the lobster as an important food source. Before long, it was regarded as poor-man's fodder, a far cry from its gourmet reputation today. Lobster appears on menus throughout New England, but the best place to try it is from the boiling cauldrons of one of the many lobster "pounds" or "shacks" along the coast roads of Maine.

A mainstay of the New

*Corn should be eaten as fresh as fresh can be: peel back the end of each ear to check it is succulent*

Englander's diet is chowder, notably clam, fish, or corn. Menus rarely exclude one of these delicious, thick creamy soups. Other seafoods that may not be familiar to outsiders include scrod (a flaky, tender white fish) and the strangely named large clam, the quahog (pronounced "ko-hog"), native to southeast New England.

**FRUITS IN SEASON** The corn season (from mid-July to early September) is short, but to be relished. Ideally, you should eat the corn within three hours of its being picked—a sweet, moist, tender treat. A favorite is the yellow and white variety called "butter and sugar." In September, just before the first frost, the orange pumpkins are harvested. Stacked against a traditional red barn, they make a sight as colorful as the autumn foliage itself.

Fall also sees the start of the pick-your-own apple season, but ready-picked apples as well as apple cider are sold at farm stands. Try Paula Reds, one of the earliest, and McIntosh, Cortland, Empire, or Northern Spy.

Blueberries are a specialty of Maine, and turn up baked into anything from muffins and pancakes at breakfast to pie at dinner. Cranberries are exported all over the world from the bogs of the southeast corner of Massachusetts.

*Above: Bean suppers, often held in church halls, are a New England custom. Visitors are always welcome*

*Education is a way of life in New England. With a number of well-regarded preparatory schools and over 250 universities and colleges, it courses through the veins of social and cultural life. As a spinoff, New England leads the field in technological and medical research.*

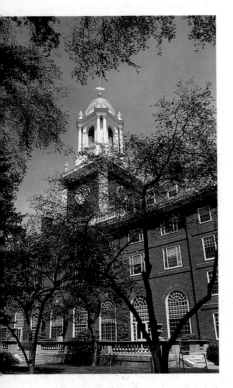

*Eliot House, typical of Harvard's elegant Georgian buildings*

❏ In October 1958, MIT student Oliver Smoot was carried prostrate by his classmates across what, to MIT's chagrin, is called Harvard Bridge. They marked off each head-to-toe length with paint and chalk. Thus the official length of the bridge is 364.4 Smoots plus one ear. The Smootmarks can still be seen today. ❏

intercollegiate football and other sports, it is for their high academic and social standing that these elitist Ivy League colleges are so revered.

The origin of the name Ivy League is uncertain: traditional ivy-covered buildings? From "I.V.," standing for Inter Varsity? Or perhaps because initially there were just four (in Roman numerals, IV) members?

❏ "You can tell a Harvard man, but you can't tell him anything." ❏

**THE IVY LEAGUE** Four of New England's universities, Harvard, Yale, Brown, and Dartmouth, together with four other eastern universities, Pennsylvania, Princeton, Columbia, and Cornell, make up that prestigious group known as the Ivy League. In the 1870s, the colleges used to meet for football games, and in those early years they were a major force in that sport. In the 1920s, however, their prowess faded somewhat and, although they still compete in

Harvard, the nation's oldest university, was founded in 1636 by the early colonists, primarily as a training ground for Puritan clergymen. Many of Harvard's first graduates in fact went on to set up other educational institutions. By 1647, towns with 50 householders had to provide primary schooling; those with 100 or more had to provide secondary schools. Today, many of America's oldest and most highly regarded colleges and universities are in Massachusetts, notably the Massachusetts Institute of Technology (MIT), which was founded in 1861.

Yale, Harvard's traditional arch rival, is in New Haven, Connecticut. New England's second oldest university was founded in 1702 at Saybrook by Harvard graduates and renamed after its benefactor. It has a collegiate system modeled on that of Oxford and Cambridge universities in England, and its fine buildings recall their architecture (see pages 102–105).

Dartmouth College in Hanover, New Hampshire, the only Ivy League college in the northern part of New England, also has a beautiful campus. Founded in 1769 as a Native American charity school, Dartmouth by tradition waives tuition fees (so exorbitant as to eliminate most locals) for any resident of New Hampshire or Vermont of Native American ancestry. Consequently, the percentage of such undergraduates, although still tiny, is greater here than in other Ivy League universities. Brown University, in Providence, Rhode Island, was

❏ Fees at the Ivy League universities are currently in the region of $30,000 per year (tuition $23,000, room and board $7,000; at Harvard, fees are closer to $40,000). Compare this with a state university, where fees for a state resident range from around $2,500 to about $4,500. ❏

founded in 1764 as a Baptist college by one of the leaders in the China trade, John Brown.

**THE FIELD OF MEDICINE** If Massachusetts is preeminent in education, it is also a major medical center, and Boston has an illustrious tradition of medical research. It was in Boston in 1846 that ether was first used as an anesthetic during an operation, the first kidney transplant was performed there in 1954, and open-heart surgery was first performed at Boston Children's Hospital in 1967.

*Below and opposite, top: Yale's Gothic Revival architecture*

*One of the rich and diverse strands that make up the fabric of New England is its cultural life. Classical music, jazz, and dance are a tradition, not just in Boston's concert halls and churches but throughout the region in universities and colleges, at festivals, and, not least, on the village-green bandstand.*

**GREAT COMPOSERS** One of America's first great modern composers was Charles Ives, who was born in Danbury, Connecticut, in 1874 and who graduated from Yale to become a successful insurance executive. In summer, outdoor concerts of classical music and jazz are held in Danbury at the Charles Ives Center for the Arts. The third movement of Ives' *Three Places in New England*, "The Housatonic at Stockbridge," was suggested by a misty Sunday morning walk with his wife along the riverbank.

The New England scenery has been inspirational to many works, including Edward MacDowell's *New England Idyls* (1902) and William Schuman's *New England Triptych*. Another important New

England composer (although the number of his works is small because he destroyed his early compositions) was Karl Ruggles, a close friend of Charles Ives. Walter Piston, whose works include the orchestral suite *Three New England Sketches*, was born in Rockland, Maine, in 1894 and was an influential teacher at Harvard, one of his most distinguished pupils being Leonard Bernstein.

❏ For more on the BSO, see page 79. For more on venues for jazz, classical, and light music in Boston, see page 85. ❏

**THE HIGHLIGHTS** For more than a century, the Boston Symphony Orchestra's concerts in Symphony Hall have been a vital element in

*Seiji Ozawa conducting the Boston Symphony Orchestra at Symphony Hall*

Boston life during the winter months (see page 79). The BSO's founding spirit was Henry Lee Higginson, and it was also he who started, in July 1885, the "Popular Concerts," or "Pops," summertime concerts of light music that were to become a national tradition. The social elite flocked to Music Hall to sit at tables arranged between potted plants, partaking of refreshments and listening to "light music of the best class." Little

baskets for a summer evening's music in the open air.

One of Colonel Higginson's friends was Isabella Stewart Gardner, a patron of aspiring musicians, conductors, and composers, as well as painters, sculptors, actors, and writers. Her magnificent creation, Fenway Court, now the Isabella Stewart Gardner Museum, a fragrant oasis of beauty in Boston (see page 69), was a meeting place for musicians and the venue for wide-ranging programs of music, song, and dance. Following in this tradition, the museum today puts on approximately 130 public concerts each year.

Tanglewood, in western Massachusetts, is the Boston Symphony's summer home, and the Tanglewood Music Festival is one of the cultural highlights of the Berkshires region, drawing hundreds of thousands of visitors annually to the open-sided Music Shed and the rolling lawns that surround it (see page 146). The Jacob's Pillow Dance Festival, held nearby at Becket from late June to late August, offers ten weeks of highly acclaimed dance programs.

*Summer music on the lawns of Tanglewood*

changed in form or content, the concerts (held in May and June) remain a highlight of the year, and the Boston Pops is the most recorded orchestra in the world.

In 1929, outdoor concerts were introduced on the Esplanade along the Charles River in Boston. Every summer, thousands of young and old continue to flock to the Hatch Shell with their blankets and picnic

The jazz scene is traditionally a strong one, with the Charles Hotel in Harvard Square, Cambridge, a long-established haunt of aficionados. Also watch for festivals, and see page 85 for more suggestions for venues in Boston and Cambridge.

Of the numerous regional festivals of music and dance, the recitals held in the opulent salons of some of Newport's mansions have become a Rhode Island summer tradition.

And all over the region, the village bandstand provides many a delightful hour of informal entertainment.

*Hollywood, past and present, has not failed to tap the rich vein of New England's diversity. In the field of drama, theater is as alive in small towns and villages as it is in the city of Boston.*

**MOVIES** Among the movies with New England associations is *On Golden Pond*, based on Ernest Thompson's 1978 play. Set on Great Pond, Maine, the movie was actually shot at Squam Lake, New Hampshire. *The Whales of August* is another movie set in New England. *Mystic Pizza* (1988) was filmed in Connecticut, not in Mystic, but nearby Stonington, on a specially built set. Steven Spielberg's *Amistad* (1997), telling the story of Africans captured by slave traders (see page 101 and panel on page 105), was partly shot at Mystic, Providence, and Massachusetts State House in Boston, and *Good Will Hunting* (1998) was set at Harvard.

Herman Melville's *Moby Dick*, with its settings on Nantucket, Henry James's *The Bostonians*, and John Updike's *The Witches of Eastwick*, set in Wickford, Rhode Island, are just three New England novels to have been made into movies.

**PLAYS AND PLAYERS** One of America's greatest playwrights,

*Madeleine Potter and Christopher Reeve in* The Bostonians

Eugene O'Neill (see page 47), set his final masterpiece, *Long Day's Journey into Night* (1957), in his boyhood summer home, Monte Cristo Cottage in New London, Connecticut. Today, the Eugene O'Neill Theater Center, in Waterford, champions new work by American playwrights.

World-class performers are regularly brought in for pre-New York shows in small-town theaters, particularly in Vermont. From 1938 to 1976, the Shubert Theater (now the Shubert Performing Arts Center) in New Haven, Connecticut, hosted many Broadway show premières (see panel on page 103), and New Haven's Long Wharf Theatre is one of the top regional theaters. Goodspeed Opera House, a resplendent Victorian concoction on the Connecticut River at East Haddam, hosts musicals. Festivals proliferate, offering strong local summertime theater programs. Those held in the Berkshires (see pages 143–147) make it a particularly popular area for theater-lovers.

*Veterans Katherine Hepburn and Henry Fonda in* On Golden Pond

# New England was

*When the Pilgrim Fathers crossed the Atlantic in 1620 and founded the first permanent European colony in New England, they did so in the wake of many earlier explorers and merchant adventurers who had been probing a land that had been home to the Algonquin peoples since time immemorial.*

*John Cabot, an Italian navigator and explorer based in London*

❏ In 1492, Native Americans in New England are estimated to have numbered about 100,000; by 1620, most were dead. ❏

It seems the ancestors of the Algonquin peoples of New England arrived in North America after the end of the last Ice Age, in a series of eastward migrations from Asia. By the time the first Europeans settled in the New World in the early 16th century, Native Americans had been inhabiting these northeastern woodlands for well over 10,000 years.

**EUROPEAN EXPLORATION** To the Native American way of thinking, land—a source of food, like water—is not something that belongs to people; it is people who belong to the land. The "People of the Dawnland," the Abenaki, once inhabited an area that extended from the Maine coast westward to Lake Champlain, and from the St. Lawrence south to the Merrimack River and northern Massachusetts. This was a forested land laced with lakes and waterways, along which they traveled in their birchbark canoes to fish and hunt. The Abenaki would have been the first natives to meet with intruders, when, possibly about AD 1000, it is believed, Leif Eriksson arrived from Scandinavia with his dreaded Vikings. Over the following centuries, a number of further forays were made across the Atlantic, many seeking the entrance to the fabled Northwest Passage across Canada. By the 1400s, fishermen from Scandinavia, Portugal, Spain, France, and Britain were coming regularly to enjoy rich pickings in the continent's then teeming offshore waters.

The excitement aroused by Christopher Columbus's voyages to the Caribbean between 1492 and 1504 tempted more and more Europeans. In 1497, King Henry VII of England authorized John Cabot to set sail from Bristol; exactly where he landed is uncertain, but Nova Scotia seems likely. Cabot staked an English claim to North America by hoisting the flag and returned home with promising

reports, but little else. In 1524, France sent the Florentine Giovanni da Verrazano (who reported a frosty welcome from the Abenaki), then, in the 1530s and 1540s, Jacques Cartier, who explored the St. Lawrence River. In 1568, David Ingram captured the imagination of all with tales of "a magic city of Norumbega," glittering with "pillars of crystal and silver."

❏ The term "New England" was coined by John Smith, English founder of the Jamestown colony in Virginia, when he wrote *A Description of New England* (1616). ❏

**ATTEMPTS TO SETTLE** The Spanish, British, and French continued to look for potential sites for settlement and began to trade with the Native Americans for furs. By the turn of the 17th century, fisheries had been established and rival trading posts were in operation. Beaver hats were by now all the rage in Europe, and fur trading was serious business. In 1605, the area was mapped by Frenchman Samuel de Champlain, who gave his name to the large lake that is set on Vermont's north-western boundary.

Attempts to establish settlements in the region, however, failed, and relationships between Europeans and Native Americans became increasingly prickly. George Popham established a

colony at Sagadahoc, but it did not survive the harsh New England winter of 1607–1608. A French Jesuit colony was set up on Mount Desert Island, but in 1613 it was burned down by the English.

**TRADING IN DISEASE** The concept of hunting animals, not for food and clothing but in order to sell their fur, was alien to Native Americans, but they were tempted by the Europeans' metal, which would improve their fishhooks, snowshoes, and canoe paddles, and welcomed their kettles and guns. However, traders also brought with them European viruses, to which the natives had no immunity, and which would in places wipe out practically the entire population. By the time the Pilgrims landed in 1620, the Native Americans were devastatingly weakened.

*Pilgrims John Alden and Mary Chilton are the first ashore*

29

*The successful establishment of the English colony at Plymouth in 1620 encouraged a flood of settlers. They came with the hopes and ideals of 17th-century England, but their vision of a new world was not easily realized.*

After a bad first winter, the Plymouth colony was soon settled and expanding, though closely dependent on contact with England and relying heavily on the advice of Native Americans for fishing, hunting, and growing crops (see pages 180–181 for more on the Pilgrims). In 1630, another group of Puritans, under the leadership of John Winthrop, founded the Massachusetts Bay Colony on a spot they named Boston, after their hometown in Lincolnshire, England. Quickly successful, it soon completely overshadowed Plymouth.

The meeting of Puritan and Native American was a meeting of two utterly different philosophies of life, yet at first, at least, they got along all right. Peace treaties made between the colonists and most of the neighboring Native Americans held firm. Gradually, however, relations began to deteriorate. Not only had the Europeans brought diseases by which, catastrophically, the native people had been crippled, they had also introduced guns and alcohol, which seriously disrupted their communities. Intertribal warfare broke out over trading, English missionaries tried to impose a foreign culture, and, as colonists needed more land, the Native Americans were increasingly confronted by that totally alien, European desire to stake a claim on territory.

**WARS OF CONQUEST** By the mid-17th century, the Puritans found themselves caught up in an unending round of skirmishes and shifting alliances between invader and native. In the Pequot War, the settlers, aided by the Narragansett, annihilated the Pequots around the Connecticut River. In what is called King Philip's War (1675–1676), however, the Puritans massacred the Narragansett, taking their land in Connecticut and Rhode Island. In the process,

*Metacom, or "King Philip," sachem of the Wampanoags, who was finally driven to leading his people into vicious war in 1675*

KING PHILIP

hundreds of settlers were killed and many towns raided. During the French and Indian War (a part of Britain's Seven Years' War with France that basically was about beaver fur), which sputtered on from the late 17th century until the final flare-up that led to French defeat in 1763, the colonists were to fight countless battles alongside British troops against the French and their Native American allies.

## A STAND FOR FREEDOM

Even within their own communities, life was not all smooth sailing for the settlers. The Massachusetts Bay Puritans were not, like some of the Plymouth colonists, Separatists who had broken with the Anglican Church. These were Puritans who were themselves dissenters in that

*John Winthrop: by 1670 his Boston colony had grown to 1,200*

they hoped to reform the Church, yet condemned any who showed signs of deviating from the (very) straight and narrow path of strict Puritanism.

Men and women such as Thomas Hooker, William Coddington, and Anne Hutchinson left to found new settlements. In 1636, a minister, Roger Williams, was banished for advocating freedom of religious thought. He went on to found Rhode Island, where church and state were always separate and religious freedom paramount.

The Puritans were equally assertive in their public administration. Even when others joined them, power remained firmly in their hands and, with England absorbed in its Civil War, they were left to their own devices. When Charles II acceded to the throne in 1660, however, he found he did not like the extent to which the colony was running its own affairs. He therefore introduced the Navigation Acts, aimed at making New England merchants trade only with Britain, and ended the Puritans' monopoly of the vote. With suffrage, the merchants (who ignored the Acts) rapidly grew both wealthy and powerful. They no longer needed, or wanted, the close contact with England; soon they would want to be their own masters.

❏ When history is told by the victor, language is easily tainted by prejudice. Thus Native Americans had warriors, Europeans soldiers; Native American victories were massacres, European victories were battles; Native Americans had chiefs, Europeans generals and kings. ❏

31

*During the early 1700s, New England was growing fat on its growing international trade. Resentment mounted at the mother country's attempts to muscle in on this wealth, with events escalating in the 1760s to the inevitable shot famously "heard round the world."*

**"NO TAXATION WITHOUT REPRESEN-TATION"** Britain emerged supreme from the French and Indian War in 1763, but it also emerged practically bankrupt. King George III decided the wealthy American colonies should pay for their own defense and also help recoup financial losses.

A series of tax-levying acts followed, but were met with protests from a core of colonists who argued that no one should have to give financial support to a government in which he had no representation.

❏ While the Sons of Liberty were hailed as heroes, the Daughters of Liberty enforced boycotts of British goods by serving herbal teas, using maple syrup instead of sugar, and wearing homespun cloth instead of imported silks. ❏

The Sugar Act of 1764 reinforced the 1733 Molasses Act, which aimed to end trade with the West Indies (in fact, it was so lax that smuggling, bribery, and therefore the rum industry continued to prosper). The Stamp Act of 1765 taxed printed matter, but met with riots and was repealed the following year. The colonists also responded to the 1767 Townshend Acts, which taxed tea, glass, paint, paper, and lead, by boycotting British goods.

In 1770, all except the tax on tea were repealed, ironically on the same day that five colonists were killed in the Boston Massacre. The colonists continued to smuggle tea in from Dutch traders.

*The Boston Massacre, as portrayed by Paul Revere. The British resemble an execution squad firing on innocents at short range. Note the Custom House is labeled "Butcher's Hall"*

32

*Disguised as Mohawks to escape detection, the Sons of Liberty tip East India Company tea into the harbor*

**THE BOSTON TEA PARTY** The Tea Act of December 1773 was seen as giving the British East India Company a monopoly on tea sales to the colonies. It so fueled resentment at the British government's power to legislate and levy taxes, that when three East India ships docked in Boston loaded with 342 chests of tea, the "Sons of Liberty," a group of patriots led by Samuel Adams, John Hancock, Joseph Warren, and Paul Revere, agreed to take decisive action. Disguised as Mohawks, they boarded the ships and threw the tea into the water. Britain retorted in 1774 with the Intolerable, or Coercive, Acts. Boston Harbor was closed.

**THE OPENING SHOTS** The American colonies united in response to these further threats to their liberty, and at the First Continental Congress plans were laid for the organization of an army (later to be led by George Washington). On April 19, 1775, the Revolutionary War began.

The British knew about a cache of arms in Concord (see panel on page 167) and sent troops to seize it. As they left Boston, Paul Revere (see page 55) made his famous ride to Lexington, on the road to Concord, to warn the Sons of Liberty there that the British were coming. There were minor scuffles in Lexington, but when the British reached Concord they met with organized resistance from the colonial Minutemen, and the "shot heard round the world," as described by Emerson in his *Concord Hymn*, was fired.

In May, Ethan Allen and his Green Mountain Boys captured Fort Ticonderoga on Lake Champlain from the British. In June, around Boston, the British won the Battle of Bunker Hill in Charlestown, but only with heavy losses, and when George Washington fortified Dorchester Heights (with arms captured from Fort Ticonderoga), they decided to quit.

The British left Boston in March 1776, never to return.

33

❏ The Battle of Bunker Hill actually took place on what in 1775 was known as Breeds Hill; Bunker Hill was nearby. In spite of the mix-up of names, the battle's name stuck and Breeds Hill was subsequently renamed Bunker Hill. ❏

The Battle of Bunker Hill, *one of a series of paintings by John Trumbull (1756–1843) recording events in the Revolutionary War*

*The history of New England is inextricably bound up with the sea. Whether it be through fishing, whaling, trading, or shipbuilding, it is the sea that has shaped the region's economy, its society, and its traditions.*

**FISHING** Even before the Europeans first established colonies on New England's shores, they were coming to fish the region's coastal waters, greedy for cod, haddock, and pollack. For 200 years, fishing was to be the mainstay of New England's trade with Europe. It declined during World War II, but there is still activity in harbors such as Gloucester, Provincetown, New Bedford, and Boston, and in the lobstering ports of Maine.

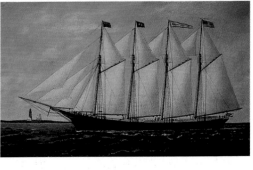

*Marine art is a proud tradition*

**WHALING** Today we look on whaling with revulsion, but during the mid-

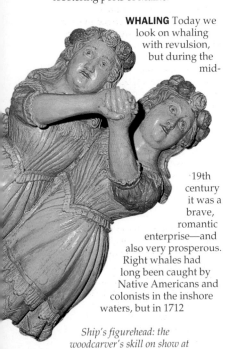

19th century it was a brave, romantic enterprise—and also very prosperous. Right whales had long been caught by Native Americans and colonists in the inshore waters, but in 1712

*Ship's figurehead: the woodcarver's skill on show at Mystic Seaport, Connecticut*

Captain Christopher Hussey caught a sperm whale which, with its oil, spermaceti, and ambergris, proved a much more valuable species. So began the Yankee enterprise that every year sent hundreds of whaling ships across the oceans of the world, to return with the oil that would light the lamps of America and Europe until the discovery of kerosene in the mid-1800s. Other exported whale products were spermaceti for candles, bones for corset stays, and ambergris for perfume. Today, this legendary era is vividly recalled in whaling museums in New Bedford, Nantucket, and Mystic.

**FOREIGN TRADE** If whaling brought wealth in the 18th century, so, too, did the infamous Triangle Trade involving slaves from Africa, molasses from the West Indies, and rum from the colonies' distilleries, a trade that thrived on smuggling and bribery. After Independence in 1776, trade was opened up with China,

❏ Maine supplied the timber for the masts of 80 percent of British Admiral Nelson's fleet. ❏

34

❏ In seaboard towns notice the "widow's walk," a balustrade along the top of some of the sea captains' houses. From here, wives would watch ships coming and going. ❏

*A shipowners' advertisement for their "first class clipper ship"*

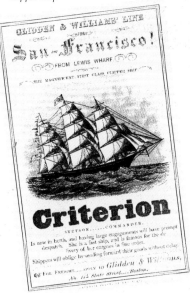

and New England entered a golden age of commercial enterprise.

The capital of maritime New England during this "Federalist Era" was not so much Boston as Salem, Massachusetts, and the elegant houses built here by the captains, shipowners, and merchants who amassed such vast fortunes are splendid monuments to their prowess. The town's Peabody Essex Museum (see page 185) displays the trinkets they brought home, along with their cargoes of tea and silks. Boston's Back Bay and Beacon Hill neighborhoods, Portsmouth, New Hampshire, and Newburyport, Massachusetts, also have their share of grand houses built on the China trade.

**SHIPBUILDING** Seafaring activity supported a wide range of other businesses—ropemakers (a 1,000-ton vessel needed 12,000 feet of rope), sailmakers, caulkers, chandlers, and, of course, shipbuilders. Northern New England's plentiful forests supplied scores of shipyards, mostly along the Maine coast. The Merrimack River was also busy, and here was invented the dory, the little workboat that fishermen would stack in nests of five or six on their seagoing boats.

*Boston Wharf in the 19th century*

This was the era in which insurance agents first began to make a killing. With premiums based on the dimensions and type of wood used for the different parts of the ship, the wise shipowner would follow their recommendations—hard (yellow) pine for the keel, Douglas fir for the deck planking, and so on. The Maine Maritime Museum in Bath (see page 118) is an excellent place for a study of boat-building.

The era of the clipper was brief, eclipsed by the steam-powered ship. New England's maritime trade began to decline, and rich merchants put their capital into manufacturing.

❏ Plaques on many houses in Marblehead, a delightful small town on the North Shore of Massachusetts, indicate the range of maritime trades. "Built for Benjamin Pritchard, Tailor, 1753," reads one; others are "Blacksmith," "Scribe," "Shoreman," "Housewright," "Mariner," and "Merchant." ❏

*During the golden years of the China trade, it was the coastal areas of New England that generated the wealth. As maritime commerce declined and new industrial technology developed toward the end of the 18th century, the waterpower of the inland river valleys became the basis for a new wave of prosperity.*

36

*Tuck* is the Algonquin word for "river with waves," and *pawtucket* is "a divided river with waves"— ideal for powering mills. It was in Pawtucket, at the mouth of the Blackstone River Valley, which runs southeast from Worcester, Massachusetts, to Providence, Rhode Island, that the American Industrial Revolution was born. Craftsmen in metal, leather, and wood, as well as handloom weavers and fullers, had worked in Massachusetts since the days of the early settlers, but in 1793 the first waterpowered cotton mill in America, Slater Mill, opened in a clapboard building beside the river in Pawtucket.

Samuel Slater had worked in Richard Arkwright's revolutionary spinning mills in Britain. With financial backing from Rhode Island's prosperous shipping merchants, including one of the Brown brothers, he reproduced the machine designs he had learned there and made use of the local craftsmen's skills to harness waterpower to drive the carders, spinning machines, and looms that launched New England's textile industry and transformed daily life across the country. The mill and other

*Thomson, on the Thames River in Connecticut, one of dozens of factory towns that sprang up during the 19th century to meet the growing demand for manufactured goods*

❑ Some mill towns—notably Lowell—are being turned into heritage parks. Immaculately restored, they barely resemble the noisy, grimy towns of the 19th century, but they do offer an excellent insight into a turning point in the region's history. ❑

❏ The exploitation of women and the use of child and slave labor were issues of great concern to 19th-century social activists such as feminist Margaret Fuller, anti-slavery campaigner William Lloyd Garrison (see panel on page 72), and the Concord circle of thinkers and writers (see pages 46–47). ❏

buildings have been restored at the Slater Mill Historic Site in Pawtucket (see panel on page 220).

**RISE...** Other merchants were quick to seize the opportunity for diversification. Alongside rivers such as the Blackstone and the Merrimack, the landscape of rolling farmland changed rapidly into a quite different scene of mills, warehouses and workers' housing, smokestacks, dams, canals, and, in time, railroads. Millbury, for instance, a town positioned to benefit from both the Blackstone River and the Blackstone Canal, had no less than six wool mills in the 1830s.

The most remarkable of these mill villages was Lowell, developed by the wealthy Boston merchant Francis Cabot Lowell on the Merrimack River northwest of Boston (see page 171). Lowell had seen the appalling conditions of some of the factory workers in Britain and planned decent company-owned housing, schools, places of worship, and recreational facilities for his workers. Women as well as men were employed, daughters of New England farmers. Letters home describe good conditions, fair treatment, and a lively social life. Lowell village became a showpiece. By 1850, it was producing 2 million yards of cloth a week and had one of the world's largest canal systems.

**...AND FALL** As mills grew larger and more numerous, more labor was needed. Workers were attracted off the land and immigrants flooded in from Europe. Some of the earliest were the Irish, who constructed the Blackstone Canal in 1828 to transport goods from Worcester to Providence, though 20 years later this was replaced by the railroad. The mills (most of which had never operated on such caring principles as Lowell's) became overcrowded and, even in Lowell, families of Irish, Portuguese, Greeks, and others were crammed into squalid tenements. Visitors to Lowell today are moved by the conditions in which people lived and worked. Child labor was introduced and all workers were desperately exploited. Wages were cut, and protests, petitions, and strikes ensued, culminating in a major strike in 1912.

Gradually, industrialists were lured by cheaper labor in the South, and by the 1920s, 50 percent of American cotton was being woven there. The Depression followed and most of New England's textile mills closed down. Industrial prosperity would only be regained with the development of the electronics industry in southern New England after World War II.

*A re-creation of the long-gone days of sweat and toil at Lowell Mill*

**37**

*The 18th century saw a steady trickle of immigrants, but by the mid-1800s foreigners began to pour into New England in numbers significant enough to have a permanent effect on society, politics, and the economy.*

**BOSTON'S IRISH AND ITALIANS** The Potato Famine in Ireland of 1845–1850 resulted in a flood of families seeking better prospects. Thousands went no farther than Boston; there, hungry and poor, they crowded into the North End district. Initially, the Roman Catholic Irish met with prejudice from Bostonians, whose blood was basically still Puritan, and their place remained at the lower end of the social ladder. Gradually, they improved their standing and proved they could hold their own in public office alongside the blue-blooded Bostonian aristocrats (with the result that the Democrats began to break the Republican hold on power).

In 1884, Hugh O'Brien became the first of many Irish mayors of Boston. In 1905 came "Honey-Fitz," as John F. Fitzgerald (grandfather of John F. Kennedy) was known, and then the colorful James Michael Curley. What Curley lacked in education he made up for in charm, and between 1920 and 1950 he was not only mayor four times, but also governor and congressman—even though he was jailed twice, once while in office. Boston Irish politicians have become legendary, and today they make up half the city council.

*"Honey-Fitz," J.F.K.'s grandfather*

The Irish of the North End were joined in the 1870s by Jewish immigrants from Eastern Europe, and in the 1890s by Italian immigrants. To this day, the area has remained an Italian quarter. In 1993 Boston elected its first Italian-American mayor, who ran unopposed for reelection in 1997.

❑ St. Stephen's Church in Boston's North End, Rose Kennedy's childhood church, has changed its denomination several times. In 1714, the New North Meeting House was founded on the site as a Congregationalist institution. In 1804, Charles Bulfinch designed the present building, and in 1813 it became a Unitarian church. In 1862, by which time the population of the North End was mostly Irish, the church, renamed St. Stephen's, became Roman Catholic. ❑

*Hugh O'Brien, first in a long line of Boston's Irish mayors*

38

**A COSMOPOLITAN MIX** Many Irish immigrants found employment building the railroads. In Vermont, for instance, descendants of laborers on the Rutland and Central Vermont lines today make up the Irish population in towns such as Burlington and Rutland (their railroad long since gone). Some of the Italian immigrants, from marble-producing areas of Italy, went to work in the marble quarries in Barre, Vermont, bringing skills with them in the same way as the Welshmen who went to the slate mines. The workforce for southern New England's textile and shoe factories was also largely formed by European immigrants. At the turn of this century, eastern Europeans formed a significant group in Providence, Rhode Island, and Connecticut's Naugatuck Valley.

The influence that many immigrants had on their adopted hometown is still felt today. Middletown, Connecticut, for instance, has had Sicilian-American mayors. Many fishing fleets were manned by Portuguese from the Azores, and those that remain—at Stonington, Connecticut, and Gloucester, Massachusetts, for example—still hold the two-day Blessing of the

> ❑ The Sicilians of Middletown, Connecticut, have for several generations come from just one village in the southeast of Sicily called Melilli. ❑

Fleet. Festivities include a parade of ships and the blessing of wreaths that are thrown into the sea.

Immigrants also came into New England from other directions. After the Civil War, French-Canadians came from Quebec, particularly to industrial cities of New Hampshire, such as Manchester, but also to Connecticut and the mill villages of Rhode Island and Massachusetts. After World War II, Jamaicans and West Indians came from the South and New York, chiefly to Boston and elsewhere in Massachusetts, Rhode Island, and Connecticut. So, too, did Hispanics, many from Puerto Rico. In Hartford, Connecticut, 20 percent of today's population is Hispanic (public notices are printed in English and Spanish).

*Top, opposite: the Blessing of the Fleet, Gloucester. Below: an Italian pizzeria in Boston's North End*

*As cities sweltered under a cloud of mid-19th-century industrial grime, New England's unsullied coast and mountains, now reached by steamship or train, began to appeal to the wealthy of the Northeast as summer homes.*

*Some of the hotels had their own railroads: the Profile and Franconia Notch ran from Bethlehem, New Hampshire, to the Profile House*

From the 1830s, the painter Thomas Cole and other artists (see page 44) had visited the little-known White Mountains region of New Hampshire, soon to be joined by the notable writers of the day, such as Hawthorne, Emerson, and Thoreau (see pages 46–47). These early "tourists" did much to publicize areas like this and, once steamships and railroads had arrived, the stage was set for the development of New England as a playground for the wealthy new industrialists. Spas proliferated, and the rich built summer "cottages," particularly in Bar Harbor and Acadia on the Maine coast, on the islands of Martha's Vineyard and Nantucket, and, notably, in Newport, Rhode Island (see pages 216–218). It is the "grand hotel," however, that best evokes these early days of tourism.

**THE FIRST RESORTS** A pioneer of the summer vacation in America was Appledore House, which opened its doors in 1848 as a resort hotel on the Isles of Shoals, off Portsmouth, New Hampshire. Boston's socialites, including literary and artistic celebrities, flocked here in the new coastal steamers to spend idyllic summer months away from the stresses of urban life. Appledore's success spawned many more grand-style summer resorts on the coast and in the mountains, and by about 1880, with the benefit of a good railroad network, the tradition of summer vacationing was firmly established.

Each year, wealthy families from the eastern seaboard would arrive at the hotels on magnificent trains such as the White Mountain Express, bringing young and old, servants and governesses—and the

lifestyle enjoyed by the top echelons of urbane society.

**THE GRAND HOTEL** In the early 1900s, there were 19 of these "grand hotels" in the White Mountains alone. Many were self-sufficient, running their own farms, stables, and ice-cooling barns. Some had post offices (envelopes stamped by a grand hotel post office are nowadays collectors' items). Each had its resident orchestra, often made up of musicians who in the winter season played for the Boston Symphony Orchestra. Artists in residence were kept busy painting souvenirs of the landscape.

Instruction was given in dancing (the tea

❑ In the White Mountains, a daily newspaper, *Among the Clouds*, used to keep hotel guests up to date with exactly who was staying where. ❑

dance being a favorite), and various sporting facilities were offered, from croquet to boating, bathing, and fishing. The more adventurous guests would go hiking or horseback riding into the mountains; some, however, would get no farther than the hotel's veranda. The veranda was an important feature of the grand hotel, built wide and long (indeed, hotels were rated by their length), with cane rocking chairs pushed well back so guests had room to promenade. Summer romances flourished.

41

The cuisine of the grand hotel chef was legendary, and menus listed up to 70 items per meal. Guests would sit at the same table, with the same waiter, for the whole season. It was important, therefore, in order to see and be seen, not to be stuck in a corner, and for this reason the dining room in the Mount Washington Hotel was octagonal.

By the 1930s, the automobile was bringing a different sort of person to the resorts, someone with less money and only a week or two to spare, looking for cheaper accommodations. It was the automobile that sounded the death knell of the grand hotel. Some were torn down, while others were gutted by fire and never rebuilt. Today, only a few remain, such as the Mount Washington Hotel and Resort in Bretton Woods and the Balsams Grand Resort Hotel in Dixville Notch, testaments to a gloriously romantic, sadly bygone era.

*Above: wish you were here—an early postcard, of the Cannon Mountain Aerial Passenger Tramway*
*Left: the Mount Washington Hotel at Bretton Woods, New Hampshire, is one of the few grand hotels still open*

*The political scene in Boston has always been active, and it is here that some of America's most influential politicians and diplomats, including five presidents, have cut their teeth.*

**THE ADAMS FAMILY** The first member of the Adams family to come to prominence was Boston-born Samuel Adams (1722–1803). A complete failure as a businessman and tax collector, he emerged as a terrierlike political agitator, a patriot whose orchestrated propaganda stirred up anti-British feeling in the years leading to Independence.

Sam Adams' second cousin, John Adams (1735–1826), was also a patriot. A more moderate man, he helped negotiate the Treaty of Versailles, which ended the Revolution, and was appointed the first U.S. minister to Britain. On his return, he became George Washington's vice president and a leading Federalist. When Washington retired in 1797, John

*Samuel Adams: an engraving of the portrait by Copley (1773)*

*President John Quincy Adams*

Adams became the second U.S. president, with his wife, Abigail, one of the intellectual women of the day, playing a strongly supportive role. Defeated by Thomas Jefferson in 1800, John Adams spent an active retirement in Quincy, Massachusetts (see page 182).

John Adams' eldest son, John Quincy Adams (1767–1848), had accompanied his father on various diplomatic missions and, after graduating from Harvard, pursued a distinguished career as a diplomat in Europe. Returning home, he became secretary of state, and in 1824, when there was no clear majority in the presidential election, he found himself chosen in preference to Andrew Jackson. John Quincy Adams' term of office was sullied by hostility from Jackson's supporters, and in the 1828 elections he was defeated. As a member of the House of Representatives, however, he put his energies into the antislavery campaign. During an impassioned speech on the subject, he had a stroke and collapsed on the floor of the House, dying two days later.

**"KEEP COOL WITH COOLIDGE"** The life and death of Calvin Coolidge (1872–1933), America's 30th president, was not so colorful. Born in Plymouth Notch, Vermont (see page 233), Coolidge was a quiet and cautious man of few words who worked his way up the ladder to become governor of Massachusetts. Elected Republican

*The Kennedy era: Robert Rauschenburg's* Retroactive *(1964)*

Rhode Island, and by the time he announced his presidential candidacy in 1960 an aura of charisma surrounded the couple.

Kennedy was the youngest man, and the first Roman Catholic, elected president. At home his main concern was social welfare, while in foreign affairs he won admiration for handling the Cuban Missile Crisis in 1962. Shortly afterward he secured the Nuclear Test Ban Treaty with Soviet leader Nikita Khrushchev and British Prime Minister Harold Macmillan. Seen by many as a symbol of hope, for America and the world, Kennedy was shot dead in Dallas on November 22, 1963.

**GEORGE BUSH** President from 1989 to 1993, George Bush grew up in Greenwich, Connecticut, and graduated from Yale. He served under presidents Nixon and Ford before becoming loyal vice president to Ronald Reagan. His presidency was marked by his involvement of American troops in the Gulf War. His summer home is in Kennebunkport, Maine (see page 137).

vice president, he became president in 1923 when Warren Harding died unexpectedly. Coolidge's two terms of office were distinguished by such government inaction that when the writer Dorothy Parker was told he had died, she is reputed to have asked, "How can they tell?"

**THE KENNEDY STYLE** President John F. Kennedy (1917–1963) was the great-grandson of an Irish immigrant. J.F.K.'s father, Joseph P. Kennedy (1888–1969), a Harvard graduate, married Rose Fitzgerald, the daughter of Mayor "Honey-Fitz" (see page 38). While Joseph made a successful career in politics and business—he was a millionaire at the age of 30—Rose bore him nine children. Four would die an early death: Kathleen, Joe, John, and Robert.

John first ran as a Democrat for Congress in 1946. In 1953, the handsome young senator married the beautiful Jacqueline Lee Bouvier in Newport,

*George Bush, U.S. president 1989–1993*

*Galleries such as the Museum of Fine Arts, the Isabella Stewart Gardner Museum, the Clark Institute, and many college museums show European art, but the work of New England's own painters is also worth seeking out.*

**COLONIAL PAINTING** Colonial America produced three artists of note. John Singleton Copley (1738–1815) painted portraits of Boston's elite. His *Watson and the Shark*, in Boston's Museum of Fine Arts, is a famous depiction of mankind's struggle with nature, but it is Benjamin West (1738–1820) who stands out as a historical painter during this period. Gilbert Stuart (1755–1828) was another eminent portrait painter (his George Washington appears on the dollar bill).

44

**THE WHITE MOUNTAIN SCHOOL** Throughout the 19th century, New England artists continued to be influenced by Europe. Thomas Cole (1801–1848) was a Romantic landscape painter and a founder of the Hudson River School. He frequently traveled about the Northeast making sketches, and in 1828 visited New Hampshire's White Mountains and was instantly captivated by the scenery. Albert Bierstadt (1830–1902), another prominent member of the school, created grandiose views of the White Mountains and the Connecticut River Valley.

*Top: from* Boy in a Boatyard *by Winslow Homer*

**COASTAL ART COLONIES** The Maine coast has been inspirational to many artists, notably Winslow Homer (1836–1910), who spent the latter part of his life at Prout's Neck. Here he painted a prodigious number of powerful seascapes. Also look for the seascapes of Fitz Hugh Lane (1804–1865). John Marin (1870–1953) was a more recent abstract landscape artist obsessive about the Maine coast. Edward Hopper (1882–1967), one of a group known as the Painters of the American Scene, also worked here, his static, silent figures set in humdrum surroundings. The area around Cushing, Maine, where Andrew Wyeth (born 1917) has his summer home, is the subject of many of his tempera and watercolor paintings. Another American Scene painter, Wyeth is best known for *Christina's World*, depicting a lonely figure in an open field.

*Shipping in Down East Waters by Fitz Hugh Lane*

Boston Common at Twilight *by Frederick Childe Hassam*

Appledore, an idyllic summer artists' colony on the Isles of Shoals, was immortalized by the leading American Impressionist, F. Childe Hassam (1859–1935). His *Boston Common at Twilight* is a favorite in Boston's Museum of Fine Arts. Childe Hassam also worked in Old Lyme, at the mouth of the Connecticut River, where Florence Griswold opened her house (now a museum) to an influential colony that became known as the Old Lyme Impressionists.

**AMERICANS ABROAD** No study of the art of 19th-century New England is complete without mention of two notable American artists whose work and influence straddled the Atlantic. These are James McNeill Whistler (1834–1903), who was born in Lowell, Massachusetts, and is perhaps best known for his paintings of London, and John Singer Sargent (1856–1925), born in Florence, Italy,

who painted portraits of Boston's prominent men and women.

**THE 20TH CENTURY** The two New England artists who have won the most widespread popularity in recent times must be the illustrator Norman Rockwell (see page 150) and Anna "Grandma" Moses (1860–1961), a primitive painter who created colorful scenes of everyday New England life (see panel on page 226).

**SCULPTORS** One of America's foremost sculptors, Augustus Saint-Gaudens (1848–1907), worked, after training in Europe, in Cornish, New Hampshire (see page 195). His work includes the 1897 *Shaw Memorial* on Boston Common.

Chesterwood in Stockbridge, Massachusetts (see page 147), was the home of another notable sculptor, Daniel Chester French (1850–1931). Best known for his seated *Abraham Lincoln* in Washington, DC, French first won acclaim with his *Minute Man* statue in Concord, Massachusetts.

*Writers in colonial times concentrated on religious tracts and journals, but after the Revolution, American literature quickly established a new identity, and New England has nurtured writers of prominence ever since.*

❏ "As the New England summer flamed into autumn, I piled cut spruce boughs all round the draughty cottage sill, and helped to put up a tiny roofless verandah along one side of it for future needs."
– From *Something of Myself* by Rudyard Kipling (1865–1936). ❏

**46**

**THE CONCORD CIRCLE** Early in the 19th century, there emerged a group of thinkers and writers based at Concord, Massachusetts (see pages 169–170), spiritual idealists known as the New England Transcendentalists. The leading figures were essayist and poet Ralph Waldo Emerson (1803–1882) and Henry David Thoreau (1817–1862), whose classic *Walden* (1854) is a record of two solitary, transcendentalist years spent communing with nature in a log cabin in the woods around Walden Pond. Novelist Nathaniel Hawthorne (1804–1864) also lived in Concord for a time, in the same house in which Louisa May Alcott

(1832–1888) spent some of her teenage years, a period she was to draw on in *Little Women*.

**THE BERKSHIRES** Nathaniel Hawthorne also lived in Lenox, western Massachusetts, where he wrote *The Scarlet Letter* (1850) and *The House of the Seven Gables* (1851), inspired by the house of that name in his birthplace, Salem. In Lenox he became good friends with Herman Melville, who was living in nearby Arrowhead completing the whaling adventure story *Moby Dick* (1851) before fading into melancholia and virtual oblivion—it was not until the 1920s that his talent was recognized. In 1902, Edith Wharton, society hostess turned novelist, built The Mount in Lenox, where she wrote her stories of trenchant social observation (such as *Ethan Frome* and *The Age of Innocence*) in between entertaining her high-flying circle of friends, including the author Henry James.

❏ "There are three kinds of lies: lies, damned lies, and statistics."
– Mark Twain, *Autobiography* (1871). ❏

**THE HARTFORD COLONY** In the Nook Farm area of Hartford, Connecticut (see pages 96–97), Samuel Clemens, alias Mark Twain, and his wife built the exuberantly Victorian house where he wrote *The Adventures of Tom Sawyer* (1876) and his masterpiece of wit and insight, *The Adventures of Huckleberry Finn* (1884). His neighbor was Harriet Beecher Stowe, a minister's wife whose *Uncle Tom's Cabin* of

*Top: Tom Sawyer's band of robbers*
*Left: Mrs. Keeley as Topsy, Uncle Tom's Cabin*

(Mᵣˢ Keeley as Topsy "Is dreffnl wicked")

**"SLAVE LIFE, OR UNCLE TOM'S CABIN."**

1852 was a widely read novel that stirred popular antislavery feeling to such an extent that it is counted by some as one of the causes of the American Civil War.

❏ Kipling and his American wife, Caroline, lived for a few years in Brattleboro, Vermont, and here he wrote some of his best-known works, including the Jungle Books. Their house, Naulakha, has been restored and is available for rent from the Landmark Trust (tel: 802/254–6868). ❏

*Longfellow, one of a circle of writers associated with Harvard*

**POETRY AND DRAMA** Henry Wadsworth Longfellow, born in 1807 in Portland, Maine, wrote many of his narrative poems, including *The Song of Hiawatha* (1855), while teaching at Harvard. Longfellow was part of an aristocratic group of New England writers closely linked with Harvard. Others were the poets Oliver Wendell Holmes and James Russell Lowell. The sensitive recluse Emily Dickinson (1830–1886) is also linked with Massachusetts (see page 176), while the poems of Robert Frost (1874–1963) are so steeped in the New England countryside he is often referred to as "The Voice of New England" (see page 209).

The only American playwright to receive the Nobel Prize for Literature, Eugene O'Neill, died in Boston in 1953. From a modest start with a one-act play performed in a wharfside playhouse in the Cape Cod fishing village of Provincetown, he rose to a position of preeminence among 20th-century dramatists. But his career was a troubled one, with much of his material being drawn from the torments of his family life. He is commemorated at his boyhood summer home, Monte Cristo Cottage, in New London, Connecticut.

*Louisa May Alcott*

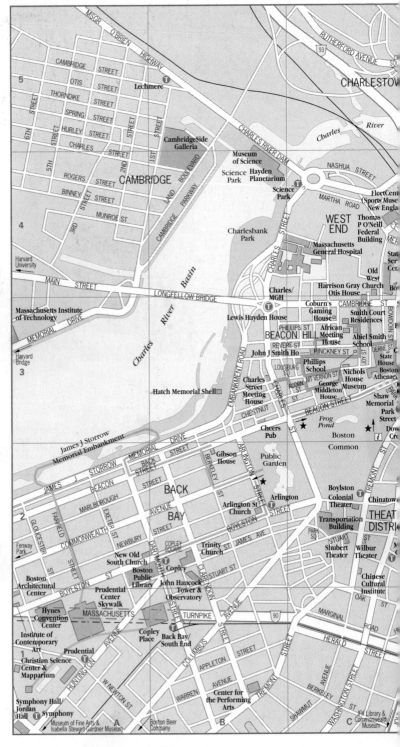

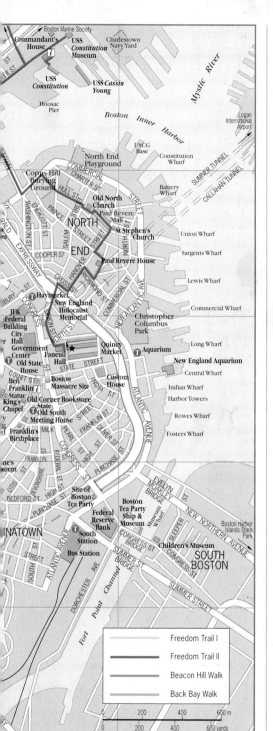

**Map Labels (image 1):**

Boston Marine Society
Commandant's House
USS *Constitution* Museum
Charlestown Navy Yard
USS *Constitution*
USS *Cassin Young*
Hoosac Pier
*Mystic River*
Logan International Airport
*Boston Inner Harbor*
USCG Base
North End Playground
Constitution Wharf
Copps Hill Burying Ground
Battery Wharf
Old North Church
Paul Revere Mall
NORTH END
St Stephen's Church
Union Wharf
Paul Revere House
Sargents Wharf
Lewis Wharf
Haymarket
New England Holocaust Memorial
Commercial Wharf
JFK Federal Building
Christopher Columbus Park
City Hall
Government Center
Quincy Market
Long Wharf
Old State House
Faneuil Hall
Aquarium
New England Aquarium
Ben Franklin Statue
Boston Massacre Site
Custom House
Central Wharf
King's Chapel
Old Corner Bookstore
Old State House
Indian Wharf
Old South Meeting House
Harbor Towers
Franklin's Birthplace
Rowes Wharf
Fosters Wharf
CHINATOWN
Site of Boston Tea Party
Federal Reserve Bank
Boston Tea Party Ship & Museum
Boston Harbor Islands State Park
South Station
Bus Station
Children's Museum
SOUTH BOSTON
Broadway

Legend:
— Freedom Trail I
— Freedom Trail II
— Beacon Hill Walk
— Back Bay Walk

0   200   400   600 m
0   200   400   600 yards

D    E

▶▶▶ CITY HIGHLIGHTS

**Charlestown Navy Yard**
*pages 66–67*

**Copley Square: Trinity Church and Boston Public Library**
*pages 63, 66*

**Faneuil Hall** *page 59*

**Freedom Trail**
*pages 58–61*

**Isabella Stewart Gardner Museum** *page 69*

**Museum of Fine Arts**
*pages 70–71*

**North End** *page 60*

**Old North Church**
*page 60*

**Public Garden** *page 73*

**State House** *page 73*

**Views from the John Hancock Tower and Prudential Center Skywalk** *pages 70, 72–73*

# Boston

**BOSTON A–Z CONTENTS**

| | |
|---|---|
| Map | 48–49 |
| Introduction | 50–51 |
| Getting around | 52–53 |
| Events | 54 |
| Focus On Paul Revere | 55 |
| Focus On The Pulse of Boston | 56–57 |
| Walks: | |
| The Freedom Trail: I | 58–59 |
| The Freedom Trail: II | 60–61 |
| Back Bay | 62–63 |
| Beacon Hill | 64–65 |
| Boston A–Z | 66–73 |
| Cambridge A–Z | 74–75 |
| Walk: Harvard and Cambridge highlights | 76–77 |
| Accommodations | 78 |
| Focus On The BSO | 79 |
| Food and drink | 80 |
| Focus On Sports | 81 |
| Shopping | 82–83 |
| Nightlife | 84–85 |

*Boston seen from the Charles River: between Boston Common, the brownstone terraces of Back Bay, and the office buildings of the Financial District rises the gilded dome of the Massachusetts State House*

**BOSTON** The cradle of American history is a city of church spires, parks, statues, and a remarkably thriving culture. To this, within the last 30 years, has been added a high-rise skyline. To most first-time visitors, the city's elements are partly familiar, partly refreshingly different. Boston also divides into strikingly contrasting neighborhoods, from the trendy elegance of Back Bay and the old-world charm of the North End to the modern skyline of the Financial District and adjacent Waterfront.

Boston looks pleased with life nowadays, with its elegant shops, gleaming office towers, refurbished wharves and historic buildings, and lively eateries and bars. Although it is by far New England's largest city—with a population of around 575,000—"the Hub" (referring to its position in the universe) often presents a pleasant surprise to visitors, who find it livable and manageable.

**FINDING YOUR FEET** Most Bostonians would tend to think of **Boston Common** and the neighboring **Public Garden** as the true heart of the city. The Common is the oldest public park in the U.S.A. and is overlooked by the State House, with its dazzling gold dome. A visitor information booth nearby marks the start of the **Freedom Trail** (see pages 58–61). To the east lies the main downtown district, with government buildings arranged around the huge plaza of **Government Center**. Here, too, is the renovated and ever popular **Faneuil Hall Marketplace** (Faneuil rhymes with manual), which comprises historic Faneuil Hall, Quincy Market, and the adjacent North and South markets. Street performers entertain the shoppers and visitors, portrait artists sketch them, and food stalls feed them: the atmosphere is conducive to lingering. The historic **North End**, the Italian quarter north of here, hosts lively street festivals on weekends in July and August, has excellent bakeries and restaurants, and has sites on the Freedom Trail.

Post Office Square is at the heart of the high-rise downtown Financial District. Nearby rises Boston's first

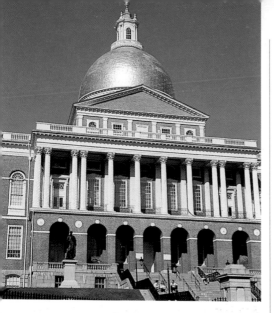

*The State House, designed by Charles Bulfinch. The dome was originally covered in copper, the work of Paul Revere*

**CITY CHEAPIES**
(See also panel on page 78 for freebies.)
● The Museum of Fine Arts has a "pay what you can" entrance on Wednesdays, 4–9:45.
● The Children's Museum offers all tickets for $1 on Fridays, 5–9.

51

"skyscraper," the Custom House, a slender Gothic-style clocktower that graces the downtown skyline. The **Waterfront** is no longer commercial, condominiums and offices having sprouted on the old wharves. It has some fine restaurants and the **New England Aquarium**. Work is well underway on a project that will put the highway that crosses the Waterfront into a tunnel and transform the area into a 73-acre park. A waterside walk from the aquarium, past Rowes Wharf and the Boston Harbor Hotel, makes the most of the Waterfront views. South of the Financial District is **Chinatown**, a colorful neighborhood with stores selling all manner of items and restaurants serving excellent food at bargain prices.

North and west of Boston Common are, respectively, the fashionable and delightful residential neighborhoods of **Beacon Hill** and **Back Bay**. South of **Copley Square** is the main hotel district, a convenient area in which to stay; eastward lies the Theater District. The **South End** is a trendy up-and-coming area of bow-fronted Victorian townhouses, where Union Park is one of the most attractive streets. The district is full of excellent eateries, and is ethnically and socially mixed.

Southwest of Back Bay is Fenway, which occupies the area around Back Bay Fens, a lakeside park. It has the pick of the city's art museums—the huge **Museum of Fine Arts** and the intensely personal **Isabella Stewart Gardner Museum**. Fenway Park, home of the Boston Red Sox, is one of the smallest and oldest baseball parks in the major leagues.

**Cambridge**, on the north side of the Charles River, is actually a separate city, although it is close enough to walk to from Back Bay over Harvard Bridge. Harvard University (the oldest university in America) and the street activity and nightlife in and around Harvard Square are among Cambridge's prime attractions. Cambridge is also home to the Massachusetts Institute of Technology (MIT) and boasts some of the finest restaurants in the Boston area.

*Close-up on the bow-fronted houses of the South End*

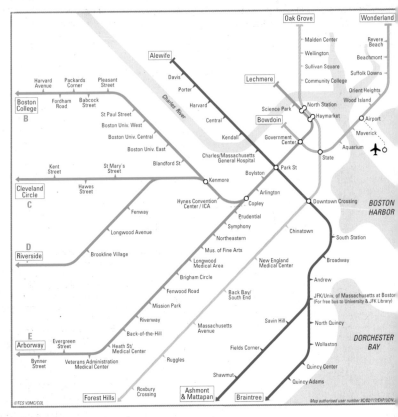

*Map of Boston's subway train network*

## BOSTON HARBOR ISLANDS

This national recreation area comprises 30 undeveloped islands (of which six can be visited), havens of wildlife that are excellent for bird-watching and hiking. They are surprisingly remote in character considering their proximity to the city. From Long Wharf it is a 45-minute ferry journey (May–mid-Oct, daily; moderate charge) to Georges Island, where there is a Civil War fort. From there you can pick up a free water taxi to five other islands (Gallops and Lovells have swimming beaches). Take your own food and water.

## Getting around

**WALKING** Everyone will tell you that Boston is a walking city. Distances downtown are small, and there is so much to see. New visitors will often find that they have walked non-stop for days on end before noticing their tired feet.

During the day, it is quite safe to wander around the central streets, although crossing them is another matter. Here, in what some people call the jaywalking capital of America, the tendency is to dodge the notoriously slow traffic lights and risk the traffic.

Compared to many other cities, Boston is safe for visitors, but some areas, such as the Common and the backstreets of Chinatown, should be avoided at night.

**DRIVING** Don't drive in Boston unless you absolutely must. The city is notorious for having some of the country's worst drivers. You'll need good nerves to cope with the traffic, to navigate through the city's confusing maze of streets, to understand the traffic patterns where no lines are painted on the road surface, and to try to find one of those elusive parking spaces. The construction of three road tunnels may help to alleviate the traffic problem after 2006, but the building work in the meantime has exacerbated the problem. If you are planning a self-drive trip around New England, seriously consider picking the car up from somewhere out of the city that is easily reached by train or subway.

**PUBLIC TRANSPORTATION** Fortunately, public transportation in Boston is excellent, running from around 5 AM (6 AM on weekends) to 12:45 AM. The subway train network, known as the "T," spreads across the city. The various lines are displayed on maps—and known to locals—by color. You need to buy tokens to ride the subway. Currently the cost is 85¢ for each ride on the T (a little more for some rides from the outer suburbs) irrespective of how many times you change lines.

The T's Visitor Passport gives unlimited travel on the T (plus discounts for certain attractions) for one, three, or seven consecutive days. However, this is unlikely to save you money on fares if you are only making a few rides each day; a better bet is to buy a stack of tokens first time around, thus saving time lining up at stations. Buses are slightly cheaper, but require a little more local knowledge.

From central Boston, visits to Cambridge, the Museum of Fine Arts, the Isabella Stewart Gardner Museum, and Logan Airport are best made by the T. The color-coded lines are reasonably straightforward, even to a newcomer: remember to look for the color and destination of the train.

**GUIDED AND SELF-GUIDING TOURS** Several companies run fleets of trolleys, with guided commentary, around the hotel area and the historic parts of the city, taking in most sights on the Freedom Trail, including the remotely located Bunker Hill Monument. All the routes cover much the same ground. You can begin at any trolley stop you like. Tickets last a day, and you can get on and off where you like, then wait a few minutes for the next trolley. Additionally, Old Town Trolley Tours take in Cambridge. The same company runs a narrated J.F.K.'s Boston tour.

Boston by Foot runs guided tours from May through October; for recorded information, tel: 617/367–3766, or for general information, tel: 617/367–2345.

**BOAT CRUISES** From spring until fall, Boston Harbor Cruises (tel: 617/227–4321) operates whale-watching, harbor, and themed Mystery and Summertime Blues cruises from Long Wharf by the New England Aquarium. The short cruise to the Charlestown Navy Yard is the most direct and pleasant way to approach it. The longer tour into Boston Harbor passes the airport and gains views of the 17th- and 18th-century fortifications on Castle Island, and there is an impressive panorama of the skyscrapers. There are boat trips to Salem (see page 184) and to Boston Harbor Islands (see panel opposite). The 80-minute Boston Duck Tours, from the Prudential Center (April–November), use brightly painted World War II amphibious vehicles. In addition to making a conventional ground tour of the city, they splash into the Charles for a river trip. Tel: 617/723–3825.

**AIRPORT TRANSFERS** See page 248.

### MORE TOURS
● Trolley tours around Boston include the Chocolate and Seafood trolleys—each with appropriate samples along the way. Tel: 617/269–7150 for both.
● Take the Orange Line to Stoney Brook for the Boston Beer brewery and museum, home of Samuel Adams Beers (*Open* tours Jul–Aug, Wed–Fri 2 PM, Sat noon, 1 PM, 2 PM; Sep–Jun, Thu–Fri 2 PM, Sat noon, 1 PM, 2 PM. *Admission: donation*).
● For tours of Fenway Park and the Federal Reserve Bank, see page 68.

### BOSTON QUIRKS
● Boston Neck, which connects the city to the mainland, was originally just 120 feet across. Much of the harbor has since been filled in.
● The city's first squares were modeled on those laid out in 18th-century London.

**53**

*Trolley tours provide an easy way to see the city*

## Events

For further information, contact the Greater Boston Convention and Visitors Bureau (see page 266).

### JANUARY
**Boston Cooks**, World Trade Center and other locations: New England's premier culinary event.
**Chinese New Year** (January/February), Chinatown: firecrackers, traditional music.
**Martin Luther King Day** (third Monday).

### FEBRUARY
**Black History Month**, centered at Black Meeting House in Beacon Hill: plays, discussion, tours.

### MARCH
**International Boston Seafood Show**, John B. Hynes Veterans Memorial Convention Center.
**New England Flower Show**, Bayside Expo Center: the world's third largest.
**St. Patrick's Day Parade** (mid-March).

### APRIL
**Boston Marathon** (Patriots' Day), from Hopkinton to Boston: the oldest marathon in America.
**Patriots' Day Parade**, City Hall to Paul Revere Mall.
**Swan Boats**, Public Garden: season begins with ceremony and first ride.

### LATE APRIL/EARLY MAY
**Ducklings Day Parade**, Beacon Hill, Public Garden: make way for the mallard family and costumed relatives.

### MAY
**Art Newbury Street**: art, special exhibits, jazz, and classical music.
**MayFair**, Harvard Square: food, fine arts, and crafts.

### JUNE
**Boston Dairy Festival** (first week): cows make an appearance on the Common (a colonial law mandates this); ice cream, butter-making, milking.
**Boston Globe Jazz Festival**, various locations.
**Bunker Hill Day and Parade**.
**Cambridge International Fair**, University Park, Cambridge.
**Harborlights** (June–September), Waterfront: music festival.

### JULY
**Boston Harborfest** (week leading up to July 4): celebration of Revolutionary War events in Boston Harbor, culminating in Revolutionary era reenactments, military parades, fireworks, concerts.
**Boston Pops**: free outdoor concerts at the Hatch Shell on the Esplanade.
**Boston Seaport Festival**, Charlestown Navy Yard.
**Chowderfest**, City Hall Plaza: sample a range of chowders produced by Boston restaurants and vote for the best.

### AUGUST
**August Moon Festival**, Chinatown.
**Caribbean Carnival**, Franklin Park.

### SEPTEMBER
**Art Newbury Street** (see May).
**Arts Festival of Boston**.
**Cambridge River Festival**.

### OCTOBER
**Columbus Day Parade**.
**Head of the Charles Regatta**: major rowing event (the world's largest) on the Charles River.
**Mixfest**: free pop concert in City Hall Plaza.
**Oktoberfest**, Harvard Square, Cambridge.

### NOVEMBER
**Holiday Happenings** (November 19–December 24): holiday festivities, including Winter Wonderland and Sleigh Bell Parade.

### DECEMBER
**Boston Tea Party Reenactment**, Tea Party Ship.
**First Night Celebration**: city-wide family celebration to ring in the New Year.
**Newbury Street Holiday Stroll**.
**Tree-lighting** Ceremonies at Prudential Center and elsewhere.

*Part of the Fourth of July celebrations in downtown Boston*

*"Listen, my children, and you shall hear/Of the midnight ride of Paul Revere…"* So begins Longfellow's **Paul Revere's Ride**, *a ballad that was to turn a silversmith into America's favorite folk hero.*

Until Longfellow's ballad was published in 1863, Paul Revere (1735–1818) was best known as a silversmith, though he dabbled in many things (see panel). An ardent patriot and an experienced express rider, he frequently carried messages for the Sons of Liberty (see page 33). On April 16, 1775, Revere rode out to Lexington to warn patriot leaders Sam Adams and John Hancock that British troops in Boston were making plans to march to Concord to seize a cache of rebel arms, and to capture Adams and Hancock in Lexington on the way. A plan was made for another message to be relayed as soon as the soldiers actually left town.

In case he was unable to escape from Boston himself, Revere asked the sexton of Old North Church, Robert Newman, to signal to Charlestown, across the Charles River, by holding up one lantern in the church steeple if the troops left by land (across Boston Neck), two if by boat (across the river). On the night of April 18, the signal was duly given, and Revere got out of Boston and headed for Lexington. He was joined there by William Dawes, and as they rode on they met Sam Prescott. All three were captured by the redcoats. Only Prescott escaped and reached Concord.

**The legend** Most newspaper reports of the night's events did not even mention Paul Revere by name. The *New York Gazette* reported him dead. A century later, however, thanks to Longfellow, Revere stepped into the annals of history. But Longfellow was a poet, not a historian, and so he could play around with the facts. He has Revere waiting for the signal in Charlestown; he has him making the heroic ride alone; and he certainly does not reveal that Revere never actually reached Concord, only Prescott. But then, "Prescott" does not rhyme as easily as "Revere."

*Left: Revere in middle age. Top: Revere as messenger*

**THE MAN**
Paul Revere was born in Boston on December 21, 1735. A silversmith like his Huguenot father, he became one of the country's finest artists in silver, gold, and copper. A remarkable man of boundless energy and talent, he also turned his hand to engraving and printing, often for propaganda purposes (see below). He made spectacles, surgical instruments, and false teeth. After the American Revolution, Revere manufactured sheet copper, some being used on "Old Ironsides" (the USS *Constitution*) and on the State House dome. Revere died in 1818, age 83, and is buried in the Old Granary Burying Ground.

**THE PATRIOT**
In March 1770, a street brawl got out of hand when some youths started throwing snowballs at British troops. The soldiers panicked, opened fire, and five men were killed. Paul Revere plagiarized an engraving of the incident by Henry Pelham (to Pelham's annoyance), fueling resentment against the redcoats or "lobsterbacks," as the British troops were derisively called. The term "Boston Massacre" was coined by Sam Adams.

*Bronze bell cast by Revere, a distinguished bell-maker*

*Boston could be forgiven for quietly basking in its venerable past and resting on its glorious cultural laurels. But life here is as much about computers as culture, and, in this capital of academia, the pace is intellectually challenging. Boston has its share of blue blood, but it is above all a dynamic, youthful city.*

**BRAHMINS AND BOSTON**
The physical development of Boston is closely linked to the Brahmins. In 1795, the society portrait painter John Singleton Copley sold land on Beacon Hill to a group of entrepreneurs. On it Bulfinch built the prestigious Beacon Hill estate into which Boston's blue-blooded elite moved, leaving their homes in the old North End en bloc. Beacon Hill was one of three major hills to be leveled off, the soil being used to fill in the swampy "Back Bay" area along the Charles River. By about 1870, Back Bay had been developed and many of the Brahmins then moved into its more grandiose houses.

*The Christian Science Center, Prudential Center (left), and John Hancock Tower*

**High-rise and high-tech** For many years the Custom Tower House was the only building in Boston higher than the State House dome. How different was the skyline then. In recent times, glassy skyscrapers and concrete office towers have risen rapidly one after the other to dwarf the elegant Victorian brownstone terraces of Back Bay. The classic architectural image of Boston is the reflection of Henry Hobson Richardson's 1870s Romanesque-style Trinity Church in the glass windows of I.M. Pei's 1970s ultramodern John Hancock Tower. And since I.M. Pei and his associates completed their commission to change the face of the blighted and downward-spiraling Boston of the 1950s and 1960s, a further proliferation of thrusting office buildings has been occupied by financial and other leading institutions, as well as computer companies.

Boston today—together with Cambridge, across the river—is a high-tech place. Go to Harvard Square on a Friday or Saturday evening, and for every browser in the bookstores there are at least twice as many parents in the computerware stores showing their kids the latest educational software. It is not insignificant that Boston's Museum of Science (see page 71) is among the best of its kind in the world. Don't miss it—it's sensational.

In recent years, Boston and Cambridge may have become "the Hub" (as Boston is known) of the computer industry, but this does not mean that their role

as leaders in medicine has in any way diminished. The place is a hotbed of research—not for nothing has the Ether Dome, the Massachusetts General Hospital's operating theater, where ether was first used as an anesthetic, been completely submerged by modern buildings (it is open to visitors, if they can find their way through to it). As for education, it sometimes feels as if virtually everyone in town is somehow connected to the 67 colleges and universities on either side of the Charles River. The start of the academic year brings chaos; the streets seem to be full of walking mattresses, as 500,000 students move into their new living quarters. It is a city full of bright and lively people.

56

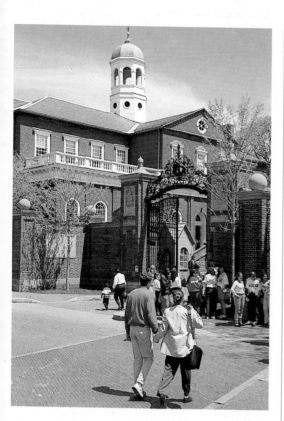

*The proliferation of academic institutions on either side of the Charles River means a huge student population: left, Harvard Hall, Harvard Yard, Cambridge*

**BAR HARBOR BRAHMINS**
Bar Harbor, in Maine, is where the proper Bostonian traditionally has a summer cottage. There is one page in the Bar Harbor telephone book on which every name, with just one or two exceptions, is that of a Boston Brahmin family.

**Boston Brahmins** In the midst of all this ferment, a small but deeply significant element of Boston society calmly carries on with life just the way it has always done. These are the members of Boston's top families, the "Proper Bostonians," the "Boston Brahmins," as the city's Establishment was termed by Oliver Wendell Holmes in the 19th century. They trace their ancestry back to the 18th-century merchants, and many claim to be related to early Puritan settlers (not, as is popularly misconceived, to the *Mayflower* Pilgrims, who landed south of Boston in Plymouth and were definitely not so upper crust).

Certainly all are characterized by Puritan qualities of frugality and self-restraint, and a sense of superiority. Breeding, rather than money, has always been paramount. Indeed, the intermarrying of Boston's top families is surely matched only by that of European royals. A Brahmin is born with a name such as Adams, Cabot, Lowell, Bowditch, Appleton, or Lodge, he is educated at Harvard (where else is there, after all?), he lives in Back Bay, and has a summer home in Maine.

In the 18th and 19th centuries, it was the Brahmins who held all the power, and to a degree their blue blood continues to course through the city's veins today. Many of the financiers and businessmen in those downtown office towers are Brahmins; but perhaps it is families like the Kennedys (of Irish ancestry) and the intellectual elite who are the new generation of Brahmins?

**THE NEW ENGLAND HOLOCAUST MEMORIAL**
Six glass and steel towers, 54 feet tall and 4 feet square, stand one behind the other in the gardens alongside Union Street, right beside the Freedom Trail and in an area of the city steeped in the history of human rights. The glass panels are etched with rows of numbers, a stark reminder of the 6 million Jews murdered by the Nazis between 1933 and 1945. The paving stones are inscribed with quotations from Holocaust survivors, and inside each tower steam rises through a grating placed over what appears to be a pit of glowing embers. The memorial is the work of architect Stanley Saitowitz.

# Walk

## The Freedom Trail: Part I

*See map on pages 48–49 (yellow route).*

Follow the red or brick line along the city sidewalks for colonial America's most historic walk. The route is the focus of Boston National Historical Park and passes many buildings associated with the Revolutionary War. Freedom Trail Players, in historic costume, patrol the trail to answer queries. Excellent free guided walks start every half-hour (in summer months) from the park visitor center at 15 State Street opposite State subway station (and the Old State House).

**Boston Common**▶, at the start of the walk, is a 44-acre, undulating grass expanse, formerly used as a pasture and parade ground. Follow the Freedom Trail across the Common up to the imposing State House with its gilded dome. Continue

*King's Chapel graveyard, where John Winthrop lies*

down Park Street to **Park Street Church** (1809), where William Lloyd Garrison made his first antislavery address in 1829 and where the song *America* was first sung in 1831. Adjacent is the **Old Granary Burying Ground**, containing graves from Revolutionary days, including those of John Hancock, Samuel Adams, Paul Revere, and the five who perished in the Boston Massacre.

At the corner of Tremont and School streets, look inside **King's Chapel**▶ (1754), Boston's first Anglican church, and later the first Unitarian church. It has well-preserved furnishings, including white box pews and a pulpit with sounding board. A finely carved gravestone in the churchyard is that of Joseph Tapping (1678), depicting Father Time extinguishing the candle of Life.

The **Old Corner Book Store** (1712; now called the Boston Globe Store), at the corner of School and Washington streets, was a literary meeting house where the works of Longfellow, Stowe, Hawthorne, and Emerson were first published. Opposite is the **Old South Meeting House**▶ (1729), a former Puritan house of worship, and at one time the largest public meeting hall in the city. Here, heated meetings took place as the British sought to impose their taxes. On December 16, 1773, Samuel Adams addressed some 7,000 citizens just before the Boston Tea Party (see page 33) and pronounced the immortal words "Gentlemen, this meeting can do nothing more to save the country." Threatened with demolition in the 1870s, the building was the first in Boston to be preserved solely for its historic importance. Its ultimate salvation was spurred by the centennial celebration for 1876. Today, it contains an exhibition focusing on the events leading to the Tea Party (*Open daily 9:30–5. Admission: inexpensive*).

Farther north along Washington Street, the **Old State House**▶ (1713) has changed much over the years but externally is now restored to its original appearance, with the (renewed) British lion and unicorn flanking the gable above the balcony from where the Declaration of Independence was read to the public on July 18, 1776. Today, the interior is a museum devoted to historical exhibitions about Boston, showing events preceding and following the Boston Massacre, plus displays on the city's neighborhoods.

A neat circle of stones embedded in a pedestrian island beside the Old State House marks the site of the Boston Massacre (see page 32).

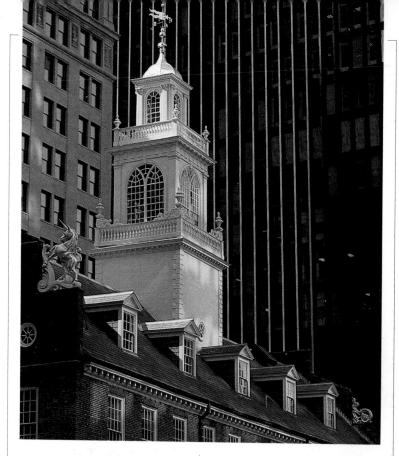

*Above: new, high-rise Boston dwarfs the Old State House. Below: Faneuil Hall Marketplace*

Nearby **Faneuil Hall**►► was donated to Boston in 1742 by Peter Faneuil, the "Bachelor of Boston," who died a few months after the building's completion of "an excess of good living." The building contains the meeting hall known as the "Cradle of Liberty" (*Open* daily 9–5. *Admission free*) where, over the years, revolutionary protests, women's suffrage, slavery, and every war except the 1990 Gulf War (the building was closed for renovation) have been discussed. Rebuilt by Charles Bulfinch, the hall is much larger today than at the time of the Boston Tea Party, when Old South Meeting House was the largest venue available for debate in the city. The top floor contains regimental memorabilia of the Ancient and Honorable Artillery Company (free tours are given by national park service rangers every 30 minutes from 9:30 to 4:30).

Behind Faneuil Hall is **Faneuil Hall Marketplace**►►►, one of the city's top attractions. This lively scene of shops, restaurants, and entertainers is centered at Quincy Market and North and South markets.

# Walk

## The Freedom Trail: Part II

*See map on pages 48–49 (red route).*

The second part of the trail leads from Faneuil Hall Marketplace, through the old Italian quarter of the North End, and past historic Charlestown Navy Yard to Bunker Hill. Some prefer to end the walk at Old North Church in the North End and take a ferry (from Long Wharf by the aquarium), trolley, or bus to Charlestown.

From Faneuil Hall Marketplace follow the trail along Union Street past the **Union Oyster House** (opened 1826), Boston's oldest restaurant, and the **Ebenezer Hancock House** (1767), home of John Hancock's brother, the deputy paymaster-general of the Continental Army. In the gardens alongside Union Street are the six glass towers of the **New England Holocaust Memorial** (see panel on page 57). Nearby, the Haymarket is a great place for bargain fruit and vegetables on Friday and Saturday.

The **North End** ▶▶ is one of Boston's oldest neighborhoods. It has been home to wave after wave of immigrants. After the original 17th-century Puritan settlers came Irish refugees fleeing from the 1840s potato famine, then Jews from Eastern Europe. Today, the North End is the Italian quarter and has some of Boston's best restaurants.

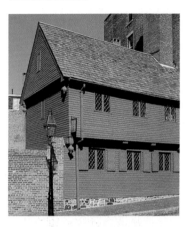

*Paul Revere House*

Something of a freak survival from the old town, **Paul Revere House**▶ (*Open* Apr–Dec, daily; Jan–Mar, Mon. Closed holidays. *Admission: inexpensive*) of about 1680, on North Square, was home to patriot Paul Revere (see page 55) and is Boston's oldest building. After Revere's time, the building functioned as a cigar factory, grocery, tenement, and bank. Restored to its original appearance, the building now operates as a small museum.

Photogenic **Paul Revere Mall** features the famous equestrian statue of Paul Revere against the magnificent steeple of **Old North Church**▶▶▶ (1723), where Robert Newman, the sexton, lit two lanterns on April 18, 1775, to warn the citizens across the river of British plans to cross by sea rather than by land via Boston Neck (see page 55). The church is a magnificent Colonial survival, with a gallery, box pews, and brass chandeliers; it is Boston's oldest church and has the tallest steeple.

**Copps Hill Burying Ground** (1660) was used by the British as a vantage point for cannon while making preparations for the Battle of Bunker Hill. It is Boston's second oldest cemetery and has some fascinating early epitaphs. The headstone of Daniel

*The North End, once a slum, is now a neat and lively district*

Malcom (to the left if entering from Hull Street and found between the broken column commemorating Prince Hall and a circular path) records "Here lies buried in a stone grave 10 feet deep. A friend to the Publick, an enemy to oppression," thus buried safe from British bullets. **North End Garage Park**, on the left side of Hull Street, is of interest as the site of the famous Brink's robbery in 1950, which netted a record $2.5 million; the FBI subsequently spent close to $29 million investigating it.

Across the bridge is **Charlestown**, founded in 1629 and named after King Charles I. It was razed by the British, and no house predates 1775. Charlestown was not incorporated into Boston until 1873. The trail continues to the entrance to **Charlestown Navy Yard▶▶▶** (see pages 66–67), today home of the warship the **USS Constitution▶▶▶** and the World War II destroyer **USS *Cassin Young*▶**, as well as the **USS Constitution Museum▶▶** and the **Commandant's House**.

Residential streets surround the **Bunker Hill Monument▶▶**, a tall obelisk that commemorates the first major Revolutionary War battle, fought on June 17, 1775. A 294-step climb is rewarded by an excellent view of the city. Musket firing takes place daily in summer, and there is an exhibition inside the lodge.

*"Old North," famous for the part it played in Paul Revere's ride*

*The Public Garden boasts the status of the nation's oldest botanical park*

# Walk

## Back Bay

*See map on pages 48–49 (orange route).*

This tour wends its way through the elegant Victorian brownstone district of Back Bay, where almost every door-way deserves attention, and past the two great high-level viewing platforms of Boston—the Prudential and Hancock towers.

Begin at the west side of the **Public Garden**▶▶ (see page 73) and cross the walkway along the center of **Commonwealth Avenue**▶▶, often rated as one of America's finest streets. This forms the central axis of Back Bay, an area subject to an ambitious landfill project in the late 19th century, when Parisian-style avenues were laid out on a grand scale and with an eye for symmetry.

Turn right onto Berkeley Street. At 137 Beacon Street, to the right, **Gibson House**▶ (*Open* May 1–Nov 1,

Wed–Sun; Nov 2–Apr 30, Sat–Sun. Tours at 2, 3, and 4. *Admission: expensive*) is a wonderfully preserved example of a Back Bay brownstone, in pristine Victorian condition. Continuing west on Beacon Street, turn right at Dartmouth Street to take the footbridge over the highway to **Charlesbank Park**, a riverside strip popular with bicycle riders, sunbathers, and joggers. The Hatch Shell, where outdoor concerts are held in summer, is to the right, while across the Charles River is the Massachusetts Institute of Technology (MIT).

Return by another footbridge over the highway to Fairfield Street. Continue to Newbury Street, an inviting detour with its restaurants, sidewalk cafés, and upscale boutiques and galleries. From Fairfield Street, turn right on Boylston Street, cross over, and go through the revolving doors and up the escalator into the **Prudential Center**, an enclosed mall with 70 shops and restaurants. Walk straight ahead, and at the Center Court turn right to the Prudential Tower. Take an elevator to the 50th floor for a panoramic view from the **Prudential Center Skywalk**▶▶▶ (see pages 72–73).

*Back Bay statue of local maritime writer Samuel Eliot Morison (1887–1976)*

Leave the Prudential Center through Huntington or Belvidere Arcade and turn right outside to visit the **First Church of Christ, Scientist complex**, immediately ahead. The complex is marked by a slender skyscraper (the **Christian Science World Headquarters**), a long oblong pond, and the **Christian Science Church▶** (1894–1906), modeled on St. Peter's in Rome and containing the largest pipe organ in the western hemisphere (*Open* tours Tue–Sat 10–4, Sun 11:30. *Admission free*). Adjacent to the church (to its right) in a room in the publishing wing of the organization, the **Mapparium▶▶** (*Open* Mon–Sat 9–4. *Admission free*) is a stained-glass representation of

*The Christian Science World Headquarters*

the globe as mapped in 1932–1935. Looking from within the sphere (with the map appearing, somewhat illogically, in concave form) you can see the whole globe in one visual sweep. The bizarre echo, with voices bouncing all around, makes this one of Boston's more offbeat experiences.

Return to the Prudential Center by escalator leading up to Belvidere or Huntington Arcade. From Center Court, take Back Bay Arcade to Copley Bridge, a covered walkway leading over Huntington Avenue into Copley Place indoor shopping center. Walk straight through on the first floor, past the indoor waterfall, then just past the staircase go left down an escalator and cross the covered walkway into the Westin Hotel lobby. Take the escalator down to emerge in **Copley Square▶▶**. On its west side is the supremely dignified Renaissance Revival **Boston Public Library▶▶▶** (1894; see page 66), the first public lending library in the world, while on the north side is the **New Old South Church** (1875; usually closed) with its flamboyant exterior, inspired by the North Italian Gothic style.

Physically, Copley Square is dominated by the huge skyscraper slab of the **John Hancock Tower and Observatory▶▶▶**, with its viewpoint 60 stories up (see page 70). Its glass reflects **Trinity Church▶▶▶** (1877), the neo-Romanesque masterpiece of Henry Hobson Richardson, with its ornate interior that includes work by John LaFarge, William Morris, and Edward Burne-Jones. Architectural fact sheets are available inside the door.

**63**

JOHN HANCOCK OBSERVATORY

*The best place to see Boston*

# Walk

## Beacon Hill

*See map on pages 48–49 (green route).*

This walk explores Beacon Hill's tight network of narrow residential streets on a sloping site. The neighborhood is a fascinating early 19th-century mixture of patrician and artisan homes. Intricate iron balconies, crisply proportioned brick façades, and carefully preserved front doors are much in evidence. Portrait artist John Singleton Copley sold land here to the Mount Vernon Proprietors, who included the great architect Charles

*Harrison Gray Otis House, built in post-Revolutionary Federal style. A plain facade hides a supremely elegant interior*

Bulfinch, and the lawyer and orator Harrison Gray Otis. Here and there you can see some of the original purple window glass imported from Hamburg in the 1820s, which discolored because of the presence of manganese oxide in the material. Another Beacon Hill quirk is that the gas lamps stay on all day.

Start from the northeast corner of the **Public Garden▶▶** (see page 73) at the intersection of Charles Street and Beacon Street. Walk eastward along Beacon Street. **Number 45**, built in 1805, was the last of three houses on "the Hill" built for Harrison Gray Otis

by Charles Bulfinch. At **number 33** lived George Parkman, the Harvard undergraduate who, in 1849, ended up in several pieces in the laboratory of a Harvard professor of medicine; the sensational trial was the major scandal of Beacon Hill.

Opposite the **State House▶▶** (see page 73), the **Robert Gould Shaw and 54th Regiment Memorial** acknowledges the role played by the first black regiment in the Civil War. Shaw, himself white, lived at 44 Beacon Street and led his regiment from here. This is the start of the Black Heritage Trail (see panel on page 66).

Turn left on Bowdoin Street. The column by the State House marks the site of the beacon that was erected here to warn the Puritans of Native Americans and foreign invasion and that gave the hill its name. The district was later to become a rough-and-ready jumble of disreputable bars and brothels, popularly known as "Mount Whoredom."

Turn left on Derne Street. From Hancock Street on the right, you can walk down to Cambridge Street and the first **Harrison Gray Otis House▶** (see page 68). If not visiting the house, continue instead along Derne Street and turn right on Joy Street, off which is Smith Court. The **African Meeting House** here is the oldest black church building still standing in the U.S.A. and the birthplace of the antislavery movement, where William Lloyd Garrison and 12 others founded the New England Anti-Slavery Society. It houses the Museum of Afro American History. **Smith Court Residences** were typical homes of Beacon Hill's free black community, who worked as servants in the 19th century.

Return along Joy Street and turn right on Pinckney Street, originally built to house service workers. Author Louisa May Alcott's family lived at **number 20**. **Number 24** (the "House of Odd Windows") was converted by a relative of Ralph Waldo Emerson from a stable into a townhouse, and **number 54** was the home of Nathaniel Hawthorne while he worked at the Custom House.

Detour right on Anderson Street and right again on **Revere Street**,

and look for a tiny entrance on the left between numbers 25 and 29. The house with columns at the end is a false facade, with a sheer drop behind.

Retrace your steps via Anderson Street to **Louisburg Square**, laid out in 1834–1844 by Bulfinch. Louisa May Alcott spent her last two years here at **number 10**. America's oldest homeowners' association maintains the square itself.

**Mount Vernon Street▶▶**, on the south side of the square, is one of Boston's finest architectural gems: Henry James called it "the only respectable street in America." Bulfinch's second Harrison Gray Otis house (1800) is at **number 85**, while the **Nichols House Museum▶** at

*The more modest houses that line lanes such as Acorn Street were built as servants' quarters*

number 55 (*Open* May–Oct, Tue–Sat 12–4:15; Nov–Dec, Feb–Apr, Mon, Wed, Sat 12–4:15. Closed Jan. *Admission: inexpensive*) provides another opportunity to see a Bulfinch interior.

Follow Walnut Street to Chestnut Street, where abolitionist poet Julia Ward Howe resided at **number 13** in 1862 and penned *The Battle Hymn of the Republic*. Turn right on Willow Street and left on **Acorn Street▶**, picturesquely cobbled and perhaps the city's most famous residential street. Finish by exploring the shops and restaurants of **Charles Street**.

*Boston Beer's award-winning brew*

### AFRICAN-AMERICAN HERITAGE
The African Meeting House, 8 Smith Court, houses the Museum of Afro American History (*Open* Labor Day–Memorial Day, Mon–Sat 10–4. *Admission free*).The nearby Abiel Smith School (46 Joy Street, tel: 617/742–5415) is home to the Boston African American National Historic Site and offers free guided tours of the Black Heritage Trail. Alternatively, the trail can be taken as a self-guiding tour with a brochure, available from the same organization or from any tourist information point.

### BOSTONIAN TERMS
The Black Maria was named after Maria Lee, who owned a disreputable hotel patronized by drunks and criminals. Police made frequent visits and took the offenders into the station by a "paddy wagon," later renamed a "Black Maria" to avoid disparaging the Irish population.
The term "gerry-mandering" originated with Governor Elbridge Gerry, U.S. vice president under James Madison, who redrew electoral boundaries for his own advantage.

### ►►► Aquarium                                    49E3
See New England Aquarium, page 72.

### ►► Boston Athenaeum                          48C3
*101/102 Beacon Street*
*Open: Jun–Aug, Mon 9–8, Tue–Fri 9–5:30; Sep–May, Mon 9–8, Tue–Fri 9–5:30, Sat 9–4. Closed for renovation until 2001. For times of free tours, tel: 617/227–0270*
*Subway: Park Street (Green and Red lines)*
Originating in 1807, this private library became the preserve of wealthy Boston intellectuals. In 1845 the Athenaeum moved into this Italian palazzo-style building. Classical statuary and choice paintings set a rarefied atmosphere. On the top floor the high-ceilinged Reading Room of 1915 has seven pairs of recessed bays looking over the Old Granary Burying Ground, and the Oval Room contains books from George Washington's library.

### ►►► Boston Public Library                    48B2
*70 Boylston Street, Copley Square*
*Open: Jun–Sep, Mon–Thu 9–9, Fri–Sat 9–5; Oct–May, Mon–Thu 9–9, Fri–Sat 9–5, Sun 1–6. Tours: Thu–Tue. Admission free*
*Subway: Copley (Green Line)*
When Charles Follen McKim's vast Renaissance-style edifice opened in 1895, it was America's first public library. Seemingly, no expense was spared: beyond the bronze reliefs on the entrance doors designed by Daniel Chester French—depicting female personifications of Music, Poetry, Wisdom, Knowledge, Truth, and Romance—the sumptuous marble foyer is revealed, its grand staircases guarded by lions sculpted by Louis Saint-Gaudens. Seek out the colonnaded courtyard, the murals by John Singer Sargent, the huge reading room, and Albert Wiggin's dioramas of printmakers at work.

### ► Boston Tea Party Ship and Museum            49E2
*Congress Street Bridge (adjacent to Children's Museum)*
*Open: summer, daily 9–6; winter, daily 9–5. Closed Dec 1–Mar 1. Admission: moderate*
*Bus: Courtesy shuttle bus from Quincy Market, at corner of State and Congress streets, in summer*
The ship moored here is a faithful replica of the brig *Beaver II*, one of the ships boarded in the Boston Tea Party protest (see page 33). You can put on quasi-Indian feather headgear and dunk a tea chest in the river, sample a cup of cold tea, and visit the small museum. Audience participation is the point: you are summoned to attend a "town meeting" such as happened (more or less) at the Old South Meeting House in 1773.

### ►►► Charlestown Navy Yard                     49D5
*Open: daily. Admission free*
*Subway: North Station (Green Line), then a 10–15-minute walk; or bus 93 from Haymarket station (Green Line); or MBTA Water Shuttle from Long Wharf by Aquarium Station (Blue Line). Trolley tours pass the Navy Yard.*

Charlestown Navy Yard served the United States Navy from 1800 until 1974. Some 30 acres of the yard now form part of Boston National Historical Park. It has retained the atmosphere of a shipyard, and visitors may enter only a few buildings. There are self-guiding and guided tours (tel: 617/242–5601), and the visitor center gives out informative leaflets.

Now fully restored, the frigate **USS Constitution▶▶▶**, the most famous of all historic American warships, was built nearby in 1797 and served in three wars. In the War of 1812, British cannonballs bounced off the vessel, earning her the nickname of "Old Ironsides," as she captured two sloops-of-war and sank two frigates (*Open* guided tours daily 9:30–4. *Admission free*).

Maritime history is brought to life in the **USS Constitution Museum▶▶**, adjacent, (*Open* May–Oct, daily 9–6; Nov–Apr, daily 10–4. *Admission: inexpensive*). The museum displays model ships, documents, and paintings, as well as some hands-on exhibits where you can try the ship's wheel or raise the sail. The **USS Cassin Young ▶** is a World War II destroyer that was hit by kamikaze raids at Okinawa (*Open* summer, daily 10–6. Guided tours on the hour. Tel: 617/242–5601 for a winter schedule. *Admission free*). The **Commandant's House** (*Open* Mar–Oct, daily 1–4) is a Federal-style building that was the home of the commanding officers of the Navy Yard from 1805 to 1974; the interior has been preserved as it was when last occupied. The **Boston Marine Society** (*Open* weekdays; tel: 617/242–0522 for hours. *Admission free*), next to the prominent octagonal Muster House of 1852, has three rooms filled with nauticalia. The **Bunker Hill Pavilion** (*Open* Apr–Nov, daily 9:30–4:30. *Admission free*) stages a 30-minute multimedia show featuring costumed mannequins that plunges you into the Battle of Bunker Hill.

## CHANGING TIMES

More than 160 ships were built in Charlestown Navy Yard. Over the years numerous buildings have been added, including boilermaker shops, a marine railroad, New England's first granite dry dock, and America's last surviving ropewalk. The yard expanded in the Civil War, and in World War II employed nearly 50,000 people. From the 1960s, it specialized in the modernization and overhaul of old vessels.

## SUMMER SALUTE

The USS *Constitution* traditionally takes part in the annual Harborfest celebration and enters Boston Harbor on July 4 to fire a national salute, a role resumed in 1996 after dry-dock restoration. Throughout the rest of the year, cannon firing takes place daily at sunset, when the flag is lowered.

67

*USS* Cassin Young *in the Navy Yard, Charlestown*

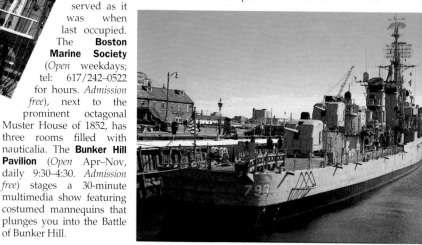

# Boston

*This giant milk bottle is actually a vintage 1930s snack bar, and can be seen outside the Children's Museum*

**THE FOUNDER OF CHRISTIAN SCIENCE MOVEMENT**
The First Church of Christ, Scientist was founded in Boston in 1879 by Mary Baker Eddy. Born in 1821 into a strict Calvinist family in Bow, New Hampshire, Mary became convinced of the power of prayer in healing after making a sudden recovery from a serious fall. She began to teach spiritual healing and in 1875 published her principal work, *Science and Health*. In 1908, aged 87, she founded the daily newspaper, the *Christian Science Monitor*. Published internationally by the Christian Science Publishing Society, it is relatively independent of its church and is highly regarded.

**BUNKER HILL**
"We wish, finally, that the last object to the sight of him who leaves his native shore, and the first to gladden him who revisits it, may be something which shall remind him of the liberty and the glory of his country."
– Daniel Webster, address on laying the cornerstone of the Bunker Hill Monument, June 17, 1825.
For more on Bunker Hill, see pages 33 and 61.

### ▶▶▶ Children's Museum 49E2
*300 Congress Street*
*Open: Sun–Thu 10–5, Fri 10–9.*
*Admission: moderate*
*Subway: South Station (Red Line)*
Adults will wish they were kids again when they see this interactive museum, one of the best of its kind. Venture aboard Boats Afloat, shop at Super Mercado, look in at the Grandparents' House, visit a Japanese home, climb a two-story maze—and more.

### ▶▶ Christian Science Center and Mapparium 48A1
See page 63 and panel on this page.

### ▶▶▶ Faneuil Hall Marketplace 49D3
See page 59.

### ▶ Federal Reserve Bank 49D2
*600 Atlantic Avenue (tel: 617/973–3000)*
*Open: tours Jul–Aug, Fri 10:30; during school terms, 1st and 3rd Fri of each month. Admission free*
*Subway: South Station (Red Line)*
This imposing, silvery 33-story slab was built in 1972–1977 by Hugh Stubbins & Associates. Here, old bills are destroyed, and at the end of the tour you are given a bag of shredded money to take home.

### ▶ Fenway Park 48A2
*4 Yawkey Way (tel: 617/267–6666 for details of guided tours)*
*Open: tours May–Sep, Mon–Fri 10 AM, 11 AM, noon, 1 PM.*
*Admission: moderate*
*Subway: Kenmore (Green Line)*
One of the most famous of all baseball grounds, Fenway Park is home to the Boston Red Sox (see page 81).

### ▶ FleetCenter Tours 48C4
*150 Causeway Street (tel: 617/624–1518)*
*Open: daily. Tours Memorial Day–Labor Day, Tue–Sat (also Sun, Jul–Aug) noon and 2 PM. Admission free; tour moderate*
*Subway: North Station (Green and Orange lines)*
The FleetCenter is home to a branch of the New England Sports Museum (see panel on page 171). Behind-the-scenes tours of Boston's state-of-the-art sports complex begin with a nostalgic look back to the days when the home of the Celtics and the Bruins was next-door Boston Garden.

### ▶ Harrison Gray Otis House 48C4
*141 Cambridge Street*
*Open: tours 11–4. Admission: inexpensive*
*Subway: Bowdoin Square (Blue Line; closed weekends) or Charles Street (Red Line)*
Dating from 1796, this was the first of the three houses built on Beacon Hill for Harrison Gray Otis, and is now home to the headquarters of the Society for the Preservation of New England Antiquities (SPNEA). The society has painstakingly researched the original wall-coverings, now fully restored, and the house contains period furnishings.

### ▶▶▶ Isabella Stewart Gardner Museum    48A1

*280 The Fenway*
*Open: Tue–Sun 11–5. Admission: expensive*
*Subway: Museum (Green Line)*

This magnificent museum is the creation of Isabella Stewart Gardner, the heiress of a wealthy New York family. Its exterior gives little hint of what lies within—a Venetian-style palazzo crammed with priceless art treasures and ranged around an exquisite four-story courtyard in which architectural fragments are surrounded by ferns and flowers in season. Each room has a theme and is arranged as Mrs. Gardner left it, giving an outstanding collection an appealing air of intimacy. As well as numeous paintings by Italian Renaissance artists, Dutch and Flemish masters, and French Impressionists, there are ancient Egyptian artifacts, sculptures, ceramics, tapestries, a lace collection, and furniture.

Concerts are held in the Tapestry Room on Saturdays and Sundays, September to May, at 1:30 PM (tel: 617/734–1359), and there is an excellent small café.

### ▶ John F. Kennedy Library and Museum    48C1

*220 Morrissey Boulevard, Columbia Point*
*Open: daily 9–5. Admission: moderate*
*Subway: J.F.K./UMass (Red Line) for free shuttle bus (every 20 minutes, 8–5)*

This striking building, designed by I.M. Pei and scenically sited on the waterfront in the southern neighborhood of Dorchester, is the nation's memorial to J.F.K. In the museum at the J.F.K. Library, the Kennedy era is re-created with replicas of the White House Oval Office, historical documents, and films on J.F.K.'s life.

See panel for the adjacent **Commonwealth Museum**.

**A STRONG CHARACTER**
Isabella Stewart Gardner was the talk of Back Bay. She wore diamonds in her hair and raised a few eyebrows by posing for her artist friend John Singer Sargent. Once she hired a boxer to perform at a ladies' tea party. She slept late in early-rise Boston. After her son died at the age of two, she suffered depression and took a trip to Europe. She returned to Boston a new woman; her Back Bay home became a fashionable salon, where she held glittering galas and balls, and she devoted much of her time to collecting art.

**69**

**COMMONWEALTH MUSEUM**
Next door to the J.F.K. Library, this museum covers everything to do with the Commonwealth of Massachusetts. Changing and permanent exhibits feature Native Americans, immigrants, towns and cities, the political system, natural history, and labor history. (*Open* Mon–Fri 9–5, Sat 9–3. *Admission free*).

*The splendid courtyard of the Isabella Stewart Gardner Museum, with its fountains, statues, and flowers*

*Nighttime view of the John Hancock Tower, an excellent observation point*

**LOCAL FINE ARTS**
New England is well represented at the Museum of Fine Arts in the sections devoted to furniture. Among the pieces on show are a late 17th-century press cupboard from Wethersfield, Connecticut, with pillars painted black to resemble ebony, and two fine Newport chests of the mid-18th century. Silverware on display includes items by Paul Revere, and many of the museum's 19th-century pictures have a New England theme, such as Frederick Childe Hassam's *Boston Common at Twilight* and Winslow Homer's *Lookout—"all's well."*

▶▶▶ **John Hancock Tower and Observatory**   48B2
*200 Clarendon Street (Copley Square)*
*Open: Hancock Observatory Apr–Oct, daily 9 AM–11 PM; Nov–Mar, Mon–Sat 9 AM–11 PM, Sun 9–6. Last admission one hour before closing. Admission: moderate*
*Subway: Copley (Green Line) or Back Bay (Orange Line)*
New England's tallest building (built 1968–1976) is a striking 60-story slab of reflective glass designed by I.M. Pei & Partners and neatly reflecting adjacent Trinity Church. It suffered numerous teething problems just after completion when window panes repeatedly fell out and landed on the street below. On the top floor the Hancock Observatory offers, like the nearby Prudential Tower, superb panoramic views over Boston and the bay, to the highlands of Massachusetts, Vermont, and New Hampshire. You can see out of three sides only, but a recorded narration describes the view from one side and gives a general survey of the city's history.

▶▶▶ **Museum of Fine Arts**   48A1
*465 Huntington Avenue*
*Open: Mon–Tue 10–4:45, Wed–Fri 10–9:45 (Thu–Fri, West Wing only after 5), Sat–Sun 10–5:45. Admission: expensive (reduced Thu–Fri after 5 and by donation Wed after 4)*
*Subway: Museum (Green Line) or Ruggles (Orange Line)*
New England's largest art gallery, often referred to as the MFA, is also one of the nation's finest. It is particularly noted for its Asian collection and its European paintings.
Most of the ground floor is devoted to a wide-ranging selection of American paintings, furniture, and decorative arts. The museum has an unrivaled collection of John Singleton Copley portraits, including John Hancock, Samuel Adams, and Paul Revere, in addition to his famous

work *Watson and the Shark*. The Hudson River School land-scape painters Albert Bierstadt, Fitz Hugh Lane, and Thomas Cole; the American Impressionists Childe Hassam, Winslow Homer, Mary Cassatt, and James McNeill Whistler; and New York's Abstract Expressionists are also well represented. A series of re-created period rooms provides a good insight into daily life in New England from the 17th to the 19th centuries. For other local themes, see panel opposite.

Also on the ground floor is the MFA's collection of Japanese woodblock prints, the largest in the world, and some fine Indian miniatures and Islamic ceramics. The Nubian collection includes pottery, sculpture, and frag-ments of furniture found in tombs and temples. The museum's Egyptian pieces include statues of King Mycerinus and Queen Kha-merer-ebty II. The rooms devoted to ancient Greece have some fine red-figure vases and the Bartlett *Aphrodite*, while among the Roman treasures are frescoes from a house in Pompeii.

The bulk of the Chinese and Japanese collection is upstairs, as is European art. Among the highlights here are J.M.W. Turner's *Slave Ship* and Constable's *Stour Valley and Dedham Church*. An outstanding selec-tion features works by French masters Manet, Degas, Gauguin, Renoir, Cézanne, and Monet, as well as Van Gogh. The Firestone Silver Collection features rare pre-1789 French silver.

The museum has a large shop and a choice of cafés and restaurants.

### ▶▶▶ Museum of Science 48B5

*Charles River Dam*
*Open: early Jul–Labor Day, Sat–Thu 9–7,*
*Fri 9–9; rest of year Sat–Thu 9–5, Fri 9–9.*
*Admission: moderate*
*Subway: Science Park (Green Line)*

One of the great science museums of the world, this has more than anyone could hope to see in a single day. With over 450 interactive exhibits, it is an almost unfailing hit with the children who come here in throngs. At the **Theater of Electricity**, you can watch high-voltage lightning sparks produced by the world's largest Van de Graaff generator. The **Observatory** delves into the unseen, including micro-scopic life and ultrasonic sounds, while **Earthworks** re-creates the process of gems growing beneath the Earth's surface. **Frontiers of Biotechnology** has interactive comput-ers providing an introduction to genetics.

Two further attractions in the museum require separate admission (each moderate); reservations are strongly advised (tel: 617/723–2500). The **Charles Hayden Planetarium** gives tours of the New England skies and offers an intergalactic journey on its multimedia "starship," as well as laser shows. The **Mugar Omni Theater** has a wraparound domed screen that is 76 feet in diameter and as tall as a four-story building; it also boasts state-of-the-art projection, and 84 speakers.

**MUSEUM TOURS**
Free tours of the Museum of Fine Arts provide an introduction to the collec-tions (Mon–Sat, except Mon holidays, 10:30, 1:30). Other themed tours take place Mon–Fri 10:30–2:30 (for details, tel: 617/267–9300).

71

*Explore the many faces of the world of nature at the Museum of Science*

**CHARLES RIVER CRUISES**
An optional extra to a visit to the Museum of Science is a 50-minute narrated cruise (Apr–Nov) on the Charles River. Departures are from CambridgeSide Galleria Mall in Cambridge. For informa-tion, contact the Charles Riverboat Company (tel: 617/621–3001).

**SPEAKING FOR FREEDOM**

In Park Street Church in 1831, William Lloyd Garrison made his first antislavery speech, a landmark in the history of the abolitionist movement. From a cramped office in Washington Street, he published the *Liberator*, an antislavery newspaper. His views incensed Brahmins and Southerners alike and, after speaking for abolition in 1835, he was attacked by an angry mob. He sought refuge in the State House (then the city hall), and the mayor put him into the safety of a jail. The cause gathered support as slaves were smuggled to freedom through the so-called "Underground Railroad."

**CHARLES BULFINCH (1763–1844)**

America's first professional architect, Bulfinch was called on after independence to give Boston—with its wooden houses concentrated in narrow streets around the waterfront—an image better suited to its role as one of the world's most prosperous seaports. With resplendent public buildings such as the State House and a revamped Faneuil Hall, a dozen churches (only St. Stephen's, in the North End, still stands), and the development of Beacon Hill as an elegant residential area, Bulfinch radically changed the city's character. He then moved on to design the new Capitol in Washington, DC.

*Whale watching with the New England Aquarium*

### ▶▶▶ New England Aquarium 49E3

*Central Wharf*
*Open: Jul–Labor Day, Mon, Tue, Fri 9–6, Wed–Thu 9–8, weekends and holidays 9–7; Labor Day–Jun, Mon–Fri 9–5, weekends and holidays 9–6. Admission: expensive*
*Subway: Aquarium (Blue Line)*

A spectacular encounter with the underwater world. The West Wing's Coastal Rhythms exhibit shows the marine and bird life of the coasts from New England shores to jungle lagoons. In the main gallery, you walk past a window onto the Aquarium Medical Center, where stranded sea creatures are treated. On the way up to the top of the ramp you will learn why fishes come in such a range of colors, shapes, and patterns; you then spiral down beside a four-story cylindrical water tank, with fish of every size—sharks among them—swimming around a replica coral reef.

Try to time your visit with a sea-lion show aboard the museum vessel *Discovery*. The aquarium also runs whale-watching cruises and educational "Science at Sea" tours on *Doc Edgerton*; for information, call 617/973–5281.

### ▶ Old South Meeting House 49D3

See page 58 and panel opposite.

### ▶▶ Old State House 49D3

See pages 58–59.

### ▶ Paul Revere House 49D4

See page 60.

### ▶▶▶ Prudential Center Skywalk 48A1

*Prudential Tower, Prudential Center, 800 Boylston Street*
*Open: daily until 10 PM. Admission: inexpensive*
*Subway: Prudential (Green Line, E train)*

Although scarcely Boston's best-loved building, the prominent Prudential Tower offers a superb view over the city from its Skywalk (50th floor), 700 feet above the streets. On a really clear day, the 360-degree panorama stretches to the Berkshire Hills and New Hampshire and

Vermont. As you walk around the gallery, displays and sound recordings highlight events and personalities from Boston's history.

### ▶▶ Public Garden 48B2

*Behind Boston Common*
*Open: dawn–dusk. Admission free*
*Subway: Arlington (Green Line)*

Well-fed squirrels and pigeons populate this charming park, graced with statues and some 350 varieties of trees. Since 1877, pedal-powered swan boats have conveyed summer visitors across the pond, past weeping willows and beneath a scaled-down replica suspension bridge (boats, weather permitting, mid-Apr–late Sep). Look for the bronze statuettes of a duck and eight ducklings, modeled on the heroes of Robert McCloskey's children's story, *Make Way for Ducklings*.

### ▶▶ State House 48C3

*Beacon Street*
*Open: Mon–Fri 9–5 (tours 10–3:30). Admission free*
*Subway: Park Street (Red and Green lines)*

Prominently sited at the top of Boston Common, the State House is the seat of government for the Commonwealth of Massachusetts. Road distances are traditionally measured from the gold-leaf dome. The State House was originally designed by Charles Bulfinch. Subsequently extended, the building has a rich marble interior. The entrance is through the **Doric Hall**. It leads to the **Nurses Hall**, hung with a trio of paintings by Robert Reid (*Paul Revere's Ride*, *James Otis Arguing Against the Writs of Assistance*, and *The Boston Tea Party*), and into the circular Hall of Flags and main staircase. The **House of Representatives** contains the Sacred Cod, a wooden fish carving that is the symbol of Massachusetts. The **Senate Chamber** and **Governor's Office** are part of the original building by Bulfinch.

### ▶▶▶ Trinity Church 48B2

See page 63.

### ▶▶▶ USS *Constitution* and Museum 48C3

See page 67.

*One of the famous and perennially popular swan boats in Boston Garden*

**MEETING HOUSES AND CHURCHES**
Old South Meeting House, with its Wren-inspired brick facade dating to 1729, replaced an earlier wooden meeting house built by Puritan settlers. These early colonists built their churches in the plain, square, meeting-house style, with a wooden spire or cupola and, inside, wooden paneling, box pews, and galleries supported on wooden columns. Reflecting the unity of Church and State, the meeting house often also served as town hall. It was not until the 19th century that new churches were built in such European-inspired styles as Gothic or Romanesque Revival.

## HARVARD'S EARLY DAYS

In 1636, the Massachusetts Bay Colony allocated £400 to establish a college, originally for 40 students, to foster the Puritan ethic and to educate potential ministers. In the 18th century, an endowment of £799 appeared. However, the headmaster stole half the money and fled.

*Japanese print at the Arthur M. Sackler Museum*

# Cambridge

Cambridge lies just across the Charles River from Boston, a short walk over Harvard Bridge from Back Bay. Yet it is a separate city in its own right—a commercial center as well as a famous seat of learning centered on Harvard University and the Massachusetts Institute of Technology (MIT). At night, Harvard Square comes alive with street entertainers and bustle. It is the busy atmosphere and the shopping, dining, and nightlife, rather than the physical appearance of Cambridge, that tend to attract visitors.

Cambridge was founded in 1630 as Newtowne and became the capital of the Bay Colony, being chosen for its protected site away from the exposed Boston peninsula. Harvard University was founded in 1636, and two years later Newtowne was renamed Cambridge after the English seat of learning. Following the battles of Concord and Lexington in 1775, provincial militias grouped on Cambridge Common to form the new Continental Army under the command of George Washington. Today, Harvard University is one of the preeminent Ivy League establishments in the country (see pages 22–23).

The Massachusetts Institute of Technology was founded in 1861 as a "society of arts, a museum of arts and a school of industrial science." For the visitor it is of chief interest for its modern architecture and sculpture. In particular seek out two buildings by Eero Saarinen: the Chapel, which reveals a dramatic interior sparkling with dots of reflected light, and the Kresge Auditorium, with an eighth of a sphere forming a triangular shell over the rest of the structure.

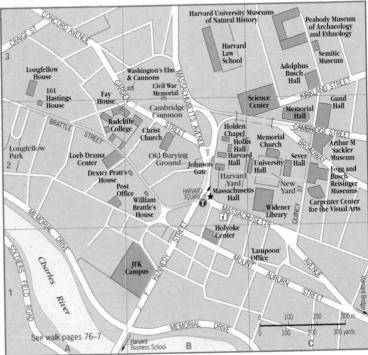

See walk pages 76–7

## ▶▶ Harvard University Museums    74C2/3

*Subway: Harvard Square (Red Line)*

The **Fogg Art Museum▶▶** and the **Busch-Reisinger Museum▶▶**, at 32 Quincy Street, are two museums in one (*Open* Mon–Sat 10–5, Sun 1–5. *Admission: moderate; free all day Wed, Sat 10–12*). The Fogg covers art from Western Europe and the U.S., featuring Italian Renaissance works, paintings by Dutch and Flemish masters, and such 19th-century Americans as Homer, Whistler, and Sargent; French Impressionists and Pre-Raphaelites are also represented. The Busch-Reisinger concentrates on art from northern Europe and Scandinavia, with Bauhaus artifacts and Expressionist paintings. The **Arthur M. Sackler Museum▶**, at 485 Broadway Street, is housed in an innovative, if controversial, candy-striped building by James Stirling. It contains beautiful and rare items from Asia and the ancient world, including Greek Attic vessels, carvings of deities, Indian and Persian miniatures, and the world's finest collection of Chinese jade.

Entrances to the Harvard University **Museums of Natural History** and **Peabody Museum of Archaeology and Ethnology▶** are at 26 Oxford Street and 11 Divinity Avenue (*Open* Mon–Sat 9–5, Sun 1–5. *Admission: moderate; free Sat 9–12; covers the three museums, but not the Peabody Museum, in this rambling building*).

Much of it is the preserve of the specialist researcher, but the public mostly comes to see the unique collection of glass flowers in the Botanical Museum, more than 700 items in all, representing giant cross sections, roots, rotting pears, and insects (see panel). A 30-minute tape tour guides you to the highlights. The other museums are the Museum of Comparative Zoology, including fossils, dinosaurs, and the world's largest collection of spiders; and the Mineralogical and Geological Museum, with an attractive stone and gem collection. The Peabody displays ethnological artifacts, including the Hall of the American Indian.

## ▶▶ Longfellow House    74A3

105 Brattle Street

*Closed for renovation until 2002; for details of opening times, tel: 617/876–4492*

*Subway: Harvard Square (Red Line)*

Henry Longfellow was 30 years old when he first saw this 1759 yellow clapboard mansion, and felt like a "prince in a villa" just to lodge here. It was bought for him and his wife Fanny as a wedding present from his father-in-law; the couple had a happy marriage and six children. Here he completed his translation of Dante and penned *The Song of Hiawatha*, *Paul Revere's Ride*, and *Evangeline*. He entertained Dickens, Twain, Emerson, Hawthorne, and Wilde. Longfellow died here after living in the house for 45 years. His personal artifacts abound: there is a crowded study, whose books reflect a passion for knowledge; a Steinway piano around which he enjoyed singing German lieder, and the chair made from the "spreading chestnut tree."

### HARVARD'S GLASS FLOWERS

George Lincoln Goodall, the first director of Harvard's Botanical Museum, wanted three-dimensional plant models for teaching purposes. He traveled to Dresden in 1886 to visit Leopold and Rudolf Blashka, father and son, who were specialists in supplying museums with glass sea creatures. In this way he established a year-round laboratory for scientific study. The final models were created by Rudolf to illustrate plant diseases.

*Longfellow House, home to the poet from 1837 to 1882*

### JUST DESSERTS?

Millionaire newspaper tycoon William Randolf Hearst achieved notoriety in his days at Harvard, where he kept a pet alligator and gave personalized chamber pots to his instructors before being expelled. Similar gratitude was shown in 1764 when a student took a book from the library of Massachusetts Hall on the eve of its burning. On returning the volume the next day, he was thanked by President Holyoke, and then expelled for taking the book without permission.

*The nation's oldest university, Harvard has become the wealthiest, too*

# Walk

## Harvard and Cambridge highlights

*See map on page 74 (yellow route).*

This is a tour of Harvard University and historic Cambridge, taking in the Common and the home of the poet Henry Wadsworth Longfellow.

From Harvard Square Red Line subway station, walk north on Massachusetts Avenue to Johnson Gate, which gives access to **Harvard Yard**, the hub of the university. The first quadrangle, **Old Yard**, contains dormitories for freshmen and the oldest campus buildings; it was here that Washington gathered his troops against the British. To the left as you enter is **Harvard Hall**, a 1764 reconstruction of the original building endowed by John Harvard and destroyed by fire. Adjacent is **Hollis Hall** (1762), whose students included Emerson and Thoreau. Dents in the steps in front of the hall were reputedly caused by the student

*Leafy Harvard Yard*

practice of placing cannonballs in fireplaces to radiate heat, and throwing them out in spring! On the right is **Massachusetts Hall** (1718), the oldest building of all, which numbers John and Samuel Adams among its luminaries.

In the center of Old Yard, the **John Harvard Statue** (1885), known as the "Statue of Three Lies," is not quite what it seems. A student, not Harvard, was the model, and the inscription "John Harvard, Founder, 1638" errs on two counts: Harvard was the benefactor, not the founder, and the university was founded in 1636.

Beyond **University Hall** (1816), designed by Charles Bulfinch, is **New Yard**, a quadrangle formed by Memorial Church (1931), Sever Hall (1880), and the **Harry Elkins Widener Library** (1913). The latter is the largest university library in the world and was endowed by the mother of Harry Widener, an avid collector of antiquarian books who perished aboard the *Titanic*. True to his mother's wishes, the building has been unaltered, and for a time all applicants had to undertake a swimming test (Harry could not swim). **Memorial Church** is dedicated to Harvard men who died in the two world wars.

Leave the yard and enter Quincy Street, opposite the concrete and glass **Carpenter Center for the Visual Arts** (1963), the only building in America designed by Le Corbusier. Turn left. Continue past the Fogg and Sackler museums to Cambridge Street, cross to the other side, and go left past the cathedral-like **Memorial Hall** (1874), built to honor all the Harvard men killed in the Civil War. Continue straight on; cross Massachusetts Avenue at the traffic lights, then cross Cambridge Common, passing the war memorial. The Common formerly functioned as the focus for Cambridge's religious, social, and political life. Three captured British cannons stand on the grass close to where Washington took command of the 9,000 men who had gathered to form the Continental Army. Washington's Elm (not the original tree) marks the spot.

Cross Garden Street by the traffic lights. To the left, the **Old Burying Ground** contains the graves of the first eight Harvard presidents, and **Christ Church** (1761) was used as a patriot barracks after its staunchly Tory Anglican congregation fled before the Revolution—its organ pipes were pilfered for use as bullets. Turn right along Garden Street, then left through the gate to **Radcliffe College**, which was founded as the Society for the Collegiate Instruction of Women in 1879, when Fay House (1807) was acquired. The college was incorporated into Harvard in 1894. Leaving Radcliffe, turn right along Brattle Street, known in the 18th century as Tory Row because of the British patriotism of its residents, to **Longfellow House**, George Washington's headquarters during the siege of Boston (see page 75). Returning along Brattle Street, see **number 56**, the home of Dexter Pratt, who was immortalized by Longfellow in *The Village Blacksmith* ("a mighty man is he, with large and sinewy hands"); the "spreading chestnut tree" is no longer there.

*Above: there's always entertainment in Harvard Square, whether it's eating out, listening to music—or watching a game of chess*

# Boston

*The handsome Lenox Hotel on Boylston Street*

**CITY FREEBIES**
● Concerts at the Hatch Shell in summer.
● New England Conservatory of Music concerts, some of which are held in the resplendent Jordan Hall (tel: 617/536–2412).
● Faneuil Hall Marketplace street entertainers and Faneuil Hall itself.
● Commonwealth Museum.
● Massachusetts State House.
● Ranger-led walking tour along the Freedom Trail.
● The Public Garden.
● The Harvard University Museums are free all day Wednesday and on Saturday 10–12.
● Charlestown Navy Yard, including USS *Constitution* and USS *Cassin Young*.
● Christian Science Church and Mapparium.
● Tours of the Boston Athenaeum and Boston Public Library.

**78**

*A visitor center will help with finding accommodations*

## Accommodations

**HOTELS** Boston has world-class hotels right in the heart of the city. The principal hotel area begins at the Theater District, just south of Boston Common, and extends westward past the Prudential Tower toward Massachusetts Avenue. Although some of the larger streets in this area are visually uninspiring, you will be within easy walking distance of Copley Square and the Freedom Trail at Boston Common. Other convenient hotels are found in the downtown and waterfront areas, and in Cambridge.

Boston accommodations are more expensive than those in rural New England. At certain periods, especially during major conventions, it can be difficult to find a room, and rates are at a premium. At times like this, consider staying out of town and visiting Boston daily by public transportation, for example from Salem or Concord using MBTA Commuter Rail—see "Canny planning," page 259. Weekends are less busy than weekdays, and accordingly rates tend to be lower. Since the converse applies in summer resorts such as the North Shore, Cape Cod, and the islands, you can make substantial savings by visiting Boston for the weekend and making for the coast during the week. Hotel rates do not usually include breakfast, and state and local room tax are added to the charge.

**BED AND BREAKFAST** If hotels are too expensive, staying at a bed-and-breakfast (B&B) provides a money-saving alternative. Several agencies organize hosted B&B accommodations, where you stay in someone's home. The most charming and convenient locations include Back Bay, Beacon Hill, and the North End (see page 268).

You can find less expensive places by opting to stay farther out from the city. The subway and rail systems take you to most far-flung locations, such as the suburb of Brookline, southwest of central Boston, which has inexpensive bed-and-breakfasts. For those on a tight budget, the Boston International AYH Hostel (for address and telephone number, see page 268) near the Prudential Center has dormitory accommodations.

*Boston has a reputation as the most musical city in the United States, a reputation that rests almost entirely on its being the home of one of the finest ensembles in the world: the Boston Symphony Orchestra.*

In October 1881, the BSO, or Boston Symphony Orchestra, gave its inaugural concert, bringing to reality the dreams of the philanthropist and amateur musician Henry Lee Higginson of founding a great and permanent orchestra in his hometown of Boston. For the first 20 years or so, concerts were given in the Old Boston Music Hall, initially under the directorship of Georg Henschel and then under a series of German and French conductors.

In 1900, the orchestra moved into Symphony Hall, which to this day remains one of the world's most acoustically perfect auditoriums. Symphony Hall also became the locale for the orchestra's hugely successful "Promenade Concerts," which had begun in 1885, fulfilling Higginson's ambition to provide a "lighter kind of music" in addition to more serious programs. Later called "Popular Concerts" and then "Pops," these have remained a favorite springtime tradition (see page 25) under the auspices of a separate ensemble, the Boston Pops Orchestra.

**The Koussevitzky era** In 1924, the Russian-born Serge Koussevitzky, a man of extraordinary talent and dynamic personality, took over as musical director. During his 25 years of illustrious leadership, the BSO began making regular radio broadcasts. From 1937 onward, the orchestra took up a summer residency at Tanglewood, in Lenox in the Berkshire Hills (see panel on page 146).

**"The aristocrat of orchestras"** Charles Munch followed Koussevitzky in 1949, introducing American audiences to quantities of French music. In the 1960s, promoted under Erich Leinsdorf as "the aristocrat of orchestras," the BSO made numerous recordings and tours all over the world.

With Seiji Ozawa as musical director since 1973 (he plans to stay until 2002), Higginson's "great and permanent orchestra" has consolidated its worldwide reputation, commissioning new works from composers such as Hans Werner Henze and John Cage, and presenting soloists of the highest caliber, such as Yo-Yo Ma, Pinchas Zukerman, and Itzhak Perlman.

*Above and left: John Williams conducts the Boston Pops*

**CONCERT INFORMATION**
The season at Symphony Hall runs from the beginning of October to the end of April. Contact Symphony Hall, 301 Massachusetts Avenue, Boston, MA 02115 (tel: 617/266 –1492 for information or 617/266–1200 for tickets; fax: 617/638–9400). For the Tanglewood Music Festival, contact Symphony Hall, as above, or Tanglewood Ticket Office, Lenox, MA 01240 (tel: 413/ 637–1600). For the Pops (May, Jun, Jul 4, and holidays), contact the Symphony Hall (see above).

**79**

**OPENING NIGHT**
When Isabella Stewart Gardner opened her Venetian-style palace (see page 69) on New Year's Night 1903, her guests were entertained in the concert hall by 50 members of the Boston Symphony Orchestra. Afterward, the doors of the hall were opened and guests had their first view of the ravishing courtyard, filled with flowering plants and lit by lanterns.

"And this is the city of Boston,
The land of the bean and the cod,
Where the Lowells talk only to Cabots,
And the Cabots talk only to God."
– James Collins Bossidy, toast at Holy Cross Alumni dinner, 1910.

"I've never seen a Lowell walk,
Nor heard a Cabot speak with God,
But I enjoy good Boston talk
And Boston beans and Boston cod."
– R.C.H. Bruce Lockhart, *In Praise of Boston*.

*Eating alfresco at Quincy Market against the backdrop of Faneuil Hall*

## Food and drink

As the birthplace of the humble baked bean, Boston is nicknamed "Beantown." However, more sophisticated fare is available. Maine lobsters, quahogs (large clams), chowders, and scrod (white fish) also feature.

Faneuil Hall Marketplace is one of the best places to eat cheaply. Food stalls in Quincy Market offer takeouts in various forms—calzones, Middle Eastern pastries, seafood, specialty milkshakes, and swordfish kebabs—but the market starts to close down after 9:30 PM.

There's another food hall, called Marché Mövenpick, in the Prudential Center, with a very appetizing selection of worldwide fare served from many food stalls.

Options for leisurely meals include restaurants on Beacon Hill's Charles Street and on Newbury Street. Chinatown has many excellent eating places: some of the best offer bargain prices with functional décor to match. The North End can boast some of the highest-quality Italian food in the Northeast, and although Bostonians as a rule tend to eat early, it is often possible to stop by in the early hours for a cappuccino or bowl of pasta.

Cambridge has so much happening in the evening that to dine out there is part of the Boston experience. A branch of Au Bon Pain, a Boston-born sandwich-bar chain, occupies one side of Harvard Square. Popular with chess players, this area is a good point from which to watch Cambridge life. Cambridge is strong on ethnic eateries, with Portuguese fare along Cambridge and Hampshire streets and a choice of Korean, Creole, and Indian restaurants.

Boston has some excellent beers: the Boston Beer Company's Samuel Adams ale and its variants are probably the best known. Some pub-restaurants produce their own brew: the Commonwealth Fish and Beer Company, Brew Moon, Cambridge Brewery, and Boston Beer Works.

*Boston means different things to different people. To some it means simply the Red Sox. Add the Celtics, the Bruins, and the Boston Marathon and you begin to form a picture of a rich sporting tradition.*

**The Red Sox** The ups and downs of Boston's baseball team are inextricably entwined in the fabric of Boston life. Strong men go misty-eyed at the mention of such legendary names as Babe Ruth, Jimmie Foxx, Carl Yastrzemski, Jim Lonborg, Ted Williams (the last major leaguer to bat over 400 for a season), and Dick "The Monster" Radatz or Roger "The Rocket" Clemens (both of whom regularly pitched at over 90 mph).

The atmosphere at Fenway Park is phenomenal, but to attend a college or local ballpark game, along with the mayor and the cheerleaders, is every bit as thrilling.

**The Celtics, the Bruins** Basketball was born at the Y.M.C.A. in Springfield, Massachusetts, in December 1891. Invented by a physical education teacher, Dr. James Naismith, to keep his students out of mischief in the winter months, it is the most widely played sport founded in the U.S.A. Naismith used two half-bushel peach baskets as targets, hence the name of the game.

Boston is home to the Boston Celtics, who won 11 of 13 titles between 1956/1957 and 1968/1969, making them one of the most successful teams in the National Basketball Association. If you look into almost any Boston backyard, you'll find a group of young Celtic fans in the team's green and white colors emulating a Larry Bird jump shot. The Celtics share the FleetCenter (successor to the venerable Boston Garden; see page 68) with the Bruins, Boston's popular hockey team.

**And more...** Other great events in the Boston sporting calendar include the Boston Marathon, held in April. The first was held in 1897 with 15 runners; now over 12,000 take part. August sees the M.F.S. Pro Championships (tennis), and in October about 1,000 boats take part in two days of races in the Head of the Charles Regatta.

**TICKET INFORMATION**
● The Boston Red Sox, Fenway Park, 4 Yawkey Way (tel: 617/267–1700; fax: 617/236–6640). The season runs from early April to early October. For tours, tel: 617/236–6666.
● The Boston Celtics and Boston Bruins, FleetCenter, 150 Causeway Street— by North Station (tel: 617/523–6050 for the Celtics and 617/624–1000 for the Bruins). The Celtics' season runs from November to April, Bruins' from October to April.
● New England Patriots Football Club, Foxboro Stadium, Route 1, Foxboro (tel: 508/543–8200). The National Football League is in action from August to early January.

*Fenway Park, much revered by Red Sox fans. It was rebuilt in the 1930s by the team's greatest benefactors, Tom Yawkey and his wife*

*Above left: the Friday and Saturday Haymarket—lively, and colorful*
*Above right: altogether quieter, a bookstore near Tremont Street*

**BARGAIN HUNTING**
Outlet shopping in New England is booming. The main places are Kittery, North Conway, Freeport, Fall River, and Worcester; the last two of these can easily be reached by bus from Boston (see pages 16–17). Whether or not these places offer the best prices is a matter of debate; some contend that the best bargains are to be had at sale time at such stores as Saks Fifth Avenue and Lord & Taylor in Boston.

**MORE SHOPPING IDEAS**
● Music: HMV, 1 Brattle Square, Cambridge; Tower Records, 360 Newbury Street.
● Secondhand books: Brattle Bookstore, 9 West Street, Boston.
● Antique maps: Eugene Galleries, 76 Charles Street.

## Shopping

**BACK BAY AND BEACON HILL** If a competition were held to find New England's most chic shopping street, **Newbury Street** would be among the front-runners. Running parallel to Commonwealth Avenue from the Public Garden through the fashionable district of Back Bay, the street has high-class designer shops, art galleries, and boutiques (including Second Time Around, selling used designer-label clothing for women) and makes for highly enjoyable window-shopping; Tower Records is a huge emporium on the corner of Massachusetts Avenue. On Beacon Hill, Charles Street is known for antiques.

**The Shops at Prudential Center** is a large and smart complex, connected to the Hynes Convention Center, the Sheraton Boston Hotel and, by footbridge, the Copley Place shopping center and the Westin and Marriott hotels—all enclosed. The 70 stores and restaurants at the Pru include shops for men, women, and children such as Saks Fifth Avenue, Levi's, Chico's, Britches, Talbots Kids, and Warner Brothers. There are also shoe and sports shops, gift shops, and several restaurants, including Legal Sea Foods. The 100-store, two-level **Copley Place** is high-class; here you will find Gucci, Louis Vuitton, Tiffany, a Museum of Fine Arts shop, and others. There are restaurants and a cinema.

Close by, at 440 Boylston Street, the world's largest teddy bear marks the entrance to **FAO Schwarz**, the city's main toy store.

**DOWNTOWN CROSSING** There are over 300 retail stores around Summer and Washington streets, including the department stores of Macy's and Filene's; **Filene's Basement** is renowned for its bargain-price clothes. **Barnes & Noble** (395 Washington Street) is the city's largest discount bookseller.

**OTHER BOSTON HIGHLIGHTS Chinatown** is great for browsing, with markets, restaurants, gift shops and supermarkets, as well as Vietnamese, Thai, and Cambodian stores. **Faneuil Hall Marketplace** is a top attraction, with over 110 shops ranging from retailers such as The Disney Store to outlets for New England crafts and souvenir stalls. Its central hall, Quincy Market, offers a variety of places to eat, including Durgin Park. By total contrast, the Haymarket is a no-frills fruit and vegetable market (Fridays and Saturdays only). Italian shops in **North End** include some outstanding food stores and bakeries around Hanover and Salem streets.

Good **museum shops** are found at the Children's Museum, Museum of Fine Arts (also at Copley Place and Faneuil Hall Marketplace), Peabody Museum in Cambridge (with a wide range of ethnic wares), and the Museum of Science.

**CAMBRIDGE Harvard Square** has a concentration of bookstores offering new and secondhand volumes. **WordsWorth**, 30 Brattle Street, offers a wide range of books at discount prices. Bookstores remain open all evening and Sundays, and you are welcome to browse for hours. There are also numerous music stores and boutiques. The **Harvard Coop Society** (known as the Coop) on Harvard Square is the major department store, serving the town since 1882, and has book and music sections. There are more books for sale inside the MIT Coop at Kendall Square. From Kendall Square you can take the free shuttle service to the **Cambridgeside Galleria,** which comprises more than 90 shops, including Sears department store. For antiques, try the four-story Cambridge Antique Market (201 Monsignor O'Brien Highway, Lechmere subway); for crafts, Cambridge Artists Cooperative, 59A Church Street on Harvard Square. Porter Exchange, north of Harvard Square, has several specialty stores.

**MORE SHOPPING** Two good places for outdoor and hiking equipment are **Eastern Mountain Sports** at 1041 Commonwealth Avenue, Boston (also winter sports gear) and **Hilton's Tent City** on 272 Friend Street near North Station.

Five miles west of Boston on Route 9, the **Mall at Chestnut Hill** is a feast for the eyes, with over 100 stores, including Bloomingdales and Filene's. Concerts take place here on weekends. Take the Green Line (D train for Riverside) to Chestnut Hill station.

Farther out of town, and accessible by commuter train, **Cape Ann**, **Marblehead**, **Ipswich**, **Essex**, and **Newburyport** each have art galleries and antiques shops.

*Quincy Market, next to Faneuil Hall, dates back to the 1820s. Today, it is always a bright and entertaining place to be*

## BOSTON DINING PERSPECTIVES

Both the Prudential Tower and John Hancock Tower have stunning high-level views of the city by night. But the 52nd-floor Top of the Hub Restaurant in the Prudential and The Bay Tower on the 33rd floor at 60 State Street allow diners to enjoy superb views at their leisure. Dinner cruises on the *Odyssey* from Rowes Wharf get a low-level but equally fascinating perspective on Boston.

## Nightlife

There's a lot going on in Boston and Cambridge at night, although it is not an all-night city in the way New York is. The liveliest areas popular with visitors are Kenmore Square and Lansdowne Street (near Boston University), Harvard Square in Cambridge (by Harvard University), Copley Square, Boylston Place, and Faneuil Hall Marketplace. The Theater District has some comedy clubs, and Roxy, a tony nightclub. A little farther out, Davis Square in Somerville has some lively nightspots.

**LISTINGS AND TICKETS** Full listings, covering theater, concerts, cinema, bars, and clubs, appear in the *Boston Globe* and *Boston Phoenix* on Thursdays, the *Boston Herald* on Fridays, *The Improper Bostonian* (biweekly; also includes restaurants), and Stuff@night, a guide to Boston's nightlife. The website www.bostonusa.com has details of all kinds of events. For bookings, contact Ticketmaster (tel: 617/931–2000), or for both advance tickets and half-price tickets on the day of performance, visit the BosTix ticket booth in Faneuil Hall Marketplace or Copley Square.

**THEATER** The Theater District, just south of Boston Common, has mainstream and avant-garde offerings. The Charles Playhouse in Warrenton Street is still showing the comedy whodunnit *Shear Madness,* America's longest-running play, in which the audience helps solve a murder mystery.

**BARS AND CLUBS** There are over 20 clubs offering everything from billiards to slam-dancing in the Lansdowne Street/Kenmore Square area. Avalon is good for dancing, and Axis for rock and roll. Jillian's Boston offers pool, billiards, and virtual-reality games; Bill's Bar is funky and relaxed. Gay venues abound in Kenmore Square and in South End. Sunday

*The Bull & Finch, familiar to many from the TV series* Cheers

night tends to be gay night at many clubs; the Club Café (Columbus Avenue) is a club and bar open seven days.

Boylston Place has several bars, such as Envy and the Sugar Shack, that attract the younger set. In Somerville, Johnny D's in Davis Square has a welcoming crowd, good food, and great music. In Beacon Hill, the Bull & Finch pub, famed for its appearance in the TV series *Cheers*, is at 84 Beacon Street. Faneuil Hall Marketplace has plenty of piano bars, pubs, dance venues, and comedy clubs.

For comedy, try Dick Doherty's Comedy Vault, 124 Boylston Street, Nick's Comedy Stop in the Theater District, and The Comedy Connection at Faneuil Hall.

**JAZZ AND BLUES** The Regattabar in the Charles Hotel, 1 Bennett Street, Cambridge, is a top-class jazz venue, booking national acts year round. Also in Harvard Square, don't miss the Sunday Gospel Brunch at the House of Blues, 96 Winthrop Street, Cambridge. Scullers, 400 Soldiers Field Road, Boston, is a favorite for lighter-style jazz. Ryles Jazz Club, 212 Hampshire Street on Inman Square, Cambridge, is for Latin music fans and serious jazz aficionados. Wally's, a tiny local joint at 427 Massachusetts Avenue in the South End, is also a major jazz attraction.

**CLASSICAL AND LIGHT MUSIC** The BSO (Boston Symphony Orchestra) performs at Symphony Hall from the beginning of October to the end of April (tel: 617/266–1200). The New England Conservatory of Music gives a series of free concerts, many in glittering Jordan Hall, 30 Gainsborough Street at Huntington Avenue (tel: 617/585–1122). The Boston Pops Orchestra performs light classics and popular favorites at Symphony Hall from early May to early July (see pages 24–25), and in early July there is a series of free Boston Pops outdoor concerts at the Hatch Shell on the Esplanade (tel: 617/266–1200). From June to September, big-name pop groups perform at the Fleet-Boston Pavilion, a 4,000-seat "tent" on the Waterfront.

Boston Lyric Opera (tel: 617/542–6772), New England's leading opera company, stages productions at the Wang Center for the Performing Arts at 270 Tremont Street and at the nearby Shubert Theater.

*The Charles Hotel's Regattabar provides a stylish ambience for an evening of jazz*

85

**BOSTON: FIRST BUILDINGS IN U.S.A.**
● First public school (Boston Latin School, 1636).
● U.S. post office (1639).
● Lighthouse (1765).
● Chocolate factory (1765).
● Branch library (1871).
● Telephone exchange (1877).

**OTHER BOSTON U.S. FIRSTS**
● Military training field (1631).
● First fire law (banning wooden chimneys, 1632).
● Law against smoking (1633).
● Football game (Boston Common, 1862).
● Computer (Differential Analyzer at MIT, 1928).

# Connecticut

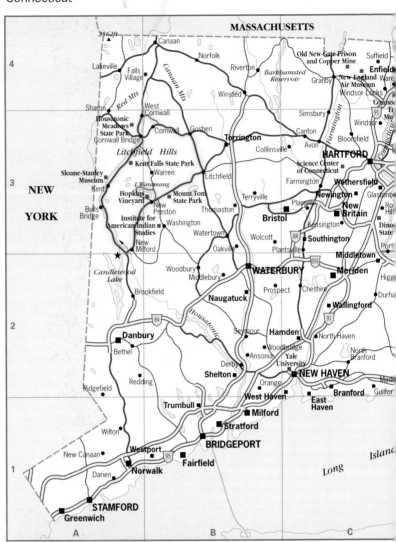

MASSACHUSETTS

NEW YORK

2562ft

Canaan
Norfolk
Lakeville
Falls Village
Riverton
Old New-Gate Prison and Copper Mine
Suffield
Enfield
Ware
Granby
New England Air Museum
Windsor Locks
Conne ft Mu

Canaan Mts
Red Mts
Sharon
West Cornwall
Winsted
Simsbury
Canton
Connecticut
Windsor

Housatonic Meadows State Park
Cornwall Bridge
Cornwall
Goshen
Collinsville
Avon
Bloomfield

Litchfield Hills
Kent Falls State Park
Torrington
HARTFORD
Science Center of Connecticut

Sloane-Stanley Museum
Kent
Warren
Litchfield
Farmington
Wethersfield

Hopkins Vineyard
Mount Tom State Park
Terryville
Plainville
Newington
Glastonb

Institute for American Indian Studies
New Preston
Washington
Thomaston
Bristol
Kensington
New Britain
Ro Hil

Bulls Bridge
New Milford
Watertown
Wolcott
Southington
Dino State

Oakville
Plantsville
Middletown
Port

Candlewood Lake
Woodbury
Middlebury
WATERBURY
Meriden
Higg

Brookfield
Prospect
Cheshire
Durh

Naugatuck
Wallingford

Housatonic
Danbury
Seymour
Hamden
North Haven

Bethel
Woodbridge
North Branford

Ridgefield
Redding
Ansonia
Derby
Yale University
NEW HAVEN
Mad

Shelton
Orange
Branford
Guilfor
East Haven

Wilton
West Haven
Milford

Trumbull
Stratford
Long
Island

New Canaan
Westport
BRIDGEPORT

Darien
Norwalk
Fairfield

STAMFORD
Greenwich

Barkhamsted Reservoir
L. Waramaug

A          B          C

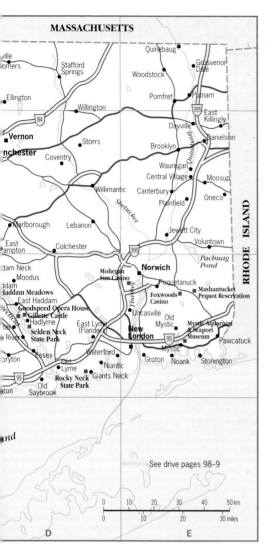

**MASSACHUSETTS**

See drive pages 98–9

| 0 | 10 | 20 | 30 | 40 | 50 km |

| 0 | 10 | 20 | 30 miles |

**CONNECTICUT** Named after New England's longest river, Connecticut extends some 90 miles east to west and 55 miles north to south. The state's rolling terrain is bisected by the Connecticut River, which flows south along a fertile valley into Long Island Sound. The shoreline has sandy beaches and quiet coastal towns, as well as more urbanized parts close to New York City. The coastal hinterland is a gentle plain, which rises farther inland into forested uplands near the New York and Massachusetts borders. Connecticut is America's third smallest state (after Rhode Island and Delaware) and is densely populated. Yet the state has genuinely rural tracts that belie its proximity to the Big Apple. In all, two-thirds of Connecticut is rural, and most of that is forested.

*Roseland Cottage in the quiet village of Woodstock*

**▶▶▶ REGION HIGHLIGHTS**

*Museums*
**Maritime Aquarium at Norwalk** *page 107*
**Mashantucket Pequot Museum** *page 95*
**Mystic Aquarium** *page 101*
**Mystic Seaport** *page 101*
**Wadsworth Atheneum** *page 95*
*Houses*
**Lockwood-Mathews Mansion** *page 107*
**Mark Twain House** *pages 96–97*
*Scenery and places*
**Litchfield Hills** *pages 98–99*
**Wethersfield** *page 97*
**Yale** *pages 103–105*

**88**

*The coastal strip looks out across Long Island Sound, where the Gulf Stream entices tropical underwater marine life*

**THE NUTMEG STATE**
Legend has it that local traders cunningly passed off wooden nutmegs as real ones, hence Connecticut's nickname.

"Here's to the town of New Haven,
The home of the Truth and the Light,
Where God talks to Jones in the very same tones
That he uses with Hadley and Dwight."
– F.S. Jones, *On the Democracy of Yale.*

"Connecticut in her blue-laws, laying it down as a principle, that the laws of God should be the law of the land."
– Thomas Jefferson, letter to John Adams, January 24, 1814.

**THE HISTORIC HERITAGE** The Connecticut River brought in the first Puritan settlers in the 1630s after Boston and Massachusetts had become too religiously intolerant for their tastes. Hartford, Windsor, and Wethersfield were the original trio of towns they established, hence the three clusters of grapes on the state's coat of arms. These settlements merged to become the Hartford Colony, later named the Connecticut Colony. The Fundamental Orders of Connecticut, adopted in 1638, are widely held to have been the world's first written constitution of a democratic government—hence the state's official nickname, the Constitution State, on every vehicle license plate. Connecticut has also been named the "Nutmeg State"—its inhabitants being "Nutmeggers" (see panel)—and, during the Revolutionary War, the "Arsenal of the Nation." The state retains plenty of mementoes of those times.

Yankee ingenuity also made Connecticut the "Gadget State." This was the birthplace of the cylinder lock, the pay telephone, the steel fishhook, the stonecrusher, and the submarine torpedo. Samuel Colt's firearms company manufactured the famous .45 revolver and other guns in Hartford, while pioneer clockmakers Seth Thomas and Eli Terry had Thomaston and Terryville named after them. Eli Whitney devised interchangeable parts, which made him in effect the father of mass production. Charles Goodyear developed rubber vulcanization, later important in car tire production, and the first American copper coins were minted here. Despite a decline in industrial activity, the state still leans heavily toward manufacturing, including the output of ball bearings, nuclear submarines, and sewing machines. The state's oldest established towns lie along the 253-mile shoreline and along the principal waterways, notably the Connecticut River. Early colonial days saw Yankee traders flourishing in shipbuilding, seafaring, and commercial ventures at Mystic, Stonington, New London, and elsewhere. The insurance industry that began in conjunction with this maritime activity gathered momentum. Today, insurance is still the state capital's raison d'être.

**VISITOR ATTRACTIONS** For the visitor, Connecticut's maritime heritage is an obvious attraction and is admirably presented in the great museums of **Mystic** and **Norwalk**. But other industrial ports bordering Long Island Sound in the state's southwestern territory have only patches of interest; one such oasis is Yale University, an architectural treasure house in **New Haven**. In the **Hartford** area, the former homes of Mark Twain, Noah Webster, and Harriet Beecher Stowe can be visited. Offbeat whimsicality can be found at Gillette Castle, in the **Connecticut River Valley**, while the Lockwood-Mathews Mansion in Norwalk, the most sumptuous house of its day, foreshadows the opulent "cottages" at **Newport** in Rhode Island. Fine art collections are found at Hartford, Yale University, New Britain, and in private houses such as the Hill-Stead Museum.

Elsewhere in the state, pristine white clapboard villages such as Litchfield, Wethersfield, Ridgefield, and Farmington await discovery, grouped around their characteristic village greens, each stubbornly refusing to concede to urbanization. By the Massachusetts border is the state's highest terrain and most scenic drive, along the fast-flowing Housatonic River in the **Litchfield Hills**, an area well endowed with arty crafts shops and galleries. The Connecticut and Housatonic rivers are both noted for fishing, the latter especially for trout, as well as for the more adventurous pursuits of tubing, canoeing, and kayaking. Near Litchfield, the White Memorial Foundation offers hiking, cross-country skiing, horseback riding and bird-watching. Connecticut also has some gentler drives through landscapes dominated by cornfields, orchards, old barns, and silos; one of the most scenic roads is Route 169 from Lisbon to Woodstock.

Several major locales exist for spectator sports. The Hartford Whalers is a major-league hockey team. The sport of jai alai can be seen inexpensively at Milford (the biggest jai alai arena in New England). Auto racing takes place at Lime Rock Park, and the Pilot Pen Tennis Women's Championships are held at New Haven. The Canon Greater Hartford Open is an annual golf event.

89

*Below: at Coventry, in the northeastern corner of the state, the Nathan Hale Homestead was built by the patriot's family in 1776, the year he was executed*

## Events

For further information, contact the state tourist office (see page 266) or chambers of commerce.

### JANUARY–MARCH
**Warm Up to Winter**, Farmington Valley area: history and good food at museums and period homes.

### MAY
**Dodge Dealers Grand Prix**, Lime Rock Park, Lakeville.
**Dogwood Festival**, Fairfield.
**Lobsterfest**, Mystic: lobster served alfresco on the waterfront.

### JUNE
**Elizabeth Park Rose Weekend**, Hartford.
**Farmington Antiques Weekend**.
**Yale–Harvard Regatta**, New London.

### JUNE–JULY
**Barnum Festival**, Bridgeport: parade and festival to honor P.T. Barnum.
**Canon Greater Hartford Open**, Cromwell: attracts top names in golf.

### JULY
**Antique and Classic Boat Rendezvous**, Mystic Seaport.
**Guilford Handicrafts Exposition**.
**Litchfield Open House Tour**: houses open their doors to the public.
**Riverfest**, Hartford/East Hartford: Fourth of July river festival.
**Blessing of the Fleet**, Stonington.

### AUGUST
**Brooklyn Fair**: agricultural fair.

**Connecticut River Powwow**, Durham: crafts, dancing, and more.
**Great Connecticut Traditional Jazz Festival**, Moodus.
**Mystic Outdoor Art Festival**: artists take over the streets.
**Pilot Pen Tennis Women's Championships**, New Haven: women's professional tournament at Yale University.
**Quinnehtukqut Rendezvous and Native American Festival**, Haddam Meadows State Park.

### SEPTEMBER
**Durham Fair**.
**Oyster Festival**, East Norwalk: tall ships, arts, crafts, oysters.
**Woodstock Fair**, South Woodstock: agricultural show, animals, crafts.

### SEPTEMBER–OCTOBER
**Chowderfest**, Mystic Seaport.
**Chrysanthemum Festival**, Bristol: parade, arts, crafts, drama.

### OCTOBER
**October Walking Weekend**, statewide: guided walks.

### NOVEMBER
**Manchester Road Race**.

### DECEMBER
**Christmas season**, Mystic Seaport: Lantern Light Tours give a one-hour "interactive play."
**First Night**, Hartford: fireworks, procession, and other entertainment.

*Mystic Seaport, venue for a variety of events and activities*

*Shelf clocks, the invention of Eli Terry, in the American Clock and Watch Museum*

## ► Bristol and Area
*86C3*

From the late 18th century until 1929, the neighboring towns of Bristol, Thomaston, Terryville, Winsted, and Waterbury formed the hub of America's clock industry. Aptly, Bristol is home today of the **American Clock and Watch Museum**►► at 100 Maple Street off Route 6 (*Open Apr–Nov, daily 10–5. Admission: inexpensive*). The collection charts the history of American horology, and in all contains 1,600 watches and 1,800 clocks. Look for the re-created 1825 clockmaker's shop and an 1860 novelty clock featuring a lion's eyes moving in time to the tick. At 95 Riverside Avenue (Route 72), the **Carousel Museum of New England**► has over 300 antique carved horses and carousel chariots (*Open Apr–Nov, Mon–Sat 10–5, Sun 12–5; Dec–Mar, Thu–Sat 10–5, Sun 12–5. Admission: inexpensive*).

Also on Route 6, opposite the church at **Terryville**, stands the **Lock Museum of America**► (*Open May–Oct, Tue–Sun 1:30–4:30. Admission: inexpensive*), close to the former Eagle Lock mills, which opened in 1854. The display features around 20,000 items, including a 1580s Spanish Armada chest.

East of Bristol, **Farmington**► has numerous Federal-style houses and has become a select satellite of Hartford. It was a key point on the Underground Railroad as well as the village where the freed *Amistad* slaves awaited return to Africa (see panel on page 105). In the village, the **Stanley-Whitman House** (*Open May–Oct, Wed–Sun 12–4; Nov–Apr, Sun 12–4. Admission: moderate*) has been painstakingly restored to its 1720 colonial appearance and contains period furnishings. The nearby **Hill-Stead Museum**►►, an early 20th-century Colonial Revival home, exemplifies good taste. It belonged to industrialist Alfred Pope (see panel). The family adorned the interior with French Impressionist paintings, including two of Monet's *Haystack* series and *The Absinthe Drinker* and *The Guitar Player* by Manet (*Open May–Oct, Tue–Sun 10–5; Nov–Apr, Tue–Sun 11–4. Admission: moderate*).

### EARLY CLOCKMAKING
Connecticut's clock-making industry, now all but defunct, originated in the late 18th century. In 1792, Eli Terry began making his name and his money by mass-producing wooden cogs at his water-powered mill in Connecticut, standardizing gears, and introducing interchangeable parts. Brass gears came in after 1800.

### HILL-STEAD'S CREATOR
Theodate Pope (later Theodate Riddle) was primarily a self-trained architect who gained much of her initial experience when she engaged the firm of McKim, Mead, and White to build Hill-Stead as a retirement home for her parents. She played a large part in influencing the vernacular New England farmstead design, which incorporated elements of Georgian and Greek Revival styles.

*Left: a carving in the Carousel Museum*
*Below: architecture from Bristol's 19th-century heyday*

**GENEALOGY AT MIDDLETOWN**

Middletown was settled in 1650 and prospered in the late 18th century, as shipbuilding and trade with the West Indies made it the richest community in the colony. The town attracts genealogists on the trail of British and European ancestors, many of whom settled here. The Godfrey Library is the chief source of information and has records for the whole U.S. before the 1850s.

*The eccentric exterior of Gillette Castle befits the reclusive actor for whom it was built*

### ▶ Connecticut River Valley 87D2

After its 407-mile journey along the New Hampshire–Vermont border and through Massachusetts, the Connecticut River finally crosses Connecticut itself before flowing into Long Island Sound. The Connecticut scenery along New England's longest river is pleasantly mild rather than spectacular, but a scattering of good sights, mostly in the county of Middlesex (at the southern end of the river's course), makes it worth taking in. Antiques shops, art shows, country fairs, concerts, and festivals are plentiful along the entire valley.

**SOUTH OF HARTFORD** At the mouth of the river is **Old Saybrook**, the earliest settlement in the valley; nearby Essex is home to the **Connecticut River Museum** (*Open Tue–Sun 10–5. Admission: inexpensive*), pleasantly sited by the river. Though not extensive, the museum's displays illustrate shipbuilding and maritime life in the context of the Connecticut River Valley. On show is a replica of the *American Turtle*, the first submarine, a one-man vessel invented to sink British ships in the Revolution.

At Essex, the **Valley Railroad▶▶**, one of only two steam railroads in New England (the other is at North Conway, New Hampshire), operates 1½-hour round trips to Chester and Haddam (May–Dec; tel: 860/767–0103 for schedule). Period passenger coaches make it a nostalgic treat: original 1920s furnishings include padded armchairs in Pullman class and cane seats in standard. An optional extra is to stop off at Deep River for a boat trip upriver to East Haddam. The **Ivoryton Playhouse** provides entertainment at nearby Ivoryton, where there is a **Museum of Fife and Drum** (*Open* Jun–Sep, Sat–Sun 1–5; performances Jul–Aug, Tue 7:30 PM).

**Gillette Castle▶▶** (*Open* late May–early Sep, Fri–Sun 10–5. *Admission: inexpensive*), high above the river south of East Haddam, is a fantasy re-creation of Rhenish medievalism, or something approaching that style. It was built in 1914–1919 for actor William Gillette, who was famous for his Sherlock Holmes performances, but, despite public prominence, was something of a recluse. A system of mirrors was placed so that he could watch from his bedroom for unwelcome visitors and decide whether to be indisposed, and his dinner table was almost comically small. His passion for railroads led to the creation of a 3-mile track (no longer existing, although one passenger coach is preserved) on the grounds. The castle's idiosyncrasies reveal themselves inside, its 24 rooms displaying wooden light switches, Javanese matting, walls made of field stones, light fixtures made with pieces of bottle glass, and bizarre lock systems.

Horse-and-carriage rides are provided daily in summer at the castle and on weekends during most of the rest of the year. A scenic approach to the castle is on the **Chester–Hadlyme ferry** (Apr–Nov). There has been a ferry here since 1769, making it one of the oldest such continuous services in the country. It is feasible to leave the car on the far side, cross the river as a foot passenger, and walk up a path to the castle. **Selden Neck State Park**, devoid of facilities and accessible only by boat, is ideal for escapists who like to rough it. Canoe rental is available from below Gillette Castle.

**Chester▶** is a village graced with an unblemished main street. Close by is the delightful **Goodspeed Opera House** (tours available Jun–Oct, Mon 1–3, Sat 11–1:30; tel: 860/873–8664), with musicals (Apr–Dec, Wed–Sun; box office

*Passengers on the Valley Railroad's early 20th-century steam train enjoy views of the Connecticut River and Valley*

## NEW ENGLAND'S LONGEST RIVER

Named by Algonquin people as the Quinnetukut ("the long river whose waters are driven by wind and tide"), the 407-mile-long Connecticut River flows from its source near the New Hampshire–Canada border through four states and is tidal from Hartford.

First charted by Dutchman Adriaen Block in 1614, the valley was, by the 19th century, an important cigar tobacco-growing area. But, as in much of New England, forest has taken over. Essex, which once had six shipyards, and other communities grew as river settlements. Shipbuilding, however, never recovered from a flood in 1936 and a hurricane two years later.

## CRUISES

Deep River Navigation (tel: 860/767–0103 or 860/526–4954) offers trips from Old Saybrook and Hartford, on Long Island Sound, and hour-long river voyages aboard the steamer *Becky Thatcher* or *Silver Star*. Camelot Cruises (tel: 860/345–8591) runs a sailing murder mystery cruise. *Sea Mist II* (tel: 203/488–8905), at Stony Creek, makes 45-minute trips around some of the 365 Thimble Islands; Money Island is where the pirate Captain Kidd reputedly used to draw in his boat.

## AIR MUSEUM HIGHLIGHTS

Despite losing 23 vintage aircraft in a freak tornado in 1979, the New England Air Museum boasts a number of choice exhibits, including:

● 1911 Ernest Hall No. 1 Blériot x1: the same design of craft as that flown by pioneer aviator Louis Blériot when he made the first crossing from England to France in 1909.

● 1934 Marcoux-Bromberg Special: an R-3 racer that won a 150-mile contest in California in 1938, achieving an average speed of 265 mph. It featured in the Clark Gable movie *Test Pilot*.

tel: 860/873–8668) usually running for six or seven weeks and audience participation on Wednesdays. You can arrive for a performance by boat, picnic on the lawn, and have drinks at the intermission on a balcony overlooking the river. A tiny one-room schoolhouse at **East Haddam** was where patriot Nathan Hale taught in 1773–1774 (*Open* late May–early Sep, Sat–Sun afternoons. *Admission free*). Its bell was made in Spain in AD 815 and is still in working order.

At Higganum, **Sundial Gardens** comprise a pretty 17th-century knot garden, an 18th-century garden, and a topiary with miniature vistas through its "outdoor rooms."

**Dinosaur State Park**, on I-91 at Rocky Hill, has in its exhibition hall (*Open* Tue–Sun) some 500 dinosaur footprints in what was a shallow, stagnant lake 185 million years ago. Life-size models, a diorama, and a com-mentary flesh out the details of their history, and there is a discovery room for children. If you bring your own plaster of Paris, you can make casts of actual dinosaur prints May–Oct, daily 9–3:30. The impressions were uncovered in 1966.

For Hartford, see pages 95–97.

**NORTH OF HARTFORD** On Route 140 at **East Windsor**, the **Connecticut Trolley Museum** (*Open* late May–early Sep, Mon–Sat 10–5, Sun 12–5; Apr–late May, early Sep–mid-Oct, Sat 10–5, Sun 12–5. *Admission: moderate*) dates from 1940. Volunteers run the trolleys along a 1½-mile section of the former Hartford–Springfield Street Railway and have rescued old trolleys from other places; one was found in a scout camp being used as a laundro-mat. On Route 75 situated close to Bradley International Airport, the **New England Air Museum▶** (*Open* daily 10–5 *Admission: moderate*) exhibits over 80 military and civil air-planes, from early biplanes to experimental fighters and modern home-built machines.

**Old New-Gate Prison and Copper Mine** (*Open* mid May–Oct, Wed–Sun 10–4:30. *Admission: inexpensive*), of Route 20 in East Granby, retains its castlelike walls. The overgrown sandstone ruins have atmosphere, and

*Cruising on the Connecticut River near East Haddam*

children will enjoy exploring the mine. The prison dates from 1773, when it was built to provide laborers to work on the copper mine. This became America's first state prison in 1776, and British loyalists were jailed here during the Revolution. The opportunities this presented, with shafts providing convenient exits and the availability of gunpowder, proved irresistible, and a mass escape by British prisoners of war and Tories occurred in 1781. The prison was abandoned in 1827.

▶ **Foxwoods** *87E2*

Foxwoods Casino, on the Mashantucket Pequot Indian reservation, has become very big business (see page 125)—it is the largest casino in the U.S. and is a huge crowd-puller. It may not be everyone's idea of heaven, but the place is so bathed in commercialism as to be an experience in itself. Financed by some of the bucks cascading into the thousands of gambling machines, the **Mashantucket Pequot Museum and Research Center▶▶▶** (*Open* late May–early Oct, daily 10–7; mid-Oct–mid-May, daily 10–6. *Admission: moderate*) is on an impressive scale, featuring a re-creation of a 1550 Pequot village, a diorama of a caribou hunt scene, a re-created 1780 Pequot farmstead, and site tours of the excavation of a 17th-century fort. Other attractions on site include the **Cinedrome 360° Theater**, the **Turbo Ride**, and **Virtual Adventures**. Nearby, on Route 2A at Uncasville, is another casino, the vast tentlike **Mohegan Sun**, based on an Indian longhouse design.

▶▶ **Hartford** *86C3*

America's insurance industry capital stands on the Connecticut River. Downtown is dominated by high-rise office buildings, the second tallest of which is the 527-foot **Travelers' Tower▶▶**, offering a 37-mile view (tours by appointment, mid-May–late October, Mon–Fri 10–3; tel: 860/277–0111. There are 72 steps). Virtually next door, at 600 Main Street, the Gothic Revival **Wadsworth Atheneum▶▶▶** (*Open* Tue–Sun 11–5; 11–8 first Thu of each month. *Admission: moderate, free Sat AM and Thu*) was, in 1842, the first public art museum in the country (see panel). The original castle has been extended to form an architectural blend of five interconnecting buildings.

(see page 125)

**WADSWORTH ATHENEUM HIGHLIGHTS**
A choice set of French Impressionist paintings includes Monet's *Beach at Trouville*, Matisse's *Woman with a Plumed Hat*, and Van Gogh's *Self Portrait*. There are also important works by Thomas Cole and Frederic Church of the Hudson River School, as well as Caravaggio's *Ecstasy of St. Francis* and Holman Hunt's *The Lady of Shalott*. Picasso, Dali, Warhol, and Rauschenberg are also represented. Other rooms are devoted to applied arts: European porcelain, 17th- and 18th-century carved chests from Connecticut and Massachusetts, costumes, textiles, and furniture.

95

*Above left: a starburst-patterned quilt in the Wadsworth Atheneum textile collection*
*Below left: local schoolmaster and patriot Nathan Hale*

**CARILLON CONCERTS**
Trinity College, a liberal, prestigious institution in Hartford, has a fine chapel modeled on the English Perpendicular (late Gothic) style and a Romanesque crypt. Carillon concerts are sometimes given.

**INSURANCE**
Hartford's insurance industry began in the 18th century to cover ship owners against loss of vessels. After the decline of shipping in the area, fire insurance grew in importance in the 19th century. Today, about 40 companies, including Aetna, Travelers, and CIGNA, are based here.

*Hartford's State Capitol: its exuberant design reflects Victorian pride*

**Bushnell Park**, the nation's first landscaped public space, cuts a green expanse across the center of the city and counts exotic rarities among its fine trees as well as a preserved carousel dating from 1914; a 1925 Wurlitzer organ provides the music. A grandiose brownstone structure known as the **Soldiers and Sailors Memorial Arch** (1886) honors citizens who served in the Civil War; its terra-cotta frieze depicts war scenes.

In the park rises the gold-domed **State Capitol▶**, built in 1878 to the design of Richard Upjohn and adorned externally with bas-reliefs of historic scenes. Its lavishly ornate legislative chambers, Hall of Flags, and gaudy silver and gold marble hall are grand gestures of civic pride. There are free tours (Jul–Aug Mon–Fri 9:15–2:15, Sep–Jun, Mon–Fri 9:15–1:15; also Apr–Oct, Sat 10:15–2:15), or you can just walk around by yourself. Since 1988, the Capitol has been connected by walkway to the new Legislative Office, an impressive addition in polished granite and starting point for tours of the Capitol Building.

At 800 Main Street is the **Old State House▶** (*Open* Mon–Fri 10–4, Sat 11–4. *Admission free*), which was designed by Charles Bulfinch and served as the state capitol from 1796 to 1878, and then as the city hall up to 1915. Today, it contains exhibitions of early Connecticut and Native American life and a visitor information center. State memorabilia and a collection of Colt firearms are displayed at the **Museum of Connecticut History** at 231 Capitol Avenue (*Open* Mon–Fri 9:30–4. *Admission free*).

West of downtown, at 351 Farmington Avenue, is the redbrick Gothic **Mark Twain House▶ ▶ ▶** (reached by bus E from the central transit station in Hartford). Samuel Clemens, alias Mark Twain (see page 46), stipulated that his 19-room house should be unique. His personality still pervades what a local newspaper in 1874 described as "the oddest house in Connecticut if not in the whole of America." Here he wrote *Huckleberry Finn*, *Tom Sawyer*, and five other major works up to 1891. Many of the original family pieces survive, including the items ranged on a mantelpiece, about which he used to tell stories to entertain his children. Each of these items had to feature in his story,

and he had to start over again if he missed anything (*Open* Memorial Day–Oct 15, Dec, Mon–Sat 9:30–5, Sun 12–5; rest of year, Mon, Wed–Sat 9:30–5, Sun 12–5. *Admission: moderate*).

Immediately adjacent is the **Harriet Beecher Stowe House▶**, the home of the author of *Uncle Tom's Cabin* (see pages 46–47) from 1873 to her death in 1896, though most items here are not original. Harriet Beecher moved here while the Twain house was being built; at that time the neighborhood was known as Nook Farm and comprised a small literary colony (*Open* Mon–Sat 9:30–4, Sun 12–4. Closed Columbus Day–Jun. *Admission: moderate*).

At 950 Trout Brook Drive, **West Hartford**, is the **Science Center of Connecticut**, which has animal and planetarium shows and hands-on exhibits (*Open* Jul–Aug, Mon–Wed, Fri–Sat 10–5, Thu 10–8, Sun 12–5; Sep–Jun, Tue–Wed, Fri–Sat 10–5, Thu 10–8, Sun 12–5. *Admission: moderate*). At 227 South Main Street, the **Noah Webster House▶**, the birthplace of the author of *An American Dictionary of the English Language* and *The American Speller*, has absorbing Webster memorabilia (*Open* summer, Thu–Tue; rest of year, Thu–Tue afternoons only. *Admission: moderate*).

Off I-91 at exit 26, the town of **Wethersfield▶▶**, settled in 1634, is one of the earliest settlements in the state. Its charming historic district, the state's largest, includes several early 18th-century sea captains' homes along Broad Street, a huge, long green with houses set back. The **Webb-Deane-Stevens Museum▶**, on Main Street (*Open* May–Oct, Wed–Mon 10–4; Nov–Apr, Sat–Sun 10–4. *Admission: moderate*), comprises three well-restored houses. At the Webb House, General George Washington and the Comte de Rochambeau planned the final campaign in the Revolution, leading to the British defeat at Yorktown in 1781. More period charm and a fascinating early kitchen are found in the historic **Buttolph-Williams House**, built in 1692, on Broad Street (*Open* May–Oct, Wed–Mon 10–4). The **Keeney Memorial Cultural Center** has good information and changing exhibitions on local history. Main Street ends at **Cove Park**, where one 17th-century warehouse survives from the days when the town of Wethersfield was a port on the Connecticut, before the river changed course.

*Mark Twain's house, in the Nook Farm district of Hartford*

**THE CHARTER OAK**
A royal charter of 1662 gave a measure of independence to the Hartford colony, but in 1687 the new royal governor insisted it should be returned. At the meeting held to discuss the matter, the candles were suddenly extinguished and the charter vanished. It remained hidden (reputedly) in an oak tree for two years until the governor returned to England. In the 19th century, Hartford's famous Charter Oak, as it had come to be known, was felled. Numerous items are said to be made from it, including the chair of the lieutenant governor in the State Capitol.

# Drive

*Early fall in the Litchfield Hills*

*Admission: inexpensive*) exhibits bygone country tools collected by the late Eric Sloane. He considered these objects as "symbols of American heritage, worthy of at least the same recognition as the popular current sculpture made from American junk." He himself was a landscape painter and his studio has been re-created. Remains of an iron furnace in the grounds recall a vanished local industry. **Kent Falls State Park** (*Open* daily 8–dusk) is a roadside picnic stopoff, with swimming pools where water tumbles down a 200-foot flight of natural steps. **Housatonic Meadows State Park** (*Open* daily 8–dusk) has picnic benches with a riverside setting and is popular with anglers. Just north, a sign on the west side of the road marks the start of the Pine Knob Loop Trail, leading up to a summit with a fine view. At **West Cornwall**, cross the covered bridge over the Housatonic River on the right.

Take Route 128 east to **Goshen**, then Route 63 to **Litchfield▶▶**, the first national historic district declared in the state and widely regarded as one of the finest towns in New England. In its heyday, it was an industrial center, with grist- and sawmills, iron forges, tanneries, fulling mills, carriage makers and clockmakers, and hatters' shops. During the Revolution, it became a depot for military stores on roads linking Connecticut with the Hudson River Valley. The obvious legacy of the past is the wealth of Federal-style architecture along North, West, South,

## The Litchfield Hills

*See map on pages 86–87 (yellow route).*

A 64-mile tour of the highlands of Connecticut, taking in the best of the Housatonic Valley and the picture-perfect town of Litchfield. The fall colors are superb.

Start from **New Milford**, with its attractive green. Take Route 7 north past **Bulls Bridge**, which boasts one of only two covered bridges in the state still open to motor traffic (off Route 7 to the left). The scenery becomes increasingly unspoiled and rugged along the **Housatonic Valley▶▶**, although foliage restricts views. The valley is known for trout-fishing and canoeing.

At **Kent**, there are more antiques and crafts shops, and the **Sloane-Stanley Museum and Kent Furnace▶** (*Open* mid-May–Oct, Wed–Sun 10–4.

*A good place for an overnight stop is in this inn at Torrington*

and East streets, which radiate from the town's prominent Congregational church (1829) on the spacious green.

In the middle of town is the **Litchfield Historical Society**▶ (*Open* mid-Apr–mid-Nov, Tue–Sat 11–5, Sun 1–5. *Admission: moderate*), which maintains an archive library and a museum. By a genealogical fluke, the society inherited the world's largest collection of pictures by Ralph Earl, an eminent 18th-century portrait painter. The collection contains examples of Litchfield County furniture. Close by, the **Tapping Reeve House** of 1773 (*Open* Apr–Nov, Tue–Sat 11–5,

Sun 1–5. *Admission included with Litchfield Historical Society Museum*) belonged to Judge Tapping Reeve, who in 1784 built America's first law college—a primitive, single-room, unheated structure—on the grounds.

Route 202 west passes the entrance to **Mount Tom State Park**▶ (*Open* daily 8–dusk), where a 1-mile trail leads to a tower at the 1,325-foot summit and a pleasant local view. At the junction with Route 45, go northwest a short distance to take in **Lake Waramaug**▶, idyllically set beneath hills and offering boating, swimming, picnicking, and camping; the far end of the lake has a tiny beach. Close by the lake is **Hopkins Vineyard**, which has free tours and tastings.

Route 202 takes you back to New Milford. An optional detour is via Route 47 to the **Institute for American Indian Studies**▶ at Washington (*Open* Apr–Dec, Mon–Sat 10–5, Sun 12–5; Jan–Mar, Wed–Sat 10–5, Sun 12–5. *Admission: inexpensive*). Highlights include a longhouse, a 17th-century Native American village, and a simulated archeological site.

99

*Litchfield, a perfect New England town*

*If there is one image that first-time visitors to New England bring with them, it is of white clapboard houses grouped around a village green, overlooked by the tall, white spire of a wooden church, and set in rolling countryside against a backdrop of glowing autumnal trees.*

100

### A CHANGING FACE

The New England village did not always present the face that is so cherished today. What is now a neat, attractive green, with its bandstand and war memorial, was once an unsightly, scrubby piece of common land. The clapboard house was not always archetypal white; until idealization set in during the 19th century, houses were painted in a range of colors: reds, russets, and blues. Even that icon, the tall, white church spire, has not always been there—many were added in the 19th century.

### FARM BUILDINGS

Although houses within the village itself are nowadays most often white, old wooden farm buildings are traditionally a deep red in color. Particularly in the colder areas of New Hampshire and Maine, farm buildings are connected, so the farmer can go from barn to shed to house protected from the weather. (This also means, as many have learned to their cost, that fire can move swiftly from barn to shed to house.)

The truth is that the New England village lives up to every expectation, serene as any calendar picture. The ingredients are always much the same. Facing onto a green is the white timber church, most often Unitarian or Congregationalist. Then there is the country store, a treasure chest that every visitor must delve into, selling anything from freshly made doughnuts and gourmet local products to cans of kerosene and farmers' rubber boots.

Larger villages often have a number of other, individually owned and equally enticing stores, selling clothes, gifts, books, or crafts. Then there will be the town hall, seat of local government. And filling in the gaps around the green, and lining the roads leading to it, are the timber-built houses that typify New England, usually painted white but occasionally in traditional dusky shades. Some may fly the flag, many have a seasonal wreath of dried flowers on the door. One or two of these houses may be inns that offer accommodations and meals. Often dating back to colonial days and furnished with antiques, inns provide a delightful way to enjoy the charm and hospitality of a New England village. Every village also has its burial ground, a plot of land set apart from the church or meeting house.

**The village way of life** Because the houses are of wood, the local fire department is often a focus of social life, organizing parades and, along with the churches, events such as barbecues and ice-cream socials. The green is a setting for regular flea markets and, during the Christmas season, for the tree that, like others, is decorated with white lights. Some villages boast a theater.

*Village scenes: (top) fall in Cohasset, Massachusetts, and (right) winter in Sudbury, Massachusetts*

### ▶▶▶ Mystic

87E2

**Mystic Seaport**▶▶▶ (*Open* summer, daily 9–5; winter, daily 10–4. *Admission: expensive*) is placed by the Mystic River, where numerous boat- and shipyards flourished before decline set in during the 1880s. The museum features an admirable re-creation of life in a late 19th-century coastal community, with period buildings that include a drugstore, sailor's tavern, and printing press. Over 400 small craft make up the biggest such collection in the world, while among the larger ships that you can board are the *Charles W. Morgan* (1841), the last surviving American wooden whaler, and a replica of *Amistad*, the notorious slave ship (see panel on page 105), built using traditional techniques and authentic materials. Indoor exhibits include superb scrimshaw and figureheads.

The **Mystic Aquarium**▶▶▶ (*Open* Labor Day–Jun, daily 9–5; Jul–Labor Day, daily 9–6. *Admission: expensive*) is one of New England's largest. Much emphasis is placed on state-of-the-art viewing: in addition to the spectacular marine life displays—which include the world's largest artificial beluga whale habitat—you can take a simulated dive to the bottom of the ocean and experience the sounds as you descend. The Challenge of the Deep is a display conceived by *Titanic* discoverer Dr. Robert Ballard, which has as its highlight a 30,000-gallon coral reef tank. There are seal-, eagle-, and whale-watching cruises in season (tel: 860/572–5955). Ocean samples are studied in Project Oceanology at Groton (see panel on page 107). The town of Mystic has a row of captains' houses standing by the waterfront and a drawbridge (raised hourly, Apr–Oct), and a specialty shopping area called **Olde Mistick Village**, replicated to look like the original colonial settlement. More delightful shoreside architecture awaits at **Noank**, a lobstering and oystering village, with views of Fisher's Island (New York state); Abbott's, something of a Connecticut institution, sells ocean-fresh lobsters straight from the boat.

The **Denison Homestead** on Pequotsepos Road has been restored in the styles of five eras, from colonial times to the 20th century (*Open* mid-May–mid-Oct, Fri–Mon 10–4. *Admission: inexpensive*).

*Masted sailing vessels moored on the Mystic River*

**STONINGTON'S SURVIVALS**
Stonington, Mystic's coastal neighbor, also has several charming 18th- and 19th-century homes recalling its maritime heyday. Settled in the mid-17th century, it became a whaling, sealing, and shipbuilding community.

**MYSTIC CRUISES**
Educational cruises, with a naturalist on board, can be taken on the windjammer *Argia* (tel: 860/536–0416). You can cruise on the SS *Sabino*, the last operating coal-fired steamer in the U.S., or on the *Resolute*, a 1917 motor launch. Or try the *Breck Marshall*, a catboat (tel: 860/572–5315).

*Life in a 19th-century seaport reenacted at Mystic Seaport*

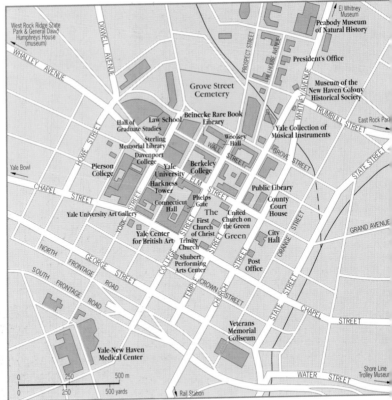

## HISTORIC HAMBURGERS

Not many fast-food establishments get onto the National Register of Historic Places. However, family-run Louis' Lunch in Crown Street, New Haven, made it by dint of being the birthplace of the American hamburger in 1900. Louis' retains its original grilling equipment. This is puritanical cuisine: toast, burger, lettuce, and tomato only—strictly no ketchup or mustard. The early 20th-century furnishings and Tiffany lamps are a far cry from McDonald's, too.

### ▶▶▶ New Haven                                86C2

Although it would take courage to rate the relative academic standards of Yale University at New Haven and Harvard University at Cambridge, Yale by far outstrips Harvard for visual interest for the day visitor. Eye-catching imitations of the medieval universities of Oxford and Cambridge in England are Yale's architectural hallmark. However, Yale and New Haven have little of the student–town interaction found between Harvard and Cambridge.

Founded in 1638 by the Puritans as an independent colony, New Haven is today a major cargo port, with a profusion of galleries, upscale shops, and good restaurants along Chapel Street.

**MUSEUMS** Most popular of the displays making up the bulk of the **Peabody Museum of Natural History▶▶** (*Open* Mon–Sat 10–5, Sun 12–5. *Admission: moderate*) is the dinosaur collection, including the first discovered specimens of brontosaurus and stegosaurus. The deinonychus ("terrible claw") inspired the vicious raptor in the movie *Jurassic Park*. In the Hall of Mammals, an 11,000-year-old ground sloth (found in a tar pit in New Mexico) is remarkable for still having part of its skin and hair attached. Elsewhere, the museum displays Egyptian and Polynesian artifacts, geology exhibits, natural history dioramas, and birds, and has a discovery room for children.

At 1080 Chapel Street, the **Yale Center for British Art▶▶** (*Open* Tue–Sat 10–5, Sun 12–5. *Admission free*) has a magnificent collection of works by Turner, Hogarth, Constable, Reynolds, and others, and puts on special exhibitions, talks, and films (for details, tel: 203/432–2800). Less well known is the **Yale Collection of Musical Instruments▶**, at 15 Hillhouse Avenue, where over 800 instruments include antique keyboards and such oddities as a 19th-century Italian-made Russian horn with a representation of a snake's head whose tongue vibrates when it is played (*Open* Tue–Thu 1–4. Closed Jul–Aug and university recess. *Admission: donation*). The **Yale University Art Gallery▶▶** at 1111 Chapel Street (*Open* Tue–Sat 10–5, Sun 1–6. *Admission free*), founded in 1832, has European paintings, a reconstructed Mithraic shrine, and a representative collection of American paintings and decorative arts.

**THE UNIVERSITY** Tours of **Yale University▶▶▶** from the visitor information center at 149 Elm Street are provided free by students Mon–Fri 10:30, 2; Sat–Sun 1:30.

The university was founded at Branford in 1701, moved to Old Saybrook the same year, and then to New Haven in 1716. Yale is the only collegiate university in the U.S.A., with students attached to the 12 colleges that belong to the university; the system is modeled on Oxford and Cambridge in England. Some 300 students live in each college, plus 100 freshmen in the Old Campus.

In the 20th century, the architect James Gamble Rogers gave Yale an "Oxbridge" look with his Georgian and Gothic-style buildings. Aging was achieved by various means: tiles were buried under different soils so that they would discolor and their edges become chipped; acid was poured on the stonework; glass was deliberately broken and releaded; and niches were left empty, as at Oxford and Cambridge, where so many statues have been stolen or destroyed down the ages.

**The Green** dates from colonial days when Puritan settlers laid out the town in neat squares, including this grazing ground. On one side, Phelps Gate leads into the **Old Campus**, where **Connecticut Hall**, built in the 1750s, is the oldest university building. The patriot Nathan Hale, industrialist Eli Whitney, and lexicographer Noah Webster were students here. Hale's statue was made in 1914 by a sculptor who had no idea of his subject's appearance, so a handsome Yale student was used as a model. The Theodore Dwight Woolsey statue is the only true likeness in the courtyard; his right foot is polished by students who rub it for good luck.

*Above left and below: Yale University is an architectural showpiece, with buildings by leading 20th-century architects rubbing shoulders with Gothic Revival and Georgian creations*

103

**WHERE THE SHOWS BEGAN**

From 1938 to 1976, New Haven's Shubert Theater was the favorite spot to première new productions before transferring to Broadway. Debut shows and plays have included *Oklahoma!, My Fair Lady, Blithe Spirit, The Sound of Music, A Streetcar Named Desire, Long Day's Journey into Night,* and *Annie Get Your Gun.* W.C. Fields, the Marx Brothers, Sarah Bernhardt, and Marlon Brando have all graced its stage. The theater reopened in 1983 and gives performances between September and June. Tours are given Sep–Jun, Mon–Fri 9–5 (tel: 203/624–1825).

*Above: home of the Yale Repertory Company*
*Right: Harkness Tower, a High Street landmark*

104

Beyond the Old Campus is the neo-Gothic **Harkness Tower** (1920), the country's tallest freestanding tower when built (221 feet) and modeled on Boston Stump in Lincolnshire, England. Around its clock are sculptures of the eight great men of Yale: Nathan Hale, E. Yale, Jonathan Edwards, Samuel F.B. Morse, Noah Webster, Eli Whitney, James Fenimore Cooper, and John C. Calhoun. **Wrexham Tower** was modeled on St. Giles Church in Wrexham, Wales (where Eli Yale is buried), and **Pierson College**'s tower is based upon the design of Philadelphia's Independence Hall. **Davenport**, ex-President Bush's college, displays the ubiquitous Gothic treatment on the street facade, but its courtyard is in a very different Georgian style.

The art deco **Hall of Graduate Studies** (1932) resembles a miniature New York skyscraper with its checkered motif and flat relief. President and Hillary Clinton attended the **Law School**, opposite whose stonework displays carvings of cops and robbers. Part of the building was inspired by King's College, Cambridge, England. The **Sterling Memorial Library**, known as the "Cathedral of Knowledge," looks intentionally like a medieval European cathedral, with cloisters decorated with stone carvings (one showing a student with a book of nude pictures and a glass of ale) and telephones masquerading as confessionals; the "altar" is the main desk. There is also a mural depicting a Mary Magdalene-like figure of Mother Yale holding the Book of Truth, with an orb of light. To the right are three men representing Art, Literature, and Philosophy (then, as now, these were the principal subjects studied at the university).

**Woolsey Hall**, a large circular building, holds regular concerts from September to May by student and visiting musicians. In the courtyard beyond is the **Beinecke Rare Book Library** (*Open* Mon–Fri 8:30–5, Sat 10–5. Closed Sat in Aug. *Admission free*), perhaps the most memorable of the

**SPORTING SPECTACULARS**
Football in the fall at the Yale Bowl has been a major feature of New Haven life since 1913. Once every two years, Yale and Harvard, the two old Ivy League rivals, battle it out in "The Game." Professional women tennis players compete each August at the Pilot Pen Tennis Women's Championships. At Milford, jai alai, a Basque sport similar to squash, takes place daily (matinees Sat–Mon; evenings Mon, Wed–Sat) from June to December. Although it is watched mainly for gambling, it is exciting, and the entrance fee is nominal.

university's modern buildings, designed in the 1960s by architect Gordon Bunshaft. The library's ingenuity is revealed inside: the outer shell of Vermont marble shields a skyscraperlike stack of priceless books and manuscripts from the sun's ultraviolet rays, while halon gas is used to protect the contents from fire. The library is

LUX ET VERITAS

best seen on a sunny day when the translucence of the marble is apparent. There is no admittance to the stacks themselves, but a complete Gutenberg Bible of 1455, one of only 22 known, is displayed in the public area. Outside, you look down into the **Sculpture Garden**, a compact landscape of geometrical shapes formed in white marble by Isamu Noguchi (the library desk has a leaflet outlining the artist's ideas).

A windowless building close by is home to secret university societies, such as George Bush's Skull and Bones Society. Note how the university's **President's Office** is purposely smaller than the other buildings: administration is seen as less important than academic life. In **Berkeley College**, Cross Campus Lawn is reputed

to be the birthplace of the game of frisbee, first played here by students using pie plates, which evidently had aerodynamic qualities.

**OUT OF TOWN** At Ansonia is **General David Humphreys House**, home of the aide to General Washington and the first U.S. ambassador (*Open* Mon–Fri 1–4:30. *Admission: inexpensive*). It is a museum with a difference, presented as a hands-on, late 18th-century experience, in which visitors dress up, spin wool, cook, and make bread and chowder in the manner of the period.

The **Eli Whitney Museum** at 915 Whitney Avenue (*Open* Wed–Fri, Sun 12–5, Sat 10–3, *Admission: inexpensive*), Hamden, pays tribute to the inventor of mass production and charts 200 years of industrial development in the New Haven area. Nearly 100 restored trolleys can be found at the **Shore Line Trolley Museum** at 17 River Street, East Haven (*Open* Memorial Day–Labor Day, daily 10:30–4; May, Sep–Oct, Sat–Sun 10:30–4; Apr, Nov, Sun 10:30–4. *Admission: moderate*), from where you can take a 3-mile trolley ride.

**THE *AMISTAD* CASE**
In 1839, 53 Africans from Sierra Leone who were taken aboard the slave ship *Amistad* revolted against their captors off the Cuban coast. They tried to force the captain to sail back to Africa, but they ended up off the U.S. coast near New London, Connecticut. The Africans were arrested and tried at New Haven. They won their case, thus making legal history; John Quincy Adams (see page 182) defended them at the appeal hearing. While funds were raised to enable them to return home, they stayed in Farmington; their living quarters and schoolrooms are open to the public (for opening times, tel: 203/678–1645).

10

*Take a trolley ride at the Shore Line Trolley Museum, East Haven*

**NEW HAVEN'S STRONGHOLD**
On July 5, 1779, 3,000 British and German Hessian troops were sighted in Long Island Sound. They succeeded in capturing the important port town of New Haven, but only after astonishing resistance from just 19 patriots ensconced at Black Rock Fort on the east side of the harbor. This fortification was rebuilt as Fort Nathan Hale and served in the War of 1812. It has since been restored and is open from Memorial Day weekend to Labor Day, free of charge.

### A DRAMATIC TRAINING CENTER

The Eugene O'Neill Theater Center at Waterford has been the training ground for hundreds of American actors; Meryl Streep and Al Pacino have been among them. Here, during the Playwright's Conference in July (drama) and August (musicals), you can watch new works in various stages of production. Performances are inexpensive, and the producer may substantially vary the presentation from one day to the next. You can listen in on rehearsals for free. (*Open* Jul–Aug, Mon–Sat; at other times of the year, you can see students rehearse and perform. Tel: 860/443–5378 for a program.)

## ▶ New London 87E2

The seafaring town of New London has a mixture of gracious houses with lawns sloping to the water's edge and a brick-built port area. A number of the houses are survivors from the town's whaling days. Also of note is the Maritime Museum inside the **Custom House** (*Open* Tue–Thu 1–4. *Admission: inexpensive*). The door timbers of this building were taken from the USS *Constitution*, the historic fighting ship of the War of 1812 (see page 67).

Captains of industry lived in Greek Revival mansions in Whale Oil Row (1832), which, together with the imposing railway station, echo former prosperity. Starr Street (1835) is strikingly uniform, its houses recently revamped. The **Joshua Hempsted House** (1678) and **Nathaniel Hempsted House** (1758) are typical of their period (*Open* Thu–Sun 12–4. Tel: 860/443–7949 for admission charges). On the harbor, a statue of the young Eugene O'Neill pays a belated tribute to the playwright, who in popular opinion was once considered no more than a drunken reprobate. His father bought **Monte Cristo Cottage▶**, close by the water, in 1880 and the summers spent here made a great impression on Eugene. The house (*Open* Memorial Day–Labor Day, Tue–Sat 10–5, Sun 1–5. *Admission: inexpensive*) was the setting of his autobiographical drama, *Long Day's Journey into Night*.

The **U.S. Coast Guard Academy** (*Open* daily), situated opposite Connecticut College, trains aspiring coastguardsmen. Below the visitors' center on the grounds, the famous tall ship *Eagle*, where sea skills are taught, can be boarded free of charge on Fri–Sun afternoons when in port (call 860/444–8270 to check). The vessel was built by the Germans in 1936, captured, and brought back after World War II.

Across the Thames River is the naval base of **Groton**, no great beauty in itself but offering a free tour of the **USS Nautilus▶** (*Open* mid-May–Oct, Wed–Mon 9–5, Tue 1–5; Nov–mid-May, Wed–Mon 9–4. *Admission free*), the world's first nuclear-powered

*The U.S. Coast Guard cutter* Eagle, *a square-rigger used by the Coast Guard Academy as a training ship*

*Ocean Beach Park, Waterford, a few miles south of New London*

submarine, and film shows about life on board. At Niantic, the **Children's Museum of Southeastern Connecticut** has plenty to keep youngsters occupied (*Open* Labor Day–Memorial Day, Tue–Sun. *Admission: inexpensive*). At Waterford, miniature golf, a 1-mile boardwalk, and a water slide are found at **Ocean Beach Park** (*Open* Memorial Day–Labor Day, daily 9–11). **Rocky Neck State Park** (*Open* daily 8–dusk), 3 miles west of Niantic, has a crescent beach and is good for swimming, fishing, and diving. There are also picnicking and camping facilities.

### ▶▶▶ Norwalk 86A1

This oystering town is home to the **Maritime Aquarium at Norwalk**▶▶▶, one of New England's most ambitious maritime museums (*Open* Jul–Aug, daily 10–6; Sep–Jun, daily 10–5. *Admission: moderate*). Housed in an old brick foundry, the museum features everything about the human and natural life of Long Island Sound, where even tropical fish can live because of the presence of the Gulf Stream. Its aquarium leads visitors through the inshore world of salt marsh habitats and out to sea. Sharks and striped bass feature in the largest tank. Other displays include oyster boats, Long Island boats, diving equipment, and boat building. Hands-on activities make the atmosphere distinctly lively, with opportunities to design your own boat and to work out how sail and wind interact. Children can try out water flows and more in the Wet Lab. Call ahead for details about lectures, events, cruises, and demonstrations (tel: 203/852–0700); reservations are recommended for the IMAX movie theater, with its screen as tall as a six-story building.

Close by, at 295 West Avenue, the astonishing **Lockwood-Mathews Mansion**▶▶ was the ostentatious 1860s precursor to the mansions of Newport (see pages 216–218), with cavernous frescoed rooms, inlaid doors, and a magnificent staircase. Its semirestored state (see panel) lends it an atmosphere of faded grandeur verging on the theatrical. Upper rooms give a good idea of the mansion's former glory and contain a wide-ranging collection of 19th-century music boxes (*Open* tours of the house mid-Mar–mid-Dec, Tue–Fri 11–3, Sat (seasonal), Sun 1–4. *Admission: moderate*).

### ▶▶▶ Yale University 86C2

See New Haven, pages 102–105.

**BATTLE SITE MARKER**
A granite obelisk of 1830 above the east bank of the Thames by Fort Griswold marks the site of the Battle of Groton in 1781, the only British victory in Connecticut. Climb the 160 steps for views of Long Island.

**SEA ADVENTURE CRUISES**
Project Oceanology, based at the Mystic Aquarium (tel: 860/572–5955), operates 2½-hour trips from Groton to Ledge Lighthouse in summer. Participants set lobster pots, examine fish life and mud samples, and learn about marine pollution. Captain John's (tel: 860/443–7259) runs whale-watching and deep-sea fishing excursions from Waterford. At South Norwalk, cruises depart for Sheffield Island Lighthouse (tel: 203/838–9444), which guarded Norwalk Harbor from 1868; its ten rooms are open to the public.

**REBIRTH OF A MANSION**
The Lockwood-Mathews Mansion was built for LeGrand Lockwood, who lost his fortune in a Wall Street crash in 1869. The house was sold to the Mathews family, then taken over by the city in 1938. The contents were sold, the floors covered with linoleum, and the rooms used to store voting machines. The mansion, which narrowly avoided a threat of demolition in 1959, has been reunited with some of its former contents. Restoration began in 1966 but will take many years to complete.

# Maine

*Near Somesville on Mount Desert Island: the island has been popular with artists and summer visitors since the mid-19th century*

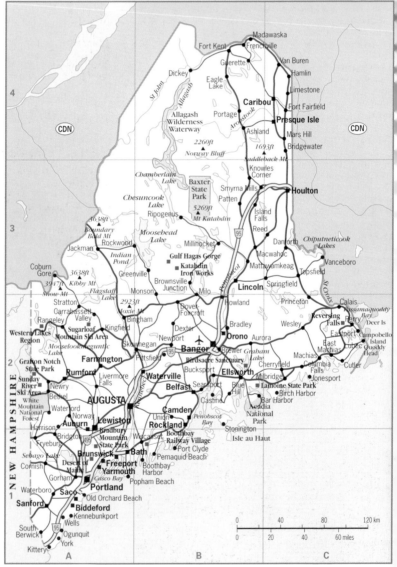

Madawaska
Fort Kent
Frenchville
Guerette
Van Buren
Hamlin
Dickey
Eagle Lake
Limestone
**Caribou**
Fort Fairfield
*St John*
*Allagash*
Portage
*Arostook*
**Presque Isle**
(CDN)
Allagash Wilderness Waterway
Ashland
Mars Hill
*2260ft*
*1693ft*
Bridgewater
*Norway Bluff*
*Saddleback Mt*
Knowles Corner
*Chamberlain Lake*
**Baxter State Park**
Smyrna Mills
**Houlton**
Patten
*Chesuncook Lake*
*5269ft*
Island Falls
Ripogenus
*Mt Katahdin*
Reed
*3638ft*
*Boundary Bald Mt*
*Moosehead Lake*
Danforth
*Chiputneticook Lakes*
Jackman
Rockwood
Millinocket
Macwahoc
Vanceboro
*Indian Pond*
Gulf Hagas Gorge
Mattawamkeag
Topsfield
Coburn Gore
*3638ft*
**Katahdin Iron Works**
Greenville
*3947ft* *Kibby Mt*
Brownsville Junction
Springfield
*Snow Mt*
*Flagstaff Lake*
Monson
Milo
**Lincoln**
Princeton
Stratton
*2923ft*
Dover-Foxcroft
Calais
Carrabassett Valley
*Moxie Mt*
Howland
Wesley
*Passamaquoddy Bay*
Rangeley
Kingfield
Bingham
Bradley
Aurora
**Reversing Falls**
Perry
Deer Is
**Western Lakes Region**
**Sugarloaf Mountain Ski Area**
Skowhegan
Newport
**Orono**
**Eastport**
Campobello Island
*Mooselookmeguntic Lake*
Dexter
Pittsfield
**Bangor**
Brewer
*Graham Lake*
Lubec
*Quoddy Head*
**Farmington**
Birdsacre Sanctuary
Cherryfield
Machias
Cutler
**Grafton Notch State Park**
**Rumford**
Livermore Falls
**Waterville**
Buckport
**Ellsworth**
Milbridge
Columbia Falls
East Machias
Jonesport
**Sunday River Ski Area**
Newry
**Belfast**
Searsport
Blue Hill
**Lamoine State Park**
**White Mountain National Forest**
Bethel
Waterford
**AUGUSTA**
Castine
Birch Harbor
Norway
Camden
**Acadia National Park**
Harrison
**Auburn**
**Lewiston**
Union
*Penobscot Bay*
Bar Harbor
Bridgton
**Bradbury Mountain State Park**
Wiscasset
Stonington
Fryeburg
*Sebago Lake*
**Rockland**
Boothbay Railway Village
Isle au Haut
Cornish
**Brunswick**
**Bath**
Port Clyde
*Desert of Maine*
Gorham
**Freeport**
**Yarmouth**
Boothbay Harbor
Pemaquid Beach
Waterboro
*Casco Bay*
Popham Beach
**Portland**
**Saco**
**Sanford**
Old Orchard Beach
**Biddeford**
Kennebunkport
South Berwick
Wells
Ogunquit
York
Kittery

**NEW HAMPSHIRE**

(CDN)

*St Croix*

0    40    80    120 km
0    20    40    60 miles

A          B          C

**MAINE** The summer vacationland of Maine is slightly larger than all the other New England states put together and has the lowest population density. Even with a massive influx of summer visitors to the coast, there are still places where you can find isolation. Easily the most crowded part is from Camden to the New Hampshire border; even here, there are areas of quiet charm if you are prepared to seek them out. Development along and around Route 1, however, is dense and often disappointingly drab. Farther up the coast and including most of Mount Desert Island is **Acadia National Park**, the jewel in the crown and the coast's only noticeably hilly area. Beyond that, the crowds thin out substantially. Even then, the intricate coast is elusive, except from a boat: drivers won't see much of it, and access on foot is limited.

**Augusta** is the state capital, but **Portland** is the cultural epicenter, and the only place that feels like a big city. Freeport and Kittery are factory outlet shopping towns.

**TREES AND MORE TREES** With forests covering 17 million acres, Maine is nicknamed the Pine Tree State. About 90 percent of the land is forested, and Maine has long lived off its appreciable lumber supplies. The state is also referred to as Downeast, as the prevailing wind pushes sailboats eastward "down" the coast. The term "Downeaster" refers to any Maine-built ship.

Many Maine villages are now gentrified, but pockets of Downeast atmosphere can still be found at numerous fishing villages and settlements along the coast. Distances between towns increase as you head north or east, and the towns get smaller and roads emptier. Inland, paper companies own vast tracts of Maine's forests; many of the roads are private. Today, papermaking accounts for nearly 35 percent of the state's total value of manufactured products.

On the few public roads in the big forests, you will encounter huge and somewhat terrifying lumber trucks every few minutes or so, which have the right of way (and should be given a very wide berth).

*Rocky shores and dark coniferous trees typify the coast of Acadia National Park*

▶ ▶ ▶ REGION HIGHLIGHTS

*Museums and houses*
**Maine Maritime Museum** *page 118*
**Portland Museum of Art** *page 134*
**Roosevelt Cottage** *page 123*
**Shore Village Museum** *page 130*
**Victoria Mansion** *page 134*
**York museums** *pages 136–137*
*Scenery, villages, and small towns*
**Acadia National Park** *pages 112–115*
**Baxter State Park** *page 119*
**Bethel and the Western Lakes** *page 120*
**Monhegan Island** *page 121*

**EARLY DAYS** The state was settled by European explorers from early times. In the early 1600s, French and English settlers established themselves on the St. Croix and Kennebec rivers respectively. Charles I then gave the territory to Sir Ferdinando Gorges and made him Lord of New England in 1635. The Massachusetts Colony purchased Maine, which remained part of Massachusetts until it became an independent state in 1820.

From colonial times up until the latter part of the 19th century, Maine supported a flourishing shipbuilding industry. America's first sawmill was built in 1634 at South Berwick, and by 1840 this number had increased to 1,400. Maine has produced more wooden sailing ships than any other state in the Union.

*Above: Sebago Lake offers boating, swimming, and fishing
Right: Maine salt of the earth*

**MAINE TRAITS** Inhabitants of Maine have a reputation for being frank and down-to-earth. They keep their cool and don't always smile at strangers (an unpleasant attitude to some).

Maine is among the nation's poorest states. While that may seem hard to believe as you scan the antiques and crafts shops in the classy resorts of Penobscot Bay, Kennebunkport, Ogunquit, and elsewhere, the remoter areas see younger people drifting out of the state, and there are high unemployment rates (particularly on the Native American reservations). Much employment is seasonal. Tourism is the biggest earner—hence the "Vacationland" on license plates. Crowds flock to the coast in summer, and fall foliage and winter sports draw visitors inland.

**MAINE AT WORK** Agricultural laborers spend August and September working on the wild blueberry harvest. Maine produces 90 percent of the nation's output of this fruit, which grows mostly in Washington County in the state's eastern corner. Potatoes are the largest crop in the state, with over 1 million tons harvested each year. From late October to early November, the Christmas wreath industry is in full swing. Maine has just the right type of balsam fir brush for this purpose, and the finished product graces the doors of many American homes.

Because of the harsh winters, the fishing and packing industries operate at maximum capacity when the weather allows it. Some three-quarters of the nation's lobsters come from Maine. Lobster is a ubiquitous menu item; even McDonald's restaurants offer lobster sandwiches in their Maine branches in summer. Meanwhile, Rockland, Prospect Harbor, and Lubec are major centers for sardine canning.

**LUMBER FACTS**
● From the 1630s to 1850s, sawmills made use of the "sash saw," an up-down moving frame. A later invention was the circular-saw blade.
● Winter is the best season for felling, when the sap is down.
● In former times, logs were placed on ice-covered lakes or rolled down to streams or rivers to be carried toward the sea each spring. As sawn logs could not be floated, sawmills could not be located close to shipping ports.

**BLUEBERRY BOUNTIES**
Blueberries are harvested by a special rake, boxed on three sides. Cherryfield, the "blueberry capital of the world," and Machias are the main processing centers.

Native Americans dried the berries for winter rations and used them to make healing potions.

# Events

For further information, contact the state tourist office (see page 266) or chambers of commerce.

## JANUARY
**White, White World Week**, Sugarloaf/U.S.A., Carrabassett Valley: winter carnival.

## FEBRUARY
**Annual U.S. National Toboggan Championships**, Camden: races, chili and chowder challenge, plus numerous other events.
**International Snowmobilers Festival**, Madawaska.
**Moose Stompers Weekend**, Houlton: snowmobile light parade, human dog-sled races, bonfire.

## MARCH
**Ice Fishing Tournament**, Moosehead Lake, Greenville.
**Log Drivers Cookout**, Mud Pond, Island Falls: torchlight parade, bonfire, and other events.
**Maine Maple Sunday**, statewide: sugar houses demonstrate the production of "liquid gold" maple syrup.
**New England Sled Dog Championship**, Rangeley.

## APRIL
**Fisherman's Festival**, Boothbay Harbor.
**Meduxnekeag River Canoe Race**, Houlton: whitewater canoe races.

## MAY
**Moosemainea**, Greenville: a month-long extravaganza of moose-related activities and events.

## JUNE
**Acadian Festival**, Madawaska: dance, food, music, heritage.
**Annual Windjammer Days Festival**, Boothbay Harbor: schooner races.
**Strawberry Festival**, South Berwick: all things strawberry.

## JULY
**Bar Harbor Music Festival**: classical and popular music (summer series).
**Native American Festival**, Bar Harbor.
**Open House and Garden Day**, Camden: houses and gardens are opened to the public.
**Yarmouth Clam Festival**, the biggest festival in Maine, with carnival, seafood, crafts, fireworks, children's parade, and other events.

## AUGUST
**Maine Festival**, Thomas Point Beach, Brunswick: arts festival.
**Maine Lobster Festival**, Rockland: a feast of Maine's most succulent crustacean in its busiest fishing port.
**Union Fair and Maine Blueberry Festival**: harvest celebration.

## SEPTEMBER
**Blue Hill Fair**, Blue Hill: on Labor Day weekend.
**Bluegrass Festival**, Thomas Point Beach, Brunswick.

## OCTOBER
**Fryeburg Fair**: Maine's largest agricultural fair.
**Harvestfest**, York: colonial celebration.
**Living History Days**, Maine Forest and Logging Museum, Orono: demonstrations of traditional crafts and foods.

## NOVEMBER
**Lighting of the Nubble**, Sohier Park, York.
**Rockland Festival of Lights Celebration**: lighted parade.

## DECEMBER
**Christmas Prelude**, Kennebunkport.

*A maple-sugaring demonstration at the annual Fryeburg agricultural fair*

## ACADIA TRIPS

Horse-and-carriage tours can be taken from Wildwood Riding Stables from mid-June to Columbus Day (tel: 207/276–3622). Sailing trips on *Blackjack* run four times daily from Northeast Harbor (tel: 207/288–3056), while two-person glider rides leave from Bar Harbor Airport on Route 3, Trenton (tel: 207/667–SOAR). Biking on the traffic-free carriage roads and on the Loop Road is possible; for rentals, contact Acadia Bike & Canoe, 48 Cottage Street, Bar Harbor (tel: 207/288–9605). In winter, the carriage roads become cross-country ski trails—the only place in New England where you can ski along the coast.

112

### ▶▶▶ Acadia National Park

*108B2*

This scenic national park is dominated by the 1,530-foot granite form of **Mount Cadillac▶▶▶**, the highest point on the U.S. Atlantic coast. Although no one can expect solitude in high summer, Acadia is undeniably the most rewarding place for hiking on the entire New England seaboard. It gives outstanding opportunities for observing wildlife, both flora (boreal northern and temperate southern species) and fauna.

In 1919, Acadia became the first national park east of the Mississippi. Mount Desert Island (the major part of the national park, connected to the mainland by bridge) was endowed a 57-mile system of scenic carriage roads by John D. Rockefeller, Jr. He considered Mount Desert Island "one of the great views of the world" and donated more than 10,000 acres to the national park. Meanwhile, Bar Harbor became the summer society rival of Newport, Rhode Island, as the Astors, Rockefellers, Vanderbilts, Fords, and others ensconced themselves here for the season. In 1947, a fire destroyed more than 60 of the millionaires' "summer cottages." Today, everything is very much visitor-oriented.

**VISITING ACADIA** In July and August, **Bar Harbor** (outside the park boundary) becomes one of the busiest points on the Maine coast. It is the most practical place for

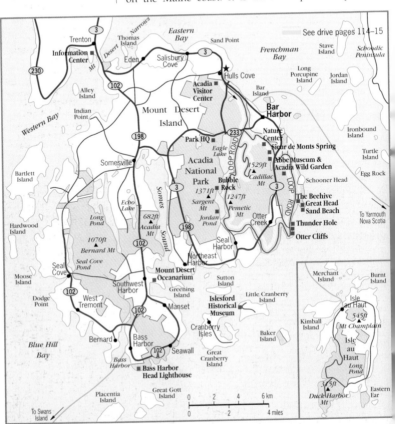

See drive pages 114–15

accommodations, eating, and shopping, as well as a starting point for whale-watching cruises, bike rentals, kayaking tours, and sailing trips. Ferries sail from here for Nova Scotia. In the town are the Natural History Museum College of the Atlantic, the Mount Desert Oceanarium, the Wendell Gilley Museum, and the Bar Harbor Historical Society.

Route 3 makes a drab entrance to Acadia, a virtually unbroken strip of motels, malls, and amusement parks, but things soon get better. Most visitors concentrate on the east side of Mount Desert Island by following the **Park Loop Road▶▶▶** (see pages 114–115).

The west side is much quieter and less dramatic, but tempting as an escape from the crowds, with few views from the wooded summits. Bass Harbor, Bernard, Southwest Harbor, and Northeast Harbor are typical Maine fishing villages, and not particularly touristy. **Echo Lake** is good for swimming by virtue of being warmer than the waters on the coast. **Northeast Harbor** is a starting point for cruises into the Sound and out to the Cranberry Isles. From the village, the **Sargent Drive** (cars and bicycles only) skirts the east side of **Somes Sound▶▶**, the East Coast's only fiord, carved by glaciers, then flooded by the sea. An undemanding 2½-mile walk from Route 102 up Acadia Mountain on the sound's western side offers an outstanding view. **Bass Harbor Head Lighthouse** (1858) ranks among Maine's most photogenic lighthouses and can be reached by car.

Route 186 leads to **Birch Harbor**, where you can follow the one-way coastal loop road to **Schoodic Point▶**, which gives views of Mount Cadillac.

Acadia's farthest-flung outpost, **Isle au Haut▶**, lies in Penobscot Bay and is reached by mail boat from Stonington (no cars taken; tel: 207/367–5193). Quiet trails wind through the island's spruce forests and along its rugged shores; there is a small campground. Ranger-led excursions are offered to **Great Cranberry Island**. **Little Cranberry Island** has a free museum (*Open* mid-Jun–Sep) covering maritime and local history. Ranger-led walks, often with a natural history content, are given free of charge in the park. Trailheads are mostly well marked from the road.

*With temperate and subarctic species, such as this wild iris, Acadia is a rich hunting ground for naturalists*

**INFORMATION SOURCES**
Thompson Island Information Center can help with accommodations and campgrounds, while the national park visitor center provides information and hiking maps.

For information and reservations, contact Acadia National Park, P.O. Box 177, Bar Harbor, ME 04609 (tel: 207/288–3338); for camping reservations, call 800/365–2267. Between June and October, the park publishes *Acadia Beaver Log*, a free newspaper listing ranger-led tours, cruises, and walks.

113

*From the loop road views extend across tiny bays backed by cliffs*

# Drive

### Acadia's Park Loop Road

*See map on page 112 (yellow route).*

This scenic (mostly one-way) 27-mile road skirts Mount Cadillac and provides a series of views that encapsulate the stunning beauty of Acadia. Although the loop can easily be driven in two hours or so, it merits a full day so that some of its trails can be experienced to the full. It may also be undertaken as a bicycle tour (there are several bike-rental shops in Bar Harbor), although some may find the traffic at peak times mars enjoyment. Parking is rarely a problem as you can stop anywhere on the right-hand side of the two-lane road along its one-way section. Week-long or seasonal passes must be bought on entering the park; entrance is free for U.S. citizens over 62 or disabled visitors with appropriate I.D.

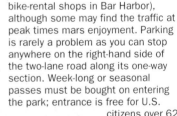

*Some of Mount Desert's early summer residents (in 1913) presented the U.S. government with lands that, in 1919, were declared a national park*

The **Hulls Cove Visitor Center▶** marks the start of the Loop Road and has a diorama of the park and a film show about Acadia's natural history. The **Acadia Wild Garden▶**, created by the Bar Harbor Garden Club in cooperation with the national park, demonstrates the range of wildflowers and vegetation that can be found in contrasting sites such as beach, bog, mountain heath, and mixed woodlands. Immediately adjacent are the Nature Center, the **Sieur de Monts Spring**, and the **Abbe Museum►** of Indian artifacts (*Open* mid-May–Jun, Sep–late Oct, daily 10–4; Jul–Aug, daily 9–5. *Admission: inexpensive*), which tells the story of the local Native American inhabitants before the Frenchman Samuel de Champlain discovered Mount Desert Island in 1604.

One of the toughest walks is the **Precipice Trail►**, which ascends lofty crags by means of rungs and ladders. In recent years, peregrine falcons have been nesting here and consequently the trail has been closed in the summer months. **Sand Beach►**, the only sandy beach in the park, has great beauty, but the water stays decidedly cool on even the hottest August day. If you turn right out of Sand Beach parking lot along the road, the trailhead for the

there and back), one of the most scenic easy walks in the national park. It runs closely parallel to the road, along the cliffs between Sand Beach and Otter Point. **Thunder Hole**, beside the road, needs bad weather, when the waves are tossed into the rock niche and the spray slants across its entrance, to look its best. Otherwise, it is little more than a minor chink in the coastline with pleasant rocks on which to sit.

The **Gorham Mountain Trail►** offers further spectacular high-level views that are similar to those on the Beehive Trail (you can make a longer walk along the ridge to take in the Beehive), but the trail itself is less demanding. Just below the trail is Cadillac Cliff, an overhanging rock with a small cave.

Where the one-way traffic ends, you can detour south past **Seal Harbor**, a sandy beach, to **Northeast Harbor**, from where you can take a cruise (see panel on page 112). Alternatively, continue north to

115

*Silver birch trees behind Sand Beach*

**Beehive Trail►** is almost immediately on the left. The short but strenuous path makes a spectacular ascent. There is an easier (less interesting) route that may be taken as a safe descent. Go right at the first path junction, and from the summit go forward, following signs for the Loop Road.

Exquisite views can be enjoyed from the **Ocean Trail►** (3.6 miles

**Jordan Pond►**, which has nature trails through the woods and along the lakeside. A longer scenic trail (**Jordan Pond Shore Path**) encircles the entire lake. The half-mile **Jordan Pond Nature Trail** to South Bubble Summit, a 768-foot protuberance with a fine panorama, passes **Bubble Rock►**, a classic glacial erratic (deposited boulder) balanced on its side.

The scenic summit road to **Mount Cadillac►►►** needs careful timing to catch the best of the light and the view, both of which can change for better or worse within a few minutes. When conditions are right you can see as far as Mount Katahdin (5,267 feet), Maine's highest point, located inland in distant Baxter State Park. Hikers who want the satisfaction of reaching a similar viewpoint without the crowds should follow the **Dorr Mountain Trail**, a short distance east of Sieur de Monts Spring.

*So prolific was the lobster in colonial days that colonists would catch it with hooks or spears in shallow waters and feed it to chickens and prisoners. Today, lobstering is one of New England's proudest traditions, and the king of seafood is dispatched to top restaurants across the world.*

**116**

## LOBSTERING LORE

Each harbor has its own close-knit society, one that guards its trade fiercely. Fishing territories are strictly defined by tradition, and each fisherman's buoys are painted in his own colors. Trespass and you may find, as one Portland fisherman did in 1993, a bomb in your trap. The scalloper who drags his nets and scoops along the ocean floor and falls foul of a lobster pot or two won't find a warm reception either.

## FOR A CLOSER LOOK

Several ports operate trips on lobstering boats in summer months, including Bar Harbor, Boothbay Harbor, and Ogunquit in Maine, and Gloucester in Massachusetts. Remember to take warm clothes.

*Lobster pounds are the best place to enjoy the day's catch—straight from the sea*

**The tradition** The American lobster, *Homarus americanus*, lives along the Atlantic coast between Labrador and North Carolina and is particularly plentiful off the coast of New England. Trapping on a commercial basis began in southern New England by 1800. By the mid-1800s, the hoop net had been introduced, which meant lobsters could be caught without damage, and Maine, by now heading the trade, was transporting live lobsters in sailing smacks to New York and Boston, where they were boiled and sold on the streets. The Maine fishery also supplied no fewer than 23 canning factories with smaller, less salable lobster. Canning ceased at the turn of the 20th century, but lobstering is still a vital part of the coastal economy. It not only attracts tourists but also provides work for local industry, producing the boats and the slatted trap that, with modifications, has been used for decades.

**The catch** Harbors bobbing with boats and wharves stacked high with traps and buoys reveal little of the tough life the trapper leads. In all weathers he (or occasionally she) heads out to his line of buoys at daybreak and winches up the strings of pots. Many trappers have up to 50 traps per string and 1,000 traps in all. Each lobster is measured to ensure it is of legal size; keepers are typically 10 inches long overall, 1–1½ pounds in weight, and about five years old. The bait (dead fish) is renewed, the lobster pots are returned to the ocean floor, and then the catch is turned in to the dealer. It's no easy way to make a living.

## ▶ Augusta
108A2

Maine's state capital is not a place that routinely attracts visitors, but it has a handful of good sights justifying a brief detour. The town lies on the Kennebec River at the site of an early Pilgrim colony. Along the river extends the green expanse of 34-acre Capitol Park. Above stands the prominent **State House▶** (*Open* Mon–Fri 9–5), dating from 1832 but extended twice since Charles Bulfinch designed it. The facade is original, although the dome replaced a cupola in the early 1900s. Wall panels provide a self-guiding tour to the building's function and history. Next door, the **Maine State Museum▶** (*Open* Mon–Fri 9–5, Sat 10–4, Sun 1–4. *Admission free*) presents displays covering aspects of the state's industry and life from the Ice Age to the present. Lumbering and ice harvesting, two of the city's former mainstays, feature in the "Made in Maine" displays, together with exhibits of the state's ship-building, sardine canning, and farming industries.

**Old Fort Western▶**, the oldest wooden fort in the U.S.A. (1754), occupies the site of a Pilgrim trading post established near the river in the 1620s (*Open* May–Jun, Sep–Columbus Day, Sat–Sun 1–4; Jul–Aug, Mon–Fri 10–4, Sat–Sun 1–4. *Admission: inexpensive*). The need for the fort arose from the colonists' fear of the French and Native Americans. It was never besieged, and it became a trading post during its 12-year history as a fort. Its design was that of a typical New England fort, with a 100-foot-long main house. William Harvard, the commander, made the fort his home from 1766 to 1810, which is why it has survived; today, it is presented as a house rather than a barracks. Reconstructions of the stockade blockhouses, with replica cannons and guns, date from 1921. Cannon firing takes place on weekends, and guides in period costume show visitors around.

Out of town, the **Matthews Museum of Maine** at Union comprises a collection of the past, including a schoolroom, a horse-drawn hearse, a cooper's shop, a colonial kitchen, spinning and weaving items, and farm tools (*Open* Jul–Labor Day, Tue–Sun 12–5. *Admission: inexpensive*).

*The Federal-style Blaine House (1833) in Augusta is the official residence of the state's governor*

117

**THE BIRTH OF MOXIE**
The locally popular soft drink known as Moxie began life at Union, near Augusta, in 1885. Its inventor, Dr. Augustin Thompson, originally sold it as Moxie Nerve Food. The Matthews Museum of Maine in the village has an interesting collection of memorabilia.

*Above and below right: ships' figureheads and marine art are among the indoor displays at Bath's maritime museum*

**118**

**KING OF BANGOR**
Author Stephen King lives on West Broadway, Bangor, and his fans frequently track him down. Many of his novels and films have a local setting. Bett's Bookstore at 26 Main Street specializes in Stephen King books and memorabilia.

**LUMBER CAPITAL**
In the 19th century, Bangor was the world's largest lumber-exporting center. The industry peaked in 1872, when 2,200 ships entered Bangor via the Penobscot River in a year, but the timber supply waned and shipbuilding declined as paper-making assumed an important role in the state. At Orono, off Route 178, the Maine Forest and Logging Museum stands on the site of Leonard's Mills (1790). It features a working water-powered sawmill, a sawing demonstration, a trapper's cabin, and more. (*Open* late Apr–late Oct, daily 10–6).

▶ **Bangor**                    *108B2*

Bangor is more a commercial center than a visitor destination. Although victim of a fire in 1911 and much redeveloped in the 1960s, the city retains some fine buildings, notably along Broadway, High Street, and the streets leading off them. The **Thomas Hill Standpipe** in Summit Park is a unique contribution to Bangor's skyline. Built in 1897, this water tower observation point is floodlit at night. The **Historical Society** operates a museum at 159 Union Street (*Open* Apr–Jun, Oct–Dec, Thu–Fri 12–4; Jul–Sep Tue–Sat 12–4. *Admission: moderate*) and runs bus tours round the city (Jul–Sep, Thu, and first Sat of the month).

Bangor's heyday is chronicled in the **Old Town Museum** on North 4th Street (*Open* Wed–Sun. *Admission free*). At the intersection of I-95 and I-395, the **Cole Land Transportation Museum** boasts over 200 vehicles, including snowplows and logging trucks from old Maine (*Open* May–Veteran's Day, daily 9–5. *Admission: inexpensive*).

▶▶ **Bath**                    *108A1*

Bath's **Maine Maritime Museum▶▶**, at 243 Washington Street (*Open* daily 9:30–5. *Admission: moderate*), is the most ambitious museum of its kind in the state. It occupies the last surviving wooden shipbuilding yard in the nation, used by Percy & Small from 1897 to 1920. The *Wyoming*, the largest sail vessel used in the country, was built here. Inside the Maritime History Building, a museum display tells the story of Maine's seafaring past from the days of the early explorers to 20th-century tourism and fishing. The museum possesses over 200 paintings and drawings, 250 models, and 100 boats. In the Percy & Small shipyard, you can see apprentices at work restoring and building wooden boats on weekdays. Five of the original buildings survive; displays include small craft and the story of lobstering. Tours of the shipyard, available from mid-April to September at no extra cost, are highly recommended.

Special cruises usually take place on Tuesdays, in addition to a regular program of 50-minute narrated boat trips on *Hardy II*. The latter pass the Bath Iron Works, the state's largest industrial employer, and a major shipyard. It is usually possible to board vessels by the museum piers, including the *Sherman Zwicker*, where you can get an idea of the tough life endured by the Grand Banks cod fishermen.

## ▶▶▶ Baxter State Park 108B3

The park is one of the more accessible parts of Maine's unpopulated mountains and forests (*Admission: moderate; payable at park entrance at Togue Pond Gate*). Wildflowers, hiking, geology, whitewater rafting, cross-country skiing, moose-spotting, hunting, canoeing, and fishing are among its attractions.

Baxter Peak (5,267 feet), the summit of **Mount Katahdin▶▶▶**, marks the northern end of the 2,035-mile Appalachian Trail to Georgia. It is the highest point in Maine and probably the only mountain in the state to have remained bare of trees since glaciation. Several trails lead to the top, including the famous **Knife Edge Trail**, which edges its way along a sharp glacial ridge, or arête. Two cirques (glacial hollows) flank the Knife Edge, which is just 3 feet wide in places and has dizzy drops on either side of up to 2,000 feet. The trail is strictly for experienced walkers in calm weather conditions.

Great Basin is the finest of seven cirques on the mountain; the Chimney Pond Trail from Roaring Brook campground gives access. Outstanding for its arctic wildflowers, the Tableland has abundant evidence of freeze-thaw weathering processes on the rocks scattered over it. Other notable trails include **Doubletop Mountain**, **South Turner**, the **Owl**, and **The Brothers**. Moose can often be seen at **Big** and **Little Niagara Falls**.

Southwest of Baxter State Park, the West Branch of the Penobscot River has its moment of glory as it gushes though **Ripogenus Gorge▶▶** (access by unpaved road). Over a mile long, the gorge has almost vertical sides up to 200 feet high, with the rock strata exposed like a school textbook diagram. It can be seen on foot or by whitewater rafting or canoeing.

Farther south, near Brownville Junction, is **Gulf Hagas▶▶**, another magnificent canyon best reached from Lloyd Pond. Here, the West Branch of the Pleasant River tumbles over five waterfalls, a memorable sight when in full spate in spring. Allow six hours for the hike.

The **Pattern Lumberman's Museum** (*Open May–Oct. Admission: donation*) has ten buildings that tell the story of the state's lumber industry.

### AN INDUSTRIAL GHOST TOWN

Gulf Hagas Canyon can be included in a visit to the site of the Katahdin Iron Works—look for signs off Route 11 south of Millinocket. Now a state historic site (*Open Memorial Day–Labor Day, daily 9–sunset. Admission free*), it retains kilns and a stone furnace as reminders of a mining town that, in the 19th century, produced almost 2,000 tons of raw iron per year and employed nearly 200 men.

119

### CAMPING AT BAXTER

For information about camping in Baxter State Park, contact Baxter State Park Authority, 64 Balsam Drive, Millinocket, ME 04462 (tel: 207/723–5140). Reservations are advisable in summer, as the numbers of campsites and lean-tos (simple shelters) are deliberately restricted.

*Baxter State Park is remote, but one of the best places in Maine for moose-spotting*

### SUNRISE CANOEING
A memorable way to enjoy the wildlife and scenery of the Western Lakes area is to take a dawn canoe trip. Look for advertisements in Rangeley—for instance, for a guided trip that offers the chance to watch beavers and moose, and be serenaded by birdsong as the mists rise.

### MOSS GARDEN
A few minutes' walk from Moose Cave in Grafton Notch State Park (look for signs at the rest area on Route 26) is this little fairy-tale clearing. A silvery carpet of reindeer moss (*Cladonia rangifera*), an exquisite erect ferny lichen, is interspersed with other mosses, some cool green and smooth, others darker and upright. With the tiny pine seedlings, it looks like a miniature forest.

*New England cameo: rocking chairs and a pumpkin on a porch of a house in Bethel*

## ►► Bethel and the Western Lakes     *108A2*

The Western Lakes Region, stretching north from Sebago Lake up to the lakes and mountains around Rangeley, includes some of New England's most beautiful countryside, with forested hills rolling down to crystal lakes and rivers. The farther north you go, the more remote and wild it all becomes. It offers excellent opportunities for walking, camping, fishing, golfing, sketching, and moose-spotting. In summer, there is boating of all sorts on the lakes and rivers, in winter every type of snow sport, and in the fall, of course, brilliant foliage.

At the heart of the region is **Bethel►**, a classic New England small town with a handful of crafts shops, inns, and restaurants. Nearby is the burgeoning Sunday River ski resort (see page 229). Alongside the road that passes the resort from Newry is one of Maine's most photographed covered bridges, **Sunday River Bridge**, built in 1870. Northwest of Newry is **Grafton Notch State Park►►** (*Open* May–Oct. *Admission: inexpensive*), an area of gorges, waterfalls, and mountains, where walks range from short hikes such as Screw Augur Falls Gorge to challenging trails up Table Rock. Northeast of the paper-mill town of Rumford, **Kingfield** has an absorbing rainy-day option in the **Stanley Museum** (*Open* May–Oct, Tue–Sun 1–4; Nov–Apr, Mon–Fri by appointment. *Admission: inexpensive*), with items relating to the versatile Stanley family, whose early 20th-century work encompassed steam-powered cars, violin-making, and photography. Nearby, **Sugarloaf Mountain►►**, Maine's second highest peak (4,237 feet) and a winter sports resort, merits taking the chairlift even outside the skiing season for the far-ranging views from its treeless summit.

**Rangeley►** is the hub of the Rangeley Lakes region, which offers canoeing, sailing, swimming, fishing, and walking. Rangeley State Park has chalets.

South of Bethel is **Fryeburg**, a canoeing center (with rentals available) famed for its agricultural fair in October. **Harrison**, set between Long Lake and Crystal Lake, is a another good center for the outdoor enthusiast. Famous for its trout and landlocked salmon fishing, **Sebago Lake►►** is ringed with small towns offering plenty for the water-sports enthusiast.

*Boothbay Harbor is a busy boating resort as well as an active fishing port*

**VISITING MONHEGAN ISLAND**
In 1614, Captain John Smith landed here, and settlers followed in his footsteps 11 years later.
  Trips are offered from Boothbay Harbor by Balmy Days Cruises (tel: 800/298–2284), and from New Harbor by Hardy Boat Cruises (tel: 800/278–3346).

### Boothbay Harbor                    *108B1*

ettled in the 17th century and developed for tourism rom the 1870s, Boothbay Harbor is the largest boating arbor northeast of Boston, as well as a busy resort town acked with boutiques and galleries. The self-proclaimed boating capital of New England" offers over 50 aily cruises, the best choice in Maine—including eal-, whale-, and puffin-watching trips, deep-sea fishing xpeditions, and tours of the coast and islands. The quarium, by the Lobsterman's Co-op, is stocked by local ishermen and contains a good variety of species.

On the east side of Route 27, near its intersection with oute 1, is **Boothbay Railway Village** (*Open* Memorial Day–Columbus Day, daily. *Admission: moderate*), a village heme park where an original train hauls you through voods inhabited by garden elves. There is a collection of e-erected buildings to explore, although for the most part ou can only look inside them from the entrances.

Some 10 miles offshore is **Monhegan Island▶▶**, only ½ miles across at its widest, but with surprising variety, ncluding some 400 species of wildflowers. The Cliff Trail uns the length of the island, and there are fine walks in he balsam-scented Cathedral Woods, as well as 160-foot liffs on the east side. The island is partly developed for isitors, with shops and restaurants. Monhegan's mpressive ocean panoramas made the island a popular rtists' haunt: Rockwell Kent and Edward Hopper are mong those who have come and painted the scene.

Across the inlet east of Boothbay Harbor is one of the oveliest parts of Maine's seaboard, **Pemaquid Point▶▶**, vhich is graced by wave-sculpted rocks. Pemaquid Point ight (1827) presides over the scene, while the former ghthouse keeper's cottage functions as a museum of ommercial fishing and a small art gallery (*Open* Memorial Day–Columbus Day, daily. *Admission: onation*). At nearby **Pemaquid Beach▶**, a sand beach rare for these parts), is the Colonial Pemaquid State Historic Site (*Open* Memorial Day–Labor Day, daily 9–5. Admission: inexpensive*), the excavated site of an early 17th-entury mariners' settlement, with an adjacent museum. ort William Henry is a replica of a 1692 fort.

121

**RAFTING**
New England Whitewater Center operates raft trips on the Kennebec, Dead, and Penobscot rivers between April and October: Box 669, Millinocket, ME 04462 (tel: 800/766–7238).

*Lobster fishing has been a vital part of Maine's economy since the 19th century*

*Massachusetts Hall, the oldest building in Bowdoin College, dates from 1799*

**RECORDED FOR POSTERITY**
The substantial film and video heritage of New England is being preserved by Northeast Historic Film, which operates from a restored 1916 cinema building in Bucksport, within sight of the massive form of Fort Knox. The exhibition "Going to the Movies" looks at the movie-watching tradition from the early days (*Open Mon–Fri 9–4. Admission free*). For information about showings, tel: 207/469–0924, or e-mail oldfilm@acadia.net; there is a website at www.acadia.net/oldfilm.

**FOREIGN VISITORS**
Visitors to Campobello Island must bring their passports. Citizens of Australia, the U.K., New Zealand, and Ireland need no visa, but should be sure not to surrender their visa waiver forms. Tell the passport control officer that you intend to return the same day. Drive over International Bridge or take a ferry from Eastport via Deer Isle.

### ▶ Brunswick                                    108A1

**Bowdoin College▶**, in the center of Brunswick, was founded in 1794 and counts among its former students the writers Henry Wadsworth Longfellow and Nathaniel Hawthorne, and President Franklin Pierce. Two fine museums (*Open Tue–Sat 10–5, Sun 2–5. Admission free*) flank the attractive campus green. Hubbard Hall, a tall and prominent tower, houses the Peary-MacMillan Arctic Museum, which tells the story of these two former students who made the first successful expedition to the North Pole in 1909. Displays feature sleighs, guns, equipment, and writings. To the right of Hubbard Hall, the Museum of Art has American colonial and federal portraits, paintings by Winslow Homer, and classical antiquities.

In town, the Pejepscot Historical Society maintains three museum properties. The Italianate **Skolfield-Whittier House** at 161 Park Row (*Open summer, Tue–Sat 10–3; fall, by appointment, tel: 207/729–6606. Admission: inexpensive*) was closed up and forgotten about from 1925 until 1982, and inhabited by a sea captain. It contains exotic items he brought back from his voyages and family possessions spanning three generations. Its north side houses the **Pejepscot Museum** of local history and genealogy (*Open Tue–Wed, Fri 9–5, Thu 9–8. Admission free*). The **Joshua L. Chamberlain Museum** (*Open summer–fall, Tue–Sat 10–4; spring, tel: 207/729–6606 for hours. Admission: inexpensive*) commemorates the college professor who achieved fame at Little Round Top in the Civil War Battle of Gettysburg.

### ▶ Bucksport                                    108B2

This small port on the Penobscot River is busy with tankers unloading petroleum products and picking up coated paper. Route 1 crosses the Penobscot by Waldo-Hancock Bridge, offering a spectacular view of the formidable **Fort Knox▶▶** (*Open May–Oct, 9–sunset. Admission: inexpensive*). Not to be confused with its more famous namesake in Kentucky, the fort was built between 1844 and 1869, originally because of the British threat from Canada. It was never completed but saw activity in the Civil War and Spanish American War of 1898. An annual Civil War encampment, with costumed actors and cannon firing, enlivens the fort on two weekends in July and August. Take a flashlight for exploring the interior.

## ▶▶ Campobello Island
### (New Brunswick, Canada)
*108C2*

Franklin D. Roosevelt's "beloved island," where he found rest and freedom from care, is just over the Canadian border, but his family summer house is jointly maintained as an international park by the U.S.A. and Canada. The park comprises 2,800 acres of deep forest, bogs, stone and sand beaches, oceanside trails, and outlooks in addition to the house. Maps are available from the visitor center near F.D.R. International Bridge. (See also panel opposite.)

The **Roosevelt Cottage▶▶** is in Dutch Colonial style and retains the original furniture. The atmosphere is personal rather than grand, with the president's books put out as if the great man had just stepped outside. The adjacent **visitor center** shows a film on Campobello and the Roosevelts (*Open* Sat before Memorial Day–Columbus Day, daily 10–6 Canada time. *Admission free*). Next door is the opulent **Hubbard Cottage**, which was home to Gorham and Sara Hubbard, an insurance businessman and a concert pianist, who became friends of the Roosevelts. One floor is open to the public.

Roosevelt spent his boyhood summers at an adjacent cottage, which his father built in 1885 (it was demolished in 1951). His family later made the existing building the summer home.

Many roads on the 9-mile-long island are unpaved but are passable in dry conditions. The northern tip offers a fine view, and whales can often be seen. **Friar's Head Outlook▶▶** (look for signs between F.D.R. International Bridge and the Roosevelt Cottage) commands an impressive view of Passamaquoddy Bay.

On the way to Campobello is **Lubec**, the most easterly town in Maine and, indeed, the U.S. It was once a busy smoked herring and sardine-canning town. Nearby are the remains of two dams, the only trace of a failed scheme in 1919 to harness tidal energy from the bay.

To the south, **West Quoddy Head▶** marks the easternmost point of the U.S. mainland. A long dirt road brings you, eventually, to **West Quoddy Light**, built in 1858 and which sends out a 20-mile beam. A 4-mile trail along high cliffs provides opportunities for spotting whales.

**123**

*Roosevelt's house on Campobello Island*

*One of New England's most familiar lighthouses, West Quoddy Light*

*"In 1492 Native Americans discovered Columbus lost at sea!" reads the T-shirt slogan. And not long afterward these so-called "American Indians" met the first European colonists on the shores of New England. This was a meeting of two cultures, which to this day are as different as night and day.*

**A PROUD TRADITION**
Keeping the tradition of basket-making alive is seen as important to the preservation of Native American culture. The Maine Arts Commission has developed a program through which basket-makers pass on their skills to apprentices. These works of fine craftsmanship may be bought at crafts festivals and through cooperatives or shops.

*A Passamaquoddy native of Maine*

Windsong, a Massachusetts Wampanoag who does not live on an Indian reservation, is a deeply spiritual man. For his traditional, sacred rituals he needs eagle feathers. But the eagle is a protected bird and only Native Americans living on registered land are entitled to their feathers. This lack of awareness of the spiritual needs of another culture is, he says, typical of a white man's society brought up on images of peace pipe-smoking "Indians" who raise one hand and call out "How!," images that have more to do with Hollywood than real life.

**Cultural and social issues** For hundreds of years, the Native People of the eastern United States have mixed with other elements in society—with blacks and, in more recent decades, with whites. Yet, although there is a degree of integration in this part of the country that may not exist in the western states of the U.S., considerable resentment does exist—and on both sides.

In the workplace, for instance, Native Americans once felt a bitter sense of discrimination as they were overlooked for promotion. Now, however, antidiscrimination regulations mean that this can no longer happen legally, and the pendulum has swung so far that the playing field is somewhat more even. Nevertheless, the clash of cultures remains, and a common stereotype suggests that the archetypal conscientious and diligent Yankee may find the Native American frustratingly casual.

Today there is far less social distinction between Native Americans and other Americans. Yet the Native American culture is still widely celebrated, notably with the opening in 1998 of the Mashantucket Pequot Museum and Research Center at Foxwoods, Connecticut (see page 95), built at a cost of $135 million.

124

### Staking a claim

So regulations are bringing Native Americans closer to full integration into New England society. At the same time, the tribes are actively reasserting their own rights. In Maine, the Penobscots and Passamaquoddy have long fought for legal control of fishing, mineral, and forest rights on their lands. In Vermont, the

Abenaki threaten legal claims on much of the land. But the hottest issue concerns the Mashantucket Pequots in Connecticut.

In 1992, the Pequots, a tribe that had all but died out, opened Foxwoods High Stakes Bingo and Casino (see panel). It currently brings in about $7.4 billion per year on slot machines alone. It is the largest casino in the Western hemisphere, a vast operation through whose ever-open doors pass 40,000 Americans a day. Awaiting them are the 5,900 clattering slot machines, bingo rooms, and blackjack, craps, baccarat, roulette, acey-deucey, money wheel, pai gow poker, and chuck-a-luck, to name but a few of the table games. In an area of dire unemployment, Foxwoods is now one of the biggest employers. Moreover, Connecticut's coffers are fatter by over $180 million per year as a result of a deal with the governor whereby 25 percent of slot machines takings are handed over in exchange for a monopoly control of all gaming machines in the state. Foxwoods looks after its employees well, but along with jobs it brings traffic, noise and, potentially at least, some of the less desirable members of society to the neighborhood. Now its owners plan to buy more land, annexing it into sovereign Indian land and thereby removing it from local control and, significantly, state and federal tax rolls. This is cause for deep concern in the nearby villages and for bitter resentment among some of New England's taxpayers.

*Top: spinning the wheel at Foxwoods*
*Left: a Connecticut Algonquin*

### SOVEREIGNTY OF LAND

A tribe that is federally recognized can assume responsibility for its own internal control. The Pequots, for instance, have established their own police force, housing authority, and ambulance and fire services, as well as their own court system. They also have their own water supply and sewage system. No federally recognized tribe pays state or federal taxes. This means that cigarettes and alcohol can be sold more cheaply on a reservation than elsewhere.

### PLAYING THE GAME

Federal law allows recognized Indian tribes to conduct gambling if the state in which they live allows gambling. Connecticut allows fund-raising, nonprofit "casino nights" (for example, church bingo evenings), and the Pequots took advantage of this, opening Foxwoods Bingo in 1986. It began to make a profit, and the state of Connecticut sued the Pequots. The case went to the Supreme Court, where the state lost. The Pequots obtained investment capital from Malaysia and opened the casino. In 1993, Rhode Island, not liking the possibility of a similar temple to gambling, repealed its law allowing fund-raising bingo.

125

*Almost extinct 100 years ago, the puffin has recently been making a comeback in the Gulf of Maine*

**REVERSING FALLS**
The falls take some effort to find. Turn off Route 1 at Pembroke, taking the road to the right of the post office. Very soon turn right and then left (follow signs to the shore), then, after 3.2 miles, turn right past a cemetery. Bear left at a fork with a dirt road. Continue for 1.4 miles, then fork left beyond a covered picnic bench up on the left: the parking lot is just beyond.

*Revolutionary memorabilia is displayed in the Burnham Tavern, Machias*

## ▶ Eastport

This is small-town Maine at its most seductively peaceful, far removed from the crafts designer stores and tourist crowds of the more frequented parts of the coast. Eastport's population numbers under 2,000 but is rated important enough to have its own city hall. High, Ray, Washington, and Water streets contain an attractive mixture of architectural styles, from Colonial to Victorian.

In the town itself, seek out Raye's Mustard, the last stone-ground mustard mill in the U.S.A., a legacy of the days when mustard was used as a preservative. In the summer months (afternoons only) you can visit the local history museum, which is housed within the old Sullivan Barracks (1809). The garrison surrendered to the British in the War of 1812 without a shot being fired.

The town, sited on Moose Island and linked by causeway to the mainland, is a sardine, granite, timber, and processed-paper port. It lies on **Passamaquoddy Bay▶▶**, site of the world's largest lobster pond, and notorious for treacherous waters that include fast incoming tides and great changes in water levels. **Old Sow**, the world's second largest whirlpool, can be seen from the car ferry to Deer Island. The curious tidal phenomenon of **Reversing Falls**, where the current goes in the contrary direction to the tide at certain times of day, occurs near Pembroke (for directions, see panel).

A little farther south, **Cobscook Bay State Park** has two trails, one leading to the coast, the other along the creek. There are ferry connections to **Deer Island**, connecting with another ferry for **Campobello Island▶▶** (see page 123). At the far end of Deer Island, a free ferry crosses to L'Etete on the Canadian mainland.

In the former lumber town of **Machias**, the **Burnham Tavern▶** on High Street (dating from 1770) is eastern Maine's oldest building. Here, patriots planned the capture of the British schooner *Margaretta* on June 12, 1775, after the British captain had ordered locals to take down their liberty pole. This was the first naval battle of the Revolution. Now a museum (*Open* mid-Jun–Sep, Mon–Fri 9–5. *Admission: inexpensive*), the tavern has Revolutionary-era furnishings and items from the British vessel.

On Route 92, half a mile from town, the Maine Wild Blueberry Company produces around 20 million pounds of berries a year; free tours (weekdays in summer; for an appointment, tel: 207/255–8364) show the processes of cleaning, freezing, and grading the berries. Route 191 leads through the town of **Cutler**, where the lobster atchery is open to the public in summer. Route 187 reaches **Jonesport**, a typical Downeast fishing village, linked by bridge to Beal Island, where clams are raised. A causeway gives access to the Mud Hole Trail (from Black Duck Cove), with good views across to the islands.

## Ellsworth                                                  *108B2*

An unassuming small town on the way to Bar Harbor, Ellsworth has a fine First Congregational church (1846), thought to be Maine's best example of a Greek Revival church. The steeple is a faithful fiberglass replica. The Old Hancock County Buildings, on Cross Street, are in similar style. The Big Chicken Barn, on Route 3 in town, is Maine's largest antiquarian bookstore and antiques shop.

Just out of town is the **Colonel Black Mansion▶** (*Open Sun–mid-Oct, Mon–Sat; tours 10–5. Admission: moderate*), built in 1824–1828 by land agent Colonel John Black. This charming Georgian home has original furnishings, a fine circular staircase, and formal gardens. The carriage house on the grounds contains old sleighs and carriages.

Out on Route 3, the **Birdsacre Sanctuary** covers 100 acres, with trails leading past ponds and nesting areas. There is a nature center (*Open* daily 10–4. *Admission: donation*), plus the Stanwood Homestead Museum, dedicated to pioneer ornithologist Cordelia Stanwood (*Open* by request). **Lamoine State Park▶**, on Route 184, has excellent views of Mount Desert Island and a safe beach. At Columbia Falls, just off Route 1, is **Ruggles House▶** (*Open* Jun–mid-Oct, Mon–Fri 9:30–4:30, Sun 11–4:30. *Admission: donation*), which dates from 1818 and was inhabited until 1920. The house is noted for its "flying" staircase (supported only at the top and bottom); the woodcarving on the staircase was executed with a jackknife over a three-year period.

### WILDLIFE SANCTUARY

Moosehorn National Wildlife Refuge, 5 miles north of Calais (pronounced "Callous"), itself north of Eastport on Route 1 on the Charlotte Road, consists of 23,000 acres of bogs, woods, and marshes, inhabited by 216 species of birds, plus moose, deer, bear, beaver, mink, and woodchuck. Some 50 miles of roads and trails are open to hikers.

### GRANITE MEMENTOES

On Route 1 between Calais and Robbinston are 12 granite milestones erected by James Shepherd Pike in 1870. Pike, a lumberman, abolitionist, ambassador, and writer, had a summer residence in Robbinston. He measured the circumference of his cartwheels, then placed the stones so as to check the speed of his horses.

127

*The 1817 Tisdale House, now Ellsworth's City Library*

## L.L. BEAN

This famous store started as a humble one-man mail-order operation and has since boomed. In 1912, Leon Leonwood Bean marketed his invention, the Maine Hunting Shoe: "designed by a hunter who has tramped the Maine Woods for the past 18 years. They are as light as a pair of moccasins with the protection of a heavy hunting boot." Today, the store sells over 16,000 products. It is still largely mail-order with its head office and main retail store in Freeport, but there are nine factory outlets: six in New England, plus branches in Delaware, Oregon, and Japan.

### ▶▶ Freeport — 108A1

Freeport, Maine's biggest visitor attraction along with Acadia National Park, consists of a main street lined wall-to-wall with factory shopping outlets. There are over 100 and most of the time sale prices are offered somewhere. Serious shoppers journey up here from New York and even farther away to make Christmas purchases.

It is a matter of dispute whether Freeport is really such good value (compared to North Conway, for instance), but the selection (candles, kids' clothes, maps and guides, crafts, sports equipment, soap, and so on) is impressive. Although village-sized, Freeport is crammed with shoppers transporting bulging shopping bags, and the traffic and parking lots are on an urban scale. Maps showing locations of the stores are given away at Bean's (see panel) and other shops. Freeport has inns, motels, and B&Bs as well as a beach, and it is the starting point for ocean cruises.

Outside Freeport is the **Desert of Maine**▶ (*Open* early May–mid Oct; guided tours every half-hour. *Admission moderate*), a curiosity. This really is a small desert, an eye-opening example of 18th-century bad farming practice where the soil was depleted and massive erosion followed. Entire farm buildings and trees were engulfed in the dunes, and telltale treetops still protrude like small bushes. From May to Columbus Day, a tour is provided of this odd tribute to human failure. Also south of town, live osprey and seals may be spotted from **Wolfe's Neck Woods State Park**▶ (*Open* Memorial Day–Labor Day. *Admission free*), which has trails and wooded shores as well as some unusual rock formations. At **Bradbury Mountain State Park** (*Open* daily) a 20-minute trail to the summit leads to views over Casco Bay.

### ▶▶ Penobscot Bay — 108B2

This is the biggest indentation in Maine's coast and the bay and its islands offer some of the loveliest panoramas along New England's seaboard. Boating has been big here for centuries. The Penobscot River once supplied over 20 towns with timber for shipbuilding, and today the ports are busy with pleasure and commercial craft. Rockland and Camden are the main boating areas. Camden is prettier and more of a resort. Be warned: the sprawl along Route 1 is unsightly, and in summer driving along it is no pleasure.

*Above: Freeport is home to the popular mail-order clothing company L.L. Bean*

*Penobscot Bay has long been busy with boats, both large and small*

**THE WEST SIDE** Port Clyde, on the west side of the bay, is the departure point for ferries making crossings to **Monhegan Island**▶▶ (see page 121). On the way to the town you pass through Tenants Harbor, a picturesque fishing village, with lobster boats moored in the harbor.

Farther north, **Owls Head Transportation Museum**▶▶ (*Open* Apr–Oct, daily 10–5; Nov–Mar, daily 10–4. *Admission: moderate*) displays New England's largest collection of pioneer vehicles. They include vintage bikes, early horseless carriages, gas-powered cars, and antique airplanes. A schedule of events features air shows and motorcycle and tractor meets (tel: 207/594–4418 for details).

Nearby **Rockland**, New England's biggest distribution center for the lobster industry and a major sardine port, has a workaday atmosphere. The local processing of seaweed gives the place a wholesome aroma.

The **Conway Homestead Cramer Museum**, Route 1 and Conway Road (*Open* Jul–Aug, Tue–Fri 10–4. *Admission: inexpensive*), is an atmospheric 1770s farmhouse and barn with farm tools, a blacksmith shop, and a maple-sugar house with sugaring demonstrations in spring.

*On the move at Owls Head Transportation Museum*

**THE BEANS OF EGYPT, MAINE**
No relation to the Beans of Freeport, the Bean family of Egypt was a fictitious invention of novelist Carolyn Chute. Her book *The Beans of Egypt, Maine* (1985) is the saga of a violent and primitive family, prisoners of rural poverty in the woods of Maine. Despite its bleak setting, the novel has moments of black humor.

**129**

**BAY ISLANDS**
Penobscot Bay's main islands make attractive hiking or bicycling country. Vinalhaven, the largest at 14 miles long, and Islesboro (12 miles long) have accommodations, but no camping is allowed. North Haven and Matinicus both have accommodations and camping by permission. Isle au Haut is part of Acadia National Park (see pages 112–113). For Monhegan Island, see page 121. Islesboro is reached by ferry from Lincolnville Beach; North Haven, Vinalhaven, and Matinicus from a car ferry at Rockland. For details, call the Maine State Ferry Service (tel: 800/491–4883).

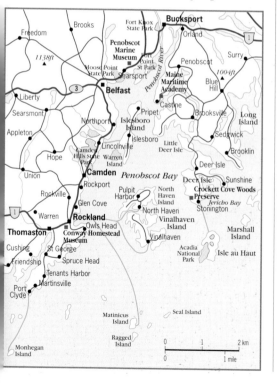

# Maine

## CASTINE'S MILITARY PAST

Castine had a strategic importance and was fought over by the French, Dutch, British, and Americans for nearly two centuries. Above the Maine Maritime Academy are the grassy ramparts of Fort George, built by the British in 1779 to protect Canadian interests and the last fort they abandoned at the end of the Revolutionary War. It still has its moat and earthworks.

Crammed into the **Shore Village Museum**▶▶, at 104 Limerock Street, Rockland, is the largest collection of lighthouse lenses and paraphernalia in the U.S.A., plus Coast Guard buoys, bells, model ships, navigational instruments, Civil War memorabilia, and 19th-century costume dolls (*Open* Jun 1–Oct 15, daily 10–4. *Admission: donation*). Also in Rockland is an outstanding art collection at the **Farnsworth Art Museum and Homestead**▶▶ (*Open* Memorial Day–Labor Day, daily 9–5; Labor Day–Memorial Day, Tue–Sat 10–5, Sun 1–5. *Admission: moderate*). The display is rotated and features Maine and New England art and artists. Winslow Homer's *Girl in a Punt* is one of the best-known works. The 19th-century Greek Revival homestead of William A. Farnsworth, the lime baron who endowed the museum, has period decor in its 12 small rooms. Andrew Wyeth had a studio at the **Olson House** on Hathorn Point Road, Cushing (*Open* Memorial Day–Columbus Day, daily 11–4. *Admission:*

*The bold and bright* Romance of Autumn *by George Bellows (1882–1925), on display at the Farnsworth Art Museum in Rockland*

*inexpensive*). He depicted the owner in front of the house in *Christina's World*, one of the most evocative of all American paintings.

**Rockport**▶ has a charming village center, little changed from the 19th century, that overlooks a marina, old lime kiln, and oceanside park. The best of **Camden**▶ lies off busy Route 1: Chestnut and Bayview streets are conspicuously attractive. Crafts shops and traffic jams are the norm in summer, with window-shoppers spilling off the sidewalks. The village keeps going all year, with events, a community theater, an opera house, and a winter carnival. In summer the village becomes the home port for a number of boat races, including the Camden–Castine Race.

Mount Battie is the crowning glory of **Camden Hills State Park**▶▶▶ (*Open* mid-May–mid-Oct), where a toll road winds up to the top for a glorious view of the bay and over the strikingly empty countryside. Hikers can walk 25 miles of park trails; it takes 1–1½ hours to ascend the mountain on foot.

Searsport is Maine's "antiques capital," well endowed with shops and flea markets. **Penobscot Marine Museum**►► in town (*Open* Memorial Day weekend–Oct 15, Mon–Sat 10–5, Sun 12–5. *Admission: moderate*) chronicles the maritime history of Penobscot Bay. Searsport once specialized in building trading ships, and several captains' houses (including the Fowler-True-Ross House and Barn) survive from those times. The museum is on several neighboring sites; one ticket covers them all. The main building has a notable collection of maritime art, a remarkable film of a 1929 voyage around Cape Horn in a hurricane, and a quaint assemblage of 200 butter dishes collected by a captain's wife. Other buildings display small craft, whaling and scrimshaw, and shipbuilding.

**THE EAST SIDE** By complete contrast, this side of Penobscot Bay has few attractions but a quiet charm of its own by virtue of its inaccessibility. A causeway links Deer Isle to the mainland, with the sleepy fishing village of Stonington at its southern tip, where ferries leave for Isle au Haut in Acadia National Park (see pages 112–113). **Blue Hill**►► rises to 934 feet just north of the village of the same name: from the village take Route 15 north, then turn right on Mountain Road; the trail starts on the left-hand side and ascends for a view over Acadia and the bay.

**Castine**►►, one of the most attractive villages in the state, has some gracious early 19th-century homes, with plaques recording their history, in Main and Perkins streets. By the common is the First Parish Church, begun in 1790 and eastern Maine's oldest church. The entire village has been designated a national historic site (see panel opposite). Berthed here is the *State of Maine*, a former troopship used by the adjacent Maine Maritime Academy for training merchant midshipmen. Regular tours are given around the ship; for hours, tel: 207/326–4311.

**Crockett Cove Woods Preserve** is a 100-acre site maintained by the Nature Conservancy and comprising coastal spruce woods and a miniature bog. A self-guiding trail leads visitors around the preserve, and brochures are available from the entrance registration booth.

**A NOSTALGIC SIDE TRIP**
At Belfast, the Belfast & Moosehead Lake Railroad (tel: 800/392–5500) runs narrated 1½-hour trips to Burnham Junction in 1920s Pullman cars. This is a 25-mile round trip (extended to 33 miles in the fall), and you get "ambushed" by comic bandits on the way. A critically acclaimed theater shares the train station, located near the water's edge. The railroad operates from early May to late October, most days in July and August, and less frequently in May, September, and October.

131

**WINDJAMMER VACATIONS**
Companies in Penobscot Bay offer vacations on schooners known as windjammers (see picture below). Participants stay for the week and can enjoy sailing trips lasting from two hours to several days on tall-masted wooden sailing ships, some of them magnificent 19th-century restorations. You can hoist the sails, take a turn at the wheel, and help navigate. Anyone sailing alone in the Boothbay or Penobscot Bay areas should have plenty of experience and be able to read a nautical chart.

*Camden has the largest fleet of windjammers*

*For lovers of the great outdoors, New England has something for everyone, whether lone fishermen or families, adventurous youngsters or active seniors. From spring to fall there is first-rate hiking, biking, fishing, and golfing. There are water sports from sailing and windsurfing to canoeing and rafting.*

### CANOEING

The Appalachian Mountain Club (AMC) publishes *Quiet Water Canoe Guide, New Hampshire/Vermont* and *River Guide, Central/ Southern New England.* Contact AMC, P.O. Box 298, Gorham, NH 03581 (tel: 603/466–2721).

Canoes can be rented and trips operate from dozens of locations, including the Rangeley Lakes area, Maine; the Lamoille and Batten Kill rivers, Vermont; the Saco River at Conway, and the Connecticut River at Hanover and Balloch's Crossing (all in NH).

**Hiking and biking** Hiking, popular throughout New England, is on marked trails (see page 257). All state parks have clearly marked trails, and bulletin boards often indicate length and difficulty. Trails range from easy to extremely challenging, but with vast areas of New England covered in forest, the terrain is not always particularly varied.

New Hampshire's White Mountains make superb hiking territory (see page 208). The lakes and forests of Maine's Kennebec Valley and the Western Lakes and Mountains are popular for both hiking and biking. Bicycles can be rented in many places. Naturalists will enjoy the trails in the wilds of Baxter State Park. As with several other ski areas in Maine, Vermont, and New Hampshire, Sunday River in Maine has a network of mountain-bike trails using the ski lifts. Cape Cod National Seashore has 40 miles of hiking and cycling trails; the Berkshires is another favorite area. Nantucket, Massachusetts, and Block Island, Rhode Island, have miles of attractive biking paths.

**Fishing and golfing** There are excellent fishing opportunities throughout New England. Lake Champlain, on the Vermont/New York border, has dozens of public access points along its 100-mile length for fishing for lake trout, landlocked salmon, bass, walleye, and the brightly colored, tasty pumpkinseed. The lake is also superb for ice-fishing, an increasingly popular winter sport.

From mid-April to the end of October, there is excellent fishing for landlocked salmon and trout in the lakes and ponds of New Hampshire and areas of Maine such as Bethel and Rangeley, the Winthrop Lakes, and around The Forks and Jackman in the north. Vermont's Northeast Kingdom region is especially popular. You'll need a map to reach the numerous "backwoods" ponds, remote and lovely beaver ponds teeming with brown trout. The Connecticut River is scenic and peaceful—a delight for anglers.

New England's spectacular natural scenery makes a glorious backdrop for hundreds of public golf courses. Some of the most magnificent courses are offered by grand resort hotels such as The

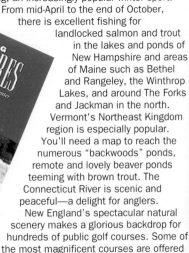

*Anywhere in New England, fishing provides beautiful scenery: above, near the Mohawk Trail*

Balsams at Dixville Notch, New Hampshire, the Mount Washington in the White Mountains, or Tory Pines, set in the Monadnock region. Outstanding courses in Vermont include the Woodstock Inn Resort as well as clubs in Stratton and Manchester Village (The Equinox). In Connecticut try Lyman Orchards in Middlefield and the Richter Park or the Hilton in Danbury. There is a fine course near Rangeley in northern Maine, and in the Berkshires Cranwell is an old country hotel with a splendid course.

**Water sports** There is good sailing from many places around the coast. Newport, Rhode Island, former home of the America's Cup, and the Penobscot Bay section of the Maine coast are the best-known areas (but much of the Maine coast has odd currents and is not for the novice—see panel on page 131). Inland, Lake Champlain and the bigger lakes in New Hampshire and Maine are popular for sailing, sailboarding, canoeing, and windsurfing, and most have boats for rent. The Connecticut River and the Housatonic provide easy canoeing. Canoeing is a peaceful way to explore the remoter areas of northern New England, offering intimate encounters with beaver, moose, and other wildlife.

Whitewater rafters await the spring runoff, when the rivers start to swirl and swell. Mecca is The Forks, in Maine, where several companies organize trips down the Kennebec, Dead, and Penobscot rivers. In the far north, experts relish the challenges of the Allagash Wilderness Waterway. In Vermont, whitewater rafting trips operate on West River. There is rafting on seven rivers from Conway, New Hampshire, and in western Massachusetts there are rafting centers on the Deerfield River.

### FISHING

Licenses may be obtained from town clerk offices, local sporting shops, or the state Fish and Wildlife Office (see below).

The Vermont Fish and Wildlife Department (103 South Main Street, Waterbury, VT 05676) publishes a *Guide to Fishing* leaflet.

Other useful addresses for further information on fishing:

● Connecticut Department of Environmental Protection, 79 Elm Street, Hartford, CT 06106.
● Maine Department of Inland Fisheries and Wildlife, 284 State Street, Augusta, ME 04333.
● Massachusetts Division of Marine Fisheries, 100 Cambridge Street, Boston, MA 02202.
● New Hampshire Fish and Game Department, 2 Hazen Drive, Concord, NH 03301.
● Rhode Island Division of Fish and Wildlife, Government Center, Tower Hill Road, Wakefield, RI 02879.

### THE APPALACHIAN TRAIL

The Appalachian Trail (2,035 miles) stretches from Maine, through New Hampshire, Vermont, Massachusetts, and Connecticut, continuing south to Georgia. Road access makes it easy to cover short stretches. The Appalachian Mountain Club estimates that of the 2,000 to 3,000 who attempt the trail each year, only 10 percent complete it.

## CASCO BAY

Casco Bay is the largest deepwater haven on the Atlantic coast; the islands that protect the bay are said to number 365.

The first secret war conference between Roosevelt and Churchill took place on a battleship off Long Island in the bay, when the Atlantic Pact was signed. Several fortifications can be spotted on the islands, including forts Scammel, McKinley, and Gorges. South Portland is the water terminal for the Portland–Montreal pipeline. Crude oil supertankers from South America and the Middle East are common sights.

*Brewed in Portland*

## CRUISES FROM PORTLAND

Casco Bay Lines' mail boat run is the longest such operating service in the U.S., stopping at Cliff, Chebeague, Long, Little, and Great Diamond islands. The company also provides cruises to Bailey Island (tel: 207/774–7871). Eagle Tours (tel: 207/774–6498) offers seal-watching and fishing trips, as well as cruises to Eagle Island.

## ▶▶ Portland                              108A1

Maine's largest city prospered as a port on the basis of its accessibility to Europe. Its decline after World War II was reversed by a revival in fortunes, spearheaded by the revival of the Old Port Exchange district, with its uniform grid of redbrick streets rebuilt in the 1860s after a disastrous fire. This part of the city is pleasant for walking and has restaurants, boutiques, and specialty shops. Portland's face is unmistakably urban, but the city has good cultural attractions. Commercial Street runs along the harbor, where you can join cruises (see panel).

The **Portland Museum of Art▶▶**, in Congress Square (*Open* Tue–Wed, Sat–Sun 10–5, Thu–Fri 10–9. *Admission: moderate*), houses one of New England's finest art collections. The American collection includes Maine scenes by Winslow Homer, Andrew Wyeth, Marsden Hartley, and Rockwell Kent. European art features sculpture by Henry Moore and Rodin, and Impressionist and Cubist works.

Next door is the **Children's Museum of Maine▶**, 142 Free Street (*Open* Mon–Wed, Fri–Sat 10–5, Thu 9–5, Sun 12–5. *Admission: moderate*), which ranks among the best of its kind in New England. At 485–489 Congress Street is the **Wadsworth-Longfellow House▶** (see panel opposite), the childhood home of Henry Wadsworth Longfellow, America's most popular 19th-century poet. His family was comfortably well-off but not wealthy, and in the house are numerous family possessions (*Open* Jun–Oct, daily 10–5; Dec, tel: 207/774–1822 for hours. *Admission: moderate*). Longfellow was inspired to write several poems about Portland, including *The Lighthouse*, *My Lost Youth*, and *The Ropewalk*. He penned *The Rainy Day* in the house.

**Portland Observatory**, at 138 Congress Street (*Open* Jun 11–Columbus Day, Mon–Sat 10–6, Sun 1–5. *Admission: inexpensive*), was built in 1807 and is a rare example of a signal tower on which signal flags would be flown to identify incoming vessels.

**Victoria Mansion▶▶**, on the corner of Danforth and Park streets, is an ornate Italianate brownstone house, built 1858–1860 and reflecting northern European taste. The interior is a lavish showpiece, with plasterwork made to resemble wood, an eye-catching chandelier, painted walls and ceilings, and a Moorish-style smoking room (*Open* May–Oct, Tue–Sat 10–4, Sun 1–5. *Admission: moderate*).

**Tate House**, 1270 Westbrook Street (*Open* mid-Jun–Oct, Tue–Sat 10–4, Sun 1–4. *Admission: moderate*), is a fine colonial period house with a riverside setting and 18th-century herb garden. A worthwhile visit is the **Neal Dow Memorial House**, at

714 Congress Street, a Federal mansion of 1829 that belonged to a leading figure in the temperance cause (*Open* Mar–Dec, Mon–Fri 11–4. *Admission free*).

**Fort Williams Park▶** occupies a fine section of rocky coast south of the city. Adjacent to the fort, Portland Head Light (1791) is the oldest lighthouse in Maine and inspired Longfellow. A museum in the lighthouse keeper's quarters tells its story (*Open* Jun–Oct, daily; Nov–Dec, Apr–May, Sat–Sun). Lighthouse devotees may also like to visit nearby **Two Lights State Park** (*Open* daily. *Admission free*). Not far away, artist Winslow Homer made his home at Prout's Neck (*Open* summer–early fall. *Admission free*).

▶ **Wiscasset**                              *108B1*

This pretty village used to be a busy shipping port. One of the old sea captains' houses here is now home to the **Musical Wonder House**, packed with musical automata (*Open* Memorial Day–Oct 31, daily 10–5. *Admission: inexpensive; tours moderate–expensive*).

**Fort Edgecomb▶** (*Open* May–Labor Day, daylight hours), off Route 1 on the east side of the river bridge, is a well-preserved wooden blockhouse of 1808–1809. It was one of four defensive forts on the Lincoln County coast. Although nothing remains inside, the setting is superb.

In town, at Lee and High streets, is **Castle Tucker** (*Open* Jun–mid-Oct, Wed–Sun 11–5. *Admission: inexpensive*), a grand house built in 1807 by Judge Silas Lee, later modified, and now displaying 19th-century furnishings. On Federal Street, the **Old Lincoln County Jail** (*Open* Jul–Aug, Tue–Sun 11–4. *Admission: inexpensive*) was built in 1811 and in use until 1953. Visitors can see the cells and jailer's house.

**135**

*Portland Head Light*

*John Hancock Warehouse, York, dates from the mid-1700s and is still used as a boathouse today*

**BLOWING CAVE**
Located between Walker Point and Cape Arundel, just east of Kennebunkport, this sea cave is a curious phenomenon. As waves enter it, air is trapped and compressed; as the water recedes, the trapped air is released, sometimes sending out a spray of seawater. Unfortunately, it is difficult to see this happen as the cave is only really accessible at low tide, but it is fun to explore just the same.

**136**

**IN LOVE WITH THE PAST**
Elizabeth Perkins and her mother fell in love with their house in York and spent their summers there. Proud of their New England heritage and ancestors, the Perkinses crammed the house with antiques and furniture, creating a comfortable rather than historically accurate house for entertaining and vacationing. Elizabeth took an interest in preserving York and was responsible for saving the schoolhouse and wooden bridge. She loved collecting antiques and installed old-fashioned beams and paneling for effect in the dining room. Both women's ashes are in the garden.

*Elizabeth Perkins House, transformed into an idyllic weekend retreat by a wealthy New York family*

#### ►► York and Kennebunkport 108A1

York is a composite place: just off Route 1 lies historic York Village, alone worth at least half a day to explore. Along the shoreline are Long Sands Beach (popular for surfing) and the famous Nubble Lighthouse (also known as Cape Neddick Lighthouse), built in 1879 on York Beach, which itself retains a graceful 19th-century air. York Harbor lies between the old village and the beaches.

**THE OLD YORK HISTORICAL SOCIETY SITES** These include a number of buildings, some with tours conducted by interpreters. Tours run from Tuesday through Saturday 10–5, Sunday 1–5 (last tour 4 PM). Jefferds' Tavern (1754), where you buy your ticket, features displays about York and is often filled with the aroma of hearthside cooking. Next door is the **Schoolhouse** (1745), which has a small exhibition on schooling and apprenticeship in Maine.

Made from two Colonial houses put together, the **Emerson-Wilcox House►** illustrates a variety of periods in its rooms, from the 1765 parlor to the 1930s dining room. The bedroom possesses the oldest known complete set of American bed-hangings, done in crewel work in 1746 and in pristine condition (notice the original spelling mistakes in the words of a hymn that have been worked into the design).

The **Old Gaol►**, in use from 1719 to 1860, took in about 14 prisoners per year; interpreters fill in the facts and legends. Jail quarters and the jailer's chambers are on show.

The **John Hancock Warehouse and Wharf►**, once owned by John Hancock, occupies a charming spot on an unspoiled creek, near a wooden bridge. The warehouse is the last commercial Colonial building in town and is still used as a working boathouse. It houses a small exhibition on shipbuilding, timber, shipping, farming, and lobstering.

By the York River is the **Elizabeth Perkins House▶▶**, a fascinating example of Colonial Revival style—a colonial house furnished during the 1920s to 1940s in an idealized conception of Colonial style itself. Its transformation began in 1898 when the Perkinses bought the 18th-century farmhouse (see panel opposite).

**ELSEWHERE ALONG THE COAST** The yachting and fishing village of **Kennebunkport** is the home and one-time Summer White House of former President George Bush, who used to jog along the beach (often with scores of red-faced reporters and photographers in tow). His house at Walker's Point can be seen from the seafront, otherwise memorable for its drawbridge. On Route 9A/35 is the Wedding Cake House, a particularly fetching yellow and white confection.

The **Brick Store Museum▶**, at 117 Main Street, Kennebunk (*Open* Mar–Dec, Tue–Sat 10–4:30. *Admission: moderate*), is a fine local history museum with rotating exhibits on both maritime and social history and on the decorative arts. Three miles north of Kennebunkport is the **Seashore Trolley Museum▶** (*Open* May–Nov, daily 10–5. *Admission: moderate*), with the world's largest collection of trolleys and the opportunity to take a nostalgic ride.

Route 1 in this area is packaged-fun country. At York itself is the **Wild Kingdom**, with a zoo and amusement park (*Open* late Jun–Labor Day. *Admission: zoo and rides, expensive; zoo only, expensive; rides only, moderate*). At Wells, the **Wells Auto Museum** (*Open* Memorial Day–Columbus Day, daily 10–5. *Admission: moderate*) has more than 80 vintage automobiles as well as an assembly of antique arcade games, nickelodeons, and other items. Saco is home to **Funtown Splashtown U.S.A.**, the **Maine Aquarium**, and **Aquaboggan Water Park**. **Old Orchard Beach**, on the coast, has a sandy shoreline and is densely developed with fast-food outlets and amusements; **Palace Playland** has yet more seaside rides.

**Ogunquit** is an upscale resort village and was once an artists' colony. Cove views are available from a pretty drawbridge leading to Perkins Cove and from a mile-long coastal path known as Rustic Way. Ogunquit's **Museum of American Art** is open from July to September (*Admission: inexpensive*), and there is a summer theater season.

**Kittery▶** has factory shopping outlets; there are over 100 such discount stores along Kittery's "miracle mile" offering savings of up to 70 percent.

137

*Travel through time at the Seashore Trolley Museum near Kennebunkport*

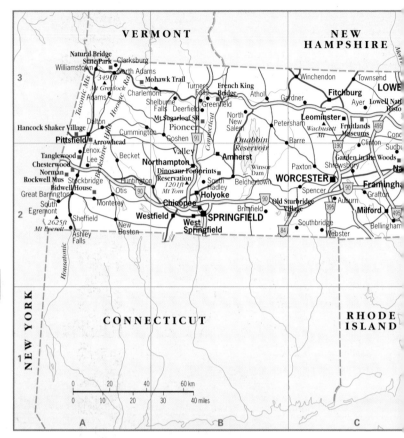

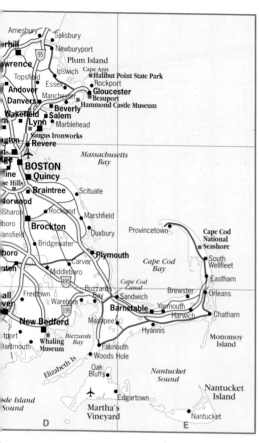

Amesbury · Salisbury
·rhill · Newburyport
·wrence · Plum Island
Topsfield · Ipswich · Cape Ann
Essex · ■Halibut Point State Park
**Andover** Manchester · Rockport
**Danvers** · **Gloucester**
**Wakefield** · Salem ■Beauport
· **Lynn** · Hammond Castle Museum
·n ■ · Marblehead
·gton · Saugus Ironworks
·d- ■**Revere**
·ge
·ine **BOSTON** *Massachusetts*
·ic Hills ■ **Quincy** *Bay*
**·lorwood** · **Braintree** · Scituate
Sharon · Rockland · Marshfield
·boro **Brockton**
·ansfield · Bridgewater · Duxbury Provincetown **Cape Cod National** ■ **Seashore**
·boro · **Plymouth** *Cape Cod* South
·nton Carver *Bay* Wellfleet
Middleboro · 495 Eastham
·all Freetown Buzzards *Cape Cod* Brewster Orleans
·ven Wareham · Bay *Canal* Sandwich
**New Bedford** **Barnstable** Yarmouth
·tport Mashpee · Harwich · Chatham
·Dartmouth *Buzzards* **Whaling** Hyannis Monomoy
*Bay* **Museum** Falmouth Island
· Woods Hole
·de Island *Elizabeth Is* Oak
*Sound* Bluffs *Nantucket*
·  Edgartown *Sound* Nantucket
**D** Martha's Island
Vineyard Nantucket
**E**

**MASSACHUSETTS** Even excluding the attractions of
Boston and Cambridge (see pages 48–85), there is plenty
in the rest of Massachusetts to excite the curious traveler.
The state is the cradle of modern America and as such is
packed with history. In 1620, the Pilgrim Fathers landed
at Provincetown, 600 miles farther north than they had
intended (they were bound for Jamestown in Virginia),
before finally establishing themselves at Plymouth. In
1775, the first shots of the American Revolution sounded
at Lexington and Concord. In the 19th century, the first
large-scale textile mills appeared in Lowell, heralding the
birth of industrial America. Massachusetts is seen as a
center of political and intellectual thought: great names
associated with the state include Ralph Waldo Emerson
(1803–1882), Henry David Thoreau (1817–1862), Herman
Melville (1819–1891), Emily Dickinson (1830–1886),
Louisa May Alcott (1832–1888), Edith Wharton
(1862–1937), and John F. Kennedy (1917–1963).

**ALONG THE COAST** Early settlers ensconced themselves
along the coast, often referred to as the North Shore and
the South Shore, with Boston at the pivot. Today, the
coast is a place for summer relaxation, though the sheer

*Leaf-peeping season on the Mohawk Trail*

numbers of visitors trying to get away from it all can be self-defeating. North Shore towns are select and picturesque, notably **Salem, Marblehead**, Rockport (on **Cape Ann**), and **Newburyport**. Each makes a feasible day trip from Boston, with good public transportation links. Of these, Salem has the most to see, with its gruesome episode of the witches' persecution told in a variety of styles.

On the South Shore is **Plymouth**, a pleasant town with several mementos of the pioneer days, most notably the re-created Pilgrim village at Plimoth Plantation and the *Mayflower II*. **Cape Cod** needs time to appreciate fully, although quirky Provincetown is an entertaining day out by ferry from Boston. Ideally, Cape Cod should be seen "out of season," and the trip should include visits to the islands of **Martha's Vineyard** and **Nantucket**, both haunts of the rich but remarkably different in character; in particular, the towns of Oak Bluffs and Nantucket have their very own, inimitable period atmospheres. New Bedford, the whaling port that took over from Nantucket, looks unappetizing as you speed through its industrial outskirts on I-195, but its old center has atmosphere and a good whaling museum.

*The huge granite blocks of a pier at Rockport on Cape Ann, mementoes of a former local granite industry*

"Listen to the surf, really lend it your ears, and you will hear in it a world of sound: hollow boomings and heavy roarings, great watery tumblings and tramplings, long hissing seethes, sharp rifle-shot reports, splashes, whispers, the grinding undertone of stones, and sometimes vocal sounds that might be the half-heard talk of people in the sea."
– Henry Beston, *The Outermost House* (1927), written in a coastal shack on Cape Cod.

**HEADING INLAND Concord** and **Lexington** lie just beyond the western suburbs of Boston; in addition to the Revolutionary battle sites, there is a rich literary heritage to explore at Concord. **Worcester**, a large industrial city, deserves a look for its armory and art museum.

Of much more mainstream appeal is the evocation of 1830s New England at **Old Sturbridge Village**—sheer pastiche, but convincingly done and atmospheric when not too crowded. Even the farm animals resemble authentic early 19th-century breeds.

Up to the late 18th century, New England extended only as far west as the Connecticut River (known here as **Pioneer Valley**), where you will find an academic center, the so-called Five Colleges Area, plus the industrial centers of Holyoke and Springfield. There are some good walks along the river, with abrupt cliffs in places. Historic Deerfield is the best sight in the valley. Here, the mile-long

*Spectacular autumn views at Shelburne Falls in western Massachusetts*

▶▶▶ REGION HIGHLIGHTS

*Museums and houses*
**Hancock Shaker Village**
*page 145*
**Norman Rockwell Museum** *page 147*
**Old Sturbridge Village**
*page 173*
**Plimoth Plantation**
*page 179*
**Sterling and Francine Clark Art Institute**
*page 144*
*Historic sites*
**Lexington and Concord**
*pages 167–170*
**Plymouth** *pages 177–179*
*Scenery, villages, and small towns*
**Berkshire Hills**
*page 143*
**Martha's Vineyard**
*pages 160–161*
**Nantucket** *pages 162–163*
**Salem and Marblehead**
*pages 184–186*

141

village street has none of the period-clad actors of Old Sturbridge, but some will find the uncommercialized and slow-paced atmosphere appealing.

**THE FAR WEST** Massachusetts now extends west of the Connecticut River into Berkshire County, which borders New York State. This hilly and predominantly rural region has much to offer in the arts: Tanglewood hosts the premier summer musical event in Massachusetts and is the summer base of the Boston Symphony Orchestra (see page 79). Artist Norman Rockwell (see page 150) is remembered near Stockbridge by an excellent museum, and at Chesterwood the house and studio of sculptor Daniel Chester French makes an absorbing visit. Hancock Shaker Village gives a fascinating insight into the almost vanished lifestyle of the Shaker sect.

**TRUSTEES OF RESERVATIONS** A useful source of information for exploring the farther-flung sights of Massachusetts is the handbook published by The Trustees of Reservations. Established in 1891, this is the world's oldest preservation society. It owns over 70 houses and areas of countryside, including woodlands, gorges, waterfalls, and wildlife refuges throughout Massachusetts. Members are admitted to most properties free of charge and to the remaining few at reduced rates. Information and membership details can be obtained from 572 Essex Street, Beverly, MA 01915-1530 (tel: 978/921–1944).

## Events

The precise dates of festivals vary from year to year. Book in advance for popular events, such as the Tanglewood summer concerts. For further information, contact the state tourist office (see page 266) or chambers of commerce.

### APRIL
**Battle of Lexington and Concord Reenactment**, Lexington.
**Daffodil Festival**, Nantucket: flower show and vintage cars.

### MAY
**Brimfield Outdoor Antiques Show**, Brimfield: New England's prime antiques event.
**Seaport Festival**, Salem: crafts, walks, exhibitions, and children's activities.

### JUNE
**Jacob's Pillow Dance Festival**, Becket: renowned modern dance event (until August or September).
**St. Peter's Fiesta**, Gloucester: Blessing of the Fleet; fireworks, parade, music.

*Plymouth Rock, the stone onto which the Pilgrim Fathers are supposed to have stepped when they came ashore from the* Mayflower

**Summer Craft Fair**, Old Deerfield.
**Tanglewood Music Festival**, Lenox: Boston Symphony Orchestra concerts (until August or September).

### JULY
**Barnstable County Fair**, East Falmouth: major Cape Cod event.
**Brimfield Outdoor Antiques Show**.
**Lowell Folk Festival**: music, crafts, and ethnic food.

### AUGUST
**Annual Teddy Bear Rally**, Amherst: dealers, teddies' hospital, entertainment, contests.
**Fall River Celebrates America**, Fall River: ships, boat races, fireworks.
**Feast of the Blessed Sacrament**, New Bedford: the country's largest Portuguese festival, with the Blessing of the Fleet, food, dance, and parade.
**Gloucester Waterfront Festival**: pancake breakfast, Yankee lobster bake, whale watching.
**Marshfield Fair**.
**Martha's Vineyard Agricultural Fair**.

### SEPTEMBER
**Brimfield Outdoor Antiques Show**.
**Harwich Cranberry Harvest Festival**, Harwich: country and western music, fireworks, and parade over ten days.
**Newburyport Waterfront Festival**: art, crafts, and entertainment.
**The Big E**, West Springfield: New England's great state fair.

### OCTOBER
**Salem Haunted Happenings**: magic, witches, costume parade, and candlelight tours at Halloween.
**Topsfield Fair**: oldest continuous fair in the U.S.A. Includes a pumpkin weigh-in competition.

### NOVEMBER
**Bright Nights at Forest Park**, Springfield (until January).
**Issac's Thanksgiving Parade**, Plymouth: Pilgrims' procession, Thanksgiving service, and dinner.

### DECEMBER
**Christmas Shoppers' Stroll**, Nantucket: carol singing, theater, house tours.
**First Night Celebration**, Cape Cod, Lowell, Newburyport, New Bedford, Northampton, Pittsfield, Quincy, Salem, and Worcester.

## ▶▶▶ Berkshire Hills    138A2

The Berkshires region forms the hilliest and westernmost part of Massachusetts and was a fashionable summer resort area for wealthy urbanites in the late 19th century. Summer nowadays is busy with arts events, with some 300,000 people attracted to Tanglewood (see panel on page 146) for the Boston Symphony Orchestra summer concert series alone. The area's fall foliage brings in more crowds later on in the year, and there are many opportunities for downhill and cross-country skiing enthusiasts in the winter. Compulsive antiques-shop browsers may like to head for the area around Route 7 between South Egremont and Ashley Falls. Note that many of the museums and houses close between mid-October and late May.

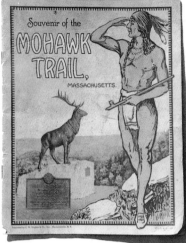

### THE MOHAWK TRAIL AND THE NORTHERN BERKSHIRES
The **Mohawk Trail▶**, the country's first designated Scenic Road (opened 1914), follows Route 2 for 63 miles from the Pioneer Valley to the New York State border. The trail dates back to 1663, when the Pocumtuck tribe invaded Mohawk territory by creating this route over the mountains from Deerfield to Troy, New York. Much of it is unspoiled even today, although motels and "Indian trading posts" (with racks of plastic totem poles and other souvenirs) dot the highway in places.

**French King Bridge▶** is a scenic crossing of the Connecticut River, the first point on the trail worth stopping for; the river is 140 feet below. Farther west,

**Shelburne Falls▶** is known for its Bridge of Flowers, an old trolley bridge graced with colorful blooms. Near the Salmon Falls dam, jagged rocks in the river attract swimmers and picnickers. The road passes the **Hail to the Sunrise Monument**, erected in 1932 by tribes and councils of the Approved Order of Red Men, showing a Mohawk with arms outstretched. Signs soon announce 4 miles of steep gradients and sharp curves, culminating spectacularly at **Hairpin Turn▶▶**, a fine lookout point. Go north along Route 8 toward Clarksburg for **Natural Bridge State Park**. Waters tumble through a small chasm gouged out by glacial meltwater and spanned by a natural bridge. Adjacent is an abandoned white marble quarry.

*The Mohawk Trail passes through some spectacularly remote scenery—and there are plenty of reminders of its origins Left: the "Hail to Sunrise" memorial at the entrance to Mohawk Trail State Forest*

**143**

### INFORMATION FOR THE BERKSHIRE HILLS
For further information, contact the Berkshire Visitors Bureau, Berkshire Common, Plaza Level, Dept. MT, Pittsfield, MA 01201 (tel: 413/443–9186, or toll-free 800/237–5747; fax: 413/443–1970; www.berkshires.org). *Berkshires Week* is a free weekly listings magazine containing information on state parks, campgrounds, sights, children's activities, shopping, and events; it is available at all chambers of commerce.

*Aerial view of
Williamstown in the
Berkshires*

**MASS MOCA**
The Massachusetts
Institute of Contemporary
Art (Mass MOCA) is a
center for visual, media,
and performing arts,
based in a converted mill
complex at 87 Marshall
Street, North Adams (tel:
413/664–4481. *Open*
Jun 1–Oct 31, daily 10–6;
Nov 1–May 31, Tue–Sun
10–4. *Admission: moder-
ate*). Here, in the center's
huge space, there are
exhibitions of modern art,
often pieces that are
rarely seen because of
their size or technological
requirements. Some
emphasis is being
placed on multimedia
technologies and telecom-
munications, so that not
only is art produced in the
workshops, but it can also
be marketed and distri-
buted from the center.

**Mount Greylock▶▶▶**, the highest peak in Massachusetts at 3,491 feet, was named after Chief Grey Lock,
who hunted here. A road climbs to the top for a grand view
over three states. Church spires dominate **North Adams**, a
redbrick mill town (for Mass MOCA, see panel). The
museum at Western Gateway Heritage State Park (*Open*
daily) narrates the history of the Hoosac Railroad Tunnel.
Away from the Mohawk Trail, the cotton mill town of
**Adams** has an atmospheric Quaker meeting house of 1782.

Founded as West Hoosac in 1750, elegant
**Williamstown▶▶** owes its name to Ephraim Williams,
who left money for the founding of an academy, stipulat-
ing that the town must take his name; the academy opened
in 1791, becoming Williams College two years later. Today,
it is among the top liberal arts institutions in America. The
superb **Sterling and Francine Clark Art Institute▶▶▶**
(*Open* Tue–Sun 10–5. *Admission: moderate; free Nov–Jun*) is
noted for French Impressionist and American paintings, as
well as British silverware (see panel opposite). The
**Williams College Museum of Art▶** (*Open* Tue–Sat 10–5,
Sun 1–5. *Admission free*) possesses 11,000 works ranging
from 9th-century Assyrian stone reliefs to Andy Warhol's
last self-portrait. The **Hopkins Observatory** contains a
museum and planetarium, open during the academic year
and on occasions during the summer.

The town of **Pittsfield** has been a paper-mill center since
the 19th century and is the largest town in the Berkshires
region. Art galleries exhibiting local work include the
Pittsfield Arts League (2 South Street). The **Berkshire
Museum▶** (39 South Street) includes art of the Hudson
River School, dolls, early electrical inventions of the
Stanley Electric Company, and domestic relics. The Crane

Paper Company's **Wahconah Mill** manufactures the paper on which American money is printed. At Dalton, east of Pittsfield, the **Crane Museum of Papermaking**, within the 1844 Old Stone Mill, tells the story of American papermaking (*Open* Jun–mid-Oct, Mon–Fri 2–5. *Admission free*). On the outskirts of Pittsfield, off Holmes Road, is **Arrowhead** (*Open* Memorial Day–Oct, daily 9:30–5. *Admission: moderate*), the home of Herman Melville and his family from 1850 to 1862. The furniture is contemporary, not original. The house contains the room where Melville wrote *Moby Dick* (1851).

    **Hancock Shaker Village▶▶▶**, the region's best-preserved Shaker village, active from 1783 to 1960, is today a living museum, well worth a full day's visit if you want to catch the events held here (*Open* Memorial Day weekend–third week in Oct, 9:30–5; guided tours Apr–Memorial Day weekend, late Oct–end Nov, 10–3. *Admission: expensive*). Originally called the "City of Peace," the village is noted for its famous round stone barn. The museum's craftsmen and craftswomen continue to live out the Shaker lifestyle (see pages 148–149), tending historic livestock breeds, maintaining an authentic herb garden, and demonstrating Shaker cooking.

*Works by Renoir and Degas form part of the notable French collection in the Sterling and Francine Clark Art Institute*

**145**

**TRUE CONNOISSEURS**
When Williamstown's Sterling and Francine Clark Institute opened in 1955, a unique collection came under the public gaze for the first time. The display was gathered by Robert Sterling Clark (1877–1956) thanks to a family fortune amassed by the Singer sewing machine empire. While living in Paris from 1911 to 1921 he married Francine Clary, who shared his passion for art; during this time he added many paintings by late 19th-century French artists. Artists represented include Homer, Sargent, Pissarro, and Monet.

*The round barn (dating back to at least 1830) at Hancock Shaker Village. People came from far and wide to study its ingenious design*

## MUSIC AT TANGLEWOOD

The Tanglewood Music Center, a training center for musicians, is the summer home of the Boston Symphony Orchestra (see page 79). The open-sided Music Shed is the main concert hall; it is cheapest to sit on the adjoining lawn for concerts (the sound does carry). Open rehearsals take place at 10:30 AM on Saturdays; you can eavesdrop from the lawn at other times, since members of the public are admitted into the grounds. While there you can visit the Little Red House, a reconstruction of the house in which Nathaniel Hawthorne wrote *The House of the Seven Gables* (1851) and *Tanglewood Tales* (1852–1853); inside is a free museum, open in summer.

## STOCKBRIDGE WALKS

Just south of Stockbridge, off Park Street, is boulder-strewn Ice Glen, so called because of the presence of ice crystals well into summer; a trail climbs up to Laura's Tower for a three-state view.

Three miles south of Stockbridge, on Route 7, the Monument Mountain Reservation overlooks the southern Berkshires, with trails encountering rock outcrops, caves, and a hillside strewn with quartzite boulders. In the 19th century, poet William Cullen Bryant waxed lyrical about the mountain: "the beauty and the majesty of the earth, spread wide beneath."

*Chesterwood, the summer home of sculptor Daniel Chester French*

**THE SOUTHERN BERKSHIRES** An amiable small-town atmosphere envelopes **Lenox▶**, well located as a base for exploring the southern Berkshires. In the late 19th century, the estates formed rural summer retreats for the wealthy; one such was **Tanglewood** (see panel), near Lenox, originally owned by the Tappan family. Another was **The Mount▶** (*Open* May–Oct, daily 9–3. *Admission: moderate*), in Lenox, summer residence of the writer Edith Wharton (see page 46) from 1902 to 1911. A sledding accident at Lenox was the basis of her novel *Ethan Frome* (1911). The restored **Lenox railroad station** (1902) also evokes the period; the Berkshire Scenic Railroad maintains a model railroad, a short section of track, and a shop.

Norman Rockwell (see page 150) put **Stockbridge▶▶** on the map with his depiction of Main Street. At the heart of the village is the Red Lion Inn, dating from 1773 and sporting the sign of George III. Even older is the **Mission House▶** (*Open* Memorial Day weekend–Columbus Day, Tue–Sun, holidays 10–5. *Admission: inexpensive*), the only elegant house in a wilderness when built in 1739 for a Congregationalist minister; its furniture is original, and there is a display on the Native

American community of Stockbridge. Across the street, **Merwin House▶** (*Open* Jun–mid-Oct, Tue, Thu, Sat–Sun, 12–5, *Admission: inxpensive*); owned and operated by SPNEA—see page 68) is a Federal-style brick house built around 1825.

Located just outside town is the **Norman Rockwell Museum▶▶▶**, (*Open* May–Oct, daily 10–5; Nov–Apr, Mon–Fri 10–4, Sat–Sun 10–5. *Admission: moderate*), which holds the world's largest collection of original works by the hugely popular artist. About a quarter of the works are on display at any one time. The reconstructed studio has Rockwell's art books, easel, and many props familiar from his paintings.

**Chesterwood▶▶** (*Open* May–Oct, daily 10–5. *Admission: moderate*; follow signs from the west end of Main Street, Stockbridge) was the summer home of sculptor Daniel Chester French from 1898. He said of Chesterwood, "I live here six months of the year—in heaven. The other six months I live, well—in New York." Tours take in his studio and house.

The best opportunity to glimpse inside a fashionable summer house in the Berkshires is at **Naumkeag▶▶** (*Open* Memorial Day–Columbus Day, daily 10–5. *Admission: moderate*). Built in 1885 by Stanford White for the Choates, it displays some of the family's eclectic possessions. Fletcher Steele later modified the gardens to create terraces with a stepped waterfall.

The **Berkshire Botanical Garden▶** (*Open* May–Oct, daily 10–5. *Admission: moderate*; Route 102 west of the intersection with Route 183) is compact but varied, with an herbarium of dyer's and medicinal herbs, rock garden, lily pond, day lilies, shrubs, and wildflowers. July and August are the best months to visit.

At Great Barrington is the **Albert Schweitzer Center**, a museum and library dedicated to the humanitarian and winner of the 1953 Nobel Peace Prize. The town is popular with antiques hunters.

**Colonel John Ashley House▶**, Ashley Falls (*Open* Memorial Day–Columbus Day, Wed–Sun 1–5. *Admission: inexpensive*), is a quintessential Colonial house of 1735 where Ashley and others drafted the petition against Britain in 1773 known as the Sheffield Declaration. In 1781, Ashley's slave, Mum Bett, was the first slave to win her freedom, doing so under the new constitution.

The pools below **Bash Bish Falls▶▶**, a fine waterfall cascading over huge rocks, are excellent for swimming. They can be reached from the lower parking lot (beyond the New York State sign). Nearby is **Mount Everett State Forest▶**, with a road leading to its summit.

*Daniel Chester French's statue of the seated Abraham Lincoln*

147

**DANIEL CHESTER FRENCH**
America's most prolific sculptor, French produced some works of worldwide renown, including his first commission, the *Minute Man* (completed in 1875 and made from ten army cannons melted down for the purpose) at Concord, the John Harvard statue at Harvard University, and the Lincoln statue in Washington, DC.

**MORE TRAILS IN THE BERKSHIRES**
October Mountain State Forest, off Route 20 near Lee, is Massachusetts' largest state forest, with 50 campsites and many trails, including the walk to Schermerhorn Gorge. To the south of Tyringham Center are good hill walks on Tyringham Cobble and the McLennan Reservation, the occasional haunts of coyotes, bobcats, black bears, and wild turkeys.

The 2,035-mile Appalachian Trail, which stretches from Georgia to Maine, crosses the length of the Berkshire Hills from south to north.

*The Shaker religious sect is now almost extinct, but, in today's complex world, the purity of its followers' way of life, the simple, functional design of their architecture and furniture, and their herbal medicines and organic farming methods have an increasing appeal.*

### SHAKER YOUR PLATE

In the summer and fall, visitors to Hancock Shaker Village can partake of a candlelight dinner. The Shaker practice of silence during meals is not observed, and the sexes may mix, but the menu is taken from Shaker cookbooks. Guests should note an extract from Rules for Visitors: "At the table we wish all to be as free as at home, but we dislike the wasteful habit of leaving food on the plate." Hence the expression "shaker your plate."

*The kitchen at Hancock, efficient and elegant*

Named because of the trembling some members experienced during worship, the Shakers were a persecuted offshoot of the Quakers in England. In 1774, their founder, Ann Lee, led eight followers from Manchester, England, to America, where religious liberty was firmly upheld, and settled near Albany, New York. Their beliefs and practices soon attracted interest and converts, and by the mid-19th century there were 18 Shaker communities in New England, New York, and the Midwest, with about 6,000 members in all.

The Shakers were originally called the United Society of Believers in Christ's Second Appearing and believed that the millennium, a thousand years of heaven on earth, had arrived with Mother Ann. The fundamental principles laid down by Mother Ann were communal living (separate from "the world") and celibacy. In the belief that Mother Ann was the female aspect of God, her followers shared leadership and work equally between men and women. Tasks indoors and out were taken in turn so no one had to endure the unpopular jobs for too long (such as looking after the small boys sent by their parents to learn a trade in the Shaker community).

**"Hands to work and hearts to God"** The Shakers aimed for perfection in all they turned their hands to. Adapting the Yankee work ethic to fit their religious ideals, they became renowned for their industry and ingenuity. Their numerous inventions include the circular saw, a rotary harrow, a threshing machine, an automatic hay-seeding device, a nondrip paint can, and the flat broom.

The Shakers were also immensely practical and kept the house very clean (this being heaven on earth, dust could not be tolerated). This explains the ubiquitous wooden peg rails for hanging clothes, kitchen utensils, mops, and their ladder-backed chairs; the built-in, floor-to-ceiling closets (no need to sweep underneath or dust on top), and the beds on rollers for ease of sweeping; it also accounts for the striking efficiency of their kitchens, and the famously progressive round barn at Hancock, Massachusetts (see page 145).

In the belief that a sound soul needs a healthy body, the Shakers ate well (their recipes are famous); they also made a wide range of herbal medicines. Assiduous gardeners, they were the first to market seeds, an enterprise that developed into a very successful industry.

*Villages such as Hancock (left) are preserved for posterity*

### SHAKER ARTIFACTS

Oval boxes, baskets, and furniture, in particular the chair, exemplify the clean, simple lines of Shaker design and their perfect craftsmanship. Everything was made purely to serve its function, without any embellishment. The chair is sturdy, but light—so it could be hung up out of the way—with a straight ladder-back. The chairs' back legs were fitted with a "button tilter," a swivel device designed to prevent wear on floors. The reproduction of Shaker artifacts is a burgeoning industry, and the Shaker villages sell beautiful examples.

### THE GIFT OF SONG

Singing and dancing were, and are, an integral part of the Shaker service of worship, and 10,000 or more of their songs have been collected. Many are based on English and early American folk tunes. Aaron Copland borrowed the Shaker "Simple Gifts" melody for his *Appalachian Spring*, scored for a Martha Graham ballet in 1944:

"'Tis the gift to be simple,
  'tis the gift to be free,
'Tis the gift to come down
  where we ought to be,
And when we find
  ourselves in the place
  just right,
'Twill be in the valley of
  love and delight."

**Shakers and "the world"** The Shaker communities adopted orphans. They also took in children indentured to the society by their parents in order to learn a trade, many of whom later joined the communities. Converts were also made from the many visitors who came to the villages, for while separation from the world was a basic principle, Shakers were happy to sell their goods—brooms, chairs, boxes, baskets, seeds, and cloaks (specially woven in bright colors for society ladies to wear to the opera)—to the "world's people."

The number of Shaker members peaked in the 1840s but, in the decades that followed, began to decline; restrictions on adoption were enforced, and the pacifism Shakerism stood for and that had once attracted converts went out of favor. Celibacy began to take its toll in falling numbers, and communities could not compete with the increasing mass production of goods.

Today, only a handful of Shakers are left, living in the town of Sabbathday Lake, Maine. They generally continue to live the traditional Shaker life, worshipping devoutly, selling their goods at fairs, farming their land (though they are more likely to be seen wearing Levis for hoeing the vegetables than the long skirts or white shirts and black vests still worn for services). Tours can be taken around the village, but most buildings may be seen from the outside only. At Canterbury Shaker Village and Enfield Shaker Museum in New Hampshire (see pages 192 and 195), and at Hancock Shaker Village in Massachusetts (see page 145), the old buildings are preserved in recognition of the purity and ingenuity of the Shaker contribution.

*"Without thinking too much about it in specific terms, I was showing the America I knew and observed to others who might not have noticed."* Norman Rockwell's portrayal of scenes from everyday life touched the nation's heart and made him one of America's most popular illustrators.

**150**

Born in New York in 1894, Norman Rockwell was given his first freelance commission at the age of 17 by the magazine publishers Condé Nast. In 1916, he took some paintings to the art editor of the *Saturday Evening Post*, the most widely circulated magazine in America, and thus began a partnership that was to turn Norman Rockwell into a household name, and his works into national treasures. Over the next 47 years he illustrated 317 covers for the *Post*, each one eagerly awaited by its readers.

**The American dream** In almost photographic detail, Rockwell depicted childhood, family, and small-town scenes, each tinged with affection and gentle humor: the family outing in the car,

*Top:* Triple Self-Portrait *(1960)*
*Above: "Freedom from Want"*

**WHERE TO SEE HIS WORK**
The largest collection of Rockwell originals is in a museum near Stockbridge, Massachusetts (see page 147). In Vermont, Rockwell's hometown of Arlington has a display of prints in a 19th-century church (see page 231), and in Rutland, the Norman Rockwell Museum has an exhibition covering his career (*Open* May–Oct, daily 10–5; Nov–Apr, Mon–Fri 10–4, Sat–Sun 10–5. *Admission: moderate*).

the boy who discovers his father's Santa Claus costume, a visit to the optician, the signing of a marriage license. When he moved with his wife, Mary Barstow, and their three sons to Arlington, Vermont, in 1939, the neighbors were "exactly the models I need for my purpose—the sincere, honest, homespun types that I love to paint." And it was just these people that he depicted in the famous wartime series of posters—"Freedom of Speech," "Freedom of Worship," "Freedom from Want," and "Freedom from Fear"—inspired by President Roosevelt's Four Freedoms Proclamation of 1941.

In 1953, the family moved to Stockbridge in Massachusetts, where Rockwell lived and worked right up to his death in 1978. His works include illustrations for calendars, such as the Boy Scout Calendar, covers for other magazines, advertisements, and greeting cards, as well as oil paintings and portraits.

Rockwell's work has always been a touch too sentimental for the fine art buffs, but among ordinary people, for whom he captures American life as it was always meant to be, Norman Rockwell remains as popular as ever.

*Cape Ann's rocky shoreline has long appealed to summer visitors and artists*

151

## ▶▶ Cape Ann                    *139D3*

Abutting the northern extremity of Massachusetts Bay, Cape Ann harbors many charming fishing ports, as well as idiosyncratic historic buildings and coastal views much depicted by artists. There are good swimming beaches and shops for browsing. Weekend traffic winds slowly along routes 127 and 127A, and parking can be very difficult, particularly in Rockport. A train service from Boston's North Station and Monday-to-Saturday bus services provide feasible alternatives.

**Manchester** has an attractive harbor and clean sands at Singing Beach (the train station is a short walk away).

**Gloucester▶** is a starting point for whale-watching trips and is also a working fishing port—founded in 1623, it is America's oldest. Fine beaches draw crowds on summer weekends. Artist Fitz Hugh Lane (1804–1865) lived in the three-gabled granite house on the waterfront, and the nation's largest collection of his work is exhibited with fishing industry displays at the **Cape Ann Historical Museum** (*Open* Tue–Sat 10–5. *Admission: inexpensive*).

**Hammond Castle Museum▶▶** in Gloucester (*Open* Memorial Day–Labor Day, daily; Labor Day–Memorial Day, Mon–Sat 10–4. *Admission: moderate*) is a sham medieval folly perched just above the shore; home of the inventor John Hays Hammond, Jr., the eye-catching edifice was built around the Hammond organ in the Great Hall (see panel). The castle comprises a labyrinth of small rooms and passages adorned with Renaissance treasures, a library with a "whispering ceiling" that picks up the slightest sounds, and a courtyard graced by a Roman sarcophagus.

*The* Gloucester Fisherman *by Leonard Craske looks out to sea*

*Fishing floats adorn the wall of Motif No. 1 (above) at the mouth of Rockport harbor (top)*

**THE PAPER HOUSE**
North of Rockport, off Route 127 at Pigeon Cove, is this all-paper building constructed between 1922 and 1942 by Elis F. Stenman as an experiment. He invented a special paste for the purpose and used some 100,000 newspapers: the furniture (made from hollow tubes) included a piano, a clock, a radio cabinet, chairs, and a desk. The walls are made of diamond-shaped blocks, with the headlines still legible. Stenman's wife created the bead curtains from old magazines.

A short drive south along the coast, though still in Gloucester, is the fantasy retreat of **Beauport▶**, the Sleeper-McCann House, with its warren of 40 rooms, many of them devoted to historical themes (*Open* mid-May–mid-Sep, Mon–Fri 10–4; mid-Sep–mid-Oct, Mon–Fri 10–4, Sat–Sun 1–4. *Admission: moderate*; owned and operated by SPNEA—see page 68). The house was built, and periodically enlarged, between 1907 and 1934, by interior designer Henry Davis Sleeper. It is full of quirky visual effects, windows with colored glass, and bottles, antiquities, and curiosities—including a secret staircase. The Pine Kitchen, recalling the simple homes of the colonial era, contrasts with the Octagon Room, elegantly French in spirit, and the Belfry Bedroom, which is sheer chinoiserie. The road continues southward to **Eastern Point Lighthouse** on the east side of Gloucester Harbor.

Picturesque **Rockport▶▶** is the most visited place on Cape Ann. The harbor scene epitomizes coastal New England and includes the fishing shack known as "Motif No. 1," one of the most photographed and painted buildings in America. **Bearskin Neck**, the heart of the old village, is a mixture of craft shops and toytown-scale fishing huts turned into homes with tiny front gardens.

Within the 54 acres of **Halibut Point State Park▶▶** is a fine panorama where a dwarf forest gives way to heathland and scrub, with drops to a rocky shore.

**Essex** stakes a claim as "king of the clam." It has lobster shacks, seafood restaurants, and over 60 antiques shops. The Essex Shipbuilding Museum expounds on 300 years of the industry in the town. Boat trips up the Essex River give opportunities for bird-watching. Crane's Beach at **Ipswich** ranks among the North Shore's finest.

*All the way up the coast, lighthouses stand as symbols of New England's maritime history. The Coast Guard has now automated the light stations, but they remain a unique and cherished part of New England's heritage.*

One of the earliest acts of Congress, signed by George Washington in 1789, provided for a program of construction and maintenance of lighthouses, beacons, buoys, and public piers. Both immigrants and traders were vital to the development of the American nation, and the safe navigation of their ships was crucial.

**Unique landmarks** Constructed of anything from wood or granite to concrete or iron, every lighthouse is different.

The tall New London Harbor Light was built in simple Colonial style by the British, while Portland Breakwater Light (1855) is in the Greek Revival style, its height typical of the shorter lighthouses found in ports. Portland Head Light, probably the most painted and photographed on the coast of New England, stands 80 feet high above the cliffs. Owls Head and Pemaquid Point in Maine are also photogenic. The red and white stripes of West Quoddy Head will be familiar to many. At Fort Point, the wooden fog-bell house still stands, one of the last of its kind. Boston Light is America's only officially manned lighthouse and is the oldest station in the country. Anyone interested in lighthouses should visit the Shore Village Museum in Rockland, Maine (see page 130).

**Keeping the lights shining** The heroic keepers have passed into history, and today many lighthouses are in poor repair. There is, however, mounting interest in preserving them, and lighthouse cruises operate from Bath's Maritime Museum and from Portsmouth, New Hampshire.

**GETAWAY**
For a "unique romantic adventure"—and a taste of what life was like for the keeper and his family—you can book bed and breakfast at Rose Island Lighthouse in Narragansett Bay (also available for longer spells, with record-keeping and maintenance chores). Contact Rose Island Lighthouse Foundation, P.O. Box 1419, Newport, RI 02840 (tel: 401/847–4242). Similarly, you can spend the night in the lightkeeper's quarters on the Monomoy Islands, a wildlife refuge (Cape Cod Museum of Natural History, P.O. Box 1710, Brewster, MA 02631; tel: 508/896–3867), or in Isle au Haut Lighthouse, Acadia National Park (Keeper's House, P.O. Box 26, Isle au Haut, ME 04645).

**153**

**TALES OF HEROISM**
Most famous of all New England's keepers was Ida Lewis (1842–1911), who took over from her father at Lime Rock Light in Newport, Rhode Island, when he was paralyzed by a stroke. She became an expert oarswoman and saved dozens of lives over half a century.

*Nobska Light, Falmouth, Cape Cod*

# Massachusetts

## CAMEOS OF NATURE

Cape Cod has several nesting areas for plovers and terns. Diamond-back terrapins, an endangered species, lay eggs at Sandy Neck Beach, Barnstable. Some 90 percent of the rare Plymouth gentian, found by ponds, grows on Cape Cod. Much of the hinterland between the two coasts consists of infertile dwarf forest, characterized by pitch pine and scrub oak: coyotes have moved in since the late 1980s. Wild cranberries proliferate. Bog plants, such as bladderwort, pitcher plant, and sundew, thrive on the salt marshes.

*Hyannis, for shops, ferries to the islands, and cruises around the harbor*

## ▶▶▶ Cape Cod and the Islands 139E1

**Cape Cod▶▶** is a busy vacation resort. Off season you may have the majestic, unspoiled beaches more or less to yourself, but in July and August traffic grinds along the roads, the beach parking lots fill up early in the day, and lodging prices are high. It's emphatically not touring territory, and there are only a few major sights. Yet it really is worth going out of your way if you are a nature lover or like a stay-put vacation with some boat trips and sights.

Physically the cape is low-lying, covered with dwarf forest and cranberry bogs, and edged by marshes and sandy beaches. It is often likened to a bent arm: severed at the shoulder by the Cape Canal, with most of the population around the biceps portion (or Upper Cape); as it turns north (the Outer Cape), the peninsula narrows to curve around at Provincetown. The towns on the south side virtually roll into one anonymous mass. The waters on the Atlantic side are cold but are often good for surfing; the bay side (facing north and west) is calmer and warmer.

**THE UPPER CAPE: SOUTH COAST** Family-style attractions (see page 246) abound on the much-developed south coast. Routes 6 and 28 cross the **Cape Cod Canal**. For a longer look at this waterway, completed in 1914 and possessing a rare vertical railroad bridge (for hoisting the tracks up to allow shipping through), view it from the largely reconstructed **Aptucxet Trading Post Museum** in Bourne. Here, the Pilgrims traded with the Native Americans using beads, and thus gave birth to American free enterprise.

Although much expanded, **Falmouth▶** preserves its conspicuously pretty village center and green. The Falmouth Historical Society maintains a handsome 1790s house, subsequently home to Elijah Swift, who pioneered the local whaling industry.

*The Glass Museum*
*at Sandwich displays*
*items from the town's*
*19th-century factory*

## SCARGO HILL TOWER

This tower is one of the few viewpoints on the Upper Cape, though it's not easy to find. From Dennis, take the road just east of the cemetery and turn left, signed "South Dennis"; the tower entrance is indicated on the left. From the top of the tower you can see right along the coast to Provincetown.

Like Falmouth, **Woods Hole▶** is a ferry port for Martha's Vineyard and Nantucket (see pages 160–163). The National Marine Fisheries Aquarium is stocked with local species, while Woods Hole Oceanographic Institution museum has displays on the wrecks of the *Titanic* and *Bismarck*.

At the Old Town Hall on Main Street, Hyannis, the **John F. Kennedy Hyannis Museum** (*Open* Mon–Sat 10–4, Sun and holidays 1–4. *Admission: inexpensive*) has displays on J.F.K.'s vacation days on the Cape with his family and friends at Hyannis Port. Steam-hauled trains run from Hyannis to Sandwich along the **Cape Cod Scenic Railroad** (*Open* May–Oct, Tue–Sun. *Admission: expensive*).

**THE UPPER CAPE: NORTH COAST** The north shore is more genteel and historic; Route 6A is the Cape's "antiques road." **Pairpoint Glass Works** on Sandwich Road, Sagamore Bridge, is the oldest glass manufacturer in America; there are glassblowing demonstrations at the factory on weekdays.

**Sandwich▶** has a tiny yet charming center, with a church and pond. Dexter Grist Mill (1640) still produces cornmeal for sale, and Hoxie House is a 1675 saltbox; both are open and stand by Shawme Pond, a haunt of waterfowl. The 1641 **Wing Fort House** has heirlooms and period pieces, and is the oldest house in America continuously lived in and owned by the same family. The **Glass Museum▶** (*Open* Feb–Mar, daily 9:30–4; Apr–Dec, daily 9:30–5. *Admission: inexpensive*) has items made by the defunct Boston Sandwich Glass Company.

The **Heritage Plantation▶▶** (*Open* mid-May–mid-Oct, daily 10–5. *Admission: moderate*) is a delightful museum of Americana, displaying custom-made cars, Currier-and-Ives pictures, toys, and old tools. The setting is enchanting: the extensive grounds are planted with over 125 varieties of rhododendron, which bloom in May.

At **Brewster▶**, the **Cape Cod Museum of Natural History** (*Open* summer, Mon–Tue, Thu–Sat 9:30–4:30, Wed 9:30–7:30, Sun 12:30–4:30; rest of year, Mon–Sat 9:30–4:30, Sun 12:30–4:30. *Admission: inexpensive*) has hands-on exhibits for children and runs outings, including trips to the Monomoy Islands (tel: 800/479–3867).

*Continued on page 158.*

155

## MARINE RESEARCH

Since the 1870s, the pleasant shoreside village of Woods Hole has been home to three important marine research establishments: the National Marine Fisheries Science Center and Aquarium, the Marine Biological Laboratories, and the Woods Hole Oceanographic Institution (WHOI). The latter exists to study rivers, coasts, seabeds, marine life, currents, pollutants, and other aspects of the oceans. In season, daily oceanographic cruises are run from here on the *OceanQuest* (tel: 800/376–2326). This is an excellent introduction to the study of the sea, enabling participants to use plankton nets and microscopes under the guidance of a scientist.

# Massachusetts

Boston

Pembroke

Bryantville

Duxbury

Gurnet Point

Kingston

Plymouth Bay

Halifax

Plympton

Plymouth

Plimoth Plantation

Manomet

44

Carver

Middleboro

South Carver

Cedarville

Lakeville

495

Great Herring Pond

West Wareham

Sagamore

Buzzards Bay

Sandwich

Long Pond

Wareham

25

Heritage Plantation

Sandy

Rochester

Onset

Bourne

Aptucxet Trading Post Museum

West Barns

6

Monument Beach

Forestdale

Mashpee Pond

Marion

Pocasset

140

Acushnet

Mattapoisett

North Falmouth

Hatchville

Mashpee

28

Centerville
Craigvi
Osterv

195

Fairhaven

NEW BEDFORD

Buzzards

West Island

28

West Falmouth

Ashumet Holly Res & Wildlife Sanctuary

Cotuit

New Seabury

Bay

Falmouth Ponds

Teaticket

East Falmouth

Great Neck

Wilbur Point

Falmouth

Round Hill Point

Falmouth Heights

Woods Hole

Nantuck

Nonamesset Island

Penikese Island

Elizabeth Islands

Naushon Island

Vineyard Haven

Oak Bluffs

State Lobster Hatchery
Joseph Sylvia State Beach

Pasque Island

Vineyard

Cedar Tree Neck Sanctuary

Lagoon Pond

Cape Poge

Nashawena Island

Sound

North Tisbury

Felix Neck Wildlife Sanctuary

Cape Poge Reservation

Cuttyhunk Island

West Tisbury

Tisbury Great Pond

Edgartown Great Pond

Edgartown

Chappaquiddick Island

Menemsha

Katama

Muskege
Channe

Aquinnah

Chilmark
Squibnocket

Long Point Wildlife Refuge

Wasque Point

Squibnocket Pond

Martha's Vineyard

No Mans Land

| 0 | 5 | 10 | 15 | 20 km |

| 0 | 5 | 10 miles |

156

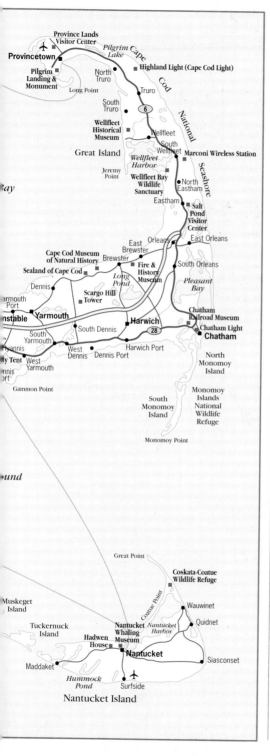

*Cape Cod National Seashore*

*Provincetown,
overlooked by the belfry
of the 1861 Center
Methodist Church*

**BEACHES**
The National Seashore
beaches are all suitable
for families; a pass covers
admission to all six of
them (free out of season
and after 5PM). To reach
Coast Guard Beach, it is
best to take the free shuttle bus from the parking
lot marked for that beach;
lots are often full in July
and August. There are
numerous town beaches
(fee payable). Le Count
Hollow and White Crest
are known for surfing,
Cahoon Hollow for surfing
and partying. Newcomb
Hollow and Longnook are
quiet family beaches. First
Encounter Beach at
Eastham is where the
*Mayflower* landed, to be
greeted by friendly Native
Americans.

**158**

**THE MONOMOY ISLANDS**
Nature lovers should not
miss a visit to the
Monomoy Islands, formed
of a barrier beach south of
the elbow of Cape Cod.
North Monomoy has
dunes, beach grass,
migrating birds, and a
large summer population
of eastern shore birds;
South Monomoy is much
larger and has a wide
range of flora and fauna,
including deer and seals.
Other sites for observing
nature on Cape Cod
include Falmouth Ponds,
Ashumet Holly and Wildlife
Sanctuary (Falmouth),
Sandy Neck (Barnstable),
West Harwich
Conservation Area, and
the beech forest at
Provincetown.

*Continued from page 155.*

**THE OUTER CAPE** The best scenery on Cape Cod is found
here, especially along the 40-mile **National Seashore▶ ▶**,
with its superb beaches and clifflike dunes. The area is
famous for its plant and bird life.

**Salt Pond Visitor Center▶** is useful for information on
natural history, trails, and ranger-led walks; it is also the
start of the **Nauset Marsh Trail▶**. The **Cape Cod Rail Trail**,
an inland course of some 20 miles, passes ponds, salt
marshes, pine woods, and cranberry bogs; it is open to
cyclists, horseback riders, and hikers.

The site of **Marconi Wireless Station** was abandoned in
1920 and only concrete foundations now remain, though a
model explains how the first overseas radio message was
transmitted from here in 1901 to Cornwall, England. **Cape
Cod Light**, the cape's oldest lighthouse, dates from 1857
and sends out a 20-mile beam.

On the west coast, **Wellfleet▶** is prettily sited overlooking an intricate pattern of marshy creeks and a
marina. To its west, the trail along the sandy spit known as
Great Island (4 miles each way) has remote beauty.

At **Province Lands Visitor Center▶** (tel: 508/487–1256),
an observation platform gives a panorama of the invasive
dunes resulting from the removal of trees, overgrazing,
and the subsequent loss of topsoil.

**PROVINCETOWN** Sand spills onto the road and is whipped
up by the wind as you approach **Provincetown▶ ▶**. On
November 11, the Pilgrim Fathers first touched American
soil here in 1620. The Pilgrims' arrival, and the signing of
the Mayflower Compact, are commemorated by the
**Pilgrim Monument▶ ▶** (modeled on the belltower of the

own hall in Siena, Italy), 252 feet high and the nation's tallest granite structure. From the top, the cape seems spread out like a map, and Boston's towers can be seen on a clear day (*Open* monument and adjacent museum Apr–Jun, Sep–Nov, daily 9–5; Jul–Aug, daily 9–7. *Admission: moderate; covers both sites*).

Provincetown itself (known as "P-town") is commercialized and touristy but great fun, with shops ranging from the tastefully arty to the outrageous. The subtle lighting effects of sun and water have drawn innumerable artists, including Edward Hopper, Jackson Pollock, Robert Motherwell, and Mark Rothko. The town's galleries include the Provincetown Art Association and Museum, the Fine Arts Work Center, and the Provincetown Gallery Guild. Provincetown also has a strong theatrical heritage: Eugene O'Neill had his first plays performed here, and Richard Gere, Marlon Brando, and Al Pacino have all acted in P-town. The artistic and theatrical ethos has gone hand in hand with the establishment of one of the East Coast's largest gay communities.

Accommodations are plentiful, and the town is easy to walk around. Trolleys tour the sights, and horse-and-buggy rides leave from the town hall.

**CRUISES AND TRIPS**
Whales can be seen around Steelwagen Bank—boats from all over the cape, and from Boston, Plymouth, and the North Shore, head over here. Passenger-only ferries connect Provincetown with Plymouth (tel: 800/242–2469) and Boston (tel: 617/457–1428). Scenic flights can be made on a classic 1930 Stinson Detroiter plane (tel: 508/487–0240). Fishing and sightseeing cruises leave from Hyannis, Provincetown, Falmouth, and elsewhere. Cape Cod Canal Cruises depart from Onset (tel: 508/778–2662), while Water Safaris at West Dennis offer the only river cruise on the Cape (tel: 508/362–5555).

*Stained-glass shop in Provincetown*

*Extending 2 miles north from Edgartown, Joseph Sylvia State Beach flanks calm, mild waters*

### GETTING AROUND MARTHA'S VINEYARD
Bike rental is available at ferry ports; the bicycle paths are safer than the roads. A public bus network connects most places, and tour buses meet the ferries. Gas is expensive: fill up on the mainland.

### WILDLIFE SANCTUARIES
● Cape Poge Reservation —salt marsh, ponds, and red cedar uplands with a range of wildlife.
● Felix Neck Wildlife Sanctuary—trails, wildfowl ponds, salt marshes, and an interpretation center.
● Cedar Tree Neck Sanctuary—good for wildlife-spotting from trails and has coastal views.
● Long Point Wildlife Refuge—butterflies and moths, spring and fall bird migrations; birds of prey.

**MARTHA'S VINEYARD** The English explorers John Brereton and Bartholomew Gosnold landed on **Martha's Vineyard▶▶▶** in 1602, and Gosnold named the island after his daughter, Martha. Brereton remarked on the "incredible store of vines and the beautie and delicacie of this sweet soil."

The East Coast's largest warm-water resort island is about three times the size of neighboring Nantucket (see pages 162–163). The rich and famous have summered here for many years: former President Clinton has repeatedly taken his vacations here, and singers Carly Simon and James Taylor are among those owning houses on the Vineyard.

Variety is a key feature in the island's places, architecture, people, weather, and scenery. The north shore is craggy, the south shore sandy with a heathy hinterland speckled with ponds. Inland, a dwarf forest of scrub oak blankets much of the scene. Weather is remarkably localized; often one part of the island can be basking in bright sunshine while another is cloaked in a hot, humid mist (a "smoky sou'wester").

Most of the island's beaches are privately owned. The main public beaches are Joseph Sylvia State Beach between Edgartown and Vineyard Haven (no surf, ideal for families); Katama (facing the Atlantic, good surf, strong swimmers only); Moshpu (by Aquinnah Cliffs, with surf); Oak Bluffs Town Beach (convenient, though often crowded, family beach); and Menemsha (quiet).

**Around the Vineyard** At the western extremity of the island, the village of **Aquinnah** (previously Gay Head) has a sizable Wampanoag community (hence the Native American crafts shops). **Aquinnah Cliffs▶▶** are a tumbled mass of multicolored clay, a spectacular natural landform of great geological interest with an excellent beach at their base, which is accessible by road. The fishing village of **Menemsha▶** has kept a weatherbeaten character, with little hint of gentrification. An excellent fishmarket is found among the tiny shacks in the harbor. You can take the ferry from here to Cuttyhunk Island, one of the Elizabeth Islands, where a monolith commemorates the first European settlement in America.

Immaculately preserved **Edgartown▶▶**, haunt of millionaires, gained its prosperous look when sea captains from the whaling days built handsome Federal-style homes. The Old Whaling Church of 1843, an outstanding example of Greek Revival architecture, has been converted into a performing arts center; walking tours begin at Vincent House—see below (for details, tel: 508/627-8619). **Vincent House** (*Open* May 1–Columbus Day, Mon–Sat 10:30–3. *Admission: moderate*) dates from 1672 and is the oldest building on the island. The town center is usually busy with window-shoppers admiring the jewelry stores and upscale boutiques.

Endowed with the longest beach on the Vineyard (scenes from the movie *Jaws* were filmed here), **Oak Bluffs▶▶▶** is a period-piece resort where the Methodists held their first summer camp in 1835. By 1850, some 12,000 people were attending the Sabbath meetings at the open-sided tabernacle. Tents were replaced by charming "carpenter Gothic" gingerbread houses, each adorned with ornate filigree work. There are now more than 300 of these cottages, and no two are quite alike. One house is now the **Cottage Museum** (*Open* mid-Jun–mid-Sep. *Admission: donation*).

**Vineyard Haven (Tisbury)▶** is a big yachting and boat-building center and possesses a state lobster hatchery. A fire destroyed much of the town in 1883, but Greek Revival houses survived along William Street. The **Seaman's Bethel**, housed in the old school (1892), was the place of refuge for seamen; gifts from those who survived storms and shipwrecks are displayed (*Open* summer, daily 11–3. *Admission: donation*).

**GETTING TO THE ISLANDS**
- The Steamship Authority (tel: 508/477-8600) runs ferries from Woods Hole to Vineyard Haven and from Hyannis to Nantucket, and has a seasonal service from Woods Hole to Oak Bluffs on Martha's Vineyard, plus interisland services.
- Hy-Line Cruises run from Hyannis to Oak Bluffs and Nantucket (tel: 508/778-2600).
- Cape Island Express Lines operate from New Bedford to Vineyard Haven and Nantucket (tel: 508/997-1688).
- Island Commuter Corporation runs a summer service from Hyannis and Provincetown to Oak Bluffs, and to Nantucket from Hyannis (tel: 508/548-4800).
- Cape Air (tel: 800/352-0714) is among several airlines serving the islands.

161

*Victorian gingerbread cottages at Oak Bluffs*

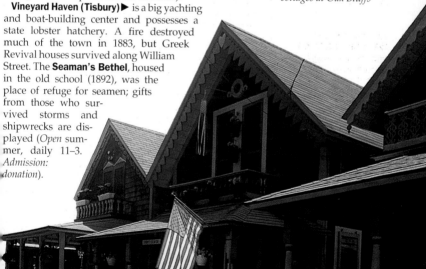

*Lighthouse guarding the entrance to Nantucket town's harbor*

**NANTUCKET** The island of **Nantucket►►►**, 30 miles of the Massachusetts mainland, deserves the accolade ". step back in time." The town (also called Nantucket) is preserved down to the last cobblestone, and the hand some houses evoke the prosperity of the whaling days. Like Martha's Vineyard, this is a million aires' vacationland, bu while the larger island i considered the territory o the newly rich, Nantucke is more the haunt of ric Yankees who choose not t flaunt their wealth, and i certainly less developed

**Nantucket town►►►** preserves an air of gentee perfection. On cobblec Main Street, the oldes houses include the Three Bricks, built in 1836–183 by Captain Joseph Starbuc for his sons. The tower o the Congregational churc offers a good view of the island. Shops tend towar artiness and good tast (although at a price antiques shops abound and there are weeken antiques auctions. Cente Street's shops have tradi tionally been run b women (dating back to th time when captains' wive had time on their hands). / local specialty is the Nantucket Lightship, a woven baske into which is inserted a scrimshaw disk.

One ticket (*Admission: moderate*) gets you into al Nantucket's museums, though apart from the Whaling Museum these are modest in scale. Housed in a forme whale oil refinery, the **Whaling Museum►►** (*Open* Ma 26–Oct 9, daily 10–5; May 1–25, Oct 10–28, Nov 24–26, daily 11–3; Apr 1–30, Oct 29–Nov 19, Sat–Sun 11–3) displays arti facts related to past whaling days, including the ship's log of the *Essex* (the vessel immortalized in *Moby Dick*), sailors souvenirs, a finback whale skeleton, and scrimshaw.

Local history collections form the basis of the **Pete Foulger Museum** (*Open* Jun–Sep, daily 10–5). **Hadwe House►** (*Open* May 26–Jun 18, Sep 5–Oct 9, daily 11–3 Jun 19–Sep 4, daily 10–5), built in imposing Greek Reviva style in 1845, belonged to the same man who owned th refinery that is now the Whaling Museum; it has Federa Empire, and Victorian furnishings. A four-vane **windmi** (1746) still grinds corn today.

The little **Life Saving Museum** covers the work of th United States Life Saving Service. Both the **Hose-Car House** (vintage firefighting equipment) and the **Old Gao** are open free of charge. The **Quaker Meeting House** wa built in 1838, though Quaker worship on the island date

**TOURING NANTUCKET**
Ferry boats (see panel on page 161) take you directly into Nantucket town, where there are plenty of taxis. In addition to public bus services, Gail's Tour runs bus tours (1 hour 45 minutes) from Federal Street Visitor Center at 10 AM, 1 PM, and 3 PM (tel: 508/257–6557). Bicycles can be rented; bicycling the island's quiet roads and bike paths is a pleasure. Numerous boat trips depart from the wharves in Nantucket town. Walking tours (tel: 508/228–5585) start from the Atheneum Library Garden in India Street at 11 AM and 4 PM.

back to 1690. Simply furnished, the **Jethro Coffin House** of 1686 is the oldest on the island and gives a good idea of early life.

**Beaches** At its maximum dimensions, Nantucket is 4½ miles long by 3½ miles wide. The northern beaches are sheltered and the waves usually gentle, whereas the south-facing ones have plenty of surf and are strictly for strong swimmers.

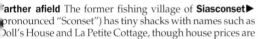

*Nantucket's southern beaches take the full force of the Atlantic surf*

Smaller beaches in and around Nantucket town have shallow waters and are suitable for children. Jetties Beach, good for watching boats and migrating birds, is an easy walk from the town (or take a shuttle bus), past the lighthouse on Brant Point; sailboards can be rented at the beach. Farther west, Dionis is a family beach.

On the south side are Surfside (public bus service) and Nobadeer beaches (the latter popular with teenagers). Madaket Beach, at the western tip, has stunning sunsets. Siasconset Beach, served by bus, has some surf.

**Farther afield** The former fishing village of **Siasconset▶** (pronounced "Sconset") has tiny shacks with names such as Doll's House and La Petite Cottage, though house prices are astronomical. In the 1930s, Hollywood stars such as Clark Gable and Carole Lombard summered here. Nearby, Sankety Head Golf Course has a 15-year membership waiting list! The **Coskata-Coatue Wildlife Refuge▶**, at the northeastern end of the island, is shaped like a fishhook and formed of a huge barrier beach. This remote and wild refuge includes around 10 miles of pristine shoreline, as well as ponds, forest, salt marshes, and tidal creeks.

163

**THE INLAND SCENE**
Nantucket's terrain is mostly scrub oak, with patches of heath and cranberry bogs. Altar Rock (111 feet) is the island's highest point. The lack of mammalian predators makes the island suitable for ground-nesting birds such as northern harriers, short-eared owls, least terns, and piping plovers.

**A WHALING TRADITION**
Settled by the English in 1659, Nantucket rapidly took off as the New World's premier whaling center, and by 1775 the export of whale oil, ambergris, and whalebone meant that Nantucketers accounted for over a third of the hard currency earned in New England. The demise in Nantucket's whaling industry after 1842 was hastened by the emergence of the whaling port of New Bedford (see page 172) and by the collapse of the British market for whale oil with the advent of gas lighting.

*Waterfront scene, Nantucket town*

*From the rocky inlets and myriad islands of the north through sandy beaches and salt marshes southward to the dunes of Cape Cod, the coast of New England supports an exceptionally rich and diverse plant and animal life. Opportunities abound for visitors to observe it all at close hand.*

*Top: dolphins may join in a whale-watch cruise*

**WHALE WATCHING**
In the 19th century, the hunting of whales was a principal source of revenue for New England; nowadays, whale-watching cruises have taken over as a burgeoning industry. In summer, boats leave from many ports, including Barnstable Harbor and Provincetown (Cape Cod); Boston, Plymouth, Gloucester, and Newburyport (MA); Portsmouth (NH); and Kennebunkport and Bar Harbor (ME). Qualified naturalists give commentaries while furthering research. Trips usually take half a day and go well out to sea. You may need warm clothes—and pills for seasickness.

**MARINE STUDIES**
A number of excellent aquariums are listed on pages 244–246, where visitors can get a close-up view of many of the creatures of the deep. For more serious naturalists, the Oceanographic Institution at Woods Hole, Cape Cod, is an international center for marine research offering study cruises (see panel on page 155). Similar cruises also run from Mystic, CT. The Shoals Marine Laboratory on Appledore Island in the Isles of Shoals, NH, offers courses for naturalists (details from Shoals Marine Laboratory, GH-14 Stimson Hall, Cornell University, Ithaca, NY 14883).

**Whales and dolphins** In the Gulf of Maine is a chain of rocky ledges and underwater sandbanks. Tidal currents around their edges are constantly churning up the plentiful nutrient-rich algae. The tiny crustaceans that feed on this green-algae soup are in turn the diet of the slim, silvery, 6-inch sand eel (or sand lance), the primary food source for several species of whale. Every summer hundreds of humpbacks come up from the Caribbean to feast in these rich feeding grounds. And every summer thousands of people go out to sea for a close-up look at these captivating creatures.

There is a good chance of seeing the massive but sleek and speedy fin (or finback) whale (they grow to over 65 feet) and the smaller (less than 30 feet) minke whale. The most commonly seen, and the most fascinating in its behavior, however, is the humpback. Anywhere up to 50 feet in length and over 40 tons in weight, humpbacks will be seen raising their flukes, or tails, out of the water and then lobbing them down with a splash. They will roll onto their sides for a bit of flipper-slapping and, most exciting of all, will "breach" or jump vertically out of the water. Each humpback has a unique and distinctive black-and-white pattern on its fluke, enabling researchers to identify and name individuals.

Just as engaging as the antics of the whales is the sight of a school of white-sided (and occasionally white-beaked) dolphins surfing the waves alongside the boat. Porpoises, too, are sometimes spotted, and the harbor seal is fairly common near port. Seabirds to look out for during the May-to-September whale-watching season include Wilson's petrel, great shearwater, gannet, herring gull, and cormorant.

**The American lobster** *Homarus americanus*, the New England variety, is known for the fearsome size of its claws. The cutter claw is used to grab and cut food (some lobsters are right-handed, some left-handed); the broader crusher claw is used to crush it. A nocturnal creature, of mottled green, yellow, and black (it turns red only when cooked), the lobster lives on the floor of the ocean and feeds on clams, sea urchins, and fish. Several times a year, it outgrows and sheds its shell.

**Bog and marsh life** The New England coast has several areas of salt marsh. Hampton Harbor and marshes are New Hampshire's largest salt marsh, rich in birdlife. Look for piping plover, whimbrel, short-billed dowitcher, black skimmer, least sandpiper, sanderling, snowy egret, osprey, and great blue heron. In Maine, the Wells

ational Estuarine Sanctuary at Laudholm Farm has
harked nature trails along the marsh, and Scarborough
Marsh Nature Center, just outside Portland, runs guided
ature walks and canoe tours (summer only). From
ssex, Massachusetts, you can glide up the Essex River
altwater estuary in a glass-bottomed boat. Two-thirds of
he fish caught off this coast have fed on the insects,
arvae, and other rich pickings
f the salt marsh "pantry."

Plants thriving in salt-marsh
abitats include sea lavender,
ea aster, seaside and grass-
eaved golden rod, cockleburr,
each grass (or "compass
rass," because it sways in
he wind) and "salt marsh
ay," used by early colonists
or cattle food, and the
rotected salt reed grass
*Spartina cynosuroides*).

Another plant that thrives on
combination of peat and
and is the cranberry. In
eptember/October, the
xtensive cranberry bogs of Cape Cod, Nantucket, and
he Plymouth area are flooded and the berries are shaken
oose to float to the surface in a spectacular sea of red.
)ne of the trails from the Cape Cod Natural History
Museum at Brewster winds through a cranberry bog.

## BLOWING BUBBLES

One humpback whale eats
up to 2 tons of food per
day (about 250,000 sand
eels). Uniquely among
whales, humpbacks blow
a "bubble net" below and
around a shoal of fish,
then rise to the surface
with mouth open wide to
swallow hundreds of fish
in one gulp.

165

*Left: a great blue heron
keeps a beady lookout*

## A LOOK AT PUFFINS

Hunted for their meat,
eggs, and feathers for over
300 years, puffins were
virtually extinct in Maine by
the late 1800s. Since the
1970s, the National
Audubon Society has
successfully encouraged
the reestablishment of
colonies in the Gulf of
Maine. Boat trips may be
taken from Rockland,
Boothbay Harbor, and
other Maine ports to nesting colonies on Eastern
Egg Rock, Matinicus Rock,
and Machias Seal Island,
in the Gulf of Maine. The
best time is during June
and July or the beginning
of August.

*Salt reed grass, found in
Cape Cod's salt marshes,
is now a protected
species*

# Massachusetts

*The sun goes down on Columbia Street, Fall River*

166

**THE BORDEN MYSTERY**
The mystery of who killed Andrew and Abby Borden has never been solved. Lizzie (their daughter) was tried but acquitted for lack of evidence. This did not stop the nation drawing its own conclusions, which were expressed in satirical verse:
"Lizzie Borden took an axe,
And gave her mother forty whacks,
When she saw what she had done
She gave her father forty-one."

**THE CON-SOCIATE FAMILY**
The Fruitlands community attempted to create a new Eden. Property was owned in common, and technology and animal products were shunned (plowing had to be done by hand). A leading member was Bronson Alcott, whose daughter Louisa (author of *Little Women*) was only ten when she was exposed to the regime's cold-bath rigors. A conflict between Charles Lane—who urged Bronson Alcott to become celibate—and Mrs. Alcott may well have contributed to the decline of the community.

**FRUITLANDS PERSONA**
Members of the Fruitlands community included Joseph Palmer, persecuted for his unfashionable beard: he was picked on in a scuffle and refused to pay a $10 fine and so went to jail for a year. Samuel Bower was an Adamite (a nudist), while Samuel Larned allegedly lived one year entirely on a diet of crackers, the next on nothing but apples.

► **Fall River**                                    *139D*

In its heyday, Fall River was one of the great textile producing centers of the world. Today, many mill survive, some empty, some as sewing-machine sweat shops, and some as factory shopping outlets. Though no picturesque, the town is set dramatically beneath the I-95 viaduct over the Taunton River.

The town's waterfront attractions begin with **Fall River Heritage State Park** (*Open* daily. Closed Mon in winter *Admission free*), which charts the checkered mill history of the town, its labor disputes, and its demise, and includes a film on Fall River's social history. The tower gives view over the harbor and its ships.

Close by, **Battleship Cove►►** (*Open* Apr–Jun, daily 9–5; Jul–Labor Day, daily 9–5:30; Labor Day–Mar, daily 9–4:30. *Admission: moderate*) features historic battleship that you can board and explore at will. The mightiest of all the vessels on display is the *Massachusetts*, known as "Big Mamie"; she served in 35 battles and carried a crew of 2,300. USS *Joseph P. Kennedy Jr.* was built in Quincy Massachusetts; everything has been displayed as if the ship is sailing. Meanwhile, the submarine USS *Lionfish* evoke the cramped lifestyle of its 76 crew members. Walk under the I-95 viaduct for the **Marine Museum** (*Open* Mon–Fri 9–5, Sat 12–5, Sun 12–4. *Admission: moderate*), which presents a history of steamers and steam power.

The **Fall River Historical Society►** (*Open* summer Tue–Fri 9–4:30, Sat–Sun 1–5; spring and fall, Tue–Fri 9–4:30. Closed winter. *Admission: moderate*) maintains a Greek Revival granite mansion at 451 Rock Street, moved in 1869 to its present location and redecorated in French Empire style. Exhibits include art, toys, china, glassware and material on the much publicized murder of Andrew Jackson Borden and his wife Abby in 1892 (see panel).

►► **Fruitlands Museums**                         *138C*

Fruitlands (in the town of Harvard, northwest of Boston owes its present form to Clara Endicott Sears, who lived in a house (now gone) by the road and who created the museums between 1914 and 1947. The site comprises four buildings. The **Fruitlands Farmhouse** was used by the Con-Sociate Family, a utopian transcendentalist community that existed for seven months in 1843 (see panels). The rural retreat was chosen for its contemplative setting overlooking mounts Monadnock and Wachusett Thoreau manuscripts are on display.

**Shaker House** (1794), used as an office by Harvard Shakers (extant 1791–1919), is now furnished with Shaker items. The **American Indian Museum** display headdresses, pottery, painted leather, baskets, and clothing. The **Picture Gallery** features Hudson River School artists and portraiture (*Open* All sites Tue–Sun, Mon during holidays 10–5. *Admission: moderate*).

### ►►► Lexington and Concord   *139D3/138C3*

The names of Lexington and Concord are inextricably linked with the events that sparked the American Revolution in 1775 (see pages 32–33 and 55). The historic sites where these events took place are all marked along the 4-mile road that links the two towns (see below).

In the 19th century, Thoreau, Emerson, Hawthorne, and Louisa May and Bronson Alcott all lived at Concord, and their homes give a fascinating insight into a remarkable circle of intellectual and literary talent (see also page 46).

**THE BATTLE ROAD** At **Lexington**, a flagpole stands on the triangular green near the statue of Captain Parker. Guides in Minuteman hats give tours on the green (tips appreciated). On Patriots' Day (the Monday nearest to April 19), you can witness battle reenactments, both here and at Concord's North Bridge. Behind the church, the Burying Ground contains 17th-century gravestones.

The Lexington Historical Society maintains three historic buildings (*Open* Buckman Tavern and Hancock-Clarke House Mon–Sat 10–5, Sun 1–5. Monroe Tavern Fri–Mon. *Admission: inexpensive*). At **Buckman Tavern►**, the American militia gathered before dawn prior to the battle on the common. A bullet hole is visible in the front door. The **Hancock-Clarke House►** was in the parsonage of the Reverend Jonas Clarke in 1775. Patriots John Hancock (Clarke's cousin) and Samuel Adams were staying here on the eve of the battle, when Revere and Dawes alerted them of the British approach. The house contains the drum that William Diamond sounded to rally men to assemble in two lines on the green prior to the firing of the first shot. The **Munroe Tavern►**, a mile from the center of town, was used by the British as a field hospital on their retreat.

**THE FIRST SHOT**
On April 19, 1775, the British marched into Lexington on their way to Concord, where they planned to seize a store of arms and ammunition. Revere and Dawes rode to Lexington to alert the colonial militia. By the time the 700 British—under Lieutenant-Colonel Francis Smith and Major John Pitcairn—had arrived, Captain John Parker and 77 American militia were waiting in two lines on Lexington Common. It will never be known who fired the first shot in the confusion, but the British ignored orders not to return fire and they shot at the fleeing Americans, killing eight.

167

*Fruitlands Farm, an early, short-lived commune, is now a museum complex dedicated to the idealists who set it up*

**THE ADVANCE TO CONCORD**
After the skirmish at Lexington, the British advanced to Concord, where they started to burn military supplies. The American militia saw the smoke and hastened to save their town. The opposing ranks met at North Bridge, and the British fired. With Major Buttrick's words "Fire, fellow soldiers, for God's sake, fire!" the Americans returned a volley and forced the British to retreat. At Lexington, Lord Percy met the British with reinforcements and the fighting intensified.

"When [the British] got about a mile and a half to a road that comes from Bedford and Bilrica they was waylaid and a great many killed. When I got there there was a great many lay dead and the road was bloody."
– Amos Barrat (1752–1829), recalling in 1825 the Battle of Old North Bridge.

*Orchard House, home to novelist Louisa May Alcott*

On Route 2A out of Lexington is the **Museum of Our National Heritage▶** (*Open Mon–Sat 10–5, Sun 12–5. Admission free*), with exhibits on American history; Lexington appears in the display "Let It Begin Here."

A self-guiding historical trail begins from the **Fiske House** site, explaining how the silence was shattered at Ebenezer Fiske's farm that fateful day. Part of the original Lexington–Concord road here is an unpaved path, giving an idea of its appearance in 1775. Virtually adjacent, the **Battle Road Visitor Center▶▶** has guided walks and talks, and a film re-creating the events leading up to the battle. The **Paul Revere Capture Site** is marked by a memorial. The **Captain William Smith House** was the residence of the captain of the Lincoln Minutemen. **Hartwell Tavern** has been restored to its appearance in 1775, when it played the role of the community meeting place (*Open daily dawn–dusk. Admission free*).

At **Concord**, an obelisk marks the spot where the first British soldier fell on April 19, 1775, at the **Old North Bridge Battle Site▶▶**. Adjacent is the famous *Minute Man* statue sculpted by Daniel Chester French (see panel on page 147). Ranger talks and activities are scheduled in summer through the nearby **Minute Man Visitor Center** (*Open mid-Apr–Nov 3, daily 9–5; Nov 4–mid-Apr, daily 9–4. Admission free*), which has historical displays, a video, and a diorama of the Lexington–Concord road.

**CONCORD** Founded in 1635, Concord has numerous 17th- and 18th-century houses, many with date plaques. In the 1850s, the town was a stop on the Underground Railroad for escaping slaves. Walking tours are held daily 2–4 PM (weather permitting), departing from the front of St Bernard's Church or the Old Burying Ground.

At the **Concord Museum▶▶** (*Open Apr–Dec, Mon–Sat 9–5, Sun 12–5; Jan–Mar, Mon–Sat 11–4, Sun 1–4. Admission: moderate*), Revolutionary exhibits include the lantern from Old North Church and a diorama of the battle at Old North Bridge. Ralph Waldo Emerson's study

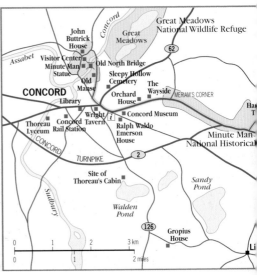

has been installed here, complete with his books and rocking chair, and there is a Henry Thoreau collection.

*Minute Men relive the Revolution at North Bridge, Concord*

**Literary Concord** The **Ralph Waldo Emerson House**▶ (*Open* May 20–Oct 15, Thu–Sat 10–4:30, Sun 2–4:30. *Admission: moderate*) has been restored and is furnished very much as it was in the time when the author lived here, from 1835 to 1882.

**Orchard House**▶▶ (*Open* Apr–Oct, Mon–Sat 10–4:30, Sun 1–4:30; Nov–Mar, Mon–Fri 11–3, Sat 10–4:30, Sun 1–4:30. *Admission: moderate*) was the home of the Alcotts; the six members of the family feature in Louisa May Alcott's novel *Little Women* (1868), written and set here. The Alcotts used to host an "at home" every week, with music, singing, and acting. They were then a poor family, and the present comfortable appearance of the house owes much to Louisa's writing income. Next door, the former Concord Summer School of Philosophy, extant 1880–1888, was established by Louisa's transcendentalist father, Bronson Alcott.

Nathaniel Hawthorne lived for a period near Orchard House at **The Wayside**▶ (*Open* May–Oct, Thu–Tue 10–5. *Admission: inexpensive*), which he bought from the Alcotts.

"By the rude bridge that arched the flood
Their flag to April's breeze unfurled,
Here once the embattled farmers stood
And fired the shot heard around the world."
– Written for the dedication of the 1836 monument at Concord by Ralph Waldo Emerson.

"To outsiders, the five energetic women seemed to rule the house, and so they did in many things; but the quiet scholar, sitting among his books, was still the head of the family, the household conscience, anchor, and comforter, for to him the busy, anxious women always turned in troublous times, finding him, in the truest sense of those sacred words, husband and father."
– Louisa May Alcott, *Little Women* (1868).

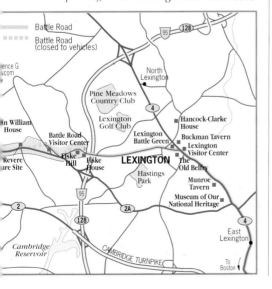

*The Old Manse, Concord, where writers Ralph Waldo Emerson and, later, Nathaniel Hawthorne lived and worked*

"I went to the woods because I wished to live deliberately, to front only the essential facts of life, and see if I could not learn what it had to teach and not, when I came to die, discover that I had not lived."
– Henry David Thoreau, *Walden* (1854).

The **Thoreau Lyceum**, headquarters of the Thoreau Society, gives lectures and classes. A furnished replica of Thoreau's cabin at Walden stands on the grounds.

The **Old Manse**▶▶, next to North Bridge (*Open* mid-Apr–Oct, Mon–Sat 10–5, Sun and holidays 1–5. *Admission: moderate*), was built by William Emerson in 1769 or 1770. His grandson, Ralph Waldo Emerson, wrote *Nature* (1836) here. The house was also rented out to Nathaniel Hawthorne and his wife Sophia for three years. All the possessions are original, including Hawthorne's tiny desk and nearly 3,000 books. Sophia loved to paint in the dining room, and she etched writing and dates on the windows.

**Sleepy Hollow Cemetery** lies off Route 62 (Bedford Street). At Author's Ridge are buried Emerson, Thoreau, Hawthorne, Alcott, and Daniel Chester French.

Thoreau made regular visits to **Great Meadows**, now a designated national wildlife refuge with headquarters at Weir Hill. This wetland is an important wildlife habitat, with well over 200 migratory and nesting bird species recorded.

At **Walden Pond Reservation**▶, Thoreau observed nature and faithfully recorded "the progress of the seasons" in a journal he kept while living in a cabin. Pieces of the cabin have long since been turned into letter openers and other souvenir items for devoted admirers. Visitors in the 19th century used to sign stones and leave them in a heap on the side of the structure. There is a trail around the edge of the lake.

Farther afield is the **Gropius House**▶▶ (68 Baker Bridge Road, Lincoln. *Open* Jun–mid-Oct, Wed–Sun; mid-Oct–May, Sat–Sun; tours 11 AM, noon, 1 PM, 3 PM, 4 PM. *Admission: moderate*; owned by SPNEA—see page 68), which was designed by the architect Walter Gropius (1883–1969), founder of the Bauhaus School of Design. Built in 1938, the house is a remarkable synthesis of tradition and innovation, ahead of its time in the use of acoustical plaster, chrome, welded steel, glass blocks, and other modern materials.

At Framingham, south of Concord, the **Garden in the Woods** (*Open* May, daily 9–7; Apr 15–30, Jun 1–15, daily 9–5; Jun 16–Oct 31, Tue–Sun 9–5. *Admission: moderate*) is the botanical garden of the New England Wildflower Society. It covers 45 acres and is planted with a mixture of wild native flowers, shrubs, ferns, and trees.

## ▶▶ Lowell
138C3

When they were first built in the 19th century, Lowell's textile mills were the wonder of the age and a landmark in the early industrialization of America (see pages 36–37). Today, after a long decline, Lowell has cleaned up its 6 miles of canal and its mills to become a much cited example of successful urban regeneration.

The **Lowell National Historical Park Visitor Center▶** (*Open* daily 9–5. *Admission free*) explains Lowell's social and industrial history through audiovisuals and exhibits. The park itself offers free ranger-led tours lasting 90 minutes and also operates a free trolley shuttle (Mar–Nov) to the Boott Cotton Mills Museum (see below). An inexpensive 1¼-hour **canal and trolley bus tour▶▶** (eight times daily) heads along the Pawtucket Canal, past guard locks where the water levels were measured, to **Pawtucket Falls**, a 32-foot drop in the Merrimack River that provided power for all the mills; it now generates hydroelectric power, supplying electricity to 120,000 homes. Those wishing to explore on foot should pick up the booklet for the Lowell Waterpower Trail.

**LOWELL'S SPORTING TRIBUTE**
The New England Sports Museum, 25 Shattuck Street (*Open* Tue–Sat 10–5, Sun 12–5. *Admission: inexpensive*), displays memorabilia of the region's sports, and touch-screens and hands-on simulations give you the chance to try rowing on the Charles River or attempt the Boston Marathon in a wheelchair. Another branch is at the FleetCenter, Boston (*Open* both branches Tue–Sat 11–5, Sun 12–5. *Admission: moderate*).

*The fully restored Boott Cotton Mills at Lowell*

At **Boott Cotton Mills Museum▶▶** earplugs are provided to counter the deafening clatter of the 88 looms. An excellent exhibition includes a model of the mill, plus videos of the 1912 strike and the reminiscences of mill workers. The **Boott Gallery** has changing exhibits of paintings and photographs, and chronicles Lowell in the Civil War.

By Boott Mill, the **Working People Exhibit▶** (*Open* Wed–Sun 10–4. *Admission free*) shows the life of the first mill girls, who were well looked after, and of the bleaker conditions of the immigrants who followed. Nearby, the mills at Lawrence were the largest in the world when built; **Lawrence Heritage State Park** (tours May–Nov) merits a two-hour visit.

**LOCAL HERO**
Jack Kerouac, father of the Beat generation, was born in Lowell. A sculpture garden was created in his honor.

# Massachusetts

## NEWBURYPORT'S ECCENTRIC

Former resident Timothy Dexter proclaimed himself "the Greatest Man in the East." He wrote a book entitled *A Pickle for the Knowing Ones*, nicknamed "the Foe of Grammar" by its detractors because it was so illiterate. One critic said it would be read "when Shakespeare and Milton are forgot... but not until." Dexter arranged a mock funeral for himself, then caned his wife because she did not shed sufficient tears. In the early 1800s, his Newburyport garden was adorned with statues of great men, allegorical figures, and Native American chiefs. These he transformed with paint into new characters when the old ones fell from fashion.

*Once a busy whaling center, New Bedford is now home to the East Coast's largest fishing fleet*

## ▶ New Bedford                                    139D1

The fishing and manufacturing town of New Bedford has an attractive old town at its heart, recalling its heyday as America's greatest whaling port. The whaling industry began in 1765, and by the 1840s there were some 10,000 seamen working here, pushing rival Nantucket into second place in the whaling league. Herman Melville enthused about the town, and some of the patrician houses he referred to in his whaling epic, *Moby Dick* (1851), can still be seen along County Street (for example, the Rotch-Jones-Duff House and Garden Museum). The decline in whaling was sparked by the loss of numerous whaling ships at sea and by the discovery of petroleum, which gradually superseded whale oil as a fuel for use in oil lamps. The town remains the nation's busiest fishing port. The **Seamen's Bethel**, with its boat-shaped pulpit, was frequently visited by mariners before they set out on a perilous voyage; it was also the setting for a chapter in *Moby Dick*.

Close by, the **Whaling Museum**▶▶ (*Open* Memorial Day–Labor Day, daily 9–8; Labor Day–Memorial Day, daily 9–5. *Admission: inexpensive*) occupies an 1821 mansion. Among a fine array of model ships is the world's largest: an 89-foot-long, half-size replica of the New Bedford whaling bark *Lagoda*. Scrimshaw, fishing gear, figureheads, harpoons, and paintings are also exhibited.

The **Fire Museum** (Bedford and South Sixth streets. *Open* Jun–Aug, daily 9–4. *Admission: inexpensive*) has antique firefighting equipment. Two vessels on the waterfront (State Pier) are the retired lightship *New Bedford* (*Open* Jul–Aug) and the schooner *Ernestina*, a fishing vessel once used for Arctic expeditions and now available for sailings.

## ▶ Newburyport 139D3

Newburyport, pleasantly set on the Merrimack estuary, is one of the most popular day-trip destinations on the North Shore. It is a center for fishing and whale-watching trips as well as for excursions along the Merrimack itself. It also has a seductive selection of antique shops and boutiques. The **Custom House Maritime Museum▶** (*Open* Apr–Dec, Mon–Sat 10–4, Sun 1–4. *Admission: inexpensive*), located within the granite Custom House, has displays covering 300 years of nautical history. Much of the town was rebuilt in brick after a fire. **High Street** has the finest architectural survivors, including the **Cushing House Museum▶** (*Open* Tue–Sat 10–4. Closed winter. *Admission: inexpensive*), a three-story brick house of 1808 with reminders of the town's maritime heyday.

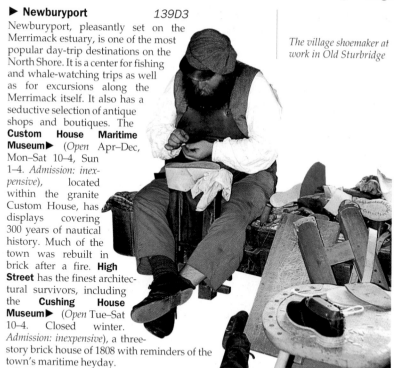

*The village shoemaker at work in Old Sturbridge*

Out of town, **Plum Island Beach▶ ▶** has 10 miles of sands and incorporates Parker River Wildlife Refuge, prolific in birdlife; in peak season, this peninsula often fills quite early in the day.

## ▶ ▶ ▶ Old Sturbridge Village 138B2

*Open: Jan–Feb, Sat–Sun 9–5; Mar, Nov–Dec, daily 9–4; Apr–Oct, daily 9–5. Admission: expensive. For details of special events, tel: 508/347–3362*

An admirable evocation of a New England village in the 1830s, Old Sturbridge opened in 1946. Actors in period dress play the part of villagers and craftsmen in the setting of a village green flanked by reerected old buildings from all over New England. Meanwhile, 19th-century cattle breeds and roaming chickens help compound the time-warp illusion. Old Sturbridge was begun by Albert B. Wells, a local industrialist who developed an interest in New England furniture, tools, and other artifacts. He opened a museum at nearby Southbridge, and his son George suggested displaying the exhibits in the setting of an early New England village. To this end he purchased a farm on the site of the present museum. Peter Pan Trailways runs buses from Boston (see page 259).

173

Peter Pan Trailways runs buses from Boston (see page 259).

**A TRIP FROM NEWBURYPORT**
From the Custom House Maritime Museum you can take a boat trip to Lowell's Boatshop at Amesbury, where boat building has been carried out since 1793 and where the flat-bottomed dory was invented. Paint encrustations, hanging like stalactites from the ceiling in the paintroom, are testimony to the long history of the site, which is very prettily located and recalls the early seafaring days of New England.

## ▶ Pioneer Valley                                138B3

In pioneer days, the Connecticut River in Massachusetts marked the western frontier of New England. Until westward expansion began in the 19th century, this was stock-farming country, and many trees were felled to feed the kilns that made bricks used to build the mills in Holyoke and South Hadley. The valley today is broad and tame, but some drama comes from the basalt ridges, where vertical splits in the rock have formed exciting cliffs and slopes. The valley's sedimentary rocks have also preserved some 200-million-year-old dinosaur footprints. These, along with fossil plants and the petrified ripple marks of a prehistoric pool, can be seen at the **Dinosaur Footprints Reservation** on the west bank of the Connecticut River near Holyoke (Route 5).

**COLLEGE NUANCES**
Holyoke, Northampton, and Amherst form the Five Colleges Area, the state's biggest concentration of academia west of Boston and Cambridge. Amherst College is prestigious, high-class, and preppy. The nearby University of Massachusetts (UMass) is a state university with a good academic reputation. Prestigious Smith College, Northampton, is an all-women's college; traditionally, Smith girls date Amherst boys. Hampshire College is expensive and ultraliberal. Mount Holyoke College, in South Hadley, is America's oldest women's college (founded 1837) and counts Emily Dickinson among its most distinguished alumnae.

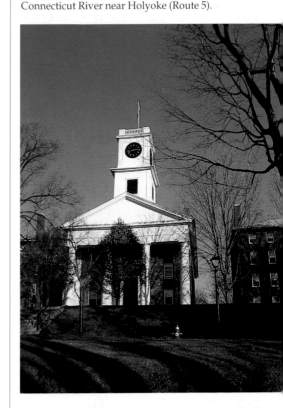

*The campus of Amherst College, founded in 1821*

**Holyoke** itself is reached by driving north from Springfield (see page 187). Here, a modest Volleyball Hall of Fame (*Open* Tue–Sat 9:30–4:30, Sun 12–5. *Admission free*) commemorates the birthplace of the sport. At **South Hadley** is the Mount Holyoke College **Art Museum▶**, one of the oldest collegiate museums in the country and containing classical and Egyptian artifacts as well as American paintings. The summer festival features student theater and concerts by student and visiting artists.

The main entrance for **Holyoke Range Park▶▶** and **Skinner State Park▶▶** is off Route 47 at Hadley. From here the park road winds up to a famous view over a loop in the river, painted by Hudson River School artist

Thomas Cole as *The Oxbow* in the 1830s. Basalt columns known as Titan's Piazza add to the drama, and mounts Monadnock and Tom are in sight. Folk, jazz, and classical concerts are given at the summit cabin in summer.

**Mount Tom**, south of Northampton, is equipped for year-round activity, with skiing, two water rides, a wave pool, and a chair lift to the summit. **Northampton** itself is a lively college town. It's centered on **Smith College**, which has an arts museum begun in 1879 that features European masters, the Hudson River School, and 20th-century sculpture (closed for renovation until 2002; tel: 413/585–2760 for details).

**AMHERST** The attractive college town of **Amherst▶**, built around a sloping common, makes one of the best bases for exploring the Pioneer Valley. The **Emily Dickinson Homestead▶** at 280 Main Street (*Open* Mar, Nov–mid-Dec, Wed, Sat; Apr–May, Sep–Oct, Wed–Sat; Jun–Aug, Wed–Sun; tours 1–4; advance booking essential, tel: 413/542–8161. *Admission: moderate*) was the home of the poet (see page 176). The world's largest collection of Dickinson memorabilia forms a display and archive in the Jones Library and is open free of charge when the archivist is there (tel: 413/256–4090). It also incorporates a large collection of material relating to Robert Frost. Next door is the **Strong House** (1740), with rooms in a range of styles including Colonial and Victorian (*Open* May–Oct, Wed–Sat, 12:30–3:30; Nov–Dec, Feb–Apr, Fri–Sat 12:30–3:30. *Admission: inexpensive*).

In Amherst College, the **Pratt Museum** exhibits natural history, and the **Mead Art Museum▶** shows ancient art, European sculpture, works by Monet, Reynolds, and Rubens, as well as paintings by American artists including Copley, Stuart, and Homer (to locate the museum, look for the churchlike tower). Just outside town is the University of Massachusetts, with concerts during the academic year.

**CONTINUING NORTH** The architectural highlight of the Pioneer Valley, **Historic Deerfield▶▶** (*Open* daily 9:30–4:30. *Admission: expensive*) is a beautifully preserved historic village displaying a variety of domestic buildings from early colonial times. First settled in 1669, the village grew rich on cattle raising. Today, it is a living village-museum but, thanks to its former residents, it is one of the best documented places in the country. Currently 14 houses are open for 30-minute tours and the Flynt Center of Early New England Life on a self-guiding tour. Combined entry tickets are valid for a week, and opening times are staggered; guided walking tours and horse-and-carriage tours are also available.

Nearby, off Route 116, is **Mount Sugarloaf State Reservation▶**; at the summit (accessed by road) fine views extend from a rocky cliff.

**ON AND IN THE WATER**
Twelve-mile cruises along the Connecticut River are offered on *Quinnetukut II* from the Riverview Picnic Area on Route 63 (tel: 413/659–3714). For canoeing, kayaking, and whitewater rafting, try the stretch from Cheapside Bridge to the Route 116 Bridge near Deerfield, or from Turners Falls Dam to Vernon Dam in Vermont. Beginners can sample the stretch from Holyoke Dam to the Northeast Utilities Power Dam in Turners Falls. The Deerfield River has mild whitewater conditions from Shelburne to Route 5 Bridge in Greenfield. Lake swimming is feasible in Upper Highland Lake at DAR State Forest on Route 112 in Goshen.

**175**

*Dwight House, an early 18th-century house; like others in Deerfield that are open to the public, it displays a fine collection of furniture*

*is, and my*
*and my heart, and all t
And all the meadows wid
ure you count, should I.
Some one the sum could
...... and al*

*In 1886, Emily Dickinson died in the house in which she had been born, in the village of Amherst in Massachusetts, a lyric poet unknown and unpublished. Her sister found 1,775 poems and numerous letters that revealed an original and exceptional talent. Equally extraordinary is the life led by this "New England mystic."*

"There's a certain slant of light
On winter afternoons,
That oppresses, like the weight
Of cathedral tunes.

"Heavenly hurt it gives us;
We can find no scar,
But internal difference
Where the meanings are.

"None may teach it anything,
'Tis the seal, despair,—
An imperial affliction
Sent us of the air.

"When it comes, the landscape listens,
Shadows hold their breath;
When it goes, 't is like the distance
On the look of death."
– Ca1861.

"It's all I have to bring to-day,
This, and my heart beside,
This, and my heart, and all the fields,
And all the meadows wide.
Be sure you count, should I forget,
Someone the sum could tell,
This, and my heart, and all the bees
Which in the clover dwell."
– Ca1858.

*After her father died in 1874, Emily Dickinson left the grounds of her house only once, when her nephew next door died*

**The recluse** Emily Dickinson was born in 1830 into a household dominated by her puritanical father, a lawyer and treasurer of Amherst College. Described by a schoolfriend as demure and shy but witty, she began to write poems when she was in her 20s, sewing them into little booklets. During her most productive year, 1862 (the height of the Civil War), she wrote 356. She tried unsuccessfully to interest a newspaper editor, Samuel Bowles, in her work, and in 1862 she asked a young man of letters, T.W. Higginson, for an opinion. He did not recommend publishing, although they remained correspondents, and from then on she refused to consider publication.

After the mid-1860s, Dickinson's output waned, and she began to withdraw from the world, seeing few friends. By the late 1860s, she had become known as an eccentric recluse, always dressed in white, who never left the grounds of her home (see page 175). From the mid-1870s, she was increasingly saddened by the deaths of many dear to her.

**The poetry** Emily Dickinson's themes of love, death, and nature are treated with an intensity and a sensitivity surprising for one who led such a secluded life. The poems and letters of the late 1850s and early 1860s reveal intense emotions, probably focused on a married Philadelphia clergyman, Charles Wadsworth. In her years of retreat, one person she did see was Otis Lord, an old family friend, and drafts of letters from these latter years suggest a tender and passionate relationship. Her poems, like her letters, are composed with scrupulous artistry: words are pared down to an epigrammatic minimum, rhythms are often irregular to assist expression of thought, and the rhymes themselves are sometimes imperfect.

### ►►► Plymouth

*139D2*

Hallowed as the birthplace of modern America, where the Pilgrim Fathers first established themselves, Plymouth preserves the spirit of the early years. Apart from Plimoth Plantation (see page 179), the attractions are small-scale, but the town has become a place of historic pilgrimage. The **Pilgrim's Path**, a designated walking route, will lead you around the town's historic sites.

Despite a dearth of evidence that the Pilgrim Fathers ever landed here, **Plymouth Rock►**, beneath its classical canopy, is, in any event, nicely symbolic of a nation that likes to think of itself as built upon a rock. **Mayflower II►** (*Open* Apr 1–Dec 3, daily 9–5. *Admission: moderate*), close by, is a faithful replica of the 104-foot-long ship in which the Pilgrims crossed the Atlantic in 1620, with period-clad actors telling the story of the 66-day voyage. The cramped conditions leave you wondering how the 102 Pilgrims dealt with frayed tempers on their long journey. The original *Mayflower* returned to England in 1621 and was scrapped a few years later.

Across the street, on Cole's Hill, a sarcophagus of 1921 contains the remains of some of the Pilgrims, and a monument honors Chief Massasoit of the Wampanoag tribe, who befriended the Pilgrims.

North Street, which leads away from the sea from here, has some fine houses. Most notable is the **Mayflower Society Museum►** (*Open* summer, daily; spring and fall, Fri–Sun. *Admission: inexpensive*), high-ceilinged and with a magnificent flying staircase that is supported only at top and bottom. Edward Winslow, a Pilgrim descendant, built the house in 1754, and Lydia Jackson married Ralph Waldo Emerson in the east front parlor in 1835.

**Spooner House** at 27 North Street (*Open* Jun–early Oct, Thu–Sat 10–4. *Admission: inexpensive*) has five generations of family possessions. The 1809 Federal-style **Hedge House►** (*Open* Jun–early Oct, Thu–Sat 10–4. *Admission: inexpensive*), opposite Town Wharf, was home to 19th-century merchant shipowner Thomas Hedge, and displays China trade porcelain, dolls, costumes, quilts, and toys.

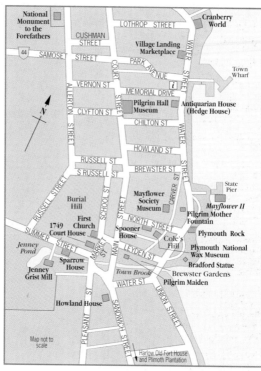

*The Mayflower Society Museum, Plymouth*

177

*Pilgrims and Native Americans share an authenticated 17th-century meal at Plimoth Plantation*

The **Pilgrim Hall Museum►** (*Open* Feb–Dec, daily 9:30–4:30. *Admission: moderate*), designed by Alexander Parris (architect of Boston's Quincy Market), focuses on the Pilgrims and their voyage. Paintings show their embarkation and landing, and there are items thought to have been brought to America as part of the *Mayflower's* cargo, including the cradle of Peregrine White, born on the voyage.

The 1749 **Court House Museum** (*Open* summer. *Admission free*) is notable as America's oldest wooden courthouse. The reconstructed courtroom was saved from demolition during major redevelopment in the 1950s. A vintage piece of 1828 firefighting equipment is displayed. **Sparrow House** is the oldest surviving dwelling in Plymouth (*Open* Apr–Dec, Mon–Tue, Thu–Fri 10–5, Sat 10–8. *Admission: inexpensive*). The house dates from 1640 and has characteristic leaded window panes and period furnishings; pottery demonstrations are given inside.

**Howland House►** (*Open* Memorial Day–Columbus Day, Thanksgiving, daily 10–4:30. *Admission: inexpensive*) is the only house where Pilgrims actually lived; *Mayflower* passengers John and Elizabeth Tilley Howland resided here and had ten children. The building was enlarged in 1750. A path along the river leads to the **Jenney Grist Mill** (*Admission free*), America's first public utility, set up by the Pilgrims in 1636. The exterior is very picturesque, with a waterwheel still turning. Along Sandwich Street is **Harlow Old Fort House** of 1677, restored to its 17th-century appearance (*Open* Jul–Aug, Fri 10–4. *Admission free*).

The **National Monument to the Forefathers►** is an astonishing example of 19th-century statuary, commemorating the Pilgrims. A gigantic central figure of Faith flanked by Law, Education, Liberty, and Morality stands high on elevated ground. Bas-reliefs depict the Departure from Delfthaven, the Landing of the Pilgrims, the Treaty with Massasoit, and the Signing of the Mayflower Compact. Etched in granite are the names of the 102 *Mayflower* passengers.

Ocean Spray, maker of cranberry juice (exported worldwide), shows its wares at **Cranberry World▶** (*Open* mid-May–Nov, daily 9:30–5. *Admission free*). Displays explain cranberry-growing and harvesting, and there are vintage Ocean Spray TV commercials. Free samples of a range of cranberry-based juices await at the end. This is one of New England's greatest freebies, especially on a thirst-inducing summer's day!

**Plimoth Plantation▶▶▶** is an impressively faithful reconstruction of the original Pilgrims' village, 3 miles south of the landing site (*Open* Apr–Thanksgiving weekend, daily 9–5. *Admission: expensive*). The "1627 Village" has all the authentic elements: partly thatched wooden dwellings, straw on the ground, wood smoke, cow dung, blankets hung out to dry in a yard. Dressed in period costume, interpreters answer visitors' questions as if they were Pilgrims, not tourist guides, and the authenticity extends to the carefully researched 17th-century accents. One woman talks of midwifery as she spins wool, a man tells of his voyage, and another explains the schisms in the Church of England. Even the chickens resemble the breeds the settlers would have had.

Also re-created here is the homesite of a native Wampanoag who acted as counselor to the new settlers. The gentle, peace-loving Wampanoags traded with the Pilgrims, but some were later taken as slaves.

> "Down to the Plymouth Rock, that had been to their feet as a doorstep Into a world unknown— the cornerstone of a nation."
> – Henry Wadsworth Longfellow, *The Courtship of Miles Standish* (1858).

> "Neither do I acknowledge the right of Plymouth to the whole rock. No, the rock underlies all America: it only crops out here."
> – Wendell Phillips, Speech at a dinner of the Pilgrim Society at Plymouth, December 21, 1855.

179

### PLYMOUTH CRANBERRIES

Plymouth County has some 12,000 acres of cranberry bogs, set within impermeable clay-lined kettleholes and dependent on supporting wetlands for their survival. In spring, the bogs look like a sea of light pink flowers. The petals fall off in mid-July, leaving a green berry that ripens spectacularly to a brilliant red and is harvested a few weeks after Labor Day. Plymouth Colony Winery, near Plymouth, claims to be New England's original cranberry winery. Cranberry juice and vodka are mixed to create the "Cape Codder" cocktail.

*Visit Cranberry World to learn about cranberry-growing and harvesting*

*Weak and weary from an uncomfortable nine-week voyage, an intrepid band of 102 English men and women arrived in Plymouth in the winter of 1620. About one-third had been driven out because of their radical Puritan faith. All had hopes set high on a new life.*

180

### BLOWN OFF COURSE?...

Tradition has it that the Pilgrims, who set off heading for the James River in Virginia, were blown off course and ended up in the Cape Cod area. However, the chances of an experienced mariner such as Christopher Jones not knowing he was 120 nautical miles too far north are remote. First, he would certainly have known the latitudes of all American East Coast landmarks; secondly, the astrolabe, a forerunner of the sextant, enabled navigators at that time to calculate all north and south distances with precision.

### ...OR A CHANGE OF MIND?

Descendants of David Thomson have claimed that when the *Speedwell* needed repair work and she and the *Mayflower* unexpectedly called at Plymouth, England, the Pilgrim leaders spoke with David Thomson about New England. The indications are that Thomson, who had been there more than once but never farther south than Cape Cod, might have recommended the Plymouth area, where his friend Squanto lived. Did the Pilgrims then change their minds about heading for Virginia?

*The* Mayflower, *an English merchant ship before she was hired to transport the Pilgrims*

### Puritans and Separatists

At a time when the English monarch was also head of the Church in more than just name, dissenting from the Anglican Church was a treasonable offense. While some Puritans attempted to reform the Church of England, one group decided in 1608 to flee to Leiden in Holland, a center of Protestantism, to escape persecution. These Protestant Separatists lived rather discontentedly in Holland for some 12 years before deciding to start a new life in America. They managed to secure finance from a group of London investors for a pilgrimage that would take them to a land where, according to all reports (and there had been many by then), they could find a better life as well as religious freedom.

The Leiden Separatists bought a small ship, the *Speedwell*, in which they sailed from Holland to Southampton, England, where they met up with the *Mayflower*. Some of the *Mayflower*'s passengers were also Puritan Separatists, but the majority were sent by the London stock company to ensure the venture's success, men such as the military officer Miles Standish (hero of Longfellow's long poem, *The Courtship of Miles Standish*). Both ships set sail from Southampton, but the

*Speedwell* proved unseaworthy and had to be abandoned at Plymouth in Devon, and all her passengers crammed onto an already crowded *Mayflower*, which set sail once again on September 6, 1620.

**Arrival in America** Amazingly, the ship and her passengers survived a 66-day journey that was not without storms or near disasters, and land was sighted on November 9. On the 11th, the *Mayflower* dropped anchor at what is now Provincetown on Cape Cod. A meeting was held on board and a famous document, the "Mayflower Compact," was drawn up by the Pilgrim Fathers (as they were only much later called) under the leadership of William Bradford. Under the terms of this agreement, the settlers promised obedience to the minority of Pilgrim leaders and, despite its one-sidedness, it remained in force until the settlement joined with the Massachusetts Bay Colony in 1691.

A reconnaissance party then sailed along the coast to Plymouth, with its safe harbor, running water, and corn-fields already cleared by the Wampanoag. It also had high ground from which the colonists could defend themselves against possible attacks from Native Americans, Spanish and French traders, or fishermen. On Christmas Day, the men began to build their new homes.

**Settling in** By the end of that first winter, half of the *Mayflower*'s passengers had died. The weather was harsh, the colonists were weak from the journey, food supplies were low, and crops not yet established. It was a rough time, until the spring came and, with it, friendly contact with members of the Wampanoag people. Like so many other Native Americans, the Wampanoag had been decimated by epidemics of European disease that had come with the traders, but one of the survivors was a man named Squanto. He had been to England (see panel) and was prepared to help the colonists.

The Pilgrims and their fellow settlers had come with a diversity of skills and interests, but most were craftsmen and not used to making a living from the land. Nevertheless, with guidance from the Wampanoag and the arrival of more goats, cattle, and other goods with further colonists from England, the Plymouth settlers became self-sufficient within a few years, and by 1640 their numbers had swelled to about 3,000.

*Top: Miles Standish makes a treaty with the Native Americans
Above: the Pilgrim Fathers give thanks after landing*

### SQUANTO

In 1605, an English captain, George Weymouth, captured five Native American men, including Squanto, and took them back to Plymouth in England. Here they became friendly with David Thomson, an apprentice to a ship's doctor. Squanto was subsequently taken on several expeditions to America, assisting the English in their explorations. On one trip, in 1614, Squanto was captured by an English ship's captain and sold into slavery in Spain. Amazingly, he escaped, made his way to England, and finally returned to New England with another expedition. In 1620 he was brought to Plymouth to act as an interpreter between the Wampanoags and the English settlers. Squanto died in 1622 while guiding Governor William Bradford on Cape Cod.

### THANKSGIVING

Thanksgiving Day, celebrated across the country with turkey and pumpkin pie, traditionally originated in the fall of 1621, when the first colonists invited the Wampanoags to join in a three-day festival of thanksgiving for their first successful harvest. Nineteenth-century romancing turned it into a New England institution, and in 1863, Thanksgiving Day was made a national holiday by President Abraham Lincoln.

*A calm evening on Quabbin*

### ▶ Quabbin Reservoir                    138B3

One of America's largest reservoirs, Quabbin supplies water to half of Massachusetts, and its zigzag form effectively divides the state into eastern and western halves. The reservoir has a 118-mile shoreline and many islands. Some 2,500 homes were lost when it was built, and 7,500 bodies from 34 cemeteries were reinterred. For the tourist, its scenic attributes make it worth a detour: an excellent view is from **Quabbin Summit ▶ ▶** at the southern end, where a tower looks to mounts Tom, Lincoln, Monadnock, and Wachusett. To locate the tower, follow signs past Winsor Dam. The reservoir offers outstanding freshwater fishing (boat rental is available for anglers), and there are nine trails, including the ¾-mile summit trail from Quabbin Hill Lookout.

North of the reservoir, at North New Salem, the Swift River's middle branch roars along **Bear's Den ▶**, a gorge with rushing waterfalls embraced by granite cliffs that are cloaked with hemlock trees. Supposedly, this was a Native American haunt in 1675 during the wars against the white settlers.

### JOHN QUINCY ADAMS

An advocate of strong federal government during his presidency, Adams was previously the U.S. minister in The Hague, Berlin, St. Petersburg, and London. As secretary of state to James Monroe, he formulated the Monroe Doctrine (1823), which defined any European colonial ambitions in the Western hemisphere as a threat to American peace and security. He was also a lawyer and in a landmark case successfully defended the Mendi Africans who were taken aboard the slave ship *Amistad* and who subsequently rebelled against their captors (see panel on page 105).

### ▶ Quincy                    139D2

Quincy (pronounced "Quinzee") is known as the "City of Presidents" because John Adams (America's second president) and his son, John Quincy Adams (its sixth), were both born here, in 1735 and 1767, respectively. The **Adams Mansion ▶** (*Open* Apr 19–Nov, daily 9–5. *Admission: inexpensive*), a large clapboard house, was home to four generations of the Adams family and now displays family pieces and paintings. In the garden, the 1870 Stone Library contains presidential books and manuscripts. Both John and John Quincy Adams were born in 17th-century saltbox farmhouses nearby, forming, with the mansion, the **Adams National Historical Site** (*Open* Apr 19–Nov, daily 9–5. *Admission: inexpensive*), the earliest surviving presidential birthplace. The **Adams Academy** (*Open* Mon–Fri, 9–4), built on the site of John Hancock's birthplace, is now the home of the Quincy Historical Society.

The National Park Service Visitor Center (opposite City Hall on Hancock Street) has brochures on historic Quincy, with information about all local sights. Quincy can be reached from Boston by the Red Line to Quincy Center.

*In 1692, the village of Salem, in the Massachusetts Bay Colony, suddenly found itself in the grip of an infamous witchcraft hysteria. It was a brush with the devil that would leave its mark forever.*

**Tituba's secret** Reverend Samuel Parris came to Salem after working as a merchant in the Caribbean. He brought back a slave girl, Tituba, who was put in charge of Parris's daughter Betty and her cousin Abigail Williams, girls at the impressionable ages of 9 and 11. Innocently, Tituba would tell them stories of her own voodoo culture, so very different from the starchy Puritan ethic the girls were brought up on. They were gripped. Soon they were bringing others into Tituba's "circle"—but for fear of eternal damnation they had to keep it all secret. Betty, however, could not cope with the divided loyalties, and it began to show in her behavior. Abigail, jealous of all the fuss now being made of Betty, mimicked her "fits" and, one by one, the other girls began to writhe and scream similarly.

**"Spectral evidence"** In 1692, most of the world believed in witchcraft, and to the Puritans of Salem this was the only explanation for the girls' behavior. But who was it who was bewitching them? The hunt was on. Tituba and others were put under pressure, false confessions were made, innocents incriminated. Things got out of control. Prisons were bursting with suspects (even the wife of the governor of Massachusetts, William Phips, was accused), and 19 "witches" were actually hanged. But everything hinged on "spectral evidence," the evidence given by the bewitched girls that they were afflicted by a specter, or the devil, in the image of someone else.

Eventually, in October, Increase Mather and his son Cotton, leading Puritans, and others protested that this meant that it was on the testimony of the devil that justices were condemning people to death. Governor Phips brought the trials to an end, prisoners were released, and convictions annulled. The girls were discredited—and Tituba was able to renounce her confession.

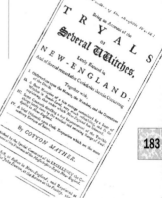

*Top: Tituba and the girls*
*Above: the title page of Cotton Mather's account of the trials*

**183**

**THE CRUCIBLE**
The names of Tituba, Abigail, and many of the other personalities involved will be familiar from Arthur Miller's play *The Crucible* (1953), based on the Salem witch trials. A French film, *Les Sorcières de Salem*, was made of the play. A remake of the film, *The Crucible*, was shot in 1995 on Hog Island, located off Ipswich, Massachusetts. The movie stars Daniel Day-Lewis and Winona Ryder.

*An all-too-common sight in 1692: a "witch" is arrested*

Map of Salem

The Puritan Roger Conant founded Salem in 1626; his statue can be found in front of the Salem Witch Museum

### ▶▶▶ Salem and Marblehead                139D3

Salem's notorious witch hunts of the past are only one aspect of the town. Its prosperity, brought about by trading (in particular with China), has left the town with a rich architectural legacy and a particular wealth of Federal-style houses. That the witch trials (see page 183) amounted to a puritanical persecution of innocent women is hardly remembered here in the ghoulish array of trinkets and souvenirs, all featuring witches in pointed hats. At least the museum-type attractions aim for something more authentic.

**History Alive! Cry Innocent▶** is worth catching (*Open Jun–Oct, daily; tours 11:30 AM, 1:30 PM, 3 PM. Admission: moderate*); this theatrical reconstruction of a witch trial is set in the Old Town Hall, with its faded classical grandeur and courtroom atmosphere. The audience plays the role of a 17th-century Puritan jury asked to judge the woman's guilt. The **Witch Dungeon Museum** (*Open Apr–Nov, daily 10–5. Admission: moderate*) also starts with a short two-person theatrical presentation, which sets the scene for the persecutions before you embark on a brisk tour of the reconstructed dungeons.

The **Witch House ▶** (*Open Jul–Labor Day, daily 10–6; rest of year, daily 10–4:30. Admission: moderate*) is a fine example of a mid-17th-century house, with period furniture. It belonged to Jonathan Corwin, one of the witchcraft trial judges. It was here that witches were examined for bodily defects. In the **Salem Witch Museum** (*Open Jul–Aug, daily 10–7; rest of year, daily 10–5; presentations every half hour. Admission: moderate*), 13 tableaux are lit to spin the witchcraft yarn; the dummies are not particularly lifelike and the commentary is over sensationalized in tone, but the story is gripping.

**TRADING AND MARITIME LEGACIES** Founded in 1626, Salem was once America's sixth largest city. So widely was the name of Salem known at the peak of its trading activity (1790–1807) that many overseas merchants thought Salem was a country and America just a part of it. At the **Salem Maritime National Historic Site►** (*Open daily 9–5. Admission free*) you can see three surviving wharves (there were once over 50). Elias Hesketh Derby, America's first millionaire, established Derby Wharf (1762), and his brick Georgian home, Derby House, can be visited along with the unfurnished Narbonne-Hale House. In the 1840s, the writer Nathaniel Hawthorne worked as a surveyor in the Custom House (1819): you can peer into his "cobwebbed and dingy" office, still used up to 1937. Behind is the Scale House (1829), where goods were weighed and taxed.

While Hawthorne worked here observing the life of Salem, he lived in a house on the grounds of his cousin's 17th-century mansion, **The House of the Seven Gables►►** (*Open Jul–Oct, daily 9–6; rest of year, daily 10–4:30. Admission: moderate*). A

*Above: The House of the Seven Gables, inspiration for Hawthorne's novel*
*Left: ship's figurehead in Salem's Peabody Essex Museum*

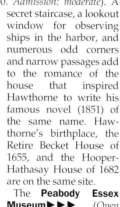

secret staircase, a lookout window for observing ships in the harbor, and numerous odd corners and narrow passages add to the romance of the house that inspired Hawthorne to write his famous novel (1851) of the same name. Hawthorne's birthplace, the Retire Becket House of 1655, and the Hooper-Hathasay House of 1682 are on the same site.

The **Peabody Essex Museum►►►** (*Open Memorial Day–Oct 31, Mon–Sat 10–5, Sun 12–5. Admission: moderate*) celebrates three centuries of Salem trade with an outstanding collection of model ships and maritime art, as well as period rooms, pictures of old Salem, witchcraft exhibits, and a splendid array of ships' figureheads.

**Chestnut Street►►** has been called America's finest street. The Stephen Phillips Memorial Trust House at number 34 and the Ropes Mansion (1727), around the corner at 318 Essex Street, are both open in summer. Salem Common was a pasture and drill ground.

**Salem 1630: Pioneer Village**, a short drive to the south of the town (*Open May–Oct. Admission: moderate*), is a re-creation of old Salem, with gardens, farm animals, and crafts, as well as costumed actors playing the roles of 17th-century Puritans.

"Halfway down a bystreet of one of our New England towns stands a rusty wooden house, with seven acutely peaked gables facing towards various points of the compass, and a huge, clustered chimney in the midst...The aspect of the venerable mansion has always affected me like a human countenance, bearing the traces not merely of outward storm and sunshine, but expressive also of the long lapse of mortal life, and accompanying vicissitudes that have passed within."
– Nathaniel Hawthorne, *The House of the Seven Gables* (opening paragraph).

*Marblehead, once a busy trading port, is today popular with yachtsmen*

## AROUND SALEM

Salem is easily reached from Boston's North Station; trains are frequent and inexpensive (with discounts for round trips) and take 30 minutes. There are also ferries from Boston's Commercial Wharf. Trolley buses tour Salem every half-hour, and there is a free shuttle bus. However, the sights can easily be taken in on foot, and Salem is a delightful town for walking. A red line marks the walking route linking the historic sights (but omits Chestnut Street); free brochures are available from the National Park Visitor Center in Museum Place or from the Chamber of Commerce in the Old Town Hall.

## TRADE WITH CHINA

The China trade began when Elias Hesketh Derby's ship, the *Grand Turk*, dropped anchor at Whampoa in 1786. By 1800, traders from Salem and Marblehead were a common sight in Canton, the only Chinese port open to them. All sorts of exotic items turned up in America as a result of this trade. From East Africa came ivory, gold, ostrich feathers, and hippopotamus teeth; from the West Pacific appeared semi-precious corals and mother-of-pearl; from the Far East, ceramics, textiles, tea, coffee, spices, sugar, and Japanese artifacts were landed.

**MARBLEHEAD** The handsome coastal town of **Marblehead** ▶ ▶ is located just to the east of Salem, and can be reached by bus 441 from Boston or Salem. Like Salem, it prospered on trade. Its tightly knit, irregular 18th-century streets have a salty charm. Today, it is a wealthy commuter satellite, known particularly for boating.

At **Public Landing** you can join cruises around the harbor and buy lobster, sea bass, and striped bass off the boats. Fort Sewell, a small fortification built for the War of 1812, Fountain Park, and Crocker Park all overlook the bay. Some 600 Revolutionary War soldiers are buried in the **Old Burial Ground**. In **Abbot Hall** (the town hall) hangs Archibald Willard's famous painting, *Spirit of '76*, epitomizing the patriotic spirit of the Revolution. The **Jeremiah Lee Mansion**▶ (*Open* mid-May–mid-Oct, Mon–Sat 10–4, Sun 1–4. *Admission: inexpensive*) has altered little since it was built in 1768; its wooden exterior was made to resemble stone in an attempt to look English.

A causeway road links **Marblehead Neck**, skirted by a loop road; affluent New Yorkers have built summer houses here in various styles such as French château and English Tudor. Chandler Hovey Park is at the northern tip of the Neck and overlooks the bay at Marblehead Light. The best sandy beaches are at Beverly; West Beach has 3 miles of sand, while Dane Street Beach is smaller.

### Springfield 138B2

This major industrial city sits at the southern end of the Pioneer Valley (see pages 174–175) and deserves a visit for its museums (*Open* Wed–Sun noon–4. *Admission: moderate*). Combined entry to four of them, all located by the Quadrangle, is available. The **Connecticut Valley Historical Museum** details the history of the valley from 1636. Dinosaur exhibits, an aquarium, a planetarium, and the story of early aviation in Springfield are attractions at the **Springfield Science Museum**. The **George Walter Vincent Smith Art Museum** has an excellent collection of Victoriana, armor, and Hudson River School paintings, as well as some outstanding Chinese cloisonné. The **Museum of Fine Arts** features French Impressionist works among its European paintings. At **Springfield Armory National Historic Site**▶, Washington set up the first arsenal in America. In 1873, the "Trapdoor" Springfield rifle was invented here. The arsenal closed in 1968 and now contains perhaps the nation's finest collection of firearms.

In 1891, Dr. James Naismith devised the game of basketball in Springfield. At 1150 West Columbus Avenue, the **Naismith Memorial Basketball Hall of Fame**▶ pays homage to the great players, teams, and coaches with reverent displays of photos and mementos, as well as "virtual reality" (*Open* Jul 1–Labor Day, Mon–Sat 9–7, Sun 9:30–5:30; rest of year, daily 9:30–5:30. *Admission: moderate*).

### Worcester 138C2

A busy industrial and commercial center, and New England's second largest city, Worcester has two notable museums. Boasting works from the ancient world, European art from the Renaissance to the 20th century, and American masters—including Whistler, Homer, Copley, and Sargent—is the **Worcester Art Museum**▶▶▶ at 55 Salisbury Street (*Open* Wed–Fri, Sun 11–5, Sat 10–5. *Admission: moderate*). The **Higgins Armory Museum**▶▶, 100 Barber Avenue (*Open* Tue–Sat 10–4, Sun 12–4. *Admission: moderate*), is spectacularly housed in a gallery modeled on the hall of a medieval Austrian castle and displays a fine collection of weapons and armor gathered together from all over the world. For details of **Worcester Common** shopping outlets, see pages 16–17.

(see pages 174–175) … see pages 16–17.

**INDUSTRIAL LEGACY**
The Blackstone River Valley close to Worcester was a busy mill district in the 19th century. Mill owners provided jobs, schools, housing, churches, and stores for their workers, who included refugees from Europe seeking religious and personal freedom. Industrial competition from the South eventually spelled economic decline. Some old mill villages survive, such as Hopedale and Whitinsville, while the Willard House and Clock Museum at Grafton honors the Willard brothers, renowned clockmakers in the 18th century.

187

*Worcester: museum visitors can choose between armory (left) and fine art (below)*

Welcome to the Worcester Art Museum

# New Hampshire

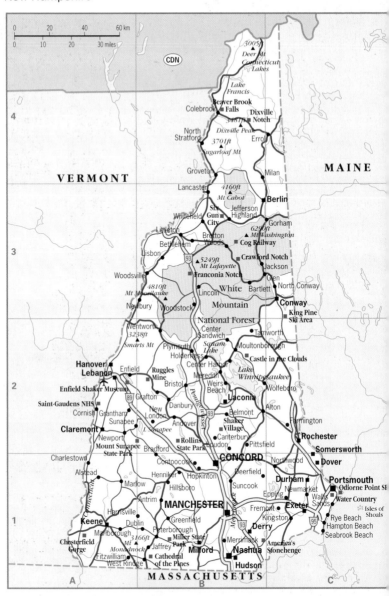

**VERMONT**

**MAINE**

CDN

3005ft
Deer Mt
Connecticut
Lakes

Lake
Francis

Colebrook
Beaver Brook
Falls
Dixville
Notch
3478ft
Dixville Peak

North
Stratford
Errol
3701ft
Sugarloaf Mt

Groveton
Milan

Lancaster
4160ft
Mt Cabot
**Berlin**

Whitefield
Ski
Gun
City
Jefferson
Highland
Gorham
6290ft
Mt Washington
Cog Railway

Littleton
Bretton
Woods

Bethlehem

Lisbon
5249ft
Mt Lafayette
**Crawford Notch**

Woodsville
**Franconia Notch**
Jackson
Glen
North Conway

4810ft
Mt Moosilauke
Lincoln
White
Bartlett

Newbury
Woodstock
**Conway**
King Pine
Ski Area

Mountain

Wentworth
National Forest
Center
Sandwich
Tamworth

3238ft
Smarts Mt
Plymouth
Squam
Lake
Moultonborough

Holderness
Castle in the Clouds

**Hanover**
Enfield
Ruggles
Mine
Center Harbor
Lake
Winnipesaukee

**Lebanon**
Meredith

Enfield Shaker Museum
Bristol
Weirs
Beach
Wolfeboro

Saint-Gaudens NHS
Grafton
**Laconia**

Cornish
Grantham
New
London
Danbury
Belmont
Alton

**Claremont**
Sunapee
Andover
Shaker
Village
Farmington

Newport
L. Sunapee
Rollins
State Park
Canterbury
Pittsfield
**Rochester**

Mount Sunapee
State Park
Bradford
Loudon
**Somersworth**

Charlestown
Contoocook
**CONCORD**
Northwood
**Dover**

Alstead
Henniker
Hopkinton
Deerfield
**Durham**

Marlow
Hillsboro
Suncook
Epping
Newmarket
**Portsmouth**
Odiorne Point SP

Antrim
Deerfield
Walls
Sands
Water Country

Harrisville
**MANCHESTER**
Fremont
**Exeter**
Isles of
Shoals

**Keene**
Greenfield
Kingston
Rye Beach

Marlborough
Dublin
Peterborough
Miller State
Park
Merrimack
**Derry**
Hampton Beach

Chesterfield
Gorge
3166ft
Mt
Monadnock
Jaffrey
America's
Stonehenge
Seabrook Beach

Fitzwilliam
**Cathedral
of the Pines**
**Milford**
**Nashua**

West Ridge
**Hudson**

**MASSACHUSETTS**

0  20  40  60 km
0  10  20  30 miles

188

*The Union Church and
covered bridge at Stark
(both 1850s) in northern
New Hampshire*

*all foliage in the White Mountains*

**EW HAMPSHIRE** The state's triangular form extends 168
miles north to south and 90 miles east to west at its maxi-
um dimensions. In shape and size, it is an inverted form
f Vermont, although its population, nudging a million, is
most twice that of its neighbor.

**HE LAND AND PEOPLE** By repute, New Hampshire
habitants are independent, hardworking, conservative,
nd proud of their state and its history. They are also
rifty, and somewhat suspicious of government. One
pical manifestation of this diehard New Hampshire
titude is that there are no income or sales taxes: much
ate revenue comes instead from "sin tax" on liquor
ence you can only purchase alcohol at state liquor
ores) and from tobacco and gambling. Another is that
e state is unique in the Union in that any resident has
e right to raise an issue at the state capitol for discus-
on. "Live free or die," words first uttered in the
evolution by Colonel John Stark, form the most cut-and-
rust of all state mottos. New Hampshire was the first
ate to vote in favor of the Declaration of Independence.
Despite its nickname, "The Granite State" does have
eas of good, fertile land, particularly in the river val-
ys. Agriculture, together with forestry, ranks third in
e state's economy after manufacturing and tourism.
ith a decline in the number of dairy farms in recent
ears have come changes in farming methods, including
e replacement of animal-feed crops with strawberries,
owers, and other produce.

▶▶▶ REGION HIGHLIGHTS

*Houses*

**Robert Frost's homes**
*pages 198, 205, 209*

**Saint-Gaudens National
Historic Site** *page 195*

**Strawbery Banke Museum
and other Portsmouth
houses** *pages 202–203*

*Museums*

**Canterbury Shaker
Village** *page 192*

**Christa McAuliffe
Planetarium** *page 193*

**Currier Gallery of Art**
*page 198*

*Scenery, villages, and
small towns*

**Lake Winnipesaukee**
*page 196–197*

**Mount Monadnock**
*page 198*

**Mount Sunapee**
*page 196*

**White Mountains**
*pages 204–208*

# New Hampshire

*Ask a New Hampshire native if he's lived there all his life and he'll reply "not yet"*

Industry, however, is New Hampshire's economic mainstay, and its factories employ a higher proportion of the population than those in New York. Textiles have declined drastically in New Hampshire since their economic heyday in the 19th century. Machinery, paper pulp, plastics, and electronics are now important in the industrial heartland in the southern part of the state, concentrated in the Merrimack Valley.

Tourism is another state money-earner. Locals will tell you that New Hampshire has better maple syrup than Vermont and the best leaf-peeping in New England. It certainly does have the distinction of possessing New England's tallest mountains and the merit of having lakes, uplands, forests, and the coast all within an hour or two's drive.

**VISITOR HIGHLIGHTS** The **White Mountains** in the north of the state are New England's tallest and finest uplands. This prime territory for fall foliage, scenic drives, and hiking has attracted artists, writers, and intellectuals since the early 1800s. Today it is busier than ever, and shopping outlets, motels, and theme parks have sprung up around its edges. As elsewhere in New England, however, many of the visitor attractions are only open during the May-to-October season.

Summer crowds also head for the seacoast and lakes regions of New Hampshire. The state's first colonial settlers came to the coast in 1623 and eked out a living supplying timber to the English. In 1679, New Hampshire became a separate royal colony from Massachusetts. Today, **Portsmouth** continues as a commercial port. The town itself has the state's biggest concentration of historic houses.

*Views from the Kancamagus Highway in the White Mountains present some of New England's finest shows of autumn color*

Elsewhere, the 18-mile coast is given over to recreation. Apart from a short empty stretch at its northern end, the seaboard is almost entirely developed, with summer cottages, motels, and fast-food outlets culminating in the 3-mile boardwalk at Hampton Beach.

The lakes number about 1,300 in all, including the smaller "ponds." **Lake Winnipesaukee** is the largest and the most obviously commercialized but is still very attractive, with abundant islands and tempting boat excursions.

The **Mount Monadnock region** in the southwest has a bucolic charm belying its nearness to the urbanized parts of New England. Bumpy back roads set a slow pace in the vicinity of Mount Monadnock itself, where the sleepy villages have quintessential white clapboard and trim greens. The mountain itself gives a view over six states and has long attracted visitors; in 1860 there was a "half-way house" and a "summit house."

*"…New Hampshire has One each of everything as in a show-case."*
– Robert Frost, *New Hampshire* (1937).

ents

r further information, contact the
te tourist office (see page 266) or the
al chambers of commerce.

**NUARY**
ckson Winter Carnival
on Mountain Independence Day
eekend, Lincoln.

**BRUARY**
rtmouth Winter Carnival, Hanover.
eat Rotary Fishing Derby,
eredith.
orld Championship Sled Dog Derby,
conia.

**ARCH**
ckingham Park Craft Festival,
lem.
ring Mania, Attitash Mountain,
rtlett.

**RIL**
rilfest, Cannon Mountain,
anconia.

**AY**
w Hampshire's Annual Lilac
stival, Lisbon.
H. Sheep and Wool Festival,
w Boston.

**NE**
arket Square Celebration,
rtsmouth.
d Time Fiddlers Contests, Lincoln
d Stark.
acoast Jazz Weekend, Portsmouth.

**JULY**
**Lake Winnipesaukee Antique and
Classic Boat Show**, Weirs Beach.
**NASCAR Winston Cup Race**, at N.H.
International Speedway, Loudon.
**Wolfeboro Antiques Fair.**

**AUGUST**
**Attitash Equine Festival**, Bartlett.
**Candlelight Tour of Historic Homes**,
Portsmouth.
**Hot Air Balloon Rally**, Pittsfield.
**League of N.H. Craftsmen Fair**,
Newbury.

**SEPTEMBER**
**N.H. Highland Games**, Loon Mountain,
Lincoln.
**Riverfest Celebration**, Manchester.
**Seafood Festival**, Hampton Beach.

**OCTOBER**
**Fall Foliage Festival**, Fremont.
**Harvest Day**, Canterbury Shaker
Village, Canterbury.
**Sandwich Fair**, Sandwich.

**NOVEMBER–DECEMBER**
**Traditionally Yours**, Jackson.

**DECEMBER**
**Candlelight Stroll**, Strawbery Banke,
Portsmouth.
**Dickens Holiday Celebration**, Hanover.
**First Night Celebrations** (New Year's
Eve), Concord, Portsmouth Wolfeboro,
Claremont, North Conway, and Keene.

*On the shores of Lake Sunapee, an all-year-
round resort*

# New Hampshire

*Canterbury Shaker Village, now a museum, was a celibate religious community, relying on conversion and adopting orphan children*

192

*The Shakers believed that every artifact should be perfectly made, to last a thousand years*

### ► America's Stonehenge 188B

*Open: daily, weather permitting; for hours, tel: 603/893–830*
*Admission: moderate*

This enigmatic 4,000-year-old site at North Salem may n quite emulate its more famous English namesake, b nonetheless it is a genuine prehistoric relic (see panel From Boston, leave I-93 at Exit 3 and take Route 111 east Island Pond and Haverhill Road. Go south on Haverhill Road to the entrance on the right.

### ►► Canterbury Shaker Village 188B2

*Open: May–Oct, daily; Apr, Nov–Dec, Sat–Sun. Admission: moderate*

Just north of Concord, this pristine example of a Shaker community, established in the 1780s, is the sixth of 18 such villages in order of founding. The last surviving female inhabitant, or sister, died in 1992, but the village has been preserved intact, with a meeting house (note the separate entrances for men and women), fire station, schoolhouse, herb garden, dwelling house (with a bell cast by Paul Revere), and a remarkably well-preserved steam-powered laundry. Th Shakers here were progressive in outlook: they had th first telephone and first car in the are and they converted to electricity in 191 five years before the statehouse i Concord did so.

The guided tour takes a look Shaker inventions, which include th wide-headed brush, an early washir machine, knitting machines, an automatic ha seeding device, and a self-sealing front doo Craft workshops, including herbal craft broom-making, and boxmaking, a held in season. For more on the Shak way of life, see pages 148–149.

### ► Concord 188B

Not to be confused with Concor Massachusetts (see pages 168–170 this commercial and administrativ

CANTERBURY SHAKER VILLAGE

Your patronage supports the preservation and interpret of Canterbury Shaker Villa

A non-profit educational m

Please wear this

center is the state capital of New Hampshire. Visitors are most likely to come for the **Christa McAuliffe Planetarium▶▶**, named after the Concord astronaut and schoolteacher who died instantly in the ill-fated takeoff of the *Challenger* space shuttle. The planetarium is one of the world's most technologically advanced. It offers a number of programs, in which you may see our galaxy in a simulated voyage through space, and home in on close-ups of the moon and the planets (*Open* Tue–Sun. Closed three weeks following Labor Day; for times and reservations, tel: 603/271–7827. *Admission: moderate*).

One of a number of granite public buildings downtown, the **State House▶** was erected by prisoner labor in 1819 and much enlarged subsequently, although the legislature still meets in the original chambers. With 400 representatives, it is the fourth largest such assembly in the world (after the government assemblies of Britain and India, and the U.S. Congress). Murals and some 200 portraits of New Hampshire dignitaries adorn the inside, as well as 88 tattered Civil War flags in the entrance hall. There are free weekend tours on the hour between 10 AM and 2 PM; during the week you can guide yourself with a leaflet available at the desk.

In Eagle Square, close by the State House, the **Museum of New Hampshire History** (*Open* Jul–mid-Oct, Dec, daily; rest of year, Tue–Sun. *Admission: moderate*) is where the renowned 1852 Concord Coach is on display (see panel). The **New Hampshire Historical Society** (*Admission free*), across from the State House, maintains changing displays looking back on the state's past. The Coach and Eagle Trail is a self-guiding walk taking in points of interest in the city center (free pamphlets are available from the State House and from the Chamber of Commerce, 244 North Main Street). The **League of New Hampshire Craftsmen**, a statewide handicraft association, has its headquarters and a gallery at 205 North Main Street.

At 14 Penacook Street, at the end of North Main Street, the **Franklin Pierce Manse** (*Open* mid-Jun–Labor Day, Mon–Fri 11–3) was the home from 1842 of the 14th president and contains a number of family pieces. Pierce had a somewhat nondescript political life and a tragic family one: two of his children died in infancy, then his third was killed in a train accident at age 13, two months before his inauguration in 1853. As a consequence, his wife could not face public appearances and so his cousin stood in for the first lady.

*Concord's up-to-the-minute planetarium*

193

**THE CONCORD COACH**
Concord's history of coachmaking dates from 1827, when J. Stephen Abbot, coach builder and wheelwright, completed the first Concord coach. He forged a partnership with Lewis Downing, and together they created 14 types of Concord coach, as well as numerous kinds of other recreational and commercial vehicles. Their company produced 3,000 coaches, some of which were used by the Wells Fargo Company in the pioneering days of the West.

*Pick your own fruit in Canterbury—and in many other places*

*Winter, with deep snow in much of the region, still provides entertainment in New England. Christmas and First Night, a New Year's Eve festival that originated in Boston's bicentennial Independence celebrations of 1976, are very special times.*

**194**

*Top: Christmas at Faneuil Hall, Boston*
*Above: snow and a welcoming wreath on the door—all part of the spirit of a New England Christmas*

**Christmas** As soon as Thanksgiving Day is over, Christmas trees, lights, wreaths, and garlands start going up all over the towns and villages. The month of December is filled with festivities, from lantern-lit sleigh rides to readings of Dickens. To highlight just three: in Portsmouth, New Hampshire, there is a Candlelight Stroll around the houses of Strawbery Banke Museum, each decorated in its own period style; lantern-bearing guides in 19th-century costume lead evening tours in Mystic Seaport Village, Connecticut; and Old Sturbridge Village, Massachusetts, celebrates a colonial-period Christmas.

Summer visitors who want to see what a New England Christmas is like should be sure to look inside one of the dozens of Christmas shops that stay open all year round. Plastic trees hung heavy with color-coordinated bows, baubles, enameled cut-outs, and crystal Santas glitter against the fake snow and piped carols. There are rolls of ribbon by the dozen, tiny stars by the yard, garlands, and wreaths ready-made or in kits. Displayed among it all are little groups of "Snowbabies," "Carolers," Annalee dolls (see panel on page 196), nutcrackers, and miniature Christmas villages—collections to build up and arrange under the tree or on the mantelpiece. There may even be a Nativity scene.

**First Night** This colorful and exciting, nonalcoholic community festival has become a well-established tradition that is spreading rapidly to dozens of towns throughout New England and elsewhere. Between the afternoon carnival procession and the midnight fireworks on New Year's Eve, there are scores of different indoor and outdoor happenings. For the cost of a First Night Button, families and friends, often wearing masks or more elaborate costumes, wander the streets imbibing jazz, dance, theater, puppets, ice carvings, storefront tableaux, and many other entertainments.

**CHRISTMAS WREATHS**
One small but thriving industry in the economically impoverished area of northern Maine is the making of decorative Christmas wreaths. Based on a particular type of balsam fir, they are sold all over eastern America.

*First Night Buttons—passport to Boston's New Year's Eve celebrations*

*Dartmouth College, the only Ivy League college in northern New England*

## DARTMOUTH'S BEGINNINGS

Dartmouth College was founded in 1769 when the Congregational minister, Eleazar Wheelock, gained a charter from the governor of New Hampshire to educate Native Americans in a log hut. The college's first sponsor was the 2nd Earl of Dartmouth, the secretary of state for the colonies under George III.

► **Hanover**                    *188A2*

In Hanover, on the Connecticut River, the town center is dominated by the 265-acre campus of prestigious **Dartmouth College►**, an Ivy League establishment (see pages 22–23). Notable among the college buildings grouped around the maple-shaded green are the Colonial-style **Baker Library** (1928) and **Dartmouth Hall** (1784). The **Hood Museum of Art** has a small but choice art collection (*Open* Tue, Thu–Sat 10–5, Wed 10–9, Sun 12–5. *Admission free*). The **Hopkins Center** features year-round music performances, plays, movies, and other cultural events.

South of town toward ► Windsor, the **Saint-Gaudens National Historic Site►►**, off Route 12A at Cornish, marks the summer home of Augustus Saint-Gaudens (1848–1907), one of America's foremost sculptors. Many of his works are on display, both in the garden that was his passion and in his studio. Pieces include copies of the *Shaw Memorial*, which stands on Boston Common opposite the State House, and the *Adams Memorial*, installed in Washington, DC (*Open* last Mon in May–end Oct, daily 9–4:30. *Admission: inexpensive*).

East from Hanover, by Mascoma Lake, is the **Enfield Shaker Museum**, retaining 13 Shaker buildings of the former Enfield community (1793–1923). Here, you can take a self-guiding tour and watch crafts demonstrations (*Open* May–mid-Oct, daily; winter, Sat–Sun. *Admission: moderate*). The nearby feast ground on Mount Assurance was chosen for its view of the lake. Farther on, at Grafton Center, a signpost points up a bumpy road to the **Ruggles Mine►** (*Open* mid-May–mid-Jun, Sat–Sun; mid-Jun–mid-Oct, daily. *Admission: expensive*). This abandoned mica, feldspar, beryl, and uranium mine (see panel) is an expensive visit for what is offered, but the site is dramatic. Entrance is through a rock tunnel into a huge open-cut mine, from which a number of manmade caverns and underground ponds can be explored (a flashlight is advisable).

## MICA AT THE RUGGLES MINE

The flexible, flaky material known as mica, which is found abundantly in the Ruggles Mine, has high resistance to heat. It was formerly used to glaze stove fronts and lanterns and to carry wires in electric toasters. The owners claim over 150 types of minerals have been found at the mine. Visitors can rent hammers and take home souvenir chunks of rock.

*The motif of Annalee's dolls*

## ANNALEE'S DOLLS
Back in 1934, Annalee Thorndike made her first doll, the first of many thousands of felt and wire creations that, with their handpainted faces and rosy cheeks, have gained something of a cult status. Near Meredith in the Winnipesaukee region is the Annalee Doll Museum and shop, on the original manufacturing site (tel: 603/279–6542. *Open* Memorial Day–Oct 31. *Admission free*). The museum exhibits some pre-World War II specimens, including the first doll ever produced; early examples can fetch $2,000 nowadays. The gift shop sells a variety of mice in top hats, Christmas shepherds, baseball players, and fishing boys.

*Lake Sunapee is popular for water sports*

### ►► Lake Sunapee                    188B2
The Sunapee area offers unspoiled lake and mountain scenery and a good alternative for those who find Lake Winnipesaukee too commercialized. The state beach on Lake Sunapee is a narrow sandy strip, ideal for families with small children as the water is shallow and the beach slopes very gently. The MV *Mt. Sunapee II* cruises the lake, with two narrated tours daily (tel: 603/763–4030). The **John Hay National Wildlife Refuge** (*Open* daily dawn–dusk. *Admission: inexpensive*), Newbury, is a former estate of a diplomat's summer mansion, The Fells (*Open* tours late May–mid-Oct, Sat–Sun, holidays. *Admission: inexpensive*). The fine grounds here slope down to the lake and contain a variety of rare alpines.

**Mount Sunapee►►** towers over the lake. Its ski lift operates all year, and the summit café offers a huge panorama encompassing Mad River Glen (73 miles) and Mount Washington (75 miles). Walks from the top include the 1,000-yard trail to a cliff high above spectacular Lake Solitude. At the base of the chair lift, at Newbury, is the site of the Annual League of New Hampshire Craftsmen Fair in August.

**Mount Kearsarge►** (2,937 feet), in Rollins State Park, has a straightforward trail up its south side (reached by road from Warner). The walk up takes 20–30 minutes; the view from the top takes in the White Mountains. **Mount Kearsarge Indian Museum** (Exit 8N or 95 off I-89 near Warner) exhibits baskets, fishing artifacts, canoes, and quiltwork of the Native Americans of the region (*Open* May–Oct, daily; Nov–Dec, Sat–Sun. *Admission: moderate*).

### ►► Lake Winnipesaukee              188B2
New Hampshire's largest lake is the center of a busy vacation area whose fortunes were boosted considerably by the movie *On Golden Pond*, filmed at adjacent Squam Lake. Its shoreline is very irregular and the charming views ever changing, although the small Victorian resort communities that fringe it are of limited interest. The best way to appreciate it is to take a cruise on the MS *Mount Washington* (late May–late Oct; tel: 603/366–5531).

*Aerial view of Moultonborough in the Lakes Region*

Ellacoya State Beach is suitable for families, with a narrow sandy strip. **Weirs Beach**, with the main steamer pier, is the most commercialized point on the lake. It is a far from sedate boardwalk village thick with fast-food stands, motels, and family-oriented action (see panel), but retains a quaintly antique array of 1950s homemade slush kiosks and amusement arcades. One of New England's last drive-in movie theaters is here, too. **Center Harbor** has a Children's Museum for ages two to ten.

**SPEEDWAY**
New Hampshire International Speedway (tel: 603/783–4931) is a big state revenue earner on Route 106 north of Canterbury. Races take place in the 75,000-seat stadium.

*The Lakes Region offers a huge range of water-sports opportunities*

**197**

The **Squam Lake Natural Science Center▶** (*Open* May 1–Nov 1, daily 9:30–4:30. *Admission: moderate*), off Route 113 near Holderness, is a wildlife sanctuary for rescued animals of New Hampshire. It is nicely done, with a ¾-mile trail leading past enclosures. Live animal demonstrations with a naturalist take place twice daily, and there are lots of hands-on activities for children. In addition to the main trail, there is a 1-mile trail up to Mount Fayal, which offers a view of **Squam Lake**. From July through October, the center also runs nature cruises on the lake for sightings of loons and other wildlife (for details, tel: 603/968–7194). Cruises are also operated by Squam Lake Tours (tel: 603/968–7577).

Quieter, traditional towns include **Center Sandwich** and **Wolfeboro▶**. The nearby **Castle in the Clouds▶**, built in 1911–1914 for millionaire Thomas Plant, is a turreted hilltop house with whimsical interior features, including an octagonal elm-paneled dining room. However, it is the setting that is most memorable. The tram that takes you up also visits the Castle Springs mineral-water bottling plant and a microbrewery (*Open* mid-May–Jun 1, Sat–Sun 9–5; Jun 1–Labor Day, daily 9–5; Labor Day–mid-Oct, daily 9–4. *Admission: moderate; tours expensive*).

At **Tamworth** is the Barnstormers Theater, New Hampshire's oldest professional summer theater. Tamworth itself glimpses Chocorua Lake, while nearby **White Lake State Park** has a beach with canoe and rowboat rentals.

**FAMILY FUN AT WEIRS BEACH**
The Winnipesaukee Scenic Railroad runs diesel trains along the lakeside from Weirs Beach, with dinner specials in the evening. There are also two open-air water parks here, one called simply Water Slide; pay for a batch of rides, or for two hours, or for the whole day. The Surf Coaster lies away from the beach and is pricier, but it also has a wave-machine surf coaster and in addition runs a miniature golf course. Across the road, another company operates go-karts and a baseball-pitching machine.

## MONADNOCK CHECKLISTS

Because the forest on Mount Monadnock was burned off around 1810, the views from the upper trails are particularly good. The open terrain here gives rise to some rare semialpine flora, including mountain cranberry, mountain goldenrod, mountain sandwort, and cinquefoil. Fauna includes moose, black bear, white-tailed deer, gray fox, red fox, woodchuck, porcupine, opossum, and raccoon.

*Andrew Wyeth is one of several artists with New England connections on show at Manchester's Currier Gallery*

## ROUTES UP MOUNT MONADNOCK

Numerous routes lead up the mountain from Monadnock State Park headquarters at Jaffrey, where free maps are available (tel: 603/532–8862). The most popular and easiest are the White Cross and White Arrow trails (3–4 hours there and back). The Pumpelly Trail is the longest, at about 5 hours' walking time. The Spelman Trail, which heads up a breathtaking series of schist rock ledges to reach Pumpelly Ridge, ascends 1,000 feet in half a mile and is the steepest. The Red Spot Trail is perhaps the most scenic. For a very full but rewarding day's walking, make a circuit by taking any trail via Bald Rock to the summit and then return via Pumpelly Ridge.

▶ **Manchester**                                          *188B1*

In the 19th century, the thriving Amoskeag Mill made Manchester the world's largest cotton cloth-producing center. Today, it is a commercial and manufacturing city, but the **Currier Gallery of Art**▶▶ makes the city worth a visit. The collection includes European and American masters, with paintings, sculpture, and decorative art from the 13th to 20th centuries (*Open* Wed–Mon. *Admission: moderate*). The gallery also organizes tours of the 1950 **Zimmerman House**, designed by Frank Lloyd Wright (*Open* Fri–Mon, reservations only, tel: 603/669–6144. *Admission: moderate*).

South of town is the **Robert Frost Homestead**▶ at Derry, the poet's home from 1901 to 1909 (see page 209). Here he "wrote more than half of my first book, much more than half of my second and even quite a little of my third." He later visited it to find it a scrapyard, and it was only after his death that his daughter Lesley Frost Ballantine restored it. The locality was used by Frost as the setting for his "Stopping by Woods on a Snowy Evening." (*Open* summer, daily; spring and fall, Sat–Sun. *Admission: inexpensive*.)

▶▶ **Mount Monadnock Region**                             *188A1*

**Mount Monadnock**▶▶▶, America's most climbed peak rises to a modest 3,165 feet, but by virtue of its isolation from New England's other high spots it gets one of the grandest views in the Northeast. The surroundings are relatively unfrequented and make a good getaway from the Boston area for those seeking accessible, low-key relaxation. Walking, kayaking, canoeing, covered-bridge spotting, looking at fall foliage, skiing, and antiques-hunting lead the pursuits.

Only reached on foot, the mountain that stands alone on the plain demands a substantial walk to the top (see panel). Rock formations to look for include the Imp, the Sarcophagus (a boulder transported and dumped on Pumpelly Ridge by glaciers in the Ice Age), and the Doric Temple (a set of composite stone blocks). The summit view on a clear day takes in points more than 100 miles away, and extends to the White Mountains, to the Boston skyscrapers, and over every New England state.

**Peterborough** is home to the MacDowell Colony, begun by composer Edward MacDowell (1861–1908), whose best-known works include his second piano concerto and the piano solos *To a Wild Rose* and *New England Idyls*. After his death the colony was for 40 years directed by his widow; it offers artistic seclusion to artists, composers and writers, but only a small part is open to the public. Those attracted here have included Leonard Bernstein

Thornton Wilder, Aaron Copland, and Virgil Thomson. Wilder's play, *Our Town*, was set in Peterborough and became one of the cornerstones of American drama. Theatrical traditions are maintained by the Peterborough Players with their summer theater and the Marionette Theater (tel: 603/924–7585), which specializes, most unusually, in opera performed by marionettes to recorded music. Fans of vintage diners should seek out the Peterborough Diner on Depot Street. **Miller State Park**▶ ▶, off Route 101 east of Peterborough, has road access for vehicles to the summit of Pack Monadnock (2,290 feet), plus picnic sites and a summit loop trail. You can walk up (nearly 1½ miles) by following the Wapack Trail from Route 101.

Blink and you'll miss **Dublin**. Along its sleepy main street is the headquarters of the *Yankee Magazine* and *Farmers' Almanac*, two famous New England–based publications; tours of the premises are given on weekdays. West of town is Dublin Pond, the haunt of blue herons and featuring a town beach with water slides, sailing, windsurfing, and swimming. Close by, Friendly Farm (*Open* summer, daily; fall, Sat–Sun) operates a petting farm for children, with a range of farmyard animals and milking demonstrations. Nearby is **Harrisville**▶, with a pretty pond and a cluster of old mill cottages; Harrisville Designs demonstrates old weaving methods (*Open* Tue–Sat. *Admission free*).

**Keene** is a commercial center rather than a tourist town but has some dignified 19th-century homes. The **Horatio Colony House Museum**, at 199 Main Street (*Open* Jun–mid-Oct, daily 11–3. *Admission free*), is a pleasing Federal-style house of 1806. The Children's Museum has displays on different parts of New England, including colonial life and a "typical" village.

West of Keene by Route 9, an easy ¾-mile loop trail follows Wilde Brook through deep **Chesterfield Gorge**. **Rhododendron State Park**▶, at Fitzwilliam, comes into spectacular bloom in mid-July and has views of Mount Monadnock. **Fitzwilliam** itself has a concentration of antiques shops, while at **West Rindge** Ed's Country Auction offers rural antiques, domestic junk, and copious local color (summer, Sat 10 AM; winter, Sat 6 PM). Near Rindge is the **Cathedral of the Pines**▶ (*Open* May–Oct, daily 9–5. *Admission: donation. See panel*).

**THE WAPACK TRAIL**
A 21-mile hiking trail leads from the base of Mount Watatic, near Ashburnham, Massachusetts, to the slope of North Pack Monadnock in Greenfield, New Hampshire. The trail takes a skyline route with views of Boston, the White Mountains, and Vermont on the way. Yellow triangle markers and stone heaps show the route.

**CATHEDRAL OF THE PINES**
Begun to commemorate Lieutenant Sanderson Sloane, shot down over Germany in 1944, this outdoor interdenominational place of worship became a national memorial in 1957. With its charming backdrop of Mount Monadnock, it focuses on a 2,000-seat "cathedral" shaded by tall white pines. The altar contains stones donated by every president since Truman, and the stone lectern contains sand and rock from every battlefield where Americans have fought. The Memorial Bell Tower, with bas-reliefs designed by Norman Rockwell, was the first memorial in the U.S. devoted to womankind.

199

*Mount Monadnock, seen from Dublin*

*Over 80 percent of New England is covered in forest. The woods, a mixture of hardwoods and softwoods, are home to an exciting variety of wildlife species. Seeing moose or beaver can be a vacation highlight, and in summer the sound of songbirds is sensational. There are also areas of enchanting alpine flora.*

**"BRAKE FOR MOOSE..."**
"...It could save your life." So read the road signs in New Hampshire. Every year there are scores of collisions between moose and cars on forest roads. A moose can severely damage not only the car, but quite possibly the driver, too. If you see a moose at the side of the road, try not to startle it and go carefully—moose are unpredictable. Dark brown in color, they are difficult to see in the dark.

**200**

**POISON IVY**
Poison ivy is common throughout eastern North America and is poisonous to touch. Its leaves have three leaflets, green turning to red/purple, and it has white berries. If you so much as brush against the plant, its poison can cause blistering and great discomfort (it can even rub off from a dog's coat onto your leg). Clothes worn a year after contact can cause poisoning. Don't go into undergrowth and always wear socks and long pants if you are going near wild vegetation. If you brush against poison ivy, wash the area quickly; don't scratch it or rub your eyes. Severe allergies are rare.

New England has two national forests: the White Mountain National Forest, which covers much of New Hampshire and creeps over the border into Maine, and the Green Mountain National Forest, in Vermont. Both are laced with trails. Away from the coastal strip, Maine is also heavily forested—and dotted with thousands of lakes. Its most northerly areas are predominantly softwood, managed by timber companies. The softwoods are mainly pine, spruce, and fir, while sugar maple, yellow birch, aspen, and paper birch are New England's dominant hardwoods.

**Forest fauna** The largest of the forest animals are moose, black bear, and white-tailed deer. The deer are ever present, and hunting them is a fall ritual. The black bear stands almost 3 feet high and is fairly frequently seen making its clumsy way through the woods of Maine, New Hampshire, and, occasionally, Vermont. It is usually harmless (but see panel opposite). The animal that attracts most attention, however, is the moose. There are numerous organized moose-watching trips (information available locally), and you may well see moose as you drive around (they like the salt that runs off the roads), particularly in northern Maine, the most northerly parts of the White Mountains, and along the Kancamagus Highway. Baxter State Park is one of the best places in New England for moose. The most likely time of day to spot moose is at dawn or dusk, especially near ponds or marshes. Moose are very ungainly creatures, with a long, pendulous snout and a hairy dewlap. They eat grasses and often stand in lakes. A full-grown male moose can be 6 feet tall at its shoulders, weigh over half a ton, and

*White-tailed deer are a fairly common sight*

have huge antlers as well—give such an animal a wide berth.

Smaller forest animals include raccoon, chipmunk, marten, woodchuck, and porcupine. Red squirrel, coyote, red fox, lynx, muskrat, skunk, and snowshoe hare are fairly common. Beaver activity in rivers and lakes is always fascinating. Their lodges (houses of sticks and mud) are up to 6 feet high, and the dams, similarly built, are amazing constructions. The beaver's favorite food is bark—watch for sticks that have been neatly stripped and gnawed. The beavers themselves are usually seen at dusk or dawn, giving themselves away with a slap of their tails as they dive.

**Mountain birds** Even if you cannot identify all the songbirds, you will enjoy the songs that fill the woods in spring and summer. Many of the birds are migratory. The most common include blackpoll and Nashville warblers, ruby- and golden-crowned kinglets, pine siskin, raven, phoebe, and chickadee, the state bird of Maine and Massachusetts and a member of the tit family. The loon, a diver sometimes heard calling from the lakes of New Hampshire, is reputedly the oldest bird species on Earth.

**Alpine flora** There are over 8 square miles of alpine zone in the White Mountains. On Mount Washington the timberline occurs exceptionally low, at 1,400 feet. Climb it (see page 208) and you will notice that the trees become more stunted as you ascend. Dense mats of vegetation called krummholz (German for "twisted tree") cover the ground.

Above the timberline, in the alpine zone, 100 different alpine flowers that are unique to Mount Washington, Labrador, and the Arctic grow among lichens, sedges, and mosses. The dwarf cinquefoil (*Potentilla robbinsiana*) is endemic to Mount Washington. Other alpine flowers that may be found here and in the alpine areas of the Katahdin Range in Maine's Baxter State Park include mountain aster, alpine violet, alpine bearberry, moss plant, mountain brook saxifrage, and goldthread.

*This young moose is one of many that inhabit the remote northern forests*

**BEAR ESSENTIALS**
Black bears are shy, preferring to stay away from people and unlikely to do any harm. Nevertheless, it is wise to be careful with food, as the smell attracts them— and this is when injuries may occur.
● Never feed bears.
● Don't leave food scraps lying around or throw them into a campfire.
● Store food (and any clothes soiled with food) in sealed containers in the trunk of your car or in a tree (so the bears don't damage your car).

**FRAGILE FLORA**
Remember that some of the flowers that have adapted to the biting winter winds and the poor soil take up to 25 years to flower for the first time, so watch where you put your feet. The best time to see wildflowers is from mid-June through August.

*Settled in the 1630s, Strawbery Banke was named after the strawberries that once grew wild there*

**STRAWBERY BANKE**
In its early days, Strawbery Banke was a prosperous merchants' center. Later, the Puritans came and, in 1653, changed the name to Portsmouth, which sounded less frivolous. Now the grid of old 1690s streets has been restored. The 42 houses show the lifestyles of their inhabitants through the ages.

**NEW HAMPSHIRE CRUISES**
Cruises to the nine islands constituting the Isles of Shoals and whale-watching trips are popular excursions. Operators around Portsmouth include:
● Portsmouth Harbor Cruises (tel: 800/776-0915).
● The Isles of Shoals Steamship Co. (tel: 800/441-4620).
● New Hampshire Seacoast Cruises (tel: 603/964-5545).
● The Atlantic Fishing Fleet, which operates the *Atlantic Queen II* (at Rye Harbor; tel: 603/964-5220).

## ▶▶ Portsmouth and the Coast  188C1

**PORTSMOUTH** Occupying the northern end of New Hampshire's short coastline, **Portsmouth▶▶** was the most important colonial town north of Boston. It has an English look, with a fine legacy of redbrick 18th- and 19th-century houses, many built for prosperous sea captains.

The original colonial settlement in the harbor was **Strawbery Banke▶▶**, now a leading historic attraction (see panel). All but one of the houses, plus a reerected four-seater privy, stand on their original sites (*Open* self-guiding tours May–Oct, daily; Candlelight Strolls two weekends in Dec, one night in Aug).

**Portsmouth Historical Society**, with the SPNEA (see page 68), maintains a number of 18th-century houses (*Open* Jun–Oct) scattered around town (the Portsmouth Harbor Trail connects the sites). If you intend to visit more than one, pick up a Portsmouth Passport for reduced admission.

In 1962, the **Warner House▶▶** (ca1716; *open* mid-Jun–Oct, Tue–Sat 10–4, Sun 1–4. *Admission: moderate*) became the first house in the country to be registered as a national historic landmark (following the restoration of the White House in Washington, DC, an action that promoted an awareness of house preservation). It was Portsmouth's first brick house, the work of John Drew, an English builder. The house retains numerous English features in its paneling and furniture. Folk-art murals date back to its construction; one of them (once covered up) shows English patriotic sentiment with its portrayal of a redcoat. Outstanding among the furnishings is a Portsmouth-made high chest on the upstairs landing.

The **Moffat-Ladd House▶** (*Open* Jun–Oct, Mon–Sat 10–4, Sun 1–5. *Admission: moderate*), a three-story blue and white building of 1763, stands amid pretty English-style gardens with grass steps. In them William Whipple, a signatory of the Declaration of Independence, planted what is now the state's tallest horse chestnut tree. The house has fine Portsmouth furniture, eye-catching wallpaper that was handpainted in Paris in 1819, and a tunnel in its kitchen that supposedly led to the wharf! The **Wentworth-Gardner House**, located at 50 Mechanic Street (*Open* late May–mid-Oct, Tue–Sun 1–4. *Admission:*

*moderate*), is a Georgian structure of 1760, and is noted for the quality of its interior carved woodwork, tiled fireplaces, and painted wallpaper.

The **John Paul Jones House** (*Open* late May–mid-Oct, Mon–Sat 10–4, Sun noon–4. *Admission: moderate*) was the lodging of the Revolutionary commander Jones while his frigate *Ranger* was being refurbished in the port. A state-of-the-art interior of 1807 is found in the **Rundlet-May House**, owned and operated by SPNEA (*Open* Jun–mid-Oct, Sat–Sun 11–4. *Admission: moderate*), featuring a contemporary roasting oven, Portsmouth furniture, and foreign wallpaper, while the **Governor John Langdon House** of 1784, also an SPNEA property (*Open* Jun–mid-Oct, Wed–Sun 11–4. *Admission: moderate*), has fine carving, Portsmouth furniture, and landscaped grounds.

In Albacore Park, Market Street, is the **USS *Albacore*** (*Open* summer, daily 9:30–5:30; rest of year, Thu–Mon 9:30–4. *Admission: inexpensive*), a navy submarine in service from 1953 to 1972 (see panel).

Horse-and-carriage tours of the old town start from the church. The **Children's Museum of Portsmouth** at 280 Marcy Street provides a variety of hands-on activities for youngsters of all ages (*Open* Mon–Sat 10–5, Sun 1–5. Closed Mon outside summer and school vacations. *Admission: inexpensive*).

**THE COAST** Just out of town, **Odiorne Point State Park▶** covers 3,050 acres of duneland, the largest tract of undeveloped land on the 18-mile New Hampshire coast. The World War II fort here is one of several historic harbor defenses. The Seacoast Science Center (*Open* daily 10–5. *Admission: inexpensive*) features aquariums showing tide pool and salt marsh ecology. There is also a fine drive on Route 1B to **New Castle Island▶** (also known as Great Island), which has old homes, forts, and lighthouses. The remainder of the New Hampshire coast is almost entirely developed, except for a few patches of marshy hinterland, but there are good state beaches at **Wallis Sands**, **Jenness**, and **North Hampton**. **Hampton Beach** has a long sandy beach but is very commercialized with an extensive boardwalk, amusements, and fast-food outlets. **Water Country**, New England's biggest water park, is on Route 1, some 3 miles south of Portsmouth (for hours, tel: 603/427–1111. *Admission: expensive*).

**203**

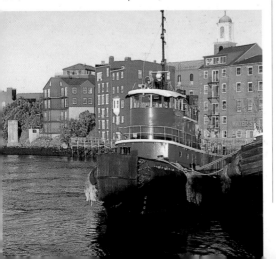

*Portsmouth's waterfront: boats have taken visitors to the Isles of Shoals from here since the mid-19th century*

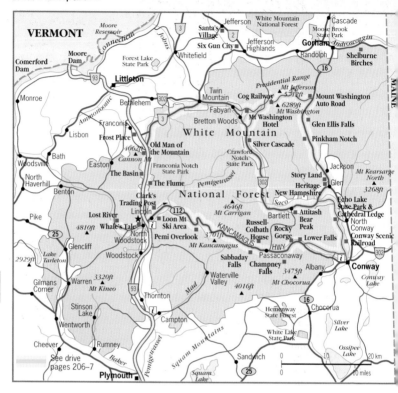

## CONSERVATION—THE EARLY DAYS

The Weeks Act, passed in 1911, introduced the national forest system. The White Mountains were the first such forest area to be designated, affording protection after the removal of many trees in the region. The soil erosion and washdown that had occurred had worried politicians who spent vacations here, and political pressure for change followed.

## ▶▶▶ The White Mountains                    188B3

The White Mountains are the highest and most dramatic uplands in New England. This is the region's finest area for mountain walking and in season draws crowds to its ski slopes and fall foliage display. The main areas for accommodations are the purely functional resort towns around the White Mountains proper. These places are well geared to tourism but not strong on atmosphere.

**North Conway** is highly rated by many for its outlet shopping malls (also known as Mount Washington Valley), which get particularly busy on rainy days in peak

*Winter in the White Mountains: Echo Lake*

*The Mount Washington Cog Railway puffs its way up an uncomfortable but scenic 1¼-hour ascent over fragile-looking viaducts and up 37-degree gradients*

season. **Woodstock** and **Lincoln** are the best bases for exploring the Kancamagus and Franconia areas. **Bethlehem** is particularly noted for its architectural gems.

**WHITE MOUNTAIN SIGHTS** At 6,288 feet, the extremely windswept peak of **Mount Washington▶▶▶** soars above the rest of the Presidential Range. It is the highest summit in New England, indeed in the entire northeast of the U.S. Numerous hiking routes lead up the slopes, but the most popular ways up are by the toll road (guided tours by van also available) and the **Mount Washington Cog Railway▶▶**, the world's oldest tourist railway (May–Oct; for reservations, tel: 603/278–5404 or 800/922–8825; note that you only have 20 minutes at the summit to ensure a return seat). At the summit, the view extends to Boston and the Atlantic Ocean. There was once a succession of grand hotels at the top; today only the Tip Top House survives (preserved as a museum; *admission free*), while the rest is a stark miscellany of antennas and small buildings.

The **Frost Place▶**, in a remote spot near Franconia, is the humble 50-acre farmstead where the New England poet (see page 209) dreamed he "could live cheap and get Yankier and Yankier." The tiny house contains original manuscripts and Frost's own writing table (*Open* last Mon in May–second Mon in Oct, daily. *Admission: inexpensive*).

**Clark's Trading Post▶** (*Open* Memorial Day–Jun 24, Sat–Sun 10–5; Jun 24–Oct 1, daily 10–5. *Admission: moderate*), near Lincoln, was set up by a family of avid collectors in the 1920s. The complex includes a reconstructed New England street, the museum (with working music boxes, vintage slot machines, and peep shows), and a topsy-turvy "haunted house." Black bears perform several times daily in summer, and a train that tours the grounds gets held up by "bandits." At Glen is **Story Land** (*Open* mid-Jun–first Mon in Sep, daily; early Sep–second Mon in Oct, Sat–Sun. *Admission: expensive*), a well thought-out children's theme park. There is a Mexican village, and rides include flying clogs and a log-boat trip down water slides.

Two other theme parks, both at Jefferson, are **Santa's Village**, including "Santa's summer home" with similar rides to Story Land, and **Six Gun City**, with a water slide and Wild West adventure. **Whale's Tale** (Route 3, North Woodstock) is a water park. **Attitash Bear Peak** and the **Fields of Attitash**, at Bartlett, features "wet and wild water slides," plus a scenic chair lift, horseback riding, and a golf driving range.

*Continued on page 208.*

"Men hang out their signs indicative of their respective trades; shoemakers hang out a gigantic shoe; jewelers, a monster watch; and the dentist hangs out a gold tooth; but up in the mountains of New Hampshire, God Almighty has hung out a sign to show that there He makes men."
– Attributed to Daniel Webster, on the Old Man of the Mountain, Franconia Notch.

**THE WORLD'S WORST WEATHER**
Because of a funnel effect, Mount Washington gets the full brunt of three continental storm systems. The fastest winds ever recorded (231 mph) have occurred here: a 10 mph breeze farther down becomes an 80 mph blast at the top. Some 175 feet down, the ground is permanently frozen. These unusual conditions give rise to 63 alpine flower species. The mountain has claimed many lives: below the summit, on the right of the railway, a wooden sign and stone marker show the spot where 23-year-old walker Lizzie Bourne died of exhaustion in 1855.

# Drive

## The White Mountains

*See map on page 204 (yellow route).*

This 94-mile loop tour is perhaps the most scenic mountain drive in New England. It takes in the Kancamagus Highway and Franconia Notch, and provides opportunities to drive up to the magnificent lookouts on Cathedral Ledge and Mount Washington. Watch out for moose, which often stray onto the roads, and keep the gas tank full.

From North Woodstock, take Route 112, the **Kancamagus Highway►►►**, famous for its fall foliage, and with choice but scattered views. Beyond **Loon Mountain ski area**, with its gondolas and outdoor activities, there are particularly fine roadside panoramas from the Pemi Overlook (with its view of mounts Kancamagus, Osceola, and Loon) and from Kancamagus Pass Overlook

*Covered bridge over The Flume in Franconia Notch*

(with Mount Kancamagus prominent). Numerous trails start from the road, including a short path to **Sabbaday Falls►**, a trio of waterfalls tumbling and twisting into a deep chasm, and another to **Champney Falls►**.

**Passaconaway Historic Site: Russell-Colbath House** (*Open* Jul–Aug, 9–4:30, but may vary. *Admission free*) is a tiny cottage formerly occupied by Ruth Colbath, the "hermit woman" postmistress whose husband walked out without explanation one night. She waited 39 years for him and left a light burning each night, but in vain. She died in 1933. The Swift River flows over great boulders at **Rocky Gorge**, where a short loop trail leads to Falls Pond. A short distance east, also by the road, Lower Falls is designated for swimming and picnicking. At the next left turn take Dugway Road, leaving Route 112 to dodge the traffic jams of North Conway. **Conway** has a pair of covered bridges.

Turn left to Echo Lake and **Cathedral Ledge►►►**. The small lake (a state park, with swimming ) is magnificently set beneath the huge granite outcrop of Cathedral Ledge, a popular cliff for rock climbing. A road ascends the top of the ledge, and a path leads out to a dizzy viewpoint.

Farther north, via Glen, is the summit of **Mount Washington►►►**

approached on foot, by toll road, or by cog railway. Retrace your drive to Glen, then follow Route 302 to the **Mount Washington Hotel**, New England's largest wooden building, the last surviving of 15 grand hotels in the White Mountains (see pages 40–41).

To the west, the **Franconia Notch road** (I-93) ▶ ▶ ▶ carves its way through awesome scenery. The drama unfolds fully from above: take the cable car up **Cannon Mountain** ▶ ▶, where the ½-mile Rim Trail looks down 2,500 feet into the valley and into New York State. By the cable car station is the **New England Ski Museum** (*Open* Dec–Mar, Fri–Tue 12–5. *Admission free*), with displays of archive photographs and equipment of various periods, plus a multiscreen slide show about skiing history.

From I-93 you can glimpse the famous **Old Man of the Mountain**, a rock outcrop some 40 feet tall that displays the uncanny profile of a human face. There is roadside parking for northbound traffic, and a short trail from a parking lot to Profile Lake for southbound traffic. **The Basin** ▶, a 30-foot-wide pothole, was gouged out by glacial meltwater and is one of a number of attractive features passed on the popular

*Glorious autumnal color is guaranteed*

Cascade Brook Trail. Better known still is **The Flume** ▶ ▶, a dark, steep-sided chasm that keeps cool on the hottest of summer days and becomes laden with 30–40 feet of ice in winter, when the wooden walkways are dismantled. A fine waterfall tumbles into its far end.

At North Woodstock, it is worth a detour west on Route 112 to **Lost River** ▶ ▶ (*Open* weather permitting, mid-May–Jun, Sep–mid-Oct, daily 9–5; Jul–Aug, daily 9–6. *Admission: moderate*). The boardwalk trail, through caves created by tumbled boulders and along a series of waterfalls, is tortuous and exciting, and requires good footwear. This remote spot was discovered by two brothers on a fishing trip, when one fell into the top entrance of a cave.

*Cycling the Kancamagus Highway*

# New Hampshire

*There is a magnificent walk from Zealand Notch up the 4,580-foot summit of Mount Guyot*

## PLANNING AND PREPARATION

National forest information centers have free leaflets detailing the main trails and sell hiking maps. The De Lorme Trail Map gives an overview of trails, with 250 descriptions.

For serious hiking, the Appalachian Mountain Club (AMC) publishes the definitive guide to mountain walks and maintains a network of mountain huts (reservations recommended, tel: 603/466–2727; www.outdoors.org). The AMC's Pinkham Notch Visitor Center and Lodge is on Route 16, near Gorham (*Admission free*). Shelters are open on a first come, first served basis. Since even the easy trails tend to be rocky, good boots with tough soles are recommended.

## HIKE HINTS

● Drinking stream water is discouraged, as the parasite giardia is prevalent (see page 263). This causes symptoms similar to dysentery.

● Parts of the White Mountains are designated as wilderness areas, where no vehicles, fires, bicycles, or radios are allowed, and camping must be at least 200 feet from the trail.

● The Appalachian Trail is marked in white on rocks and trees. Side trails into it are blue; other trails are yellow. Two blazes together denotes a junction. A pile of sticks across a trail means that that trail is closed.

*Continued from page 205.*

**WHITE MOUNTAIN WALKS** The White Mountains are laced with trails of all degrees of difficulty. The Presidential Range has the highest summits. **Mount Washington** is popular but must not be underestimated; a recommended ascent is from Pinkham Notch and up Tuckerman's Ravine. Ask at the Appalachian Mountain Club (AMC) here first about conditions (see panel). Another rewarding hike is the **Zealand Trail** to the Zealand Falls AMC hut (3–3½ hours there and back). From the AMC building at Crawford rail depot on Route 302, an easy climb up **Mount Willard** follows a well-graded trail, an old carriage road, which takes in ledges and cliffs above Crawford Notch Zealand Campground (allow 2–2½ hours).

Along the Kancamagus Highway, photogenic **Mount Chocorua** can be approached from the trailhead leading to **Champney Falls**. The less demanding 3¼-mile **Boulder Loop Trail**, starting at Covered Bridge Campground, offers views from high rock ledges. Easier still is the **Lincoln Woods Trail** from Hancock Campground, which follows the course of an old railroad and gives river views before reaching Franconia Falls (allow 4 hours).

Northeast of Glen, Town Hall Road leads into Slippery Brook and becomes a dirt road. Farther on is the trail encircling lonely **Mountain Pond**, set beneath Slope Mountain. One of the best ridge walks above the treeline is along the **Franconia Ridge Trail**, reached from Lafayette Campground on I-93 (allow 5 hours). Ascend via the Falling Waters Trail and climb Mount Lincoln (5,089 feet); descend via the Bridal Path. **Mount Kearsarge North** (3,268 feet) is a 2,700-foot climb north of North Conway, and takes roughly 3 hours each way.

For a very arduous day's walking (for experienced and fit hikers only), an exceptionally fine route is from Route 16 south of Gorham up **Mount Jefferson**.

Further ideas for short walks are covered in the drive on pages 206–207.

*The poet Robert Frost is best known for his simple themes, his language, and his rhythms. His appeal lies in his sharp observation of daily rural scenes, which he describes in conversational language, but with delicacy and a hint at deeper meanings. In setting and in character, Frost's poetry is deeply rooted in New England.*

**Early days** Robert Frost's father, William, a teacher and newspaper editor, was a New Englander. His mother, Isabell Moodie, also a teacher, was born in Scotland, of Orkneyan origin. Robert was born on March 26, 1874, in San Francisco, where his father was working on a newspaper, but after his father's death he was taken back to New England, at the age of ten.

Frost's mother was to exert a strong influence, teaching him and his sister and encouraging the enjoyment of literature. He briefly attended both Dartmouth College in Vermont and, later, Harvard, but left to teach and to write poetry. In 1901, he began working on a farm in Derry, New Hampshire, given him by his grandfather (see page 198). Farming was to be a recurring theme of his life, one never taken very seriously as a living, but something that brought him close to nature and, in particular, botany.

**"The voice of New England"** Some of Frost's best-known poetry was written in Derry, but he received no recognition there. In 1912, he moved with his wife, Elinor Miriam White, and their children to Britain, to live in Beaconsfield, Buckinghamshire. During this time, two collections of poems written in Derry, *A Boy's Will* and *North of Boston*, were published in Britain, and to great acclaim.

After the outbreak of World War II, Frost returned with his family to America, unexpectedly famous. He bought another farm, in Franconia, New Hampshire (see page 205), and began a long association as teacher and poet-in-residence with several academic institutions, including Amherst College in Massachusetts.

Four times Pulitzer Prize winner, Robert Frost died in Boston in 1963, almost 90 years of age.

*Top: the poet's grave in Bennington*
*Above: Robert Frost on his 85th birthday*
*Below: the Robert Frost Homestead in Derry*

"I'd like to get away from earth awhile
And then come back to it and begin over.
I'd like to go by climbing a birch tree,
And climb black branches up a snow-white trunk
Toward heaven, till the tree could bear no more,
But dipped its top and set me down again.
That would be good both going and coming back.
One could do worse than be a swinger of birches."
– From "Birches."

*Yachting is big in Rhode Island, and in Newport in particular*

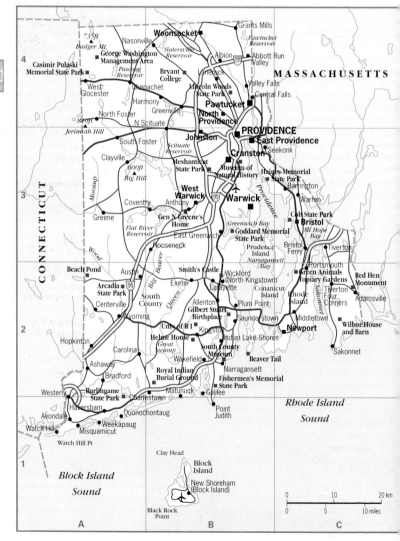

**MASSACHUSETTS**

**CONNECTICUT**

Grants Mills
**Woonsocket**
Nasonville
Pawtucket
Reservoir
*735ft*
*Badger Mt*
Slatersville
Reservoir
Albion
Abbott Run
Valley
**Casimir Pulaski**
**Memorial State Park**
George Washington
Management Area
Pascoag
Reservoir
Bryant
College
Limerock
Valley Falls
West
Glocester
Chepachet
Lincoln Woods
State Park
Central Falls
Harmony
**Pawtucket**
*810ft*
*Jerimoth Hill*
North Foster
Greenville
**North**
**Providence**
N Scituate
**PROVIDENCE**
**Johnston**
**East Providence**
South Foster
Scituate
Reservoir
**Cranston**
Seekonk
Clayville
Meshanticut
State Park
Museum of
Natural History
Haines Memorial
State Park
*600ft*
*Big Hill*
**West**
**Warwick**
Anthony
**Warwick**
Barrington
Coventry
Warren
Greene
Flat River
Reservoir
**Gen N Greene's**
**Home**
Greenwich Bay
**Colt State Park**
**Bristol**
*Mt Hope*
*Bay*
East Greenwich
**Goddard Memorial**
**State Park**
Prudence
Island
*Narragansett*
*Bay*
Bristol
Ferry
Tiverton
Mooseneck
**Beach Pond**
Austin
**Smith's Castle**
Wickford
(North Kingstown)
Portsmouth
**Green Animals**
**Topiary Gardens**
**Red Hen**
**Monument**
**Arcadia**
**State Park**
Exeter
Lafayette
Conanicut
Island
Tiverton
Four
Corners
Centerville
South
County
Allenton
**Gilbert Stuart**
**Birthplace**
Plum Point
Rhode
Island
Adamsville
Wyoming
**Univ of R I**
Kingston
Saunderstown
Middletown
**Newport**
**Wilbor House**
**and Barn**
Hopkinton
**Helme House**
*Great*
*Swamp*
Indian Lake Shores
Carolina
**South County**
**Museum**
Sakonnet
Ashaway
Wakefield
Narragansett
Bradford
**Royal Indian**
**Burial Ground**
**Beaver Tail**
Westerly
**Burlingame**
**State Park**
Charlestown
Matunuck
**Fishermen's Memorial**
**State Park**
Galilee
**Rhode Island**
**Sound**
Avondale
Haversham
Quonochontaug
Point
Judith
Watch Hill
Weekapaug
Misquamicut
Watch Hill Pt

Clay Head
Block
Island
**Block Island**
**Sound**
New Shoreham
(Block Island)
Black Rock
Point

0    10    20 km
0    5    10 miles

A                    B                    C

**RHODE ISLAND** Officially, this is Rhode Island and Providence Plantations, the state with the longest name but the smallest area, roughly 48 miles by 37 miles at its maximum dimensions. The state capital, **Providence**, lies at the northern end of Narragansett Bay, a scenic 28-mile inlet that is speckled with islands and that almost splits the state in two. The hinterland is low-lying. To the east it is densely urbanized and industrialized, while to the west it is more rural, with pockets of solitude such as the 2,600-acre Great Swamp. But it is the intricate coastline, measuring 419 miles, that most attracts visitors. Rhode Island is one of the finest sailing areas on the East Coast, and the state proudly proclaims itself as "America's first resort." Its major island, **Block Island**, has an open terrain with cliffs and a rolling countryside that remind some visitors of Scotland.

The state's remarkable architectural legacy includes 20 percent of all the nation's registered national historic landmarks. Most famous of all are the **Newport** mansions, the summer "cottages" of magnates of the coal and railroad age, but there are also fine earlier survivors. Both Newport and Providence have impressively intact colonial districts. A ferry service enables Providence, Newport, and Block Island to be enjoyed without a car.

**EARLY DAYS** Rhode Island began as a haven in a time of religious intolerance. Roger Williams, a clergyman, founded the state in 1636 after being expelled from the Puritans' Massachusetts Bay Colony for his heretical views. Williams and his followers established a settlement on the banks of the Moshassuck River and named the place Providence, as God's providence was thought to have led them there. In 1644, he traveled to England and gained a charter, reinforced in 1663, uniting the various settlements in the area as the Colony of Rhode Island and Providence Plantations. The charter gave the inhabitants a degree of independence and "full liberty in religious commencements." Hence the state became a sanctuary for religious refugees. Jews and Quakers came to Newport and made a significant contribution to the town's success. The Native American population declined after 1676, when an unsuccessful attempt by Philip, king of the Wampanoags, led his people, the Narragansetts and Nipmucks, in a war against the English colonists.

Rhode Island was the first colony to declare its independence from Britain (May 1776) but the last to become a state (1790); it celebrates May 4 as well as July 4. Providence became a commercial center with the boom in shipping and trade. The China trade, pioneered by John Brown of Providence, and the notorious Triangle Trade (see page 34) enhanced the state's prosperity. In 1793, the opening of Slater's Mill at Pawtucket touched off the move to the mass production of textiles, a landmark in America's industrialization. Skilled immigrant workers, notably from Britain, Ireland, Italy, and French Canada, heralded an expansion of the cities and the emergence of the state's tradition of industrial excellence.

▶▶▶ REGION HIGHLIGHTS

*Architecture*
**Newport Casino**
*page 216*
**Newport mansions**
*pages 216–218*
**Touro Synagogue, Newport**
*page 215*
**Benefit Street, Providence** *page 220*
**John Brown House, Providence** *page 220*
**State Capitol, Providence** *page 220*
*Museums*
**RISD Museum of Art, Providence** *page 220*
*Scenery*
**Block Island** *page 213*
**Cliff Walk, Newport**
*page 214*
*Gardens*
**Green Animals**
*page 218*

## Events

For further information, contact the state tourist office (see page 266).

### MARCH

**Irish Heritage Month**, Newport: month-long, citywide celebration of Irish heritage.

### APRIL

**Waterfire Providence**: bonfires along the Providence River.

### MAY

**Gaspee Days**, Warwick: arts and crafts festival, with colonial encampment.
**May Breakfasts**, over 100 held across the state.
**Used Boat Show**, Newport.

### JUNE

**Annual Newport Outdoor Art Festival**.
**Block Island Race Week**.
**East Greenwich Navy Days**.
**Festival of Historic Houses**, Providence: private houses and gardens specially open for tours.
**Newport International Film Festival**.
**Rhode Island National Guard Open House and Air Show**, North Kingstown.
**Schweppes Great Chowder Cook-Off**, Newport: best chowder competition.

### JULY

**Black Ships Festival**, Newport: celebration of American-Japanese trade, with sumo wrestling and kite flying.
**Civic, Military, and Fireman's Fourth of July Parade**, Bristol: the nation's oldest (1785).
**Miller Lite Hall of Fame Tennis Championships**, Newport: major professional men's grass-court tennis tournament.

**Newport Music Festival**: two weeks of classical music in the mansions.
**South County Hot Air Balloon Festival**, Kingston.
**Wickford Art Festival**: one of the East Coast's oldest, largest, and best.

### AUGUST

**Ben & Jerry's Newport Folk Festival**: the best and biggest in the country.
**Charlestown Chamber Annual Seafood Festival**.
**Newport JVC Jazz Festival**.
**Providence Waterfront Jazz Festival**.

### SEPTEMBER

**Annual Tuna Tournament**, Galilee.
**Newport International Boat Show**.
**Rhode Island Heritage Festival**, Providence.
**Rhythm and Roots Festival at Ninigret Park**, Charlestown.
**Taste of Rhode Island**, Newport.
**Waterfront Festival**, Providence.

### OCTOBER

**Edgar Allen Poe Day**, Newport.
**Newport Harvest-by-the-Sea Festival**: month-long celebration.
**Octoberfest**, Newport.
**Woonsocket Autumnfest**.

### NOVEMBER

**Ocean State Marathon**, Warwick–Providence.

### DECEMBER

**Christmas in Newport**: much of the town and several mansions are lavishly decorated, and there are candlelight tours and concerts.
**Festival of Lights**, Wickford Village.
**First Night Providence**: family-oriented citywide arts and entertainment celebration.

212

*Fishing boats on their moorings in Galilee*

## ▶ Block Island 210B1

lock Island is something of an underrated getaway.
ormed of rock debris dumped by two glaciers in the Ice
ge, the island has 200-foot clay cliffs, 365 glacial ponds,
nd an open terrain. Known by Native Americans as
lanisses ("Island of the little God") and mentioned by
e Italian explorer Giovanni da Verrazano in 1524, the
land was explored by and named after the Dutchman
driaen Block before being settled by the English in 1661.
In the 19th century, Block Island became a weekend
leasure resort, but by the 1960s much of it was boarded
p and its Victorian charm lay crumbling and forgotten.
oday, it has been spruced up, but not overdone; the
ictorian character is jealously preserved, and nightlife is
istinctly sleepy. There are more bicycles than cars out-
de the main town, and its attractions are deliberately
w-key. In fact, the island is nowhere near as busy as
lartha's Vineyard or Nantucket. The authorities are pro-
oting the island for "green" tourism as it has appeal for
aturalists and for hikers, with coastal and inland trails;
ut beware of the deer ticks, for Lyme disease (see pages
2–263) is prevalent.

The island is 7 miles by 3 miles at its maximum dimen-
ons, and is small enough to bike around at leisure (bicy-
es can be rented at the port). Alternatively, taxi drivers
ill give a tour for about $20 (the older drivers tend to
ave the best anecdotes), or you can see the island on
orseback. **Black Rock Point**, at the island's southern tip,
nd **Clay Head** (with trails), at the northeastern end, have
ne cliffs. The Greenway Trails are recommended for
ora and fauna, and there are guided nature walks for
sitors during the summer.

The main town is officially called **New Shoreham**, but is
sually known as Block Island, and has a small beach.
eaches on the south coast have no undertow (unlike
ose on the mainland) and are ideal for families. **Corn
eck**, at the north end, has the longest beach. Surfers
ould head for the south coast, while **Chaqum Pond** is the
lace for windsurfing.

### GETTING TO BLOCK ISLAND

The fastest ferry crossing is from Galilee (1 hour 10 minutes). Other ferries operate from Providence, Newport, New London (Connecticut), and Montauk (Long Island); for car reservations, tel: 401/783–4613. Flights can be taken from Westerly (New England Airlines, tel: 401/596–2460).

### BLOCK ISLAND WILDLIFE

213

In 1991, the Nature Conservancy listed Block Island among the 12 "Last Great Places" in the Americas, and 23 percent of the island is now held for nature conservation. The island is the home of the rare northern harrier and is one of only two habitats in the U.S.A. for burying beetles and regal fritillary butterflies. May brings out the snow-white flowers of the shad bush, while in the fall there is a spectacular bird migration of some 150 overwintering species.

### A FREAK VIEW

West Side Baptist Church on Block Island is the only church in the U.S.A. from where you can see the sun both rise and set over the Atlantic Ocean.

*A view along the dramatic Mohegan Bluffs toward Southeast Lighthouse, at the southern end of Block Island*

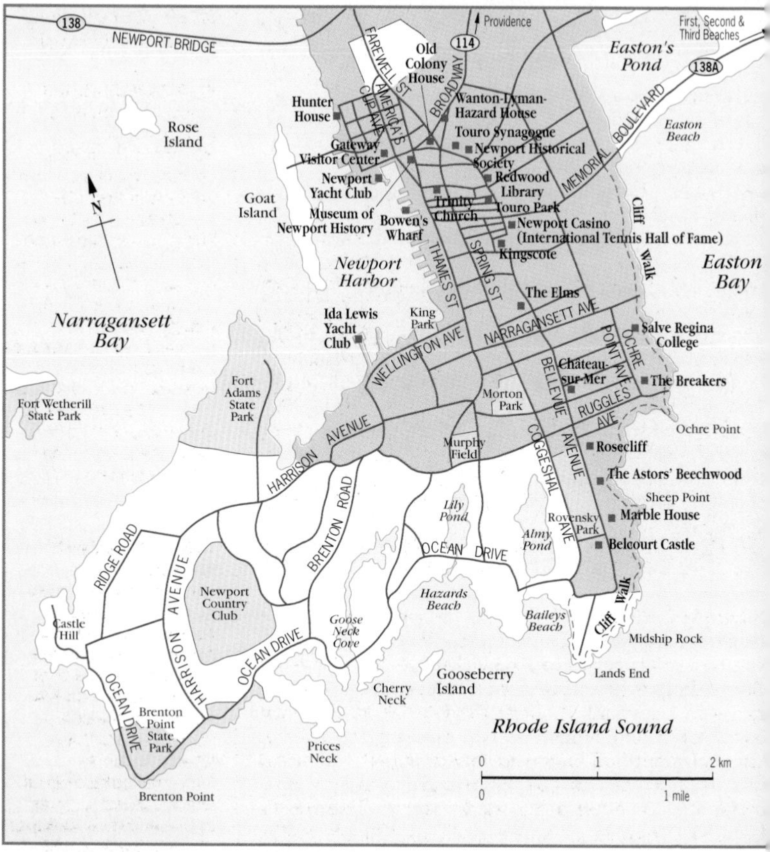
NEWPORT BRIDGE
138
114
Providence
First, Second & Third Beaches
Easton's Pond
138A
Old Colony House
FAREWELL ST
AMERICA'S CUP AVE
BROADWAY
Hunter House
Wanton-Lyman-Hazard House
Touro Synagogue
Newport Historical Society
Rose Island
Gateway Visitor Center
Newport Yacht Club
Redwood Library
Touro Park
MEMORIAL BOULEVARD
Easton Beach
Goat Island
Museum of Newport History
Bowen's Wharf
Trinity Church
Newport Casino (International Tennis Hall of Fame)
Kingscote
Cliff Walk
N
Newport Harbor
THAMES ST
SPRING ST
Easton Bay
The Elms
Narragansett Bay
Ida Lewis Yacht Club
King Park
NARRAGANSETT AVE
Salve Regina College
WELLINGTON AVE
OCHRE POINT AVE
BELLEVUE
Château-sur-Mer
The Breakers
Fort Adams State Park
Fort Wetherill State Park
Morton Park
RUGGLES AVE
Ochre Point
HARRISON AVENUE
Murphy Field
COGGESHAL AVE
AVENUE
Rosecliff
The Astors' Beechwood
Sheep Point
BRENTON ROAD
Lily Pond
Rovensky Park
Marble House
RIDGE ROAD
Almy Pond
OCEAN DRIVE
Belcourt Castle
Newport Country Club
Hazards Beach
Castle Hill
Goose Neck Cove
Baileys Beach
Midship Rock
HARRISON AVENUE
OCEAN DRIVE
Gooseberry Island
Lands End
Cherry Neck
Brenton Point State Park
Rhode Island Sound
Prices Neck
0 1 2 km
0 1 mile
Brenton Point

*Newport Bridge, leading over Narragansett Bay*

## ▶▶▶ Newport

*210C2*

With the combined attractions of its historic summer mansions and colonial architecture, its jazz festival, its sailing and regattas, its golf, its beaches, and its nightlife, Newport has a lot to offer visitors. Although the town gets busy on summer weekends, accommodations are plentiful, with a large concentration of B&Bs.

Newport is an important lobster town; lobsters can be bought fresh off the boats at Aquidneck Lobster Co. in Bowen's Wharf near the harbor, at the hub of the town's crafts and gift shops. The three main beaches are called, unsurprisingly, First Beach, Second Beach, and Third Beach. Additionally, there are a couple of small beaches off Ocean Drive. Parking fees at the beaches are expensive, but it is only a mile or so to bike out from the center of town. Good views of the ocean can be had from the 3½-mile **Cliff Walk▶▶**, which snakes above rocky shores and beaches and offers fascinating glimpses of some mansion backyards and gardens. Good shoes are needed to walk it in its entirety.

Newport in its early days was a center for religious tolerance, thanks to the liberal attitude of Roger Williams (see page 211), the founder of Rhode Island. In colonial times, Jews and Quakers made it their home, and this cultural diversity was instrumental in the town's success

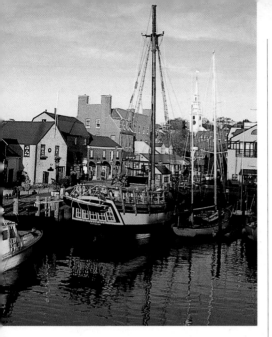

*Looking toward Trinity
Church's white steeple*

**COLONIAL NEWPORT** Despite devastation in the Revolutionary War and a long period of neglect, colonial Newport still survives to a remarkable extent: there are 200 buildings over 200 years old (the biggest such concentration in the country). Until the late 1960s, the town looked drab and numerous houses were tar-covered. Although many buildings were torn down, 60 were saved by Operation Clapboard, a campaign to encourage people to buy and renovate a historic house, and Newport's dreamed-of face-lift became a reality. Pineapple motifs are found on many of Newport's older buildings, the fruit being a symbol of hospitality in the state (sailors returning from the tropics used to display a pineapple in their windows to show they were home and receiving visitors).

Today, **Town Green** looks like a typically timeless New England green, dominated by **Trinity Church▶** (1726), which still has box pews and a galleried interior. In fact, the green was a 20th-century beautification scheme: houses were moved here after buildings were cleared.

In **Touro Park** is the town's most celebrated enigma, an open-sided stone structure in the center of a green (see panel). Nearby is the library, opened in 1748 and the oldest in the U.S.A. It is a classical, wooden building, designed to resemble stone.

The **Touro Synagogue▶▶** (*Open* Tue–Sun for tours. *Admission free*) is the oldest Jewish place of worship in the country and dates from 1763. A century earlier, Portuguese and Spanish Jews, fleeing religious persecution, found sanctuary in Newport. The elegant interior is a real surprise and contains the famous letter from George Washington to warden Moses Seixas extolling religious tolerance.

At 54 Washington Street is **Hunter House** (1748), a colonial-era house. It has period furniture made locally and a charming old-world garden.

At 17 Broadway, the restored **Wanton-Lyman-Hazard House** (1675) is Newport's oldest colonial house (*Open*

**215**

*Aerial view of The Breakers, showing the cliff walk that skirts its grounds*

## NEWPORT CASINO

This American Renaissance period piece began in 1880 as a social and residential club, gaining popularity with old-money families as lawn tennis boomed. Newport Casino hosted the U.S. National Tennis Championships (later to become the U.S. Open) from 1881 to 1914, and today hosts the men's ATP Tour Tournament, the only grass-court competition in North America. In addition to lawn tennis and court (real) tennis, Newport Casino offers croquet. The 13 grass tennis courts are the only ones in the nation available for public use. For more information, tel: 401/849-3990 or 800/457-1144.

summer; for times, tel: 401/846–0813. *Admission: inexpensive*). On Thames Street is the **Museum of Newport History▶**, a treasure house commemorating Newport's remarkable past, with exhibits on fishing, crafts, religion and social history (*Open* May–Dec, Mon, Wed–Sat 10–5, Sun 1–5; Jan–Apr, for hours tel: 401/846–0813. *Admission: moderate*). The **Doll Museum**, at 520 Thames Street, has over 600 antique and modern dolls (*Open* Mon, Wed–Fri 11–5, Sat 10–5. *Admission: inexpensive*).

The **Newport Casino▶▶** has never had anything to do with gambling, taking its name from the Italian for "little house" (see panel). Inside the casino is the **International Tennis Hall of Fame▶▶** (*Open* daily 9:30–5. *Admission: moderate*), the world's largest tennis museum and a shrine to the tennis greats, where new additions undergo an induction ceremony. In addition to the displays of vintage equipment, there are entertaining interactive videos.

**THE MANSIONS** In the 19th century, Newport became a summer playground for the elite. Mansions modeled on Italian palazzi, French châteaux, and English stately homes appeared along **Bellevue Avenue▶▶▶** and **Ocean Drive▶▶▶**. No expense was spared as European craftsmen were employed and the rooms were packed with costly objets d'art. First came the old-money families; later the new-guard Vanderbilts and others added flamboyance and entertained in their fabulous "summer cottages."

Today, numerous mansions are open to the public. It is best to select a few contrasting types, then drive or bike along Bellevue Avenue and the 9½-mile Ocean Drive to enjoy the scenery. The Preservation Society of Newport County maintains 11 properties in Newport; eight are covered here (pages 216–218), including the mansions of Kingscote, The Elms, Château-sur-Mer, The Breakers, Rosecliff, and Marble House, plus Hunter House and Green Animals (*Open* summer, daily; winter, several open on weekends; The Elms open all year, daily. *Admission: moderate; The Breakers expensive; reduced admission if more than two properties are visited.* For more details, tel: 401/847–1000).

**Kingscote►**, a gray clapboard Victorian Gothic house of 1839–1841, is notable as being Newport's first "cottage" and is more modest than its successors. The house contains family pieces of William Henry King, a China trade merchant. McKim, Mead, and White, architects of the Newport Casino, added the dining room.

**The Elms►►** (1899–1901), a French Renaissance château built by Horace Trumbauer for a coal magnate, was modeled on the Château d'Asnières near Paris.

**Château-sur-Mer►►** (1851–1852) was the first truly grand cottage, with its French-style mansard roof. Inside, a wall-painting of the Tree of Life accompanies the staircase, with overhead paintings of sky, birds, and foliage. This was a year-round rather than a summer residence and was enlarged by Richard Morris Hunt in the 1870s, his first commission in the High Victorian grand manner, although he later reverted to French and Italian styles.

**The Breakers►►►**, on Ochre Point Avenue, was designed by Richard Morris Hunt for Cornelius Vanderbilt and took 2,500 workers two years to complete in 1895. It was modeled on a 16th-century Italian palazzo, with French additions, and no expense was spared. The music room was constructed in Paris and shipped over, and there is a huge hall of Caen marble. The grandest gesture is the formal dining room, festooned with gilded garlands of fruit and cherubs, decorated with wall paintings and alabaster pillars, and lit by chandeliers. It is perhaps testament to the Vanderbilts' wealth that the house was seen only as a "summer cottage," used for about ten weeks each year; accordingly, the youngest daughter inherited it.

**Rosecliff►►**, a graceful building of 1889–1902, was modeled by Stanford White on the Grand Trianon palace at Versailles and features a Court of Love and a heart-shaped staircase. *The Great Gatsby* was filmed here.

**217**

*The ballroom at Rosecliff, the grandest of all ballrooms in Newport, where leading socialites were entertained and many dazzling soirées held*

# Rhode Island

## THE COAL MAN'S RETREAT

In 1894, while cruising in Narragansett Bay, Pennsylvania coal magnate Augustus van Wickle and his wife Bessie set their hearts on owning a summer retreat at Bristol, north of Newport. Their first house burned down in 1906, but their new 45-room "cottage," Blithewold, survives and is open to the public (*Open* mansion mid-April–mid-Oct, Wed–Sun 11–3:30. Grounds all year, daily 10–5. *Admission: mansion moderate; grounds inexpensive*). It is a delightful amalgam of English manor, Colonial, and Dutch styles, with gardens filled with exotic trees and flora.

At **The Astors' Beechwood▶** (1856), costumed guides treat visitors as though they were guests at a dinner party with the Astors in the 1890s and play the part of servants and debutantes. Special events include tea-dance tours, grand parties, cotillions, and murder mystery tours. The house lacks the physical glamour of many of the others, but many visitors prefer this livelier approach (*Open* Feb–mid-May, Fri–Sun 10–4; mid-May–Oct, daily 10–5; Nov, daily 10–4. *Admission: moderate*).

**Marble House▶▶▶** (1888–1892) was the first of the "gilded era" houses and was modeled on the Grand and Petit Trianons at Versailles. Although smaller than The Breakers, it is even more ornate. It was built for William Vanderbilt by Richard Morris Hunt, who was also involved in designing the pedestal of the Statue of Liberty and the New York Public Library. A whimsical Chinese Tea House stands close to the Cliff Walk.

**Belcourt Castle▶▶** (1891), modeled on the Louis XIII hunting lodge at Versailles, has an intimate half-timbered courtyard and 60 rooms filled with European treasures, including 13th-century stained glass and a 13,000-piece

*The magnificent ballroom at The Astors' Beechwood*

## NEWPORT FIRSTS

● In 1803, Newport was the first town in the U.S.A. to have gas street lighting.

● A Newport man was the first person brave enough to eat a tomato (previously thought to be poisonous).

● The town's synagogue was America's first (1763), as was its ferry (1657), open golf tournament (1895), and free public school (1640).

crystal chandelier from Imperial Russia (*Open* Feb–Memorial Day, Sat–Sun 10–4; Memorial Day–mid-Oct, daily 9–5; mid-Oct–Nov, daily 10–4. *Admission: moderate*).

Along Ocean Drive are the America's Cup Museum and the summer home of the New York Yacht Club, where hundreds of regattas are held each year. The mansions here are private; look for "Normandy," designed in the style of a Normandy farmhouse.

North of town, at Portsmouth, is **Green Animals▶▶**, a bewitching topiary garden featuring 21 animal and bird creations ingeniously formed from privet and yew and numerous other geometrical boxwood figures, as well as a toy museum. For **Blithewold Mansion, Gardens, and Arboretum▶▶**, see top panel.

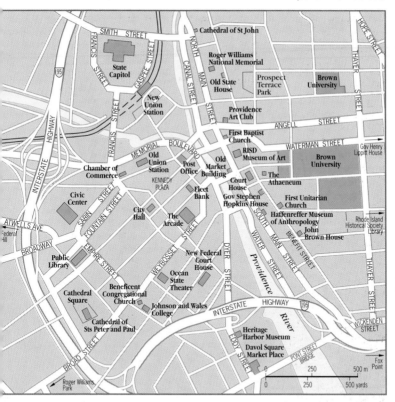

## ▶▶ Providence

*210B3*

Easily reached by commuter train or bus from Boston, Providence is well worth a visit as an example of a city renaissance. Founded by Roger Williams in 1636, it prospered as a China trade and Triangle Trade seaport. Its downtown is still compact enough to explore on foot and has a skyline graced by church spires, the State Capitol, and the art deco Fleet Bank—a mini-skyscraper known as the Superman Building. The presence of both **Brown University**, founded in 1764 and centered on College Green, and the **Rhode Island School of Design** (**RISD**) lend the downtown area a college-life air, with plenty of cafés, funky boutiques, nightclubs, and numerous bookstores along Thayer, Hope, and Wickenden streets. At the fore of the recent climate of change has been the ongoing rejuvenation of the river, with the creation of walkways and a park; in summer gondolas operate and outdoor concerts take place. In an attempt to enliven the whole downtown shopping area, artists have been enticed with tax-free incentives; many stores stand empty still. At 65 Weybosset Street, **The Arcade**, the nation's oldest covered shopping mall (1828), is a three-tier Greek Revival structure that houses food stalls and shops.

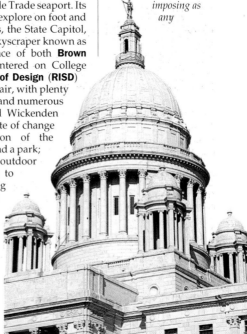

*Marble marvel: the smallest state boasts a state capitol as imposing as any*

*The Carrie Tower, a landmark of Brown University's campus*

**TOURS OF PROVIDENCE**
Guided walking tours start from the old schoolhouse at 21 Meeting Street, and trolley tours start from Kennedy Plaza. Tours of Narragansett Bay on board the *Vista Jubilee* are offered by Bay Queen Cruises and leave from Warren (tel: 410/245–1350 or 800/439–1350).

**BIRTH OF A BOOM**
North of Providence is the Blackstone River Valley, once a hive of textile mills and the cradle of the American Industrial Revolution—the catalyst for huge social change later in the 19th century. The nation's first mass production of cotton yarn using waterpowered machines took place in 1793 at Slater Mill in Pawtucket. Samuel Slater had been a manager at Arkwright Mills in Derbyshire, England, and brought technical know-how with him. The mill now functions as a museum and gives demonstrations (*Open* Jun–Labor Day, Tue–Sat 10–5, Sun 1–5 *Admission: moderate*).

The **State Capitol▶▶** (*Open* self-guiding tours Mon–Fri 8:30–4:30. *Admission free*), built of Georgia marble, was modeled on the Capitol at Washington, DC, and boasts the world's fourth largest self-supporting marble dome. Gilbert Stuart's famous portrait of George Washington hangs in the Executive Chamber, and the 1663 Charter granted by King Charles II is displayed at the entrance to the Senate.

Set on College Hill close to downtown, historic East Side displays fine Colonial, Federal, Greek Revival, and Victorian domestic architecture, 19th-century industrialists' mansions, and steep cobbled streets. Its pride and joy is **Benefit Street▶▶▶**, the city's "mile of history." Restoration began in the 1950s with the founding of the Providence Preservation Society, which bought up houses and pushed for conservation laws. A fine view extends from **Prospect Terrace**, a park where Roger Williams is buried on Congdon Street. Elsewhere along Benefit Street peep inside the **Old State House** (*Open* Mon–Fri 8:30–4:30. *Admission free*), with its tiny general assembly room, and the **Athenaeum▶**, a Greek Revival building of 1838, where Edgar Allen Poe met Sarah Helen Whitman in the book stacks (she is thought to have inspired his poem *Annabel Lee*). The **First Baptist Church▶** (1775) has a magnificent 185-foot steeple, a galleried interior and a Waterford crystal chandelier. The Browns, who endowed Brown University, were Baptists and intended it to be a Baptist ministry school; it has become an eminent and ultraliberal Ivy League university, but some commencement ceremonies are still held in the church.

At 224 Benefit Street, the **RISD Museum of Art ▶▶** has an outstanding collection that includes paintings by U.S. masters, French Impressionists, and modern artists. Highlights among artifacts of the ancient world are a wooden Buddha (ca1150) from Japan and a 4th-century Roman mosaic (*Open* Tue–Sun 10–5, Fri 10–8. *Admission: inexpensive; free Sat*). Foremost among the historic houses open to view is the **John Brown House▶▶**, built at 52 Power Street in 1786 for a wealthy China trade merchant, and later extended. It contains John Brown's chariot of 1782 (the earliest American-made vehicle in existence) and a spectacular early 20th-century bathroom with tiled murals of water nymphs (*Open* Jan–Feb, Fri–Sat 10–5, Sun 10–4; Mar–Dec, Mon holidays, Tue–Sat 10–5, Sun 12–4. *Admission: moderate*). Other museum attractions include the **Haffenreffer Museum of Anthropology** on South Main Street (*Open* Jun–Aug, Tue–Sat 11–5; May and Sep, Sat–Sun 11–5. *Admission: inexpensive*), with numerous Native American artifacts.

**Federal Hill** is the Italian quarter, with lively festivals and good restaurants; it is at its most animated around Atwells Avenue. South of downtown, **Roger Williams Park** (*Open* daily 7–9. *Admission free*) is a

Victorian creation with bandstand concerts, lakes, a natural history museum and planetarium, and a zoo.

## ▶ South County                    *210A2*

South County makes up Rhode Island's southwestern corner. Swimming and beaches are the main draw of the coast itself, although wildlife reserves here and in numerous inland wetlands attract naturalists.

Sedate **Watch Hill** is both a fishing port and resort town, with long beaches. Its Flying Horse Carousel, built in 1867, is the oldest in America. At Misquamicut, **Water Wizz** offers amusements, miniature golf, a giant water slide, and a roller-skating rink (*Open* Memorial Day–mid-Jun, Sat–Sun 10–6:30; mid-Jun–Labor Day, daily 10–6:30. *Admission: expensive*). There are several beaches between the resort towns of **Charlestown** and **Narragansett**. Near the latter, the **South County Museum**▶ displays a range of reconstructed New England buildings, including an old-time store and a cobbler's shop (*Open* May–Oct, Wed–Mon 10–5. *Admission: inexpensive*).

The quaint community of **Wickford**▶, off scenic Route 1A, has a pretty view of the harbor and abounds in antiques, crafts, and specialty shops. John Updike set his novel *The Witches of Eastwick* here. Look for signs on Route 1A for the **Gilbert Stuart Birthplace**, near Saunderstown (*Open* Apr–Oct, Thu–Mon 11–4. *Admission: inexpensive*), the home of the artist who created the portrait of George Washington seen on dollar bills. In Kingston, the **Old Washington County Jail** (1792) has changing local history exhibits and original jail cells and rooms (*Open* May–Oct, Tue, Thu, Sat 1–4. *Admission free*).

*Native American monument, Narragansett*

**THE BIRTHPLACE OF THE DINER**
Rhode Island can claim to be the true birthplace of that uniquely American institution, the diner. The semimobile cabins that can still be seen throughout the U.S. (there is a fine surviving example in the center of Providence, just off Kennedy Plaza) had their origins during the early Industrial Revolution in the Blackstone Valley, when workers were fed from horse-drawn food carts.

**A MARINE FEAST**
Bargain-priced fresh lobsters can be bought at Galilee, near Point Judith, when the boats come in at around 4–5 PM. Take a plastic bag.

*Galilee: fishing is important all along Rhode Island's coastline*

221

# Vermont

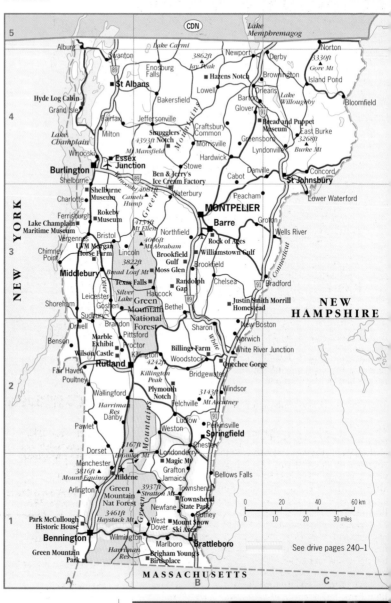

*Vermont retains the character of a retreat from the busier outside world*

*The Northeast Kingdom, with signs of the season*

**VERMONT** Vermont is a survivor, a rural state of mountains and forests, much of it unspoiled. The landscape is folded; its very name, derived from the French words for "green mountain," is descriptive enough for much of the year (although the forests you see today have taken over after cleared farmland was abandoned a century or so ago). Towns are distinctly on the small side; even Burlington is far from being a buzzing metropolis, and Montpelier, the state capital, has a villagelike quietness at night. A few days' driving around the state will leave memories of quiet, winding roads and huge red barns, of handpainted signs pointing out ATMs and homemade maple syrup outlets, of fashionable designer shops and country stores. Vermonters thrive on crafts, music, and literature, and are strongly involved in the visual arts of painting and sculpture. The events calendar always looks busy.

**THE RURAL HERITAGE** In the second quarter of the 19th century, Vermont was the wool capital of the world. Spain had been forced to sell off a great number of its flocks of sheep in 1811 to pay off Napoleonic War debts, and many of them came here. Wool production only declined in Vermont after the Civil War, when the railroads in the West allowed sheep from Wyoming and Montana to dominate the wool trade. Foreign competition from Australia accompanied this downturn.

▶▶▶ **REGION HIGHLIGHTS**

*Houses*
**Hildene**  *page 230*
**Plymouth Notch and Coolidge Birthplace**
*page 233*
*Museums*
**Ben & Jerry's Ice Cream Factory**  *page 232*
**St. Johnsbury Athenaeum**
*page 236*
**Shelburne Museum**
*page 237*
*Scenery, villages, and small towns*
**Bennington**
*pages 226–227*
**Lake Champlain**
*page 227*
**Mount Mansfield**
*page 233*
**Northeast Kingdom**
*pages 236–237*
**Woodstock**
*pages 242–243*

*Right: red barns and silos are a common sight*

"They hewed this state out of the wilderness, they held it against a foreign foe, they laid deep and stable the foundation of our state life because they sought not the life of ease but the life of effort for a worthy end."
– President Theodore Roosevelt, 1902.

**FIRSTS IN THE NATION**
Vermont was the first state in the U.S.A:
● to manufacture a postage stamp (at Brattleboro, 1846).
● to offer troops in the Civil War.
● to found a Boy Scout Club (at Barre, 1909).
● to install a chair lift (at Mount Mansfield, 1940).
● to abolish slavery (1777).

*The first pumpkins of the season: they must be picked before the frosts arrive*

Today, cows and sheep no longer outnumber the inhabitants, but dairy farming is by far the largest agricultural industry. Fruit and vegetable farming, producing hardy crops that can survive the harsh winters, also takes place. Other industries include granite and marble extraction.

The fragile character of "Vermontness" has been preserved, but only just. Proximity to the Big Apple and to Boston might change all that, although large advertising signs are banned in this last bastion of rural perfection. A state law lays down ten tough environmental conditions to be met by all new large developments, including a requirement that any buildings constructed should not adversely affect the "aesthetics, scenic beauty, historic sites, or natural areas" of the vicinity.

**VERMONT FOR VISITORS** The southern part of Vermont, with its relatively affluent communities of **Bennington**, **Manchester**, and **Woodstock**, is seductive vacation territory. Northern Vermont is appreciably quieter and emptier, except for the area around **Burlington** and **Shelburne**. The Northeast Kingdom (the northeast corner of the state) is less sophisticated, ideal for those who like to make their own discoveries.

For hikers, the 260-mile Long Trail crosses the state from the Massachusetts line to the Canadian border, via the Green Mountains and Mount Mansfield (4,393 feet), the highest peak in Vermont. You can look down on Vermont's endless mantle of forest from the top of ski lifts (many are open in summer) such as at Killington, the premier winter-sport destination in the Northeast. Other ski areas are on the small side, but there's plenty of scope for visiting several in a week.

Also firmly imprinted on Vermont's tourist map are Ben & Jerry's Ice Cream Factory near Waterbury, and the wonderfully eclectic bits-and-pieces collection of Americana at the Shelburne Museum, not far from Burlington.

# Events

For further information on any of the following events, contact the state tourist office (see page 266) or alternatively the local chambers of commerce.

**JANUARY**
**Brookfield Ice Harvest**.
**Stowe Winter Carnival**: top winter event.

**FEBRUARY**
**Fisk Trophy Race**, Woodstock: this is the oldest continually run ski race in the U.S.
**Stratton Winter Carnival**.

**MARCH**
**Maple Festival**, Woodstock.
**U.S. Open Snowboarding Championships**, Stratton.

**APRIL**
**Vermont Maple Sugar Festival**, St. Albans.

**MAY**
**Champlain Valley Quilt Show**, Shelburne.
**Spring Farm Festival**, Woodstock.
**Lilac Weekend**, Shelburne: visitors come to see over 400 lilac bushes in full bloom.

**JUNE**
**Discover Jazz Festival**, Burlington.
**Hot Air Balloon and Craft Festival**, Quechee.

**JULY**
**Bennington Museum Antiques Show**.
**Fiddlers' Contest**, Hardwick.
**Marlboro Music Festival**, Marlboro College (ends August).
**Old Time Farm Day and Grand Old Fourth Celebration**, Shelburne.
**Vermont Mozart Festival**, takes place at various locations in the state (ends August).
**Vermont Quilt Festival**, Northfield: the largest quilt event held in New England.

**AUGUST**
**Bennington Battle Day Celebration**.
**Stowe Antique and Classic Car Meet**.
**Vermont Antique Dealers Association Antiques Show**, Stratton.
**Vermont Craft Fair**, Manchester.

*Autumn color comes to the Northeast Kingdom*

225

**SEPTEMBER**
**Apple Days**, Brattleboro: hayrides, cider pressing, and an apple pie contest.
**Bennington Antique Auto and Motorcycle Show**.
**Champlain Valley Exposition**, Burlington: dairy days, fairground rides.
**Harvest Festival**, Shelburne.
**National Traditional Old-Time Fiddlers' Contest**, Barre.
**Stage Race**, Killington: bicycle race featuring Tour de France stars.
**Stratton Arts Festival**, Stratton Mountain (ends October).
**Vermont State Fair**, Rutland.
**Vermont's Northeast Kingdom Annual Fall Foliage Festival**, held at various locations (ends October).

**OCTOBER**
**Apples and Crafts Fair**, Woodstock.
**Mount Snow Craft Fair**, West Dover.
**Stowe Foliage Craft Fair**.

**NOVEMBER**
**Vermont Hand Crafters Craft Show**, Burlington.

**DECEMBER**
**Wassail Christmas Festival**, Woodstock.
**Prelude to Christmas**, Manchester.

# Vermont

*The archetypal New England clapboard church, Bennington's Old First Church*

## THE BATTLE OF BENNINGTON

On August 16, 1777, British General Burgoyne sent Hessian and Indian troops to capture military supplies stored in Bennington as part of his attempt to split the colonies in two in an advance down the Hudson River. Brigadier General John Stark countered by sending two detachments to head off the British. The battle actually took place at Walloomsac Heights (now in New York State), 5 miles from Bennington; it began at 3 PM and two hours later the British were forced to retreat.
The British failure to procure supplies resulted in defeat at Saratoga two months later, and in surrender on October 7.

## GRANDMA MOSES (1860–1961)

Born in New York State, Grandma Moses lived in Virginia and later in Bennington. As an artist she was self-taught, and her primitive, even child-like style, which captured the public imagination, is immediately identifiable. Typically her work shows village scenes or hill landscapes with tiny figures. She was perhaps more significant for recording a particular time and region in America's past than for her gifts as an artist.

### ▶ Barre                                    222B3

Pronounced "Barry," this is a blue-collar town adjacent to the **Rock of Ages▶**, the world's largest granite quarry, which covers a 50-acre site. Self-guiding tours (May–Oct, Mon–Sat 8:30–5, Sun 12–5) and narrated bus tours (Jun–mid-Oct, Mon–Fri 9:15–3. *Admission: inexpensive*) from the visitors' center give a view of the quarry, where huge blocks are lifted by derricks, and of the manufacturing division and the finished products. **Hope Cemetery**, established in 1895, has choice examples of memorials crafted from Barre granite.

### ▶▶ Bennington                              222A1

Bennington is doubly famous for its college and for the Battle of Bennington, a turning point in the Revolution (see panel). A bronze panther marks the site of the Catamount Tavern where Ethan Allen and the Green Mountain Boys plotted against the British for the capture of Fort Ticonderoga. Allen's house was beside the **Old First Church** (1805), whose magnificent steeple dominates the old village, up the hill from the modern town. The churchyard has a good number of fine carved tombstones. Among these are the graves of Revolutionary War soldiers from both sides, as well as the resting place of the poet Robert Frost (see page 209), whose epitaph records "I had a lover's quarrel with the world." The entire district of Old Bennington is worth taking in for its crisp examples of Federal-style homes. The **Bennington Battle Monument** (*Open* mid-Apr–Oct, daily 9–5. *Admission: inexpensive*), a 306-foot memorial tower, rises close to the site of the storehouse that sparked the battle. An elevator whisks you up Vermont's tallest structure for a view over three states.

**Bennington Museum▶** (*Open* Jun–Oct, daily 9–6; Nov–May, daily 9–5. *Admission: moderate*) has a collection of Grandma Moses paintings (see panel opposite), as well as numerous examples of Bennington glassware and pottery, plus musical instruments, Revolutionary War exhibits, and the oldest Stars and Stripes flag in existence.

Route 67 passes the **Park McCullough Historic House▶** (*Open* late May–late Oct, Thu–Mon 10–3. *Admission: moderate*) on West Street, North Bennington, a cheerful yellow 35-room Second Empire Victorian mansion. Built as a summer cottage in 1875 and occupied by four generations of one family up to 1965, it retains original furnishings and even the owners' clothing, diaries, and 37,000 documents. It hosts regular music recitals.

Also on Route 67A, **Bennington Center for the Arts** is an exclusive, liberal, and progressive institution, the home, from April through October, of the professional Oldcastle Theatre Company (tel: 802/447–0564). Here, plays, readings, and an August music festival are presented.

### ▶ Burlington
222A4

Set beside Lake Champlain on the state's western border, Burlington is a college town whose population increases drastically in the fall. Apart from the considerable attractions of Lake Champlain, the largest city in Vermont hosts numerous arts and music events and is a place worth stopping at for its shops. It has a range of "environmental" stores, sidewalk cafés, and the pedestrian zone of Church Street Marketplace. Of the town's four beaches, North Beach is the best.

**Lake Champlain▶ ▶**, 128 miles long, up to 12 miles wide, and the largest body of fresh water in the U.S.A. outside the Great Lakes, lies between the Hudson River and New York to the south and the Richelieu River and Montreal to the north. Lake views can be enjoyed from a number of points on the shore, notably Red Rocks Park in South Burlington and Sand Bar State Park at Milton (where there are windsurfer and boat rentals). To appreciate the lake's shoreline and sunsets, try a cruise (late May–mid-Oct) on the *Spirit of Ethan Allen II* from Burlington (tel: 802/862–8300).

The **Lake Champlain Maritime Museum at Basin Harbor▶**, near Vergennes (*Open* mid-May–mid-Oct, daily 10–5. *Admission: moderate*), has historical and maritime displays, boat-building demonstrations, and a working forge. On Grand Isle, **Hyde Log Cabin** dates from 1783 and is one of the country's oldest log cabins. Built by surveyor Jedediah Hyde, Jr., whose family stayed here for 150 years, the cabin houses maps and memorabilia.

**CHAMP**
Lake Champlain has its own version of Scotland's Loch Ness Monster, known as Champ. This creature gets occasional "sightings." In 1982, the Vermont House of Representatives passed a resolution to protect the beast from "any willful act resulting in death, injury, or harassment."

**ACROSS THE LAKE**
The ferry from Burlington to Port Kent, New York State, is handy for visits to Ausable Chasm (*Open* mid-May to mid-October). This sandstone gorge, with rapids and whirlpools surging beneath 200-foot cliffs, can be seen from a boat ride and a ¾-mile walkway. Farther south, on Route 74, a ferry gives access to the New York side at Fort Ticonderoga, begun in 1755 by the French to block the British and now mostly reconstructed and marketed for the tourist industry. Between mid-May and mid-October, costumed guides explain the history of the fort, and cannon firing and period music supply the background atmosphere.

227

*The lively Church Street Marketplace, Burlington*

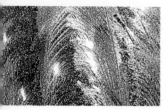

*New England's long, cold winters bring plenty of snow, and New Englanders certainly know how to make the most of it. Resorts, though generally small, offer great variety; locals flock to them at weekends. To make the most of a full week you may wish to sample a range of places or activities.*

## FURTHER INFORMATION

● The brochure *Skiing in New England* is available from Discover New England (see page 266).
● Maine Handicapped Skiing assists those with disabilities with programs at Sunday River; tel: 207/824–2440; fax: 207/824–0453.
● The American Skiing Company's ME ticket covers Killington, VT; Mount Snow, VT; Sugarbush, VT; Sugarloaf U.S.A., ME; Sunday River, ME; Attitash Bear Peak, NH; The Canyons in the Rockies, Steamboat, CO; and Heavenly, CA/NV.

## ICE CLIMBING

Frozen waterfalls are targets for ice climbers. For details, contact the International Mountain Climbing School, Main Street, P.O. Box 1666, North Conway, NH 03860 (tel: 603/356–7064; e-mail: guides@ime-usa.com).

*Many gondolas are open to nonskiers*

**Downhill (Alpine) skiing and snowboarding** Vermont, New Hampshire, and Maine are the prime downhill destinations, and snowmaking virtually guarantees good conditions from November to April in many areas. You can rent equipment at all resorts, child care is available, the standard of instruction is very high, and most skiers are well mannered. Total beginners might consider learning in mid-week: there are inexpensive packages available, covering accommodations and rentals, and you avoid the weekend crowds. Bromley in southern Vermont is one of several smaller, family-oriented places ideal for learning, where the more expert runs are well separated from the rest. Passes are less expensive than at nearby Stratton, the birthplace of snowboarding, which is a single mountain with a full range of runs and a resort. Snowboarding has gained massive popularity with teenagers in particular; beginners will find themselves falling a lot at the outset, but learning is rapid. Some areas have special snowboard parks, with jumps and half-pipes. On a much larger scale is Killington (and adjacent Pico), New England's biggest winter resort, with some very long beginner runs and plenty of challenging terrain.

From Stowe, you can take in Mount Mansfield or the easier runs on Spruce Peak, or you can ski to Smugglers' Notch, New England's premier family winter resort. Wachusett, the closest ski area to Boston, is excellent for children, beginners, and intermediates. Massachusetts' main skiing is in the Berkshires, including Jiminy Peak.

The White Mountains ski areas each have enough skiing for three days or so (if you plan to stay longer, the Ski New Hampshire Pass is useful). Of these, Bretton Woods is best for families and beginners, Waterville Valley, Attitash

Bear Peak, and Loon are all-rounders (Loon has plenty for nonskiers, including an animal park and a skating rink), and Cannon appeals to intermediates and experts.

Maine's resorts, out of range for day trips from Boston or New York, avoid the weekend crowds. Sunday River encompasses eight mountains, 3 miles across, with something for everyone, including long, easier runs with views all the way. This can be combined with Sugarloaf, where the treeless summit offers the highest skiing in New England (a 2,820-foot drop from the 4,237-foot summit) and superb views over three states and Canada.

**Cross-country (Nordic) skiing** Much of this sport's appeal lies in its sense of freedom: there's no waiting around for lifts, you can take prepared trails at your own pace, and you can stop where you like. However, while cross-country on flat trails is easily mastered, even experienced downhill skiers should have some instruction in the technique for steeper descents, and long uphill sections can make considerable physical demands. Passes and equipment rentals are much less expensive than for downhill skiing.

The Von Trapp family (of *Sound of Music* fame) introduced cross-country skiing to the U.S. at Stowe, which now has New England's premier network. The Von Trapp trails have glorious views toward Mount Mansfield, and high up in the woods is a tiny log cabin where skiers are greeted with an open fire and bowls of soup. Vermont's many other cross-country centers include Blueberry Hill near Goshen and Mountain Top near Killington, named after just two of the many cozy inns from which you can ski from the door. Additionally, you can ski from inn to inn along the Catamount Trail (for details, contact Roy Jackson Country Inns, tel: 802/247–3300; www.inntoinn.com).

In the White Mountains there are fine views of the Presidential Range from the Bretton Woods and Great Glen ski areas (both of which are good for beginners), as well as from the more challenging trails at Jackson, New Hampshire's main cross-country center.

In Maine, Sunday River and Sugarloaf both lie below the downhill resorts of the same name. Acadia National Park offers coastal skiing on its carriage roads.

**WINTER VARIATIONS**
There are good networks of snowmobiling routes in Vermont, in the White Mountains, and in the Rangeley Lakes area of Maine. These machines have impressive traction, can be rented, and are easy to drive; youngsters aged 12 to 18 must have instruction. Snowshoeing needs no instruction at all, and shoes can cope with steep slopes and ice. You can also try out tubing—hurtling down a run on a rubber tire—or take a horsedrawn sleigh ride.

*Several resorts have special snowboard parks, although most ski slopes are also open to snowboarders*

▶ **Manchester** 222A1

Pristine-looking old Manchester Village, with its white houses and marble sidewalks, has been a pleasure resort and spa since the 1850s. Nowadays the village merges into Manchester Center, often something of a traffic jam owing to the popularity of its outlet shopping and crafts and country stores.

On the southern fringes of the village is **Hildene**▶▶ (*Open* mid-May–Oct, daily 9:30–4. *Admission: inexpensive*), a 24-room Georgian Revival mansion, the home of Robert Todd Lincoln, son of Abraham and Mary Lincoln. Mary discovered this elite mountain village retreat, and the Lincolns spent the summer here in 1863 to recuperate in the midst of the Civil War. Robert made Hildene his home, and his descendants lived here until 1975. Today, the house, with its family furnishings and memorabilia, offers interesting insight into the lives and times of the Lincolns. Highlights include landscaped grounds and a self-playing Aeolian organ. Also in Manchester is the **American Museum of Fly Fishing** (*Open* May–Oct, daily 10–4; Nov–Apr, Mon–Fri 10–4. *Admission: inexpensive*), with the rods and reels of President Eisenhower, Bing Crosby, and other celebrities.

**230**

**COVERED BRIDGES**
Spanning rivers and streams all over the region, wooden covered bridges, built from the 1830s onward, are now recognized as historic landmarks. These pretty structures—often painted in reds, greens, or blues, and by the nature of their setting almost inevitably highly picturesque—are immortalized by photographers (particularly in the fall). Their *raison d'être* seems to be to protect the wooden bridge from the weather, particularly snow—though some say they prevented horses from taking fright. They are usually named after their builder or the river they cross.

*Manchester, with its upscale stores, is popular as a base for fishing and other outdoor sports*

Manchester lies beneath the commanding peak of **Mount Equinox▶▶** (3,835 feet). The highest point in the Taconic Range, it is reached by the Sky Line Drive toll road (*Open* May–Oct, daily 8 AM–10 PM. *Admission: moderate per car*).

At Arlington, south of Manchester, the **Norman Rockwell Exhibit** comprises reproductions of the famous illustrator's work (see page 150). A 15-minute film show is included (*Open* May–Oct, daily 9–5; Nov–Dec, Feb–Apr, daily 10–4. *Admission: inexpensive*). Northwest on Route 30, **Dorset▶** is a showcase village in a conspicuously attractive setting and has a summer playhouse (tel: 802/867–5777).

▶ **Middlebury and the Green Mountains**    *222A3*

Middlebury is a small but bustling college town, picturesque and unfussy, dominated by the four-tiered, wedding-cake steeple of its Congregational church. Crafts are popular, with the nonprofit Vermont State Craft Center based with other craft outlets in the old mill complex in Frog Hollow. On Park Street, the **Sheldon Museum**, displaying furniture and decorative arts (*Open* summer, daily 1–5; winter, Mon, Wed 1–4, Tue, Thu–Fri 3–5. *Admission: inexpensive*), has been open since 1882.

Out of town on Route 23, past a rare two-way covered bridge, the **UVM Morgan Horse Farm** (*Open* May–Oct, daily 9–4. *Admission: inexpensive*) still breeds the famous versatile Morgan horses and gives tours of its stables (see panel). Farther north is **Vergennes**, with over 100 craft and other shops in its Factory Marketplace. At Ferrisburgh is **Rokeby Museum▶** (*Open* mid-May–mid-Oct, Thu–Sun), a fascinating 11-room Quaker family home that was once a focus of abolitionist activity and a stop on the Underground Railroad.

West of **Orwell** is a relic of the Revolutionary War: Mount Independence, a peninsula jutting into Lake Champlain that was fortified to defend against a British attack from Canada. The visitor center fleshes out the historical background, and trails lead past blockhouses, a stockade, and the remains of batteries.

The **Green Mountain National Forest** describes an area of densely wooded, rounded hills covering much of western Vermont. The majority of it is unspoiled and offers countless opportunities for walking. On Route 125, the 1-mile **Robert Frost Interpretative Trail** begins close to the site of the poet's summer cabin: Frost's verses are placed along the route, which crosses damp bogs and passes through scrub and woodland. **Silver Lake**, east of Leicester, has a ½-mile shoreline interpretive nature trail, and there is a shorter circuit around the nearby **Falls of Lana** (both in Branbury State Park). More dramatic hikes include the hour-long walk to **Sunset Ledge** from Lincoln Gap, east of Lincoln. **Bristol Ledges** (1,825 feet) is the highlight of a 1-mile trail above the pleasant town of Bristol and provides views of the village and of Lake Champlain. More ambitious is the 3–4-hour walk on the **Long Trail** to Mount Abraham from Lincoln Gap, with its rocky 4,006-foot summit rising above the timberline.

**Kingsland Bay**, on Lake Champlain northwest of Vergennes, and **Lake Dunmore** in Branbury State Park are good for swimming.

**MORGAN HORSES**
In the 18th century, a Massachusetts school-teacher named Justin Morgan came to Vermont and created the country's first horse breed. He was second owner of a rough-coated, hardy colt born in 1793 called Figure, which had attributes of both draft and riding horse and was muscular and compact with plenty of stamina but a gentle disposition. Figure, renamed Justin Morgan, was first used as a working horse, then for breeding in Woodstock. From 1878, Colonel Joseph Battell Hardy continued the stock line. Morgans seen at Middlebury's UVM Morgan Horse Farm and elsewhere look much now as they did then, and they commonly live to 30 years.

231

# Vermont

*The golden dome of the State House, Montpelier, seen against the early autumn sky*

**MOUNTAIN GREENERY**
As you ascend Mount Mansfield, notice the changes in vegetation as the climate gets harsher. The typical New England trees are found lower down (sugar maple, yellow birch, and beech). Farther up the slope are pine, white birch, red spruce, and balsam fir, and finally tundra. At the summit is the largest community of arctic-alpine flora in Vermont.

*"Vermont's Finest"— Ben & Jerry's ice cream*

▶ **Montpelier**                                    *222B3*

Vermont's state capital is scarcely more than a country town graced by the golden dome of the State House. A good local view of the town can be obtained by climbing from Elm Street to Winter Street and up into Hubbard Park, where a stone tower in the woods provides an all-round panorama. Life continues at an amiable pace in a town small enough to make a relaxing base. Alongside the alternative lifestyle of the Horn of the Moon Café, on Langdon Street, Montpelier has the New England Culinary Institute and a large insurance industry.

The **State House▶** (*Open* Mon–Fri 8–4. Guided tours Jul–mid-Oct, Mon–Fri 10–3:30, Sat 11–2:30. *Admission free*) has been restored to its original 1859 appearance internally and is the third building on its site—the first State House became too cramped, and its 1838 successor was the victim of an exploding stove. Next door, the **Vermont Historical Society Museum** (*Open* Tue–Fri 9–4:30, Sat 9–4, Sun 12–4. *Admission: inexpensive*) has well-displayed, changing exhibitions about various aspects of state life

**Ben & Jerry's Ice Cream Factory▶▶** (see also page 234), near Waterbury on Route 100 north of I-89, has become Vermont's biggest visitor attraction (*Open* daily. *Admission: inexpensive*). The free samples are the lure; although the tour omits the factory on Sundays, the samples are larger. The tours are very popular: you may have to wait hours, but there are kids' activities (face-painting and so on) and ice cream to be eaten. Cow souvenirs of the wackiest kind proliferate in the gift shop. There is also a Hall of Fame, featuring the ink-scrawled napkin used by former school friends Ben Cohen and Jerry Greenfield to plan their ice cream pickups on their marathon promotion journey ("Scoopathon") across the U.S.A. giving free samples of their super premium ice cream as they went. It proved a hugely successful public relations venture. From humble beginnings in an abandoned filling station in Burlington in 1978 on a $12,000 investment, their ice cream business has become an international success.

Other Vermont specialties are produced at the **Morse Farm Sugar Works**, outside Montpelier, and the **Cold Hollow Cider Mill**, on Route 100.

## ► Mount Mansfield and Stowe     222B4

Vermont's highest peak, Mount Mansfield (4,393 feet), rises amid some of the state's grandest scenery. At Stowe Mountain Resort, on Route 108 some 6 miles north of Stowe, are the toll road and gondola (*Open* mid-Jun–mid-Oct, daily 10–5. *Admission: expensive*) up the mountain. The toll road winds up the slopes for 4½ miles; bicycles are not allowed (*Open* late May–mid-Oct, daily 10–5. *Admission: expensive per car*). Farther north along Route 108, at Spruce Peak on the right, a chair lift gives access to the Alpine Slide, a summer sled ride. At **Smugglers' Notch**, the road rises to 2,162 feet, with 1,000-foot cliffs on either side. During the War of 1812, when trade with Canada was forbidden, much cattle smuggling took place here.

Stowe, the main skiing and recreation center for the area, has a wide choice of high-class dining and lodging. Many of the hotels in the town have an Austrian appearance, including the Trapp Family Lodge (tel: 800/826–7000), still owned by the Von Trapps of *The Sound of Music* fame, although the original lodge structure has been replaced. The **Stowe Recreation Path** gains lovely riverside views.

## Plymouth Notch     222B2

This tiny and remote hamlet was the birthplace and home of "Silent Cal," Calvin Coolidge (1872–1933), president of the United States between 1923 and 1929 (see pages 42–43). Today, the hamlet is part museum, and one ticket covers all the sites (*Open* late May–mid-Oct, daily 9:30–5. *Admission: moderate*). The modest homestead that was the **Coolidge Birthplace** is much as it was, with a quilt and a miniature chest of drawers he made himself; the **Coolidge Homestead** is the family's later home. The visitor center tells of the president's life, while the (still-functioning) store displays a "Drink Moxie" sign—a memento of his favorite drink. Upstairs in the latter building, the **Coolidge Hall** served as the Summer White House: the nation's affairs were conducted with a staff of two from this humble place. The huge barn next to the visitor center houses family carriages.

The village **cheese factory**, built in 1892, offers hand-made cheddar-type products, including an extra-sharp cheese matured for two years. Cheese-making takes place from Monday to Wednesday, when visitors are welcome.

**MOUNT MANSFIELD**
The remarkable resemblance Mount Mansfield has to an upward-facing head has meant that each protuberance is named accordingly on the map: the Forehead, the Adam's Apple, the Chin, and the Nose. Native folklore speaks of the mountain as a sleeping giant. The Chin, reached by a 1¼-mile trail, is the true summit.

**233**

*Stowe: a classic landmark*

**SILENT CAL**
A dinner party guest once jested, "Mr. President, I have made a bet with my friends that I can get more than two words out of you this evening." Coolidge replied, "You lose."

*Out of Vermont's rolling hills and lush valleys come a range of distinctive products. There are the famous traditional cheeses (including cheddar, colby, and Monterey jack); there are McIntosh apples and there is cider; there is honey, chocolates, and hams. And then there is maple syrup, and Ben & Jerry's.*

### LIQUID GOLD

Maple syrup is sold in a variety of grades: Fancy, or Grade A Light Amber (delicate flavor, light color); Grade A Medium Amber (the most popular); Grade A Dark Amber (stronger flavor, dark color); and Grade B (robust color and flavor, good for cooking). You can sample them all at the New England Maple Museum in Pittsford (see page 235) or the Maple Grove Maple Museum and Factory in St. Johnsbury (see page 236). During the maple-sugaring season (March and April), visitors are welcome at farms listed in the brochure *Maple Sugarhouses Open to Visitors*, available from Vermont Department of Agriculture, 116 State Street, Drawer 20, Montpelier, VT 05620-2901 (tel: 802/828-2416).

*Vermont farm produce includes maple syrup (below) and cider (right)*

**Vermont's finest** All over Vermont there are black-and-white cows. A good many are the Holstein (Holstein-Friesian) cows grazing in the fields; others are Woody Jackson's Holy Cows. Woody Jackson is an artist, and his famous symbols of Vermont appear on anything from mugs and boxer shorts to the T-shirts produced for Ben & Jerry's.

Ben & Jerry's makes Vermont's Finest All Natural Ice Cream, in over 50 "euphoric flavors." But making great ice cream (and frozen yogurt) is only part of the Ben & Jerry's story that has so captured the public imagination. For Ben Cohen and Jerry Greenfield, serving the community is just as important as making a profit: some 7.5 percent of pretax profits go to nonprofit organizations working for progressive social change, and half the proceeds of the Waterbury factory tours (see page 232) go to Vermont charities. So popular have Ben and Jerry found their ice cream to be, that they have now taken them abroad, notably to Britain.

**Maple syrup** See steam billowing up from the sugar houses that dot the Vermont landscape and you know spring has arrived. Ideally the temperature will be about 40°F in the daytime, but there will still be a light frost at night. Under these conditions, sap rises up the sugar maple tree (*Acer saccharum*), and the sugar farmer gets "a good run"—any warmer and the tree bursts into bud and the sap stops rising.

The farmer drills holes in the trunk, into which he fits spouts through which the sap drains, either into galvanized buckets or into long plastic pipes that feed directly into a holding tank in the sugar house. The buckets (up to three per tree) take several hours to fill, and about 40 gallons of sap will have to be boiled down to make 1 gallon of syrup.

### ▶ **Proctor** 222A2

roctor and its larger neighbor, Rutland, e at the heart of Vermont's marble-roducing district (see panel). **Rutland** is plenty of budget accommodations rving the huge **Killington** ski area (see ges 228 and 243). Massive blocks of ck are cut and dressed at the Vermont larble Company, whose **Vermont larble Exhibit** ▶ (*Open* mid-May–Oct, ily 9–5:30. *Admission: moderate*) dis-ays the virtues of marble here in the rm of a marble chapel (complete with eonardo da Vinci's *Last Supper*, also in arble) and a series of bas-reliefs epicting every U.S. president.

**Wilson Castle** ▶, south of Proctor, was uilt in 1874 by Dr. Robert Johnson for s wife Sarah, who had set her heart on ving in a castle in the Green Mountains. nfortunately, the marriage broke up st as the 32-room castle was being com-eted. It is still lived in and feels like it, ith a welcome lack of roping off. espite being an architectural hodge-odge with Dutch gables and French enaissance-style mansards and turrets,

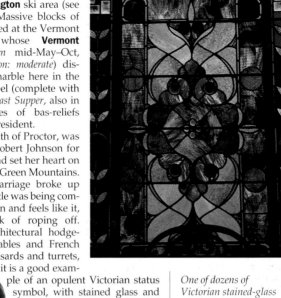

it is a good exam-ple of an opulent Victorian status symbol, with stained glass and painted ceilings. European and Far Eastern antiques adorn an interior dramatically bathed in golden light (*Open* late May–mid-Oct, daily 9–6. *Admission: moderate*).

North of Pittsford on Route 7, the **New England Maple Museum** (*Open* Mar–Dec, daily. *Admission: inexpensive*) is at the back of a huge gift shop selling syrup by the gallon, maple candy, and numerous other Vermont special-ties. The exhibition shows the many maple sugar-making meth-ods used over the ages, along-side the most complete collec-tion of old sugar-making e q u i p m e n t known; there is also a film and free samples.

**235**

*One of dozens of Victorian stained-glass windows in Wilson Castle*

**VERMONT MARBLE**
This material is extracted from Dorset Mountain near Danby, the largest underground marble quarry in the world. The qualities of the 400 million-year-old rock are advertised in an extrava-gant marble bridge in Proctor. More famous examples of its use are at the Beinecke Rare Book and Manuscript Library at Yale University in New Haven, the U.S. Supreme Court in Washington, DC, and the UN Building in New York City.

*A sculptor works in Vermont marble*

# Vermont

## ST. JOHNSBURY'S ATHENAEUM

This pristine Victorian-style art gallery is the oldest unaltered example of its kind in the U.S.A. It was presented to the townspeople by businessman Horace Fairbanks in 1873 to house *Domes of Yosemite*, a major work by Hudson River School artist Albert Bierstadt, whose works form a major part of the collection. Critics despaired of "a profound loss to civilization," claiming that the painting would be "doomed to the obscurity of a Vermont town where it will astonish the natives." Nevertheless, its installation drew visitors from all over the world.

**236**

*St. Johnsbury and the forests, hills, and valleys of the Northeast Kingdom that surround it*

## ▶▶ St. Johnsbury and the Northeast Kingdom
222C4

The modestly sized town of **St. Johnsbury**▶, known locally as St. Jay, harbors a few surprises. One is the main street itself, a fetching Victorian survival, with its brick mansions and granite churches. Another is the room at the back of the town library housing the celebrated **Athenaeum**▶▶ art museum (*Open* during library hours. *Admission free*; see panel). Also on the main street, the **Fairbanks Museum and Planetarium** (*Open* Jul–Aug, Mon–Sat 10–6, Sun 1–5; Sep–Jun, Mon–Sat 10–4, Sun 1–5. *Admission: moderate*) is yet another Victorian period piece; the museum houses natural history exhibits, tribal artifacts, and dolls in its old-fashioned barrel-vaulted hall. At the tiny **Maple Grove Maple Museum and Factory** you can watch the sugar-making process and see maple candies being packed—and find your shoes sticking to the floor (*Open* Mon–Fri 8–4. *Admission: inexpensive*.)

St. Johnsbury is a good base for excursions into the three northeastern counties that comprise the remote-feeling **Northeast Kingdom**▶▶. North of the town, **Burke Mountain** (3,267 feet) is accessible by toll road and boasts 120-mile panoramic views. **Lake Willoughby**▶, beside Route 5A, is popular for windsurfing, boating, and fishing, and swimming for those hardy enough. Hikers can take the 7-mile circular route up adjacent **Mount Pisgah** (2,751 feet). Adventurous naturalists might care to seek out **Victory Bog**, a huge wetland preserve harboring rare plants, as well as moose and black bear. The rural character of the area is exemplified by the **Bread and Puppet Museum**▶, south of Glover on Route 122 (see panel opposite). At Cabot is the farmers' Cabot Creamery Co-op (*Open* Jun–Oct, daily; Nov–Dec, Feb–May, Mon–Sat. *Admission: inexpensive*), renowned for its sharp cheddar cheese.

**Craftsbury Common**▶, conspicuously attractive high up on a ridge road (part of a military route to Canada built in the 1780s), was painted white for Alfred Hitchcock's *The Trouble with Harry* (1955) and has stayed that way ever since. Route 14 north of here and the unclassified road southwest to Route 15 give a good idea of the quiet beauty of the Northeast Kingdom. Willey's General Store at nearby **Greensboro** is one of the best stocked in Vermont; its outside wall serves as the local bulletin board.

At **Brownington**, an out-of-the-way hamlet in the far
north where the paved road turns to a dirt one, is the **Old
Stone House**, the former county grammar school built by
Reverend Alexander Twilight, a black minister, in the
1830s. It now houses a local history museum (*Open
Jul–Aug, daily 11–5; mid-May–Jun, Sep–mid-Oct, Fri–Tue
11–5. Admission: moderate*), run on a shoestring, with
everything donated by locals.

### ▶ ▶ Shelburne                                    222A4

At Shelburne is the remarkable **Shelburne Museum ▶ ▶ ▶**
(*Open late May–late Oct, daily 10–5; late Oct–late May, tour
of selected buildings 1 PM. Admission: expensive*), an
unrivalled collection of buildings, reassembled and
packed with Americana and American folk art, which was
the creation of Mrs. Electra Havemeyer Webb. Her love of
everyday objects started as a hobby, the collection being
housed in a public museum when the first building, a
schoolhouse, was moved here in 1947. Other structures
then followed, including a general store, jail, inn, and covered bridge. To see the wide-ranging collection properly—
over 80,000 items in nearly 40 buildings—a full day is
needed (tickets are valid for two consecutive days). Do not
miss the quilt collection, the 1890 private rail car, the
*Ticonderoga* (America's last surviving vertical-beam side-
wheel steamboat, once in service on Lake Champlain), and
the Electra Havemeyer Webb Building (a stylish New York
apartment adorned with Impressionist paintings).
To the north, **Shelburne Farms ▶** was an agricultural
experiment set up with Vanderbilt money (see panel).
Today, it plays a semieducational role in demonstrating
stewardship and farm animals, with a family-oriented,
hands-on activity area, cheese-making, a farm trail,
90-minute tours, and farm animals. Also of interest are the
**Vermont Teddy Bear Co.** on Route 7, and **Vermont
Wildflower Farm**, in Charlotte (*Open May–Oct, daily 10–5.
Admission: inexpensive*).

*The SS Ticonderoga
is preserved at the
Shelburne Museum*

**BREAD AND PUPPET**
Glover is the home of the
Bread and Puppet Theatre
troupe, founded in New
York in 1962 but based in
Glover since 1974. Its
rickety looking barn, a
free "museum" (*Open
May–Oct, daily 10–5*),
displays the giant
Expressionist-style
puppets, masks, and
props used in previous
shows and pageants.
Sourdough bread is given
to audiences, symbolizing
that theater is as much a
necessity as bread.
Performances in the field
across the road attract
audiences of 20,000-
strong. Some camp out
the night before. The
troupe regularly tours the
U.S.A. and Europe.

"I did not want to create a
village...I was anxious to
create something in
arrangement and
conception that had not
been tried."
– Electra Havemeyer
Webb, founder of the
Shelburne Museum.

**A FARM OF THE FUTURE**
Shelburne Farms was
founded in the late 19th
century by Dr. William
Seward Webb and Lila
Vanderbilt Webb as a
grand agricultural experiment. Dr. Webb purchased
32 farms and hired the
services of landscape
architect Frederick Law
Olmsted, designer of
Central Park in New York
City, and forester Gifford
Pinchot, known in the U.S.
today as the father of
forestry. Architect Robert
H. Robertson designed the
three main buildings on
the property. The
Shelburne House, once
the Webbs' family
residence, is now the comfortable Inn at Shelburne
Farms and restaurant
(*Open mid-May–mid-Oct*).

*Quilts and rugs, weather vanes and whirligigs, trade signs and decoy ducks, baskets, boxes, and wooden toys—New England's myriad antiques shops, its dozens of crafts shops, and many of its museums are stuffed with examples, old and new, of these folk crafts.*

## STENCILING

Kitchen utensils, containers, walls, and pieces of furniture were commonly painted and decorated with motifs. Some of these patterns were applied with stencils, and itinerant stencilers would work from pattern books, using milk-based paints in dusky shades.

**238**

*Right: a spinner practices an ancient craft*
*Top: crazy quilting*

## DO-IT-YOURSELF

Visitors interested in patchwork and quilting will enjoy a browse in the many shops that sell everything needed. Keepsake Quilting (Senter's Marketplace, Centre Harbor, New Hampshire; catalog available) claims to be America's largest quilt shop, with thousands of small prints as well as plains. Paints for stenciling can be found in craft supply shops but are also readily available in many hardware stores.

## SPRUCE GUM BOXES

Lumbermen whiling away the evenings in the logging camps of Maine, New Hampshire, and Vermont used to carve little wooden boxes for a wife or sweetheart to hold a gift of spruce gum. These were often in the shape of books and fitted with a slide at one end, and were typically carved with hearts and a cross.

**Quilts and coverlets** Winters have always been hard in New England, and the early colonists certainly needed the quilted bed coverings that had long been traditional in Europe. Cloth was in short supply, so the tradition of piecing scraps of leftover fabric together was an economic necessity. Some patchwork designs crossed the Atlantic with the early settlers: "Log Wood," used in the north of England, for instance, became known as "Log Cabin," and some Pennsylvania quilts, made by settlers from Germany, used designs known in Europe since the Renaissance. Other patterns, such as "Bear's Paw," were clearly inspired by new experiences. As material became

more available, small pieces were appliquéd onto larger areas, often representing the farmhouse, its occupants, and animals, so that the quilt was a personal journal of its creator's life. Old quilts are collector's items, while modern ones are sold widely across New England.

The colonial coverlet, woven in cotton in overshot patterns, traditionally in blue and cream, is another craft that dates back hundreds of years. Popular as throws, modern versions of these cotton blankets in various, usually pastel colors may be found in numerous crafts outlets.

**Baskets and boxes** Market baskets, half-bushel and bushel baskets, fish baskets, berry baskets, clothes baskets, sewing baskets, feather baskets (in which to collect feathers until you had enough to stuff a pillow)—in the days before containers were made of mass-produced material, the Native Americans made baskets in dozens of shapes and sizes, traditionally using the brown ash (*Fraxinus nigra*). The Native Americans are still noted for their basketry, though now it is made for the tourist trade. Glass beads may have been replaced by plastic, and colored strips are no longer dyed with berries, but basketry is an unbroken tradition, passed from generation to generation. The Shakers, who made a unique contribution to

*Scrimshaw jagging wheels or pie-crimpers*

### SCRIMSHAW

Dating from the whaling boom of the early 19th century is the type of carving called scrimshaw. Using a sail needle or jackknife, sailors out at sea carved exquisitely detailed designs on whalebone or teeth, which they then etched in black. There are many examples of scrimshaw in maritime museums and the old captains' houses.

### CIGAR STORE FIGURES

The Shelburne Museum in Vermont (see page 237) has a room full of these carved figures. Up to 6 feet high, they normally depicted Native Americans, wearing or carrying the tobacco leaves that they introduced to the colonists.

*Weather vanes are now more decorative than functional*

merican crafts, were famed for their baskets as well as or their oval boxes and furniture (see pages 148–149).

**arving** Native Americans introduced the early colonists o the use of duck decoys in hunting. Made at first of skin nd feathers, they were later made of wood, carved and ainted more and more realistically until the decoy ecame a folk art form. The Shelburne Museum in ermont has the largest decoy collection in the world. New England's was a seafaring and farming community, ependent on the weather, and many buildings would ave a weather vane on the roof, cut from metal or carved wood in a variety of shapes. Along the coast, fish, meraids, and ships were popular designs, while a farm uilding would often be topped by a cow or sheep. A varint, the "whirligig," had paddles that kept it turning in a ind; the noise it made, they say, kept the moles at bay. o sought-after are these traditional pieces of folk art ow that thieves have been known to go to the extent of ropping a line from a helicopter to grab an antique off a of. Reproductions are popular, decorative items.

Boat-builders turned their skills to woodcarving, too, nd some made magnificent figureheads for the ships ey built. Woodcarvers produced signs to hang outside hops, painted to advertise their specialty. They also ade little models of subjects dear to them: a mapleugaring scene, a team of working horses, or farmers ain-sawing.

*Southern Vermont is prime territory for crafts, from the fancifully ornate to such simple items as these turned dishes at the Weston Bowl Mill*

# Drive

## Southern Vermont

*See map on page 222 (yellow route).*

This is a tour of southern Vermont's choicest rural retreats. Allow a very full day to sample the craft shops and the village atmosphere, and maybe to enjoy a walk in Townshend State Park.

Start from **Manchester▶** (see pages 230–231). A few miles east, Bromley Ski Area stays open all year round and operates an alpine slide and a chair lift up to a 360-degree lookout, with views over five states. There are a number of hiking trails from the summit.

Then stop off at **Weston▶**, home to the Vermont Country Store, to browse in its quintessentially Vermont-style craft shops, of the homespun rather than the designer variety. Clustered around the green and village bandstand are the old sawmill, now housing a tinsmith's workshop and a display of antique tools, and the Weston Playhouse, Vermont's oldest professional summer theater (tel: 802/824–5288). Just to the north, in an appealingly ramshackle old sawmill that began life in 1902, the Weston Bowl Mill carries inexpensive wooden products. Southward, the Toy Works stocks wooden toys, marionettes, and more. The Farrar-Mansur House (*Open* Memorial Day–Jun, Sat–Sun 1–4; Jul–Labor Day, daily 1–4. *Admission: donation*) is a former colonial tavern.

**Chester▶** is quiet and prosperous-looking, with some classic old-fashioned shops, including a drugstore with an enamel sign and the famously offbeat Inn at Long Last along its main street. The National Survey Charthouse ("Clear, correct, complete" boasts its motto) has local hiking maps. A rare group of stone houses is found a mile out of Chester by turning off the main street by Jiffy Mart.

Rising from a bridge, immaculate **Grafton▶▶**, a former wool-making

*Covered bridge at Brattleboro*

and soapstone-quarrying village, was rescued from partial dereliction and is now one of Vermont's best-looking villages. It makes a point of having plenty of nothing to do, though there are historical society and natural history museums. Crafts fans can observe a smithy at work and see cheddar cheese being made at the Grafton Village Cheese Company. A covered bridge can be seen in Townshend Road.

On Route 35 to Townshend, the road is briefly unpaved. Continue 2 miles

more of a cultural than a rural center. The Museum and Art Center in Union Railroad Station opens May to October. Connecticut River Tours offers cruises on the *Belle of Brattleboro* (Wed–Sun in summer and at foliage time; tel: 802/254–4565).

Maple syrup stalls accompany Route 9 west. **Marlboro College**, a liberal arts establishment that is one of America's smallest colleges, with just 260 students, hosts a major summer chamber music festival, founded in 1951 by the legendary Rudolf Serkin,

*The Old Tavern Inn, in the pristine village of Grafton*

west of Townshend on Route 30, past the **Scott Covered Bridge**▶ on the left, then turn left across the dam to **Townshend State Park**▶ (*Open* mid-May–Columbus Day. *Admission: inexpensive*). Here you can walk 1,100 feet up Bald Mountain, which rises above the treeline and has fine views of Mount Monadnock and West River Valley. The 1.8-mile trail has both steep and gentler routes. Nearby, Townshend Dam (*Admission free*) offers swimming and canoeing from a manmade sand beach.

**Newfane** offers a touch of grandeur around its green, with its county courthouse, Congregational church, and old inns. **Brattleboro**, a redbrick administrative and manufacturing town, is

which attracts big names. Its Tyler Gallery is a showcase of regional artistic talent (*Open* Mon–Fri during the school year. *Admission free*).

Westward, the road climbs to **Hogback Mountain**▶, giving an extensive view south, with the prominently pointed Haystack Mountain (3,420 feet) visible to the northwest. Close by, the slopes of Mount Olga offer pleasant walks in Molly Stark State Park. **Wilmington** is a small resort town on the main road, but there are quieter accommodations nearby in the Mount Snow resort area to the north. Continue west to **Bennington**▶▶ (see pages 226–227) before turning north to explore **Arlington** and to enjoy the spectacular scenic drive up **Mount Equinox**▶▶ (see page 231) on the way back to Manchester.

# Vermont

**FOR BUDDING SCIENTISTS**

The Montshire Museum of Science at Norwich (north of Windsor) is a leading children's attraction in central Vermont. Sited on the Connecticut River, it has outdoor nature trails, an aquarium, and a snake show, plus a bubble room and tunnels to explore. Emphasis is firmly toward hands-on activities (*Open* daily 10–5. *Admission: moderate*).

*A fisherman faces the challenges of the Quechee Gorge*

**ALONG THE RIVER**

The Connecticut River flows 250 miles along the Vermont–New Hampshire border, and was the waterway along which numerous early settlers came to these parts. North Star Canoe Rentals (tel: 603/542–5802) offers canoeing to the covered bridge and to the Sumner Falls from Cornish, New Hampshire, as well as winter sleigh rides.

▶ **Windsor** 222B2

Windsor has the longest covered bridge in New England, spanning 460 feet over the Connecticut River and the border with New Hampshire. On Main Street are the Vermont State Crafts Center and the former Elijah West tavern, known as the **Old Constitution House** (*Open* Memorial Day–Columbus Day, Wed–Sun 11–5. *Admission: inexpensive*). Vermont's constitution was signed here in 1777, and a historical display relating to this event accompanies period furnishings, toys, and artifacts. From June through September and at fall foliage time a train runs from Bellows Falls to the Chester area for admiring the foliage. On South Main Street, the **American Precision Museum**, housed in an 1846 armory and machine shop, is a tribute to historic technical innovations (*Open* Memorial Day–Oct, daily 10–5. *Admission: moderate*).

North of Windsor, **White River Junction**, once a busy railroad junction with 50 passenger trains daily and an eight-track crossing, has tours of Catamount Brewery. Southwest of Windsor, **Mount Ascutney**▶ (3,144 feet) can be ascended by following hiking trails from routes 44, 44A, and 131, or by taking the 3.8-mile toll road. Its summit, a ½-mile walk from the parking lot, looks over the Green and White mountain ranges.

You get a good idea of the rural feel of Windsor County by taking Route 106 through **Felchville**, with its miniature-looking buildings, then along the flat valley bottom, past

cornfields and maple syrup outlets. **Stoughton Pond** lies just off the main road and has swimming, a picnic site, and a nature trail in very pretty surroundings. **Perkinsville** is grander but still unspoiled, with white chainlink fencing around its green.

▶▶ **Woodstock** 222B2

A self-consciously pretty village at the heart of Vermont, with its own covered bridge and numerous handsome Federal-style homes, Woodstock has captured the public imagination as epitomizing that elusive quality called "Vermontness." However, the crowds of visitors and the concentration of boutiques, galleries, and designer shops have also given it the veneer of a sophisticated all-year resort. Money was poured into Woodstock by the

Rockefellers, who had family ties with the Billings Farm and Woodstock Inn. The **Dana House Museum** on Elm Street offers a glimpse inside one of Woodstock's many well-preserved Federal-style architectural gems (*Open May–Oct, Mon–Sat 10–5, Sun 12–4. Admission: inexpensive*).

To get to the **Billings Farm and Museum▶** (*Open May–Oct, daily 10–5. Admission: moderate*), follow Elm Street out of the village and turn right past the bridge on River Road. This premier local attraction provides a rare chance to look around a working farm, with butter-making, crafts, and milking demonstrations. Established in 1871, the farm has had an outstanding Jersey herd since the 1880s, and in the pristine milking parlor each cow's name, birthday, pedigree, and honors are recorded above its stall. The museum offers farm artifacts and a film, while a renovated 1890s farmhouse gives a glimpse of a well-to-do farming household. The **Vermont Raptor Center**, 1½ miles from town on Church Hill Road (*Open Mon–Sat. Admission: moderate*), displays around 26 species of owls, hawks, and eagles that, because of their injuries, cannot survive in the wild.

Route 4 east of Woodstock crosses the **Quechee Gorge▶▶**, dubbed the "Little Grand Canyon" of the Ottauquechee River. The 165-foot chasm can be looked into from the road bridge itself or from the half-mile trail to the bottom. An old riverside mill in the former textile village of **Quechee** is home to Simon Pearce Glass, where you can watch glassblowers and potters at work. The **Theron Boyd House**, a survivor from the preelectric era and the state's oldest unaltered dwelling, is currently closed awaiting restoration funding (tel: 802/295–7900 for information).

West of Woodstock lies **Bridgewater**, offering tours of the Mountain Brewery, makers of Long Trail Ale, and **Killington**, the largest ski area in Vermont (see panel and page 228). Easily accessible by chair lift, 4,241-foot Killington Peak has a nature trail, enabling study of its mountain plants, and views extending to the Adirondacks and White Mountains.

## EUREKA: A SCHOOL

At Springfield, south of Windsor, Eureka Schoolhouse stands next to an 1870 covered bridge and is Vermont's oldest one-room schoolhouse. Completed in 1790, it was abandoned in 1900 and underwent wholesale restoration in 1968. It is now open to public view (*Open Memorial Day–Columbus Day, Tue–Sun. Admission free*).

**243**

## KILLINGTON IN SUMMER

Even when the snows have gone at Killington, New England's biggest ski area, the resort keeps busy. The Killington/Pico Adventure Center has waterslides, a climbing wall, an in-line skate and skateboard park, and hiking trails. The Alpine Slide traverses 3,410 feet over ski trails. There are more than 50 miles of mountain-bike trails (bike rental available): you take the lift up and bike down at full speed. The resort also offers an 18-hole golf course, and a playhouse (tel: 802/422–9795). For details of all the activities, tel: 802/422–6200; www.killington.com.

*Attractive Woodstock offers some chic shopping*

**CHILDREN'S MUSEUMS**
● **Connecticut**
Manchester, Mystic
Seaport, New Haven,
and Niantic.
● **Rhode Island**
Pawtucket.
● **Maine** Portland.
● **New Hampshire**
Portsmouth, Londonderry,
Keene Science Center at
Holderness.
● **Massachusetts**
Boston, Dennisport, and
Falmouth on Cape Cod,
Acton, Dartmouth, Easton,
Foxboro, Holyoke, and
Plymouth.

244

**AMUSEMENT PARKS**
● **Connecticut** Quassy
Amusement Park, by Lake
Quassapaug, Middlebury.
● **Maine**
Funtown/Splashtown
U.S.A., Saco, biggest chil-
dren's park in southern
Maine; Aquaboggan Water
Park, Saco.
● **Massachusetts**
Riverside Park, Agawam,
near Springfield, largest
amusement park in New
England; Water Slide and
Family Fun Center,
Westport, near Fall River;
Cartland, Wareham, buddy
and indy-style carts,
bumper boats; Water
Wizz, Wareham, wet and
wild thrills and spills.
● **New Hampshire** Plenty
around Weirs Beach, Lake
Winnipesaukee (see panel
on page 197), and at
Hampton Beach on the
coast. In the White
Mountains are Santa's
Village, Six Gun City,
Whale's Tail Water Park,
Attitash Bear Peak, and
Story Land.

*One way of getting
supper: an improvised
fishing expedition*

# New England for children

**THE GREAT OUTDOORS** In summer, take a whale-watching cruise or lobster-trapping outing (see pages 164 and
116); join a moose search or a sunrise beaver-spotting
canoe trip (see page 201); go for a swim, sail on a lake, or
take a picnic on a walk in a forest park. There are rental
facilities on many rivers for canoeing and rafting.

In the mountains and forests of the northern states there
is excellent mountain biking (ski lifts carry the bikes to the
mountaintop), and there are miles of bicycle trails on
Cape Cod National Seashore (see pages 154–159). At
many ski resorts you can take a cable car to the top of the
mountain for a spectacular view (especially in the fall). In
some places (such as Bromley Mountain in Vermont and
Attitash Bear Peak in New Hampshire) you can take a
chair lift up and a slide down. In the winter, there is the
whole gamut of snow sports (see pages 228–229), and as
for spectator sports, there are hockey and basketball
games galore to watch.

**MUSEUMS AND ATTRACTIONS** "Hands-on" is the buzz
word. Children's museums can be found throughout the
region (see panel) and many others have special rooms,
exhibits, or events for children. Listed below are just some
of the dozens of attractions featured in official state
guides. Aquariums and a selection of amusement parks
are listed separately in the panels, and most places are
covered in more detail elsewhere in this guide.

## CONNECTICUT
**Mystic Seaport** and **Maritime Aquarium at Norwalk** are
popular with older children who like ships, history, and
the sea. The **Denison Pequotsepos Nature Center** near
Mystic has nonreleasable birds of prey and 7 miles of
trails. In the Connecticut River Valley, the **Essex Steam
Train and Riverboat Ride** combines a train ride with a
riverboat cruise. The **Science Center of Connecticut**,
West Hartford, has hands-on exhibits and a planetarium.

You can see inside a lighthouse by visiting the **Old Lighthouse Museum** in Stonington, handle a live python in the discovery room of the **Peabody Museum of Natural History**, New Haven, and you can dissect a model human body at the **Children's Museum of Southeastern Connecticut** in Niantic (see page 107).

## MAINE

The four-level **Children's Museum of Maine** in Portland is one of the best of its kind in New England—meet Mr. Bones, the bicycling skeleton, and read the news on television. The **Maine Maritime Museum** at Bath has a variety of interesting exhibitions in its restored shipyard buildings. The **Seashore Trolley Museum** at Kennebunkport has the world's largest streetcar and railway car collection, while at **Boothbay Railway Village** (see page 121) you can take a train ride through gnome-inhabited woods. York's **Wild Kingdom**, on Route 1, is a zoo and amusement park. When in Maine, you should also try to visit a lighthouse.

## MASSACHUSETTS

**In and around Boston** The city is so visually exciting that most children will get a thrill out of just being there: take them up one of the skyscrapers (**Prudential Center Skywalk** or **John Hancock Observatory**), enjoy the free entertainment of **Faneuil Hall Marketplace**, ride the swan boats in the **Public Garden,** take in **Harvard Square**, visit the **Mapparium** and USS *Constitution* in **Charlestown Navy Yard**. Older children will find **Filene's Basement** fun for bargain shopping. The **Children's Museum**, the **New England Aquarium**, and the **Museum of Science** are all big crowd pleasers. Sports fans can take tours of **Fenway Park** and the **FleetCenter** (see pages 68 and 81). On a hot summer's day, take a boat trip from Long Wharf to Georges, the largest of the Boston Harbor Islands, for a picnic. Water taxis go from there to the other islands, where you can explore old forts.

At Salem on the North Shore (see pages 184–185) you can go into a jail cell, attend a mock trial, and do some gravestone rubbing at the **Salem Wax Museum**. At Plymouth (see pages 177–179), **Plimoth Plantation** and the *Mayflower II* make an expensive but unforgettable outing. The **New Bedford Whaling Museum** is one of the best.

**The Springfield area and the Pioneer Valley** History really comes alive at **Old Sturbridge Village**, a re-creation of life in the 1830s (see page 173). Young dinosaur experts will insist on seeing the quarry of dinosaur tracks at **Dinosaur Land** in South Hadley and on meeting *Tyrannosaurus rex* in the **Springfield Science Museum**. See page 175 for the **Words and Pictures Museum** in Northampton, in the Pioneer Valley, and page 187 for the **Basketball Hall of Fame**.

*History comes alive at Old Sturbridge Village*

### FOR THE SPORTS ENTHUSIAST

Young basketball fans will want to try their skill at the Basketball Hall of Fame in Springfield, Massachusetts (see page 187). Tennis players should visit the International Tennis Hall of Fame in Newport (see page 216). The action-packed New England Sports Museum in Lowell (see panel on page 171) and at the FleetCenter in Boston (see page 68) gives a hands-on taste of everything sporty.

### AQUARIUMS

● New England Aquarium, Boston.
● Mystic Aquarium and Maritime Aquarium at Norwalk, Connecticut.
● Maine Aquarium, Saco, Maine.
● Aqua Circus Aquarium and Zoo, West Yarmouth, Cape Cod, Massachusetts.

*Boston Common's very famous ducklings*

**VACATION READING**
Small children will love Robert McCloskey's 1940s classic *Make Way for Ducklings* (available in several languages), the endearing story of a mother duck looking for a home for her family by Boston's Charles River. Bring the book to life by taking a guided walk from Boston Common along the route described in the book, with readings and stops to feed the ducklings' descendants. Children leapfrog the bronze duck sculptures in the Public Garden.

**Cape Cod and the Islands** Here are miles of sandy white beaches for windsurfing, swimming, and sailing. At Brewster is the excellent **Cape Cod Museum of Natural History** (see page 155), while the Wellfleet Bay Sanctuary has programs for the under-sixes and canoe trips for the over-12s (who must be accompanied by an adult).

## NEW HAMPSHIRE

At the **Ruggles Mine**, near Grafton, you can tap away with a hammer and explore the old mine. The **Christa McAuliffe Planetarium**, Concord, is one of the world's most advanced, while **New Hampshire International Speedway**, near Canterbury, is the biggest venue of its kind in New England. **Clark's Trading Post** is a museum, railroad, and bear show. **Story Land** at Glen is a theme park for younger children. Not to be missed is the cog railway up **Mount Washington** (see page 205). In Portsmouth, on the coast, children can join in workshops in some of the **Strawbery Banke** buildings (see page 202).

## RHODE ISLAND

**Roger Williams Park** in Providence hosts a zoo, natural history museum, and planetarium, and there's boating in the park. Older children will learn about the factory age at the **Slater Mill Historic Site**, birthplace of the American Industrial Revolution (see panel on page 220), at Pawtucket, while younger ones will enjoy a trip on the canal. Many of the **Newport Mansions** will impress young and old alike. For Newport's **International Tennis Hall of Fame** in the Casino, see page 216.

## VERMONT

Fun is the word, too, at **Ben & Jerry's Ice Cream Factory** (see pages 232 and 234). Take in a visit to a maple syrup museum and sample the candy at **New England Maple Museum**, Pittsford, or **Maple Grove Maple Museum and Factory**, St. Johnsbury. The **Shelburne Museum** (see page 237) is one for all ages. Birds of prey are sheltered at the **Vermont Raptor Center**, near Woodstock, while at Norwich the **Montshire Museum of Science** is an excellent hands-on museum (see panel on page 242).

*A Ben & Jerry's could well be the highlight of the day*

# Travel Facts

## Arriving

### Airports

Boston's **Logan International Airport** is the international terminal for New England, and terminals C and E have the usual assortment of car rental desks and tourist information facilities (*Open* Mon–Fri 8 AM–9:30 PM, Sat–Sun 11 AM–9:30 PM), as well as a hotel reservation desk covering the whole of New England (no commission charged to customers; *open* daily 8:30 AM–11:30 PM).

A number of smaller airports are handy for destinations in other parts of New England. **Bradley International Airport**, in Windsor Locks, Connecticut, north of Hartford, is convenient to southern Massachusetts and all of Connecticut. **Theodore Francis Green State Airport**, just outside Providence, Rhode Island, is another major airport. Additional New England airports served by major carriers include those in Manchester, New Hampshire; Portland and Bangor, Maine; Burlington, Vermont; and Worcester, Massachusetts. Among U.S. airlines serving the region are: **American** (tel: 800/433–7300), **Continental** (tel: 800/525–0280), **Delta** (tel: 800/221–1212), **Northwest** (tel: 800/225–2525), **TWA** (tel: 800/221–2000), **United** (tel: 800/241–6522), and **US Airways** (tel: 800/428–4322).

### Getting into Boston

Excellent public transportation gets you into downtown Boston. From Logan International Airport's terminal building, leave the main exit and cross to the courtesy bus stop, where buses marked with a circled T provide a free shuttle service to the Airport subway station, on the Blue Line (see pages 52–53). From here it is a few stops to the downtown area. Alternatively, the Airport Water Shuttle carries passengers to Rowes Wharf in the Financial District (Mon–Thu 6 AM–8 PM, Fri 6 AM–11 PM, Sat 10 AM–11 PM, Sun 10 AM–8 PM). A courtesy bus (with frequent service) picks passengers up at stops outside the terminal building. The water shuttle takes only a few minutes to cross Boston Harbor and provides good views of the Boston Tea Party Ship, the Bunker Hill Monument, and most of the city's tallest buildings.

On weekdays, a nonstop Logan Express shuttle van (tel: 800/23–LOGAN) operates from the airport to South Station in the Financial District. Taxis are available at all terminals; in 2000, fares to downtown Boston and

Cambridge averaged about $10–18 compared to 85¢ on the subway, $10 on the water shuttle. There are also buses to South Station (tickets $6).

If you are renting a car at the airport, remember to carry some cash—you will need to pay a toll at the Sumner Tunnel in order to reach Boston.

### What to take

The principal rule on weather in New England is that there are no rules. A cold, foggy morning can and often does become a bright, 60°F afternoon. A summer breeze can suddenly turn chilly, and rain often appears with little warning. Thus, the best advice on how to dress is to layer your clothing so that you can peel off or add garments as needed for comfort.

*The Connecticut Valley Railroad is one of only two steam railways in New England*

Showers are frequent, so pack a raincoat and umbrella. Even in summer, you should pack long pants, a sweater or two, and a waterproof windbreaker, for evenings are often chilly and the sea spray can make things cool on a whale-watch or deep-sea fishing trip. If you'll be walking in the woods, take heavy boots and expect to find mud. Winter requires heavy clothing, gloves, a hat, warm socks, and waterproof shoes or boots.

Casual sportswear—walking shoes and jeans—will take you almost everywhere, but swimsuits and bare feet will not: shirts and shoes are required attire at even the most casual venues. In Boston, the most cosmopolitan New England city, you may want to dress up. Jacket and tie are required in better Boston restaurants, at a number of inns in the Berkshires, and in the occasional more formal dining room elsewhere.

In summer, take a hat and sunscreen. Also pack insect repellent—and use it! Recent outbreaks of Lyme disease (see pages 262–263) all over the East Coast make it imperative (even in urban areas) that you protect yourself from ticks in early spring and right on through the summer.

Pack an extra pair of eyeglasses or contact lenses in your carry-on luggage. If you have a health problem that requires a prescription drug, pack enough to last the duration of the trip. Pharmacies, especially in rural areas, may be closed on Sunday. Don't pack prescription drugs in luggage that you plan to check in, in case your bags go astray. Pack a list of the offices that supply refunds for lost or stolen traveler's checks.

**249**

*A ride around Faneuil Hall Marketplace provides an easy introduction to Boston*

## Essentials

### Climate and seasonal considerations

New England's climate is characterized by warm summers, pleasant if somewhat unreliable spring and fall seasons, and extremely cold winters.

Spring can bring glorious weather, with warm days and cool nights; there are fewer tourists than in summer and fall, so room rates are lower. Maple sugaring takes place in northern New England. Inland, April is "mud season," while blackflies (whose bites are not so much painful as annoying) proliferate in late May and early June in parts of the north.

Memorial Day is the start of the migration to the beaches and the mountains, and summer begins in earnest on July 4. Those who are driving to Cape Cod in July or August should know that Friday and Sunday are the days weekenders clog the overburdened Route 6.

More museums and houses open their doors in summer than at any other time of year. July and August see the coastal and lake resorts crowded and the roads jammed with traffic. At this time the events calendar is packed with festivals.

Brilliant foliage attracts visitors from all over the world in the fall, making this the busiest season; hotel rates are high and the famous foliage areas, such as the Berkshires, White Mountains, and Green Mountains, become very busy. The first scarlet

*Winter invariably brings snow to many parts of New England*

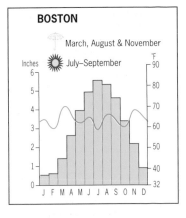

**BOSTON**

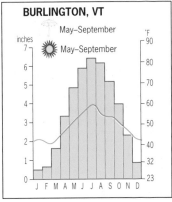

**BURLINGTON, VT**

and gold colors emerge in mid-September in northern areas; "peak" color occurs at different times from year to year. Generally, it is best to visit the northern reaches in early October and then move southward as the month progresses (see box on page 18 for Fall Foliage Hotlines).

Conversely, the coast sees fewer crowds after Labor Day. The days are mild, the nights cool. There are also plenty of events, such as country fairs and crafts markets, at this time, and roadside produce stalls are common.

A marked lull occurs after the leaves fall in late October, but much happens at Christmas and First Night

> ❏ "There is a sumptuous variety about the New England weather that compels the stranger's imagination—and regret...in the spring I have counted one hundred and thirty-six different kinds of weather inside four-and-twenty hours."
> – Mark Twain, speech given in New York City, December 22, 1876. ❏

(see page 194). Winter brings enough snow to many areas to make New England a major winter sports destination (see pages 228–229), and when natural snow is lacking, the region has the greatest snowmaking capacity in the U.S. T.V. and radio forecasts and ski reports in New England keep people informed about the weather.

### Money matters
**A.T.M.s** Many automated teller machines are tied to international networks such as Cirrus and Plus. You can use your bank card at A.T.M.s to withdraw money from an account and get cash advances on a credit-card account if your card has been programmed with a personal identification number (P.I.N). Check in advance on limits on withdrawals and cash advances within specified periods. On cash advances, you are charged interest from the day you receive the money from A.T.M.s as well as from tellers. Transaction fees from A.T.M. withdrawals away from your home turf may be higher than for withdrawals at home. For specific Cirrus locations in the United States and Canada, call 800/424–7787. For U.S. Plus locations, call 800/843–7587 and press the area code and first three digits of the number you're calling from (or of the calling area where you want an A.T.M.).

*Patience pays off at an A.T.M.*

251

**Wiring money** You don't have to be a cardholder in order to send or receive a MoneyGram from American Express for any sum up to $10,000. To send a MoneyGram, go to a MoneyGram agent in a retail or convenience store or American Express travel office and pay up to $1,000 with a credit card and anything over that in cash. You are allowed a free long-distance call in the U.S. to give the transaction code to your recipient, who need only present identification and the reference number to the nearest MoneyGram agent to pick up the cash. MoneyGram agents are in more than 120 countries (for locations, tel: 800/926–9400). Fees range from 3 percent to 10 percent, depending on the total and how you pay. You can also use **Western Union**. To wire money, take either cash or a cashier's check to the nearest office or call and use MasterCard or Visa. Money sent from the United States or Canada will be available for pickup at agent locations in 78 countries within minutes. Once the money is in the system, it can be picked up at any one of 22,000 locations (tel: 800/325–6000 for the one nearest you).

**Sales tax** Sales tax is added to certain items, including meals and lodging. Connecticut sales tax is 6 percent (12 percent meals/lodging); Rhode Island, 7 percent (no tax on clothing and meals, 5 percent on lodging); Massachusetts, 5 percent (except clothing purchases under $175 in Boston and Cambridge, which are not taxed; no tax on meals but 9.7 percent on lodging); Vermont, 5 percent (9 percent meals/lodging); and Maine, 5.5 percent (no tax on meals; 7 percent on lodging); New Hampshire, no tax payable except 8 percent on meals and lodging.

### Opening times

Many museums close on Monday and on public holidays. Smaller museums and many houses open between Memorial Day and Labor Day or mid-October. Attractions often open 10 AM–5 PM (be there by 4 PM for guided tours); few places open before noon on Sunday.

Information on hours is given for guidance only. We have tried to ensure accuracy, but things do change. Check locally before your visit.

### Public holidays

Roads and attractions are often busy, and accommodations get booked up during New England's holiday weekends. The busiest holidays are New Year's, Memorial Day, Fourth of July, Labor Day, Thanksgiving, and Christmas. In addition, there are a number of holidays (listed below) that are celebrated in just some of the New England states. Stores usually remain open on these days, but some attractions and services (particularly those that are maintained by the state) are closed.

● **Lincoln's Birthday** February 12 (Vermont only).
● **Town Meeting Day** First Tuesday in March (Vermont only).
● **Evacuation Day** March 17 (Suffolk County, Massachusetts, only).
● **Patriots' Day** Monday nearest April 19 (Massachusetts and Maine only).
● **Fast Day** Fourth Monday in April (New Hampshire only).
● **Bunker Hill Day** June 17 (Suffolk County, Massachusetts, only).
● **Victory Day** Second Monday in August (Rhode Island only).
● **Bennington Battle Day** August 16 (Vermont only).
● **Election Day** First Tuesday after first Monday in November (New Hampshire, Rhode Island, and Vermont only).

*The Fourth of July is celebrated with fireworks, pageants, and parades*

## Tours and packages

Fully escorted tours and independent packages take the hassle out of planning and provide a better idea of how much a vacation will cost. Year-round, escorted tours are usually sold in three categories: deluxe, first-class, and tourist or budget class. Top operators in the deluxe category include:

● **Maupintour** (Box 807, Lawrence, KS 66044, tel: 800/255–4266).

● **Tauck Tours** (11 Wilton Road, Westport, CT 06881, tel: 800/468–2825).

In the first-class category are:

● **Brush Hill/Gray Line** (39 Dalton Avenue, Boston, MA 02199, tel: 617/236–2148).

● **Caravan Tours** (401 North Michigan Avenue, Chicago, IL 60611, tel: 312/321–9800 or 800/227–2826).

● **Collette Tours** (162 or 180 Middle Street, Pawtucket, RI 02860, tel: 401/728–3805 or 800/340–5158).

● **New England Vacation Tours** (Box 560, Mount Snow Village, West Dover, VT 05356, tel: 802/464–2076 or 800/742–7669).

● **Parker Tours** (255 Executive Drive, Plainview, NY 11803, tel: 516/349–0575 or 800/833–9600).

Most itineraries are jam-packed. To judge just how fast-paced the tour is, review the itinerary carefully.

Independent packages are offered by tour operators that may also do escorted programs and by many other companies—from large, established firms to small, new entrepreneurs. Airline operators include:

● **American Airlines Vacations** (tel: 800/321–2121).

● **Continental Airlines Vacations** (tel: 800/634–5555).

● **TWA Getaway Vacations** (tel: 800/438–2929).

● **United Airline's Vacation Planning Center** (tel: 800/328–6877).

Also look into **Americantours International** (347 5th Avenue, 3rd floor, New York, NY 10016, tel: 212/683–5337 or 800/340–7284).

*Wherever you are staying in the summer months, there's usually a festival nearby: (above) jazz in Burlington, and (below) the Maple Festival in St. Albans, Vermont*

## ting around

**ing** Because the six New England states form a relatively compact region with an effective network of interstate highways and other good roads linking the many cities, towns, and recreational and shopping areas that attract visitors, a car is the most convenient means of travel. Yet driving is not without its frustrations; traffic can be heavy on coastal routes and beach-access highways on weekends and in midsummer, and Newport in summer and Boston all year long are inhospitable to automobiles. Each of the states makes available, free on request, an official state map that has directories, mileage, and other useful information in addition to routings. The speed limit in much of New England is 65 mph (55 mph in more populated areas).

**Roads** Apart from the heavily congested roads of downtown Boston, driving in New England is a pleasurable experience.

Country roads are obviously more interesting for touring, but can be slow going, with speed limits down to 25 mph at some curves (look for the signs) and police radar checks enforcing the law at the most unlikely spots. Signs are not especially good in New England, with turns appearing without prior warning; the problem seems particularly bad in Massachusetts.

Visitors to New England often encounter rotaries (traffic circles) for the first time. Designed to keep traffic moving through busy or complicated intersections, rotaries often have the exact opposite effect. Traffic already on the rotary has the right of way, and you can only enter the rotary when there is a clear break on the left. Once on the rotary, stay in the inside (left) lane unless you are getting off at the next exit, but remember that this traffic rule—like most driving etiquette—is ignored by many Boston drivers.

**Car rentals** All major car rental companies are represented in New England, including **Alamo** (tel: 800/327–9633), **Avis** (tel: 800/331–1212), **Budget** (tel: 800/527–0700), **Dollar** (tel: 800/800–4000), **Hertz** (tel: 800/654–3131), **National** (tel: 800/227–7368), and **Thrifty** (tel: 800/367–2277).

A good way to dodge the worst of the traffic is to ride the train out of Boston or New York, and rent your vehicle out of town. For example, **Enterprise** (tel: 800/325–8007) can pick you up from the train station if you travel out from Boston northward to Lynn or southward to Quincy, or from New York northeastward to Stamford. Depending on season and location, unlimited mileage rates typically range from $45–$55 per day and $225–$275 per week for a small car, and $65–$75 per day and $325–$375 per week for a large car. This does not include tax, which varies from state to state.

Be aware that picking up the car in one city and leaving it in another may entail substantial drop-off charges or one-way service fees. The cost of a collision or loss-damage waiver (see below) can also be high. Some rental agencies will charge you extra if you return the car before the time specified on your contract; ask before making unscheduled drop-offs. Fill the tank when you turn in the vehicle to avoid being charged for refueling at what you'll swear is the most expensive pump in town.

Major international car rental companies have programs that discount their standard rates by 15–30 percent if you make the reservation before departure (anywhere from 24 hours to 14 days), rent for a minimum number of days (typically three or four), and prepay the rental. More

*Mopeds for rent on Martha's Vineyard—a good way to get around the island*

**255**

economical rentals may come as part of fly/drive or other packages, even bare-bones deals that combine only the rental and an airline ticket.

Before you rent a car, find out exactly what coverage, if any, is provided by your personal auto insurer and by the rental company. Don't assume that you are covered. If you do want insurance from the rental company, secondary coverage may be the only type offered. You may already have secondary coverage if you charge the rental to a credit card. Only Diners Club (tel: 800/234–6377) provides primary coverage in the United States and worldwide.

In general, if you are involved in an accident, you are responsible for the automobile. Car rental companies may offer a collision damage waiver (CDW), which ranges in cost from $17 to $19 a day. You should decline the CDW only if

you are certain you are covered through your personal insurer or credit card company. In many states, laws mandate that renters be told what the CDW costs, that it's optional, and that their own auto insurance may provide the same protection.

**Hazards** In winter, roads are kept reasonably clear by snowplows, but even so they can still be treacherous; cat litter or sand can be put down to ease the car out if it becomes stuck in the snow. Snow tires are essential for winter driving in New England.

During the winter, pay attention to highway signs warning about "Low-Salt Areas." Concern about salt filtering into drinking water supplies has led highway maintenance departments to take alternative—and often less effective—measures for keeping roads clear of ice. Exercise similar caution if you see signs indicating that a "Bridge Freezes Before Road Surface." Springtime uncovers one of New England's more unpleasant winter side effects— potholes and frost heaves. Road surfaces expand and contract after a winter of heavy freezes and sudden thaws. The result is a series of craters, fissures, and cracks in the asphalt.

*Driving in downtown Boston can be a hair-raising experience for first-time visitors and is best avoided if at all possible*

Beware of moose, which like the salt that runs off the road and are seemingly oblivious to traffic; colliding with one can cause a fatal accident. Moose are particularly prevalent in the White Mountains and inland Maine. Also keep an eye out for deer. If you collide with a skunk it may spray your car; the pungent smell is no joke.

**Parking** Boston and other large New England cities have public parking lots and garages as well as the usual parking meters, but demand for spaces often exceeds supply on weekdays. A better bet around Boston is to park near one of the outer stops on the MBTA (see pages 52–53 and 258), and from there take a train or subway into the city.

**Traffic lights** Massachusetts was one of the last states to adopt a policy of right-turn-on-red. This stubborn refusal has left a legacy of "No Right Turn on Red Light" signs at some intersections, so don't take this maneuver for granted.

**School buses** Remember that New England pioneered the idea of enforced traffic stops (on both sides of the road) when a school bus stops. This law is strictly observed—even around Boston. Watch for flashing lights on the bus or stop signs that pop out from its cab.

**Biking**
In Boston, the **Dr. Paul Dudley White Bikeway**, approximately 18 miles long, runs along both sides of the Charles River. **The Bicycle Workshop** (259 Massachusetts Avenue, Cambridge, MA 02140, tel: 617/876–6555) rents bicycles, fixes flat tires while you wait, and delivers bicycles to your hotel. Elsewhere in New England, there are plenty of opportunities for the bicyclist, with ready-made bike trails on Cape Cod and in the Pioneer Valley, for example, and scenic country roads in the Berkshires and northern Vermont; biking is also a feasible option in and around Newport. Mountain biking is very popular (particularly in the White Mountains), and ski resorts often offer this facility when the snows have gone. The loop road in Acadia National Park is scenic (although traffic gets busy in summer), and there is not a lot of distance to cover. Nantucket and Block Island are excellent for exploring by bike; Martha's Vineyard has dangerous roads (too narrow to accommodate traffic safely) but some bike paths.

Free information is available from the Maine Publicity Bureau (Box 2300, Hallowell, ME 04347, tel: 207/623–0363 or 800/932–3419), the Massachusetts Office of Travel and Tourism (see page

266), the New Hampshire Bureau of Trails (Box 1856, Concord, NH 03302, tel: 603/271–3254), and the Vermont Travel Division. Other sources include **Maine Sport** (Rte. 1, Rockport, ME 04856, tel: 888/236–8797), and **Vermont Bicycle Touring** (Box 711, Bristol, VT 05443-0711, tel: 800/245–3868). Cycle route maps are available from the **Adventure Cycling Association**, 150 East Pine Street, P.O. Box 8308, Missoula, MT 59807-8308 (tel: 406/721–1776 or 800/755–2453).

### Hiking

Country walking for pleasure is mainly confined to state and forest parks, where ready-made trails are well marked. There is usually an indication of the time needed, and the length and difficulty of the walk, and free maps are generally available. The finest areas in New England for walking are the White Mountains and Acadia National Park, although there are many smaller parks with one or two outstanding trails. Naturalists particularly enjoy the trails in Maine's Baxter State Park.

Many of the best routes are mentioned in this book. Because of the prevalence of tree cover, good views can be hard to find; you often see nothing until the summit. Ask locally which routes go above the timberline. Long-distance walks include the **Appalachian Trail**, which stretches for 2,035 miles between Georgia and Maine, and Vermont's 260-mile **Long Trail** over the Green Mountains and Mount Mansfield.

A range of practical walking guide-books covers the region. For further information contact the **Appalachian Mountain Club** (A.M.C), Box 298,

*Left: Signposts and road numbers can leave some visitors scratching their heads*

Gorham, NH 03581 (tel: 603/466–2727), the Berkshire Region Headquarters, 740 South Street, Pittsfield, MA 01202 (tel: 413/442–8928), the **White Mountains National Forest**, 719 North Main Street, P.O. Box 638, Laconia, NH 03247 (tel: 603/528–8722), or the **Green Mountain National Forest**, 231 North Main Street, Rutland, VT 05701 (tel: 802/747–6700).

### Boating and sailing

In most lakeside and coastal resorts, sailboats and motorboats can be rented at a local marina. Newport, Rhode Island, and Maine's Penobscot Bay are famous sailing areas. Lakes in New Hampshire and Vermont are splendid for all kinds of boating. The Connecticut River in the Pioneer Valley and the Housatonic River in the Berkshires are popular for canoeing.

257

*A coastal bicycle trail gives the freedom to look around as you travel*

## Public transportation

**Selected train trips** Commuter rail services from Boston and New Haven are inexpensive, and tickets can be bought immediately prior to travel. Long-distance Amtrak services can fill up and should be booked in advance. Some basic trips are suggested below.

● **Amtrak** (tel: 800/USA–RAIL). Northeast Corridor: Boston South Station, Providence, Mystic, New London, Old Saybrook, New Haven, New York, Philadelphia.

● **Metro-North** (tel: 800/METRO–INFO; in New York, tel: 212/532–4900). New York (Grand Central), Rowayton, South Norwalk, New Haven, with connections to New Canaan, Danbury, and Waterbury.

● **MBTA Commuter Rail** (tel: 617/222–3200). Boston North Station to Fitchburg via Concord (MA); Rockport via Salem (for bus to Marblehead), Manchester

*The "T" is useful for traveling between Boston and the North and South Shores*

(MA), Gloucester; Ipswich. Boston South Station to Providence.

**Selected bus trips** Boston services leave from South Station and/or Logan International Airport. Services vary in frequency and are periodically altered or withdrawn completely; check before traveling.

Bus companies tend to be organized regionally; for example:

● **Concord Trailways** (tel: 800/639–3317): covers much of New

*Trolley tours operate in Boston*

Hampshire and parts of Maine, including Concord (NH), and Maine to Bangor via Camden.
● **Plymouth and Brockton** (tel: 508/746–0378): serves Cape Cod (including Provincetown).
● **Bonanza Buses** (tel: 888/751–8800): Connecticut, Rhode Island; the Maine coast, the Berkshires (from New York), Cape Cod for ferries to the islands. Includes Providence, Fall River, Portsmouth, Portland, Bangor.
● **C & J Trailways** (tel: 800/258–7111): the coastal towns of New Hampshire and Maine, including Newburyport and Portsmouth.
● **Peter Pan Trailways** (tel: 800/343–9999): western Massachusetts and Connecticut, covering Amherst, Hartford, Foxwoods, Old Sturbridge, Lowell, New Haven, and New York.
● **Greyhound International** (tel: 800/231–2222): Hartford, Springfield; long-distance routes across the U.S.A.
● **Vermont Transit Lines** (tel: 802/864–6811): numerous towns in Vermont, New Hampshire, and Maine, notably Lowell, Montpelier, Burlington, Brattleboro, Portland, Portsmouth, Augusta, and Bangor.

**Selected ferry trips** See gazetteer entries for Block Island (page 213), Martha's Vineyard (pages 160–161), Nantucket (pages 162–163), and Provincetown (pages 158–159). One option is to tour Rhode Island by ferry from Providence, stopping at Newport and continuing to Block Island (Interstate Navigation, tel: 401/783–4613). There is also a ferry from Boston's Commercial Wharf to Salem.

**Regional flights** Boston's Logan International Airport and many of the smaller airports mentioned in the "Arriving" section (see page 248) are ideal jumping-off points for flights to other parts of New England. Flying is the most expensive travel alternative within New England, but makes a getaway weekend possible.
Major carriers within the New England region include:
● **Cape Air** (tel: 800/352–0714).
● **Delta** (tel: 800/221–1212).

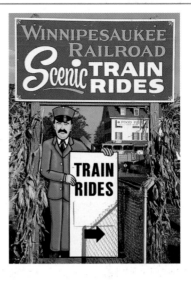

259

*Most trains running in much of the north of the region will be those on tourist railways*

● **Island Airlines** (serving Nantucket, tel: 800/248–7779).
● **Northwest Airlines** (tel: 800/225–2525).
● **US Airways** (tel: 800/428–4322).
In addition, short-hop charter flights or scenic aerial tours can be arranged at many small airports.

**Canny planning**
Public transportation can help you overcome the busy times of year. For example, during conventions in downtown Boston, consider commuting from an outlying town such as Concord, Salem, or Quincy, all of which are pleasant bases with good accommodations, and excellent transportation links enabling you to reach Boston in a short time. Bus, train, and air services also take the hassle out of trying to plan a circular car tour of New England, but beware of one-way drop-off charges (see page 254).
You could further dodge the crowds by visiting New England in spring, by visiting the coast in fall or even winter, by venturing into the mountains in the summer, or by going to the busier resorts during the week and saving money on hotel bills by staying in Boston at the weekend.

## Communications

### Language
New England has seen more centuries of immigration and assimilation into the "melting pot" than just about any other part of the U.S. Each incoming ethnic group, whether French Canadian, Irish, Portuguese, or Hispanic, has left a lasting mark on the way New Englanders speak.

Nevertheless, visitors to New England expect locals to speak like the Kennedys. That accent, with its characteristic broad *a*'s and ignored *r*'s, is at its most pronounced around Boston and along the New England coastline. Some linguists maintain that it is close to the accent of those original settlers from the eastern part of England. Distinctively "English" pronunciations of words such as "half," "can't," "aunt," and "path" are beginning to be lost in the face of the mass media, but each generation of Bostonians learns to "pahk the cah in Hahvid yahd."

The accent of western New England played a large role in how much of modern America speaks. Western New Englanders moved north from the Middle Atlantic states rather than west from Boston. They then were the first to settle the Midwest in great numbers, laying the linguistic foundations for future generations in Ohio, Illinois, Michigan, and beyond.

New England pronunciations shouldn't pose difficulties for first-time visitors, but a number of words and phrases might need explaining.

| New England | "American" |
| --- | --- |
| Bay State | Massachusetts |
| frappé | milkshake |
| frost | milkshake |
| the Hose | the Red Sox |
| the Hub | Boston |
| package store | liquor store |
| quahog (pronounced "ko-hog") | a hard-shelled clam |
| rotary | traffic circle |
| scrod | tender baby cod |
| ten, quarter of… (telling time) | ten, quarter to… |
| tonic | soda pop |

### Media
**Newspapers** The *Boston Globe* and *Boston Herald* are both dailies, with listings on Thursday and Friday respectively. The daily *Boston Phoenix* Thursday edition carries listings and comments on the city's entertainment. The *Christian Science Monitor*, highly regarded for its unbiased reporting, is published on weekdays and has international news.

*Hot off the press: this newsstand does brisk business in Harvard Square, Cambridge*

**Television** Television stations in Boston, Providence, Hartford, and other New England cities link up with the major networks, and a host of UHF and cable stations cater to local interests. Satellite and cable TV are common in the more mountainous and remote areas, where reception has traditionally been poor.

Local stations have long recognized the importance of tourism in the region. Weather reports on the evening news often feature items on peak foliage viewing or on ski conditions.

**Radio** Local radio derives a great deal of input from the diverse ethnic makeup and from the many colleges and universities in the region. Even commercial FM stations recognize that there is a highbrow audience in this cultural area, so expect to find Berlioz and Bach rubbing shoulders with Bon Jovi on the radio dial.

Politics is a spectator sport in Boston, and listening to AM talk shows is a good way to follow the heated and occasionally witty arguments of local politicians. Professional spectator sports also spawn a number of call-in programs. Expect to hear variations on the following themes: the pitiful state of the Patriots; the glory days of the Celtics and Bruins; and why the Red Sox self-destruct each September.

In rural New England, much of the air time is filled with easy listening, golden oldies, or mainstream pop, but you can also pick up some useful insider's knowledge about upcoming antiques fairs, church bazaars, town meetings, or lobster suppers. If you're lucky, you might even hear about where the trout, striped bass, and bluefish are biting.

### Telephones
Find out your hotel's policy on telephones. Local calls are sometimes free, but don't bank on it. Other calls from hotels are usually marked up considerably, so exercise caution. Remember that most state and regional tourist offices have toll-free numbers.

**Area codes** In New England there is one code per state in most cases, except for Massachusetts, with five, and Connecticut, with two.

- **Boston** 617.
- **Connecticut** 203, 860.
- **Maine** 207.
- **Massachusetts** (western) 413.
- **Massachusetts** (southern and eastern) 508.
- **Massachusetts** (northern) 978.
- **Massachusetts** (Greater Boston, outer areas) 781.
- **New Hampshire** 603.
- **Rhode Island** 401.
- **Vermont** 802.

**Overseas call code** International calls can be made from any phone. For the international operator, dial 0. Omit the first 0 if applicable from local area code:
- **Australia** 011 61.
- **Canada** no extra code needed.
- **Ireland** 011 353.
- **New Zealand** 011 64.
- **United Kingdom** 011 44.

**Weather information** For current weather conditions and forecasts for cities in the United States and abroad, plus the local time and helpful travel tips, call the **Weather Channel Connection** (tel: 900/WEATHER; charged at 95¢ per minute) from a touch-tone phone.

*Public telephone booth in Boston's Chinatown*

## Emergencies

### Crime
Robert B. Parker and George V. Higgins have put Boston on the crime fiction map, but neither Boston nor New England is swamped by a crime wave. In fact, many parts of the region are charmingly relaxed, with houses and cars left unlocked and bicycles left standing against lampposts.

However, it is wise to be on guard in quiet city areas, particularly at night, to lock your car doors if you are driving, and to be careful about where you choose to park.

Central Boston is generally very safe in daytime, and even its notorious "Combat Zone" (a red-light district between downtown and Chinatown) has had something of a face-lift in recent years. Some southern neighborhoods are crime-ridden, but few visitors have reason to go there. There are some other notable no-go areas in the city of Brockton (south of Boston) and in larger cities in the region such as Providence, Hartford, and Bridgeport.

If confronted by a mugger, do not resist him. A wise precaution is to carry a $20 bill separately from other valuables, in the hope that this will satisfy the attacker.

*Boston is a safe city but normal precautions should be taken at night*

### Police
There are no county police in New England. Local matters are dealt with by city or town police; state police patrol highways regularly.

### Emergency numbers
The best advice is simply to call the operator and explain the difficulty. Boston and Cambridge police can be reached by dialing 911.

### Consulates
Boston has consulates dealing with matters involving nationals of the following countries:
● **Canada** 3 Copley Street, Suite 400 (tel: 617/262–3760).
● **Ireland** 535 Boylston Street (tel: 617/267–9330).
● **United Kingdom** Federal Reserve Plaza, 25th Floor, 600 Atlantic Avenue (tel: 617/248–9555).

### Natural hazards
Deer ticks are tiny insects that can fall on you unawares and burrow into the skin, causing **Lyme disease**, an unpleasant condition that normally starts with a circular rash. It is followed by flulike symptoms and lethargy, leading in some instances to numbness, tingling, arthritis, meningitis, or heart failure. It is important to get treatment as soon as symptoms occur, as the condition can worsen rapidly. The highest risk areas are Connecticut, Rhode Island, and

*In rural areas, watch out for poison ivy and ticks*

Massachusetts. To reduce the chance of contracting the disease, wear light-colored clothing (so that the dark ticks can be spotted and brushed off), tuck your pant legs into your socks when walking in the countryside, get a companion to inspect your back and head, and wear repellents. If bitten by a tick, remove it with tweezers, and seek medical attention if the mouthpart has been lodged in the skin. Blood tests can determine whether or not you have been exposed to Lyme disease.

Stream water may carry **giardia**, a parasitic protozoan that causes serious intestinal problems; only drink stream water if it has been purified (iodine tablets are best), filtered, or thoroughly boiled (for at least five minutes). **Poison ivy** can cause a painful rash if the skin rubs against it (see panel on page 200.)

**Bears** frequent the northern woods of New England. Although generally timid, they can turn aggressive if you get between a mother and cub, or if they are otherwise surprised. Loud noises usually frighten them off (see also panel on page 201.)

With so much of New England heavily wooded, pay attention to warnings about **forest fires**, particularly in the months of July and August. Rangers and other officials at state parks and forests can provide useful advice about precautions and any local ordinances about campfires and barbecues.

New England is blessed with some of the country's best beaches, but remember that swimming in the ocean can be dangerous. Children must keep within roped-off areas attended by a lifeguard.

Always check whether a particular beach has an **undertow**, which can take even strong swimmers unawares.

### Lost property
In the event of loss, damage, or theft on domestic flights, airlines' liability is $1,250 per passenger, excluding valuable items such as jewelry, cameras, and more that are listed in the fine print on your ticket. Excess-valuation insurance can be bought directly from the airline at check-in. Your homeowner's policy may fill the gap; if not, firms such as **The Travelers Companies** (1 Tower Square, Hartford, CT 06183, tel: 860/277–0111 or 800/243–3174) sell baggage insurance.

### Lost credit cards
● **American Express** (tel: 800/528–4800).
● **Diners Club/Carte Blanche** (tel: 800/234–6377).
● **MasterCard/Access** (tel: 800/826–2181).
● **Visa** (tel: 800/847–2911).

### Lost traveler's checks
● **American Express** (tel: 800/221–7282).
● **Thomas Cook** (tel: 800/223–7373).

## Other information

### Antiques
Boston, Cape Cod, and the Berkshires harbor active artists' communities and many antiques shops, but the days of bargain prices have passed. Local newspapers and the bulletin boards of country stores carry notices of flea markets, shows, and sales that can be lots of fun—and a source of bargains as well. The **Cape Cod Antiques Dealers Association** (P.O. Box 463, Barnstable, MA 02630, tel: 508/362–2025) publishes a directory of the area's antiques dealers and auctions. Send an SASE to the **Vermont Antiques Dealers Association** (c/o Murial McKirryher, 55 Allen Street, Rutland, VT 05701) or the **Maine Antiques Dealers Association** HC68, Box 130-L, Cushing, ME 04563, tel: 207/354–8055) for copies of their annual directories.

### Beaches
Long, wide beaches edge the New England coast from southern Maine to southern Connecticut; the most popular are on Cape Cod, Martha's Vineyard, Nantucket, and the shore areas north and south of Boston in Massachusetts; in the Kennebunk area of Maine; on Long Island Sound in Rhode Island; and the coastal region of New Hampshire. Many are maintained by state and local governments and have lifeguards on duty; they may have picnic facilities, rest rooms, changing facilities, and concession stands. Depending on the locale, you may need a parking sticker to use the lot. The waters are at their warmest in August, though they're cold even at the height of summer along much of the Maine coast. Inland, there are small lake beaches, most notably in New Hampshire and Vermont.

### Camping
New England has hundreds of campgrounds, both private and state-owned. Each state tourist office publishes lists of campgrounds at state parks, which are public recreation areas usually set up with hiking trails and picnic facilities. Prices are reasonable, but grounds in the more frequented areas, such as Acadia National Park, tend to fill up rapidly in summer.

Campers should keep food in sealed containers, well out of the reach of bears (for example, on a high, slender branch). Look out for ticks and inspect yourself regularly (see "Natural hazards" on pages 262–263).

### Maple sugar and produce
Opportunities abound for obtaining fresh farm produce from the source; some farms allow you to pick your own strawberries, raspberries, and blueberries, and there are maple-syrup producers who are willing to demonstrate the process to visitors. The **Massachusetts Association of Roadside Stands** (P.O. Box 243, Southampton, MA 01073, tel: 413/529–2471) prepares a list of pick-your-own fruit farms in that state. The **Massachusetts Maple Producers Association** (Box 377, Watson-Spruce Corner Road, Ashfield, MA 01330, tel: 413/628–3912) has a list of sugarhouses. The **New Hampshire Department of Agriculture** (Box 2042, Concord, NH 03302, tel: 603/271–3551) publishes lists of maple-syrup producers and farmers' markets in New Hampshire.

### Photography
Many museums prohibit flash photography; a tripod may therefore be useful. All types of film are available, but it can be hard to track down film for color slides in smaller places. Film should be kept as cool as possible. A skylight filter helps to reduce haze and protect the lens on an SLR camera.

### Places of worship
The Boston Yellow Pages lists churches in the Greater Boston area under "Churches;" these include Baptist, Catholic, Greek Orthodox, Congregational, and Evangelical.
● **Jewish Religious Information Services** 177 Tremont Street, Boston (tel: 617/426–2139).
● **The Islamic Center of New England** 470 South Street, Quincy (tel: 617/479–8341).

### Visitors with disabilities
Newer hotels and restaurants as well as those that have recently been

*Acadia National Park in Maine has several campgrounds—for more information, contact the park headquarters in Bar Harbor (see panel on page 113)*

renovated are apt to be equipped for travelers with mobility problems and sensory impairments; the passage of the Americans with Disabilities Act in 1990 should mean increasing accessibility. The official Vermont state map indicates which public recreation areas at state parks have facilities for travelers using wheelchairs. In addition, both the **Vermont Travel Division** and the **New Hampshire Office of Travel and Tourism Development** publish statewide directories of accessible facilities.

**Getting around** For the price of a single fare, **Greyhound Lines** (tel: 800/231–2222) will carry a person with a disability and his or her companion. **Amtrak** (National Railroad Passenger Corp., 60 Massachusetts Avenue NE, Washington, DC 20002, tel: 800/872–7245, or for text telephones TTY 800/523–6590) advises that you request any redcap service, special seats, or wheelchair assistance you may need when you make your reservations. (Not all stations are equipped to provide these services.) All passengers with disabilities, including children, are entitled to a 15 percent discount on the lowest available fare. The free brochure *Access Amtrak* outlines available services for the elderly and people with disabilities.

Parking lots all have parking spaces for people with disabilities; Boston's subway stations have elevators as an alternative to stairs; and public buildings are wheelchair accessible.

*Many towns and villages have several places of worship*
*Left: Cohasset in Massachusetts*

### Tourist offices

Gathering free information on an area is no problem in New England, where each state issues a free road map, as well as brochures describing its visitor attractions. In addition to the state-run tourist offices, nearly every important town has a chamber of commerce, stocked with tourist information. Many inns and hotels have leaflets about local attractions.

**Discover New England**, P.O. Box 3809, Stowe, VT 05672 (tel: 802/253–2500; fax: 802/253–9064; www.discovernewengland.org) is the international marketing arm of the six states. **DestINNations**, 572 Route 28, Suite 3, West Yarmouth, MA 02673 (tel: 508/790–0566; fax: 508/790–0565) specializes in arranging tour itineraries, with accommodations, around New England.

### State tourist offices

**Greater Boston Convention and Visitors Bureau** 2 Copley Place, Suite 105, Boston, MA 02116-6501 (tel: 617/536–4100 or 888/SEE–BOSTON; fax: 617/424–7664; www.bostonusa.com).

**Connecticut Office of Tourism** 505 Hudson Street, Hartford, CT 06106 (tel: 860/270–8080 or 800/282–6863; fax: 860/270–8077; www.tourism.state.ct.us).

**Maine Office of Tourism** State House Station 59, Augusta, ME 04333 (tel: 207/287–5711; fax: 207/287–8070; www.visitmaine.com).

**Massachusetts Office of Travel and Tourism** State Transportation Building, 10 Park Plaza, Suite 4510, Boston, MA 02116 (tel: 617/973–8500; fax 617/973–8525; www.massvacation.com).

**New Hampshire Office of Travel and Tourism** 172 Pembroke Road, P.O. Box 1856, Concord, NH 03302 (tel: 603/271–2665; fax: 603/271–6784; www.visitnh.gov).

**Rhode Island Tourism Division** 1 West Exchange Street, Providence, RI 02903 (tel: 401/222–2601; fax: 401/273–8270; www.visitrhodeisland.com).

**Vermont Department of Tourism and Marketing** 6 Baldwin Street, Montpelier, VT 05633 (tel: 802/828–3237; fax: 802/828 3233; www.travel-vermont.com).

*The tourist information office in Chatham, Massachusetts, is one of several on Cape Cod*

# Accommodations & Restaurants

# ACCOMMODATIONS

The following recommended hotels and restaurants have been divided into three price categories:

- **budget** ($)
- **moderate** ($$)
- **expensive** ($$$)

Some straddle two categories.

New England inns range from genuine period hostelries filled with antiques and collected bits and pieces to large, deluxe modern buildings. Bed-and-breakfasts (B&Bs) are often upscale; you pay extra for the privilege of staying in someone's home, but breakfast is included.

Some hotels and inns include rentals of town houses and cottages. The cheapest accommodations are generally motels, which are usually adequate in comfort and facilities but not strong on atmosphere (although there are some in fine settings).

It is often possible to negotiate deals by telephone. Some motels will give you a discount over the phone if it seems that you might go elsewhere, but not if you turn up on the spot.

Always check to see if sales and state tax are included. Some accommodations also make an additional charge for service.

Many hotels and inns have packages including Full American Plan (accommodations with breakfast, lunch, and dinner) and/or Modified American Plan (accommodations with breakfast and dinner). Useful statewide organizations include:

## Connecticut
- Lodging reservations can be made in Connecticut by calling 800/CT–BOUND. Lists of accommodations can be obtained from state tourist offices (see page 266) or at www.ctbound.org.

## Maine
- For information on where to stay, tel: 888/624–6345 or visit www.mainetourism.com for a copy of *Maine Invites You.*

## Massachusetts
- Tel: 800/447–MASS (in U.S.A. and eastern Canada) or visit www.massvacation.com for a copy of the *Massachusetts Getaway Guide.*

## New Hampshire
- The New Hampshire Office of Travel and Tourism distributes the *New Hampshire Guidebook*, which includes lodgings listings (tel: 800/FUN–IN NH); it's also available online at www.visitnh.gov.

## Rhode Island
- Request a *Rhode Island Travel Guide* from the Rhode Island Tourism Division (see page 266). Bed and Breakfast Rhode Island (Box 3291, Newport, RI 02840; tel: 401/849–1298 or 800/828–0000;

www.visitnewport.com/bedandbreakfast) handles statewide B&B reservations.

## Vermont
- Contact the Vermont Department of Tourism and Marketing (see page 266) for a *Vermont Vacation Planning* packet. *Four Seasons Vacation Rentals*, a guide to cottage, condo, and vacation home rentals, is available from P.O. Box 1564, Montpelier, VT 05601 (tel: 802/229–2433; www.vermontproperty.com).

Useful international organizations include:
- Homelink, P.O. Box 650, Key West, FL 33041 (tel: 800/638–3841; www.homelink.org), a house exchange organization.

## Boston and Cambridge (Massachusetts)

### Agencies
**B&B Agency of Boston**
*47 Commercial Wharf, Boston, MA 02110*
*tel: 617/720–3540 or 800/248–9262*
*fax: 617/523–5761*
*www.boston-bnbagency.com*
The biggest B&B agency in the city, with some excellent locations, such as the Waterfront, Beacon Hill, Back Bay, and the North End. Also apartments from studio size upward.

**Bed and Breakfast Cambridge & Greater Boston**
*Box 1344, Cambridge, MA 02238*
*tel: 617/720–1492 or 800/888–0178*
*fax: 617/227–0021   www.bandbcambridge.com*
Has information on accommodations in private homes, apartments, and short-term apartment rentals, primarily in Cambridge.

**Host Homes of Boston**
*Box 117, Waban Branch, Boston, MA 02468*
*tel: 617/244–1308 or 800/600–1308*
*fax: 617/244–5156*
Provides accommodations, including some apartments, in private "hosted homes."

### Accommodations

**Boston International AYH Hostel** ($)
*12 Hemenway Street, Boston, MA 02115*
*tel: 617/536–9455  fax: 617/424–6558*
*www.bostonhostel.org*
Dormitory accommodations, self-service kitchens, daily activity programs. Nonmembers welcome.

**Boston Park Plaza Hotel** ($$$)
*64 Arlington Street, Boston, MA 02116*
*tel: 617/426–2000 or 800/225–2008*
*fax: 617/426–5545  www.bostonparkplaza.com*
A stylish, grand hotel built in 1927. There are 960 rooms, including 82 luxurious rooms on the 15th-floor Concierge Level.

**A Cambridge House Bed & Breakfast** ($$–$$$)
*2218 Massachusetts Avenue, Cambridge, MA 02140  tel: 617/491–6300 or 800/232–9989  fax: 617/868–2848*
*www.acambridgehouse.com*
An upscale 15-room B&B near Davis Square, complete with period furnishings in an 1892 house and carriage house.

**Charles ($$$)**
*1 Bennett Street, Cambridge, MA 02138*
*tel: 617/864–1200 or 800/882–1818*
*fax: 617/864–5715 www.charleshotel.com*
A modern hotel, appointed with patchwork quilts
and Shaker furniture, in a convenient Harvard
Square location. Home of the excellent Rialto
restaurant and the well-regarded Regattabar jazz
club (see pages 279 and 85 respectively).

**Copley Square ($$–$$$)**
*47 Huntington Avenue, Boston, MA 02116*
*tel: 617/536–9000 or 800/225–7062*
*fax: 617/267–0351*
*www.copleysquarehotel.com*
This Victorian hotel offers acceptable comfort at a
reasonable price. Try its Café Budapest for formal
dining and an informal bar.

**Fairmont Copley Plaza ($$$)**
*138 St. James Avenue, Boston, MA 02116*
*tel: 617/267–5300 or 800/527–4727*
*fax: 617/247–6681 www.fairmont.com*
Built in 1912, this is one of the grand old hotels of
Boston. Go in for a look just to see the decor.

**Fifteen Beacon Hill ($$$)**
*15 Beacon Street, Boston, MA 02108*
*tel: 617/670–1500 or 877/XVBEACON*
*fax: 617/670–2525 www.xvbeacon.com*
A stylish 61-room boutique hotel in a converted
1902 office building near the State House. Home
of the fashionable restaurant The Federalist.

**Inn at Harvard ($$$)**
*1201 Massachusetts Avenue, Cambridge,
MA 02138 tel: 617/491–2222 or
800/458–5886 fax: 617/492–4896*
*www.theinnatharvard.com*
Near Harvard Square; although it is run by
Doubletree Hotels, it is owned by Harvard
University. Pleasantly appointed, with art on loan
from the Fogg Museum.

**Lenox ($$$)**
*710 Boylston Street, Boston, MA 02116*
*tel: 617/536–5300 or 800/225–7676*
*fax: 617/267–1237 www.lenoxhotel.com*
An early 20th-century building in a good location by
Copley Square. It has 212 well-appointed rooms.

**Le Meridien Boston ($$$)**
*250 Franklin Street, Boston, MA 02110*
*tel: 617/451–1900 or 800/543–4300*
*fax: 617/423–2844*
*www.lemeridienboston.com*
Housed in the old Federal Reserve Building in the
heart of the downtown Financial District. There are
326 deluxe rooms and the outstanding Julien
restaurant (see page 278).

**Regal Bostonian ($$$)**
*Faneuil Hall Marketplace, Boston, MA 02109*
*tel: 617/523–3600 or 800/343–0922*
*fax: 617/523–2454*
*www.regal-hotels.com/boston*
Excellent comfort and service. A European-style
hotel in a building dating from 1824.

**Ritz-Carlton ($$$)**
*15 Arlington Street, Boston, MA 02117*
*tel: 617/536–5700 or 800/241–3333*
*fax: 617/536–9340 www.ritzcarlton.com*
Considered by many to be Boston's top hotel, with
its views of Newbury Street and the Public Garden
and its traditional decor.

**Susse Chalet Inn ($)**
*211 Concord Turnpike (Route 2 East),
Cambridge, MA 02140 tel: 617/661–7800 or
800/524–2538 fax: 617/868–8153*
*www.sussechalet.com*
This is a feasible budget option with convenient
access to downtown by Red Line.

## Connecticut

### Connecticut River Valley
**Bishopsgate Inn ($$)**
*7 Norwich Road, Goodspeed Landing, East
Haddam, CT 06423 tel: 860/873–1677
fax: 860/873–3898 www.bishopsgate.com*
An 1818 Colonial house, close to the Goodspeed
Opera House. Six rooms furnished with antique
and reproduction furniture; four have fireplaces.

**Copper Beech Inn ($$–$$$)**
*46 Main Street, Ivoryton, CT 06442*
*tel: 860/767–0330 or 888/809–2056*
*www.copperbeechinn.com*
Named after the tree that shades the 19th-century
main building. The rooms in the main house and
carriage house are all furnished with period
antiques; some have cathedral ceilings. The restau-
rant serves elegant country French cuisine with a
menu that changes seasonally; reservations are
essential on weekends.

**Griswold Inn ($–$$)**
*36 Main Street, Essex, CT 06426*
*tel: 860/767–1776 fax: 860/767–0481*
*www.griswoldinn.com*
The earliest three-story frame building in
Connecticut (built in 1776); its structure remains
largely unaltered. The antique-filled rooms may be
small, but they have lots of character. There is
also the 1738 barroom, cozy Gun Room,
riverboat-style Steamboat Room, and a dining
room constructed from a covered bridge, serving
traditional New England and American dishes.

**Inn at Chester ($$–$$$)**
*Route 148, 318 West Main Street, Chester,
CT 06412 tel: 860/526–9541 or
800/949–STAY fax: 860/526–4387*
*www.innatchester.com*
A traditionally decorated country inn, with 18th-
century reproduction furnishings. There are 41
rooms and one suite. The Post and Beam dining
room serves renowned New England cuisine.

**Saybrook Point Inn ($$$)**
*2 Bridge Street, Old Saybrook, CT 06475*
*tel: 860/395–2000 or 800/243–0212*
*fax: 860/388–1504 www.saybrook.com*
Furnished with flair, more a hotel than an inn, this
modern lodging has 80 rooms, many with water
views. It has a health club and spa, plus indoor
and outdoor pools. Highly recommended.

### Hartford
**Goodwin Hotel ($$$)**
*1 Haynes Street, Hartford, CT 06103*
*tel: 860/246–7500 or 888/212–8380*
*fax: 860/247–4576 www.goodwinhotel.com*
An upscale hotel in an ornate turn-of-the-20th-
century building opposite the Hartford Civic Center.
There are 124 rooms, a fitness center, and
business services.

269

# Accommodations and Restaurants

## Litchfield Hills

### Boulders Inn ($$$)
*Route 45, East Shore Road, New Preston,*
*CT 06777 tel: 860/868–0541 or*
*800/55BOULDERS fax: 860/868–1925*
*www.bouldersinn.com*
This small inn, built in 1895, has a superb view of
Lake Waramaug, complete with waterfront activities and boating. The 17 rooms in the main
building and adjacent guest houses are furnished
with antiques and country-style fixtures. There is
also a fine restaurant.

### Cornwall Inn ($$)
*270 Kent Road, Scenic Route 7, Cornwall*
*Bridge, CT 06754 tel/fax: 860/672–6884 or*
*800/786–6884 www.cornwallinn.com*
Six rooms and a restaurant in the 1810 main inn,
plus eight rooms in the adjacent mountain lodge.
The rooms have feather beds. Outdoor pool.

### Tollgate Hill Inn ($$)
*Route 202 and Toll Gate Road, Litchfield,*
*CT 06759 tel: 860/567–4545 or*
*800/445–3903 fax: 860/567–8397*
A travelers' way station since 1745, out of town
on the Torrington road. This charming Colonial
building has 21 rooms. The restaurant serves
New England cuisine.

### Tucker Hill Inn ($–$$)
*96 Tucker Hill Road, Middlebury, CT 06762*
*tel: 203/758–8334 fax: 203/598–0652*
*e-mail: tuckerhill2@yahoo.com*
Not a historic inn, but a 1923 clapboard house. It
makes a pleasant and welcoming base, and is
strategically located southwest of Waterbury.

## Mystic

### Antiques and Accommodations ($$–$$$)
*32 Main Street, North Stonington, CT 06359*
*tel: 860/535–1736 or 800/554–7829*
*fax: 860/535–2613*
*www.visitmystic.com/antiques*
A primrose-yellow Victorian house with five rooms,
furnished with an eye for detail and graced with
choice antiques, some of which are for sale. You
can also rent the adjacent "House in the Garden,"
with three bedrooms. Nature tours.

### Old Mystic Inn ($$–$$$)
*52 Main Street, Box 733, Old Mystic,*
*CT 06372 tel: 860/572–9422*
*fax: 860/572–9954*
*www.visitmystic.com/oldmysticinn*
Charming 1784 house with carriage house annex
and gazebo on the lawn. Eight bedrooms, including
family-size rooms. Quiet location.

### Randall's Ordinary ($$–$$$)
*Route 2, Box 243, North Stonington, CT 06359*
*tel: 860/599–4540 fax: 860/599–3308*
*www.randallsordinary.com*
There are 16 rooms in the 1685 farmhouse and
1819 converted barn, plus a log cabin that sleeps
six. Furnished simply and harmoniously.

## New Haven

### Three Chimneys Inn ($$$)
*1201 Chapel Street, New Haven, CT 06511*
*tel: 203/789–1201 or 800/443–1554*
*fax: 203/776–7363*
*www.threechimneysinn.com*

An 11-room Victorian mansion with antiques, plus
modern amenities, including two-line phones.

## New London

### Queen Anne Inn ($$–$$$)
*265 Williams Street, New London, CT 06320*
*tel: 860/447–2600 or 800/347–8818*
*fax: 860/443–0857 www.queen-anne.com*
This characterful 1903 mansion has ten charming
rooms, complete with antiques and stained-glass
windows.

## Norwalk

### Silvermine Tavern ($$–$$$)
*194 Perry Avenue, Norwalk, CT 06850*
*tel: 203/847–4558 fax: 203/847–9171*
From Merritt Parkway, exit 40A. One of the oldest
lodgings in the state, dating from the mid-1700s.
Ten rooms (and one suite) with lots of character.
The restaurant serves New England fare.

# Maine

## Acadia and Bar Harbor

### Bayview ($$–$$$)
*111 Eden Street, Bar Harbor, ME 04609*
*tel: 207/288–5861 or 800/356–3585*
*www.barharbor.com/bayview*
Prime position by the ocean, on the edge of town.
Three contrasting accommodations categories:
the three-story townhouses, the modern main
hotel, and the period inn.

### Cleftstone Manor ($$–$$$)
*92 Eden Street, Bar Harbor, ME 04609*
*tel: 207/288–4951 or 888/288–4951*
*fax: 207/288–2089 www.cleftstone.com*
A 16-room Victorian extravaganza, ideal for a
romantic retreat. Built in 1881 as a private
summer home, and converted to an inn in 1948.

## Bath

### Fairhaven Inn ($)
*118 North Bath Road, Bath, ME 04530*
*tel: 207/443–4391 or 888/443–4391*
*fax: 207/443–6412*
*www.mainecoast.com/fairhaveninn*
This charming cedar-shingle house of 1790
overlooks the Kennebec River. The eight rooms
boast handmade quilts and mahogany four-poster
beds. Two rooms share a bath.

## Baxter State Park

### Pamola Motor Lodge ($)
*973 Central Street, Millinocket, ME 04462*
*tel: 207/723–9746*
The nearest motel to Baxter State Park; it also
has a restaurant.

## Bethel, Rangeley, and
## the Western Lakes

### Bethel Inn and Country Club ($$$)
*1 Broad Street (Box 49), Bethel, ME 04217*
*tel: 207/824–2175 or 800/654–0125*
*fax: 207/824–2233 www.bethelinn.com*
The main hotel for Bethel, a 1913 mansion
expanded into a sport and health resort with
conference facilities. Condominiums are also
available.

**Herbert** ($–$$)
*Main Street, P.O. Box 67, Kingfield, ME 04947*
*tel: 207/265–2000 or 800/THE–HERB*
*fax: 207/265–4594*
*www.mainemountaininn.com*
An atmospheric 28-room beaux arts inn of 1918 with many original features, including the tin ceiling of its colonnaded dining room. Moose and deer heads adorn the walls of the lobby, where there is a grand piano and open fire. Only a few rooms have TVs. Packages are available for skiing at nearby Sugarloaf.

**Hunter Cove on Rangeley Lake** ($$–$$$)
*Mingo Loop Road, Rangeley, ME 04970*
*tel: 207/864–3383 fax: 207/864–5173*
*www.rangeleymaine.com/hunter*
Eight lakeside cabins, each sleeping 2–6, with full kitchens, baths, and living rooms. There is a sand beach, swimming, and boat rentals.

## Eastport
**Motel East** ($)
*23A Water Street, Eastport, ME 04631*
*tel/fax: 207/853–4747*
*e-mail: moteleastport@acadia.net*
Has 14 well-equipped rooms, some with kitchenettes, plus views across the bay toward Canada.

## Freeport
**Freeport Inn** ($–$$)
*31 U.S. Route 1 South, Freeport, ME 04032*
*tel: 207/865–3106 or 800/99VALUE*
*fax: 207/865–6364 www.freeportinn.com*
A modern building set back from the main road, a short drive from the factory outlet shops at Freeport. They also own the nearby café where you have breakfast, and the larger Muddy Rudder restaurant.

**Harraseeket Inn** ($$–$$$)
*162 Main Street, Freeport, ME 04032*
*tel: 207/865–9377 or 800/342–6423*
*fax: 207/865–1684 www.harraseeketinn.com*
A modern re-creation of a traditional inn: Federal-style beds, fireplaces, and a formal dining room.

## Moosehead Lake
**Birches Resort** ($–$$)
*The Birches Road, Box 41, Rockwood,*
*ME 04478 tel: 207/534–7305*
*or 800/825–9453 fax: 207/534–8835*
*www.birches.com*
Located on an 11,000-acre wilderness preserve on Moosehead Lake, with trails for hiking, mountain biking, and cross-country skiing. There are 16 cottages, sleeping 2–16; a lodge with four rooms; and yurts with wood stoves, beds, and tables.

## Penobscot Bay
**Castine Inn** ($–$$)
*Main Street, Castine, ME 04421*
*tel: 207/326–4365 fax: 207/326–4570*
*www.castineinn.com*
An attractive location by the harbor, with a wraparound porch and good views from the top floor. There are 19 rooms, plus a restaurant that serves sophisticated New England cuisine.

**Craignair Inn** ($–$$)
*533 Clark Island Road, Spruce Head,*
*ME 04859 tel: 207/594–7644 or*
*800/320–9997 fax: 207/596–7124*
*www.craignair.com*
A remote backwater ideal for a quiet escape: this cozy inn has creaky floors, antiques, and pretty rooms; there is a more modern feel to the Vestry, a former chapel. The dining room serves fresh fish.

**East Wind Inn and Meeting House** ($–$$)
*Mechanic Street, Box 149, Tenants Harbor,*
*ME 04860 tel: 207/372–6366 or*
*800/241–8439 fax: 207/372–6320*
*www.eastwindinn.com*
Has 26 simple rooms, 19 with private bath. The restaurant menu features poultry and seafood.

**Keeper's House** ($$$)
*Box 26, Isle au Haut, ME 04645*
*tel: 207/367–2261 www.keepershouse.com*
A former lighthouse keeper's house with four rooms. No roads lead to it (access is by mail boat), and there is no electricity (it is lit by lanterns and candles).

**Norumbega** ($$–$$$)
*63 High Street, Camden, ME 04843*
*tel: 207/236–4646 or 877/363–4646*
*fax: 207/236–4990 www.norumbegainn.com*
A spectacular 1886 castle near Route 1, with lavish interiors and Empire furnishings. Many rooms have garden and bay views.

271

**Pentagoet** ($$$)
*Main Street, Castine, ME 04421*
*tel: 207/326–8616 or 800/845–1701*
*fax: 207/326–9382 www.pentagoet.com*
Has 16 country-style Victorian bedrooms, some in the 1894 main inn and others in an older Colonial building next door. The restaurant serves formal dinners; reservations recommended.

**Whitehall Inn** ($$)
*52 High Street, Camden, ME 04843*
*tel: 207/236–3391 or 800/789–6565*
*fax: 207/236–4427 www.whitehall-inn.com*
A traditional 50-room inn in an 1834 former captain's house with a later wing. American cuisine is served in the dining room.

## Portland
**Pomegranate Inn** ($$–$$$)
*49 Neal Street, Portland, ME 04102*
*tel: 207/772–1006 or 800/356–0408*
*fax: 207/773–4426 www.pomegranateinn.com*
Eight antiques-filled rooms in a quiet, backstreet B&B with a tasteful, crisp interior.

## York and Kennebunkport
**Black Point Inn** ($$$)
*510 Black Point Road, Prout's Neck,*
*Scarborough, ME 04074 tel: 207/883–2500*
*or 800/258–0003 fax: 207/883–9976*
*www.blackpointinn.com*
This charming inn is at the end of a peninsula. Cottages on the grounds will appeal to families.

**Captain Jefferds Inn** ($$–$$$)
*5 Pearl Street, Box 691, Kennebunkport,*
*ME 04046 tel: 207/967–2311 or*
*800/839–6844 fax: 207/967–0721*
*www.captainjefferdsinn.com*
A clapboard sea captain's house, built in 1804. The 15 rooms (some with fireplaces) have old dressers and chests, books, paintings, ceramics, and glass.

# Accommodations and Restaurants

## Massachusetts

### The Berkshires
**Blantyre ($$$)**
*16 Blantyre Road, Lenox, MA 01240*
*tel: 413/637–3556 fax: 413/637–4282*
*www.blantyre.com*
A Tudor-style castle on fine grounds, with superb guest rooms. The rooms in the carriage house and cottages are slightly less grand.

**Red Lion Inn ($$–$$$)**
*30 Main Street, Stockbridge, MA 02162*
*tel: 413/298–5545 fax: 413/298–1691*
*www.redlioninn.com*
This celebrated old inn, situated right in the village center and immortalized by artist Norman Rockwell, has an antique-laden interior befitting its status. Some rooms in the main building are quite small. The dining room offers New England specialties such as oyster pie and scallops.

**River Bend Farm ($)**
*643 Simonds Road, Williamstown, MA 01267*
*tel: 413/458–3121*
A 1770 house on National Register of Historic Places. Four-poster beds, washstands, and spinning wheels adorn the four bedrooms, which share two bathrooms.

**Williams Inn ($$)**
*On the Green, Williamstown, MA 01267*
*tel: 413/458–9371 or 800/828–0133*
*fax: 413/458–2767*
This large, comfortable inn is in prime position at the top of the village green.

**Williamsville Inn ($$–$$$)**
*Route 41, West Stockbridge, MA 01266*
*tel: 413/274–6118 fax: 413/274–3539*
*www.williamsvilleinn.com*
An old inn by itself on a lonely country road. There are 16 pretty rooms with antiques in the 1797 farmhouse and adjacent restored barn. There is also storytelling on Sunday nights in winter.

### Cape Ann
**Inn on Cove Hill ($)**
*37 Mount Pleasant Street, Rockport, MA 01966  tel: 978/546–2701 or 888/546–2701  www.cape-ann.com/covehill*
A traditional inn dating from 1792, and furnished with period pieces. There are 11 rooms, nine with private bath.

**Old Corner Inn ($–$$)**
*2 Harbor Street, Manchester, MA 01944*
*tel: 978/526–4966 or 800/830–4996*
Built in 1865, this inn was formerly a Danish summer embassy. Some of the eight rooms have four-poster beds, claw-foot tubs, and fireplaces.

**Sally Webster Inn ($)**
*34 Mount Pleasant Street, Rockport, MA 01966*
*tel: 978/546–9251 or 877/546–9251*
*www.rockportusa.com/sallywebster*
Decorated in the Colonial style, this eight-room B&B is prettily furnished with rocking chairs and candle lanterns.

### Cape Cod
**Captain Freeman Inn ($$–$$$)**
*15 Breakwater Road, Brewster, MA 02631*

*tel: 508/896–7481 or 800/843–4664*
*fax: 508/896–5618  www.captfreemaninn.com*
Once a Victorian sea captain's home, this inn has pretty rooms, and is in the village center but a short walk from the beach. There is a pool. B&B only; there is a restaurant across the road.

**Captain's House Inn ($$$)**
*369 Old Harbor Road, Chatham, MA 02633*
*tel: 508/945–0127 or 800/315–0728*
*fax: 508/945–0866*
*www.captainshouseinn.com*
A charming inn, with 19 good-size rooms in four buildings.

**Dan'l Webster Inn ($$–$$$)**
*149 Main Street, Sandwich, MA 02563*
*tel: 508/888–3622 or 800/444–3566*
*fax: 508/888–5156  www.danlwebsterinn.com*
A traditionally furnished inn on an old village street, built in 1971 on the site of a 1692 parsonage. There are good-size rooms and public areas. The restaurant offers a lunch menu of sandwiches, salads, and soups, Sunday brunches, and more expensive dinners of seafood and meats.

**Mostly Hall ($$)**
*27 Main Street, Falmouth, MA 02540*
*tel: 508/548–3786 or 800/682–0565*
*fax: 508/457–1572  www.mostlyhall.com*
A fine 1849 house with a cupola and wraparound veranda in a parkland setting. There are six stylishly furnished rooms; B&B only.

### Marblehead
**Harbor Light Inn ($$–$$$)**
*58 Washington Street, Marblehead, MA 01945*
*tel: 781/631–2186 fax: 781/631–2216*
*www.harborlightinn.com*
This old-fashioned inn offers creature comforts and excellent Continental breakfasts. It has 21 rooms plus a pool.

### Martha's Vineyard
**Daggett House ($$–$$$)**
*59 North Water Street, Box 1333, Edgartown, Martha's Vineyard, MA 02539*
*tel: 508/627–4600 or 800/946–3400*
*fax: 508/627–4611  www.mvweb.com/daggett*
A 17th-century tavern with a secret staircase, period interiors, and fine views.

**Oak House ($$–$$$)**
*Sea View Avenue, Box 299, Oak Bluffs, Martha's Vineyard, MA 02557*
*tel: 508/693–4187 or 800/245–5979*
*fax: 508/696–7385*
*www.vineyard.net/biz/inns/oakhouse*
A Victorian house with pretty rooms, near the beach; quieter rooms are at the back.

**Outermost Inn ($$$)**
*Off Lighthouse Road, RR1, Box 171, Aquinnah (formerly Gay Head), Martha's Vineyard, MA 02535  tel: 508/645–3511*
*fax: 508/645–3514  www.outermostinn.com*
This civilized seven-room hideaway has a restrained contemporary decor and views of the Aquinnah lighthouse. A sailboat is available for charter.

### Nantucket
**Hosteling International Nantucket ($)**
*Surfside Beach, Nantucket (mailing address:*

31 Western Avenue, Nantucket, MA 02554)
tel: 508/228–0433, off-season reservations
617/531–0459 www.hi-travel.org/nantuck.htm
The cheapest accommodation on the island,
reached by a 3-mile ride on a bike path from town
out to Surfside Beach. Closed from mid-October to
mid-April.

**Jared Coffin House** ($$–$$$)
29 Broad Street, Nantucket, MA 02554
tel: 508/228–2405 or 800/248–2405
fax: 508/228–8549 www.jaredcoffinhouse.com
Located in the historic heart of Nantucket town,
this inn has 60 rooms in four buildings centered
on a brick mansion. Oriental carpets and antiques
set the tone; other rooms have reproduction
furniture. There is formal dining in the restaurant.

## Newburyport
**Clark Currier Inn** ($$)
45 Green Street, Newburyport, MA 01950
tel: 978/465–8363 or 800/360–6582
www.clarkcurrierinn.com
An eight-room stylishly restored Federal-period
mansion with antique furnishings. There is also
a library and garden.

## Old Sturbridge
**Old Sturbridge Village Lodges and
Oliver Wight House** ($–$$)
Route 20 West, Sturbridge, MA 01566
tel: 508/347–3327 or 800/SEE–1830
fax: 508/347–3018 www.osv.org
Owned by Old Sturbridge Museum. The house
dates from 1789 and has Federal-style furnishings
in the ten rooms. There are also 47 single-story
village units.

## Pioneer Valley
**Deerfield Inn** ($$$)
81 Old Main Street, Deerfield, MA 01342
tel: 413/774–5587 or 800/926–3865
fax: 413/775–7221 www.deerfieldinn.com
In the heart of the historic village; there are 23
rooms, with antique and reproduction furnishings.
Enjoy country breakfasts and candlelit dinner in the
pretty restaurant, whose menu often features
recipes from the Historic Deerfield museum's
cookbooks.

**Lord Jeffery Inn** ($–$$)
30 Boltwood Avenue, Amherst, MA 01002
tel: 413/253–2576 or 800/742–0358
fax: 413/256–6152
www.pinnacle-inns.com/lordjefferyinn
A 48-room inn facing the green in the town
center, a minute's walk from the college. The
rooms are decorated in Colonial style. The
restaurant is casually sophisticated, with a
menu that features poultry, fish, and game.

**Whately Inn** ($)
193 Chestnut Plain Road, Whately Center,
MA 01093 tel: 413/665–3044 or
800/942–8359 fax: 413/665–4969
www.whatelyinn.com
This inn (located between Northampton and
Deerfield) has four well-appointed rooms with
antiques and four-poster beds. The large dining
room hosts dinners and Sunday lunches;
reservations recommended.

## Plymouth
**Blue Spruce** ($–$$)
710 State Road, Plymouth, MA 02360
tel: 508/224–3990 or 800/370–7080
fax: 508/224–2279
www.bluespruce-motel.com
A modern motel with 28 rooms and four townhouse
units. On Route 3A, some 6 miles south of town.

**Pilgrim Sands Motel** ($–$$)
150 Warren Avenue, Plymouth MA 02360
tel: 508/747–0900 or 800/729–SANDS
fax: 508/746–8066 www.pilgrimsands.com
South of town near Plimoth Plantation. There is a
private beach and sea views.

## Salem
**Amelia Payson Guest House** ($–$$)
16 Winter Street, Salem, MA 01970
tel: 978/744–8304
www.salemweb.com/biz/ameliapayson
An 1845 Greek Revival house with a grand piano in
the parlor. Four cozy rooms with wicker furniture,
canopies, and brass beds. Near the town center.

**Hawthorne Hotel** ($$–$$$)
18 Washington Square West, Salem,
MA 01970 tel: 978/744–4080 or
800/729–7829 fax: 978/745–9842
www.hawthornehotel.com
A traditional redbrick inn on the green. The 89
rooms are appointed with 18th-century reproductions. There is a formal restaurant and casual bar.

## Westminster
**Wachusett Village Inn and Conference
Center** ($$–$$$)
9 Village Inn Road, Westminster, MA 01473
tel: 978/874–2000 or 800/342–1905
fax: 978/874–1753
www.wachusettvillageinn.com
This comfortable resort, beside Route 2, is set
out like a stylized New England village. It offers
outdoor family activities, including skiing, sleigh
rides, hay rides, and hiking.

# New Hampshire

## Cornish
**Chase House** ($$)
RR2, Box 909, Route 12A, Cornish, NH 03745
tel: 603/675–5391 or 800/401–9455
fax: 603/675–5010 www.chasehouse.com
Near Cornish-Windsor covered bridge and Saint-
Gaudens National Historic Site. Nine traditionally
appointed rooms in the elegantly restored home of
the man who was chief justice of America under
President Lincoln. Meadow and river views.

## Hanover
**Hanover Inn** ($$$)
Main and East Wheelock streets, Hanover,
NH 03755 tel: 603/643–4300 or
800/443–7024 fax: 603/646–3744
www.hanoverinn.com
This highly acclaimed Georgian inn fronts the green
at the hub of the Dartmouth campus and is also
adjacent to the Hopkins Center for the Performing
Arts. The inn's Daniel Webster Room is one of the
state's top restaurants; lighter meals, as well as a

273

# Accommodations and Restaurants

large selection of wines by the glass, are available in Zins Winebistro.

## Lake Sunapee

**Dexter's Inn and Tennis Club ($$)**
*258 Stagecoach Road, Sunapee, NH 03782*
*tel: 603/763–5571 or 800/232–5571*
*e-mail: dexters@kear.tds.net*
A small, idyllically set inn above the lake with good tennis facilities.

**New London Inn ($$)**
*140 Main Street, New London, NH 03257*
*tel: 603/526–2791 or 800/526–2791*
*fax: 603/526–2749 www.newlondoninn.com*
This 1792 Federal-style inn has 26 rooms and faces the village green.

## Lake Winnipesaukee

**Nutmeg Inn ($)**
*80 Pease Road, Meredith, NH 03253*
*tel: 603/279–8811*
*www.bbhost.com/nutmeginn*
Made from old ship's timbers, this 18th-century black-shuttered house has rare, wide "king's boards" that were reserved from the Royal Navy. It has a quiet position between Route 104 and the lake.

**Red Hill Inn ($$–$$$)**
*Route 25B, Box 99M, Center Harbor, NH 03226*
*tel: 603/279–7001 or 800/573–3445*
*fax: 603/279–7003 www.redhillinn.com*
A finely sited 26-room inn overlooking Squam Lake.

**Tamworth Inn ($$)**
*Main Street, Tamworth (mailing address:*
*15 Cleveland Hill Road, Tamworth, NH 03886)*
*tel: 603/323–7721 or 800/642–7352*
*fax: 603/323–2026 www.tamworth.com*
The 15 country-style rooms are full of personal touches, so each is slightly different. There is an outdoor pool, plus a restaurant serving new American cuisine.

**Wakefield Inn ($)**
*2723 Wakefield Road, Wakefield, NH 03872*
*www.wakefieldinn.com*
Seven rooms in a restored house and stagecoach inn dating back to 1815.

## Mount Monadnock region

**Amos Parker House ($)**
*146 Route 119, Box 202, Fitzwilliam,*
*NH 03447 tel: 603/585–6540*
This attractive house near a village green has four rooms.

**Benjamin Prescott Inn ($–$$)**
*Route 124 East, Jaffrey, NH 03452*
*tel/fax: 603/532–6637 or 888/950–6637*
*www.benjaminprescottinn.com*
A small historic inn set by itself in rolling country-side. The ten-room house is full of artifacts and knickknacks.

**Inn at East Hill Farm ($$–$$$)**
*460 Monadnock Street, Troy, NH 03465*
*tel: 603/242–6495 or 800/242–6495*
*fax: 603/242–7709 www.east-hill-farm.com*
A year-round farm vacation resort that caters for families. Indoor and outdoor pools, tennis, horseback riding, boating, fishing.

## Portsmouth and the coast

**Martin Hill Inn ($)**
*404 Islington Street, Portsmouth, NH 03801*
*tel: 603/436–2287*
*www.portsmouthnh.com/martinhillinn*
Close to the historic district; the seven rooms are decorated with antique furnishings.

**Rock Ledge Manor ($$–$$$)**
*1413 Ocean Boulevard, Rye, NH 03870*
*tel: 603/431–1413 www.rockledgemanor.com*
A Victorian house with three guest rooms, a wraparound porch, and sea views.

**Sise Inn ($$–$$$)**
*40 Court Street, Portsmouth, NH 03801*
*tel/fax: 603/433–1200 or 800/267–0525*
A former merchant's house of 1881 of a suitably comfortable, Victorian character.

## White Mountains region

**Balsams Grand Resort Hotel ($$$)**
*Route 26, Dixville Notch, NH 03576*
*tel: 603/255–3400 or 800/255–0600*
*fax: 603/255–4221 www.thebalsams.com*
The last word in luxury, among the finest hotels in the state. Resort facilities include an outdoor pool, cross-country ski center, a small downhill ski area, and children's programs. Stunning views. The restaurant is one of the finest in the state, serving American and Continental cuisine; jacket and tie.

**Christmas Farm Inn ($$$)**
*Box CC, Route 16B, Jackson Village,*
*NH 03846 tel: 603/383–4313 or*
*800/HI–ELVES fax: 603/383–6495*
*www.christmasfarminn.com*
An 18th-century inn with cottages, dairy barn suites, a log cabin, and a saltbox building. The restaurant's mixed menu includes "heart healthy" dishes.

**Cranmore Inn ($)**
*80 Kearsarge Street, North Conway, NH 03860*
*tel: 603/356–5502 or 800/526–5502*
*fax: 603/356–6052 www.cranmoreinn.com*
A welcoming 18-room guest house that has been in North Conway since the late 1800s.

**Darby Field Inn ($$–$$$)**
*185 Chase Road, Conway, NH 03818*
*tel: 603/447–2181 or 800/426–4147*
*fax: 603/447–5726 www.darbyfield.com*
There are memorable mountain views from each of this inn's 15 rooms. Several rooms have whirlpool tubs, some have fireplaces. The pine-paneled dining room has commendable specials.

**Mount Washington Hotel and Resort, Bretton Arms Country Inn, and Bretton Woods Motor Inn ($–$$$)**
*Route 302, Bretton Woods, NH 03575*
*tel: 603/278–1000 or 800/258–0330*
*fax: 603/278–8838 www.mtwashington.com*
A range of styles and prices, at the foot of Mount Washington, The resort owns the railway up the mountain, as well as cross-country and downhill ski areas, tennis courts, and a golf course. Mount Washington Hotel itself is an amazing 1902 sur-vival, a grand hotel, complete with ballroom. Bretton Arms has classic inn rooms and a fine restaurant; the Motor Inn is a good budget family option.

**Woodstock Inn ($–$$)**
*Main Street, Route 3, North Woodstock,*
*NH 03262 tel: 603/745–3951 or*

*800/321–3985 fax: 603/745–3701*
*www.woodstockinnnh.com*
There are inexpensive but pretty Victorian-style rooms in the main inn, with shared bathrooms, and private bathrooms in the annexes. It also features a pub with its own microbrewery partly within an old (reerected) railroad station.

# Rhode Island

## Block Island
**Manisses, 1661 Inn and Guesthouse** ($$$)
*Spring Street, Block Island, RI 02807*
*tel: 401/466–2421 or 800/626–4773*
*fax: 401/466–3162*
*www.blockisland.com/biresorts*
The Hotel Manisses, an elegantly furnished Victorian hotel on the National Register of Historic Places, has 17 rooms. In the 1661 Inn, some of the nine rooms have ocean views. The more contemporary guest house has nine rooms. In season, a lavish buffet breakfast is served at the 1661 Inn for guests at all three properties.

## Newport
**Cliffside Inn** ($$$)
*2 Seaview Avenue, Newport, RI 02840*
*tel: 401/847–1811 or 800/845–1811*
*fax: 401/848–5850 www.cliffsideinn.com*
A grand 1880s house filled with Victorian pieces; close to Cliff Walk. 16 rooms and 26 fireplaces!
**Francis Malbone House** ($$$)
*392 Thames Street, Newport, RI 02840*
*tel: 401/846–0392 or 800/846–0392*
*fax: 401/848–5956 www.malbone.com*
Harbor views are enjoyed from this grand historic inn. Polished floorboards, reproduction furniture, and fireplaces adorn the interior.
**Ivy Lodge** ($$$)
*12 Clay Street, Newport, RI 02840*
*tel: 401/849–6865 or 800/834–6865*
*fax: 401/849–2919 www.ivylodge.com*
This Victorian house offers the only B&B accommodations in the mansions district. The rooms are of a good size.

## Providence
**Old Court** ($$)
*144 Benefit Street, Providence, RI 02903*
*tel: 401/751–2002 fax: 401/272–4830*
*www.oldcourt.com*
A B&B in the city's prettiest quarter; complete with Victorian decor.
**Providence Biltmore** ($$–$$$)
*11 Dorrance Street, Providence, RI 02903*
*tel: 401/421–0700 or 800/294–7709*
*fax: 401/455–3050*
A 1920s art deco building, the hotel features good service and a handy downtown location.

## South County
**Richards** ($$)
*144 Gibson Avenue, Narragansett, RI 02882*
*tel: 401/789–7746*
A Victorian house with high ceilings and antiques, on a quiet residential street. There are two rooms, plus two suites. Bed and breaksfast only, but the breakfasts are inspired.

**Shelter Harbor Inn** ($$–$$$)
*10 Wagner Road, Westerly, RI 02891*
*tel: 401/322–8883 or 800/468–8883*
*fax: 401/322–7907*
A secluded retreat with creature comforts; a cluster of buildings around a renovated 19th-century country inn. The restaurant's menu changes frequently and there is a wine list as long as your arm.

# Vermont

## Bennington
**Molly Stark Inn** ($–$$)
*1067 Main Street, Bennington, VT 05201*
*tel: 802/442–9631 or 800/356–3076*
*fax: 802/442–5224 www.mollystarkinn.com*
An 1890 inn on the road to Brattleboro; quieter rooms are situated at the rear. There are also two suites in the adjacent sugarhouse-style building, plus a cottage.
**South Shire Inn** ($$–$$$)
*124 Elm Street, Bennington, VT 05201*
*tel: 802/447–3839 fax: 802/442–3547*
*www.southshire.com*
A prettily decorated and furnished inn with five rooms in the main house, and four in the adjacent carriage house. Near the town center.

## Burlington
**Inn at Essex** ($$$)
*70 Essex Way, off Route 15, Essex Junction, VT 05452 tel: 802/878–1100 or 800/727–4295 fax: 802/878–0063*
*www.innatessex.com*
A modern hotel and conference center styled after a country inn. The New England Culinary Institute operates the restaurants and room service.

## Grafton
**Old Tavern at Grafton** ($$–$$$)
*92 Main Street, Box 9, Grafton, VT 05146*
*tel: 802/843–2231 or 800/843–1801*
*fax: 802/843–2245 www.old-tavern.com*
This painstakingly restored inn of 1788 has antiques, four-posters, and canopied beds in its 12 rooms. Across the street are 18 more rooms. There are two dining rooms, one with Georgian furniture, the other with a low ceiling, paneling, and exposed beams. Here, you can sample New England specialties and local cheeses.

## Killington
**Inn at Long Trail** ($$)
*Route 4, Box 267, Killington, VT 05751*
*tel: 802/775–7181 or 800/325–2540*
*fax: 802/747–7034 www.innatlongtrail.com*
A welcoming rustic lodge near the Pico/Killington ski slopes and the Appalachian Trail. There are 14 rooms, including two family rooms, plus five suites. Winter weekend packages include breakfast and dinner. An Irish pub serves light meals.
**Inn of the Six Mountains** ($$$)
*2617 Killington Road, Killington, VT 05751-9709 tel: 802/422–4302*
*www.sixmountains.com*
Modern comforts at this 103-room hotel a mile from the base lift at Killington ski resort.

275

# Accommodations and Restaurants

## Manchester

**Alpenrose Inn ($)**
*Winhall Hollow Road, P.O. Box 187, Bondville,*
*VT 05340 tel: 802/297–2750*
*www.alpen-rose.com*
A peaceful, Alpine-style house conveniently placed
for Stratton and Bromley ski areas.

**Cornucopia of Dorset ($$–$$$)**
*3228 Route 30, Dorset, VT 05251*
*tel: 802/867–5751 or 800/566–5751*
*fax: 802/867–5753 www.cornucopiaofdorset.com*
Four rooms in a turn-of-the-20th-century house,
plus a cottage, with wraparound veranda.

**Hill Farm Inn ($–$$)**
*458 Hill Farm Road, Arlington, VT 05250*
*tel: 802/375–2269 or 800/882–2545*
*fax: 802/375–9918 www.hillfarminn.com*
This long-established inn has an unspoiled river
setting. There are five rooms in the 1830 main inn
and six rooms in the 1790 guest house next-door,
with New England farmhouse-style decor.

**Marble West Inn ($–$$)**
*Dorset West Road, Dorset, VT 05251*
*tel: 802/867–4155 or 800/453–7629*
*www.marblewestinn.com*
A gracious and personal house with stenciled hall-
way, open gas fires in the library and breakfast
room, and a grand piano in the sitting room. The
eight bedrooms enjoy tranquil rural views and have
polished wood furniture; there are no TVs.

**West Mountain Inn ($$–$$$)**
*West Mountain Inn Road (off Route 313),*
*Arlington, VT 05250 tel: 802/375–6516*
*fax: 802/375–6553 www.westmountaininn.com*
A former farmhouse in a secluded mountainside
location. Hiking and ski trails are within the
grounds, and there are two pet llamas.

## Marlboro

**Whetstone Inn ($)**
*550 South Road, Marlboro, VT 05344*
*tel: 802/254–2500 or 877/254–2500*
This reasonably priced inn is convenient for the
Marlboro summer music festival. There are eight
rooms with private bath, four with shared bath.

## Middlebury

**Blueberry Inn ($$$)**
*Forest Service Road, Goshen, VT 05733*
*tel: 802/247–6735 www.blueberryhillinn.com*
This 1813 farmhouse is a peaceful retreat high up
in the Green Mountains. It has its own cross-
country ski area and offers hiking and biking in
the summer.

**Middlebury Inn ($–$$$)**
*14 Court House Square, Middlebury,*
*VT 05753-0798 tel: 802/388–4961 or*
*800/842–4666 fax: 802/388–4563*
*www.middleburyinn.com*
A large village inn dating from 1827. Special
programs include hiking and nature packages.

**Swift House Inn ($$–$$$)**
*25 Stewart Lane, Middlebury, VT 05753*
*tel: 802/388–9925 fax: 802/388–9927*
*www.swifthouseinn.com*
This former home of a Vermont governor
comprises three buildings; the main house
dates from 1815.

## Montpelier

**Inn at Montpelier ($$–$$$)**
*147 Main Street, Montpelier, VT 05602*
*tel: 802/223–2727 fax: 802/223–0722*
*www.innatmontpelier.com*
Two Greek Revival and Colonial-style buildings
from the early 1800s house a variety of rooms
within walking distance of the town.

## Rutland

**Mountain Top Inn ($$$)**
*195 Mountain Top Road, Chittenden,*
*VT 05737 tel: 802/483–2311 or*
*800/445–2100 fax: 802/483–6373*
*www.mountaintopinn.com*
This inn is remotely located north of Rutland, on a
hillside overlooking Chittenden Reservoir and the
Green Mountains. Games and sports activities are
included in the room price—there are sleigh rides,
skating, golf, and cross-country skiing trails.

## St. Johnsbury and
## the Northeast Kingdom

**Inn on the Common ($$$)**
*1162 Craftsbury Road, Craftsbury Common,*
*VT 05827 tel: 802/586–9619 or*
*800/521–2233 fax: 802/586–2249*
*www.innonthecommon.com*
The inn occupies three small buildings in a pretty
village; guests eat together. There is also a
croquet lawn, tennis, and a swimming pool.

## Shelburne

**Inn at Shelburne Farms ($$–$$$)**
*1611 Harbor Road, Shelburne Farms,*
*Shelburne, VT 05482 tel: 802/985–8498*
*fax: 802/985–8123 www.shelburnefarms.org*
Built in 1899 by Lila Vanderbilt Webb and William
Seward, this Queen Anne Revival-style inn has original furnishings and is similar to the mansions of
Newport, RI. It makes for a romantic setting by the
lake. There are 24 rooms, 17 with private bath.

## Stowe

**Gables Inn ($$–$$$)**
*1457 Mountain Road, Stowe, VT 05672*
*tel: 802/253–7730 or 800/GABLES–1*
*fax: 802/253–7730 www.gablesinn.com*
A former 1850s farmhouse furnished in early
American style; the more expensive rooms are in
the Carriage House and in the two Riverview
Suites. Imaginative, hearty breakfasts.

**Inn at the Brass Lantern ($$)**
*Route 100, 717 Maple Street, Stowe,*
*VT 05672 tel: 802/253–2229 or*
*800/729–2980 fax: 802/253–7425*
*www.brasslanterninn.com*
Nine rooms in an 1810 farmhouse and adjacent
carriage house, decorated with quilts and period
antiques. Fine views of Mount Mansfield.

**Trapp Family Lodge ($$–$$$)**
*700 Trapp Hill Road, Stowe, VT 05672*
*tel: 802/253–8511 or 800/826–7000*
*fax: 802/253–5740 www.trappfamily.com*
Still owned by the Von Trapps of *Sound of Music*
fame—the family grave is here too—this Austrian-
style lodge replaced the original structure, which
was destroyed by fire in 1980. Rooms have floral

stenciling and Austrian print fabrics, and enjoy mountain views; most have balconies. Flowers were important to Maria von Trapp, and the lodge employs two florists to present spectacular shows of greenery in the public areas.

**Ye Olde England Inne ($$–$$$)**
433 Mountain Road, Stowe, VT 05672
tel: 802/253-7558 or 800/477-3771
fax: 802/253-8944  www.oldenglandinne.com
English owners have given this inn a distinctive Old English tone, with scones set out for fireside afternoon tea. There are modern suites in the Bluff House annex, in addition to traditional rooms in the inn, and two-bedroom cottages are available. The Pickwick pub has some 150 ales.

## West Dover

**Four Seasons Inn ($)**
Route 100, West Dover, VT 05356
tel: 802/464-8303
The Four Seasons has pretty Victorian decor and sloping ceilings.

## Weston

**Darling Family Inn ($–$$)**
815 Route 100, Weston, VT 05161-5404
tel/fax: 802/824-3223
e-mail: dfi@vermontel.net
A former farmhouse with handcrafted quilts and American and English antiques. There are five guest rooms, plus two cottages that are good for families.

# RESTAURANTS

Quantities are usually generous in New England's restaurants and diners. The obvious attractions are the seafood, often served with drawn (melted) butter. Prices often include a salad. For more general information about New England cuisine, see pages 20–21.

Reservations are recommended in the most popular places, especially at the peak of the season. Casual dress is generally acceptable, although more upscale restaurants may require a jacket and tie. Many places have a no-smoking policy. A number of the inns listed under the accommodations section (see pages 268–277) also have restaurants that serve good-quality, often local dishes.

You can also eat very adequately and inexpensively at diners, pizza parlors, and other places. There is no problem in asking for a "doggie bag" at most of these places. Vegetarian food is not widely available; even the more upscale establishments have a very limited choice for those who exclude fish as well as meat from their diet. State tax is normally added to the cost of a meal, and tips of 15 percent are expected.

## Boston and Cambridge

**Ambrosia on Huntington ($$$)**
116 Huntington Avenue, Boston
tel: 617/247-2400
The presentations are breathtaking, and the fusion cuisine is exquisite at this spacious restaurant.

**Anthony's Pier 4 ($$)**
140 Northern Avenue, Boston
tel: 617/423-6363
A favorite Waterfront restaurant offering traditional New England fare.

**Aujourd'hui ($$$)**
The Four Seasons, 200 Boylston Street, Boston  tel: 617/451-1392
Overlooking the Boston Public Garden, this top dining destination provides the perfect setting for its exquisite regional dishes.

**Barking Crab ($$)**
88 Sleeper Street at Northern Avenue, Boston
tel: 617/426-2722
Good New England seafood, served in a wooden shack by the water's edge. Eat outside in summer.

**Biba ($$$)**
272 Boylston Street, Boston
tel: 617/426-7878
One of the most celebrated restaurants in Boston; check out the funky art on the walls, the chic clientele, and most importantly, the eclectic American fare that features dishes such as lobster pizza.

**Blue Diner ($$)**
150 Kneeland Street, Boston
tel: 617/695-0087
A celebrated Boston institution near South Station; opens Fri–Sat 24 hours, Sun–Thu 11 AM–4 AM. Hearty meat dishes, plus classic and updated diner fare.

**Bomboa ($$–$$$)**
35 Stanhope Street (off Clarendon Street), Boston  tel: 617/236-6363
The Latin-fusion trend has come to Boston with this stylish French-Brazilian restaurant. Popular for drinks as well as dinner.

**Border Café ($)**
32 Church Street, Cambridge
tel: 617/864-6100
A casual Tex-Mex eatery in Harvard Square. Wildly popular with students; expect to wait for a table.

**Boston Sail Loft ($)**
80 Atlantic Avenue, Boston  tel: 617/227-7280
The best budget seafood on the Waterfront, as well as a Sunday brunch, noon–3 PM.

**Casablanca ($$)**
40 Brattle Street, Cambridge
tel: 617/876-0999
A landmark Harvard Square bar/restaurant, filled with the ghosts of famous Bostonians, which since its overhaul in the early 1990s has become a dining destination for its innovative Mediterranean cuisine.

**Chez Henri ($$)**
1 Shepard Street (off Massachusetts Avenue), Cambridge  tel: 617/354-8980
Classic French bistro fare with a Cuban accent may be an unusual idea, but it seems to work at this lively, relaxed spot between Harvard and Porter squares. The prix fixe dinner is also excellent value.

**Clio ($$$)**
The Eliot Hotel, 370A Commonwealth Avenue, Boston  tel: 617/267-1607
Understated elegance defines this hushed, supper-club style restaurant that opened in 1997. The food—French with Asian accents—is the star, and the staff add to the experience by being attentive and knowledgeable.

# Accommodations and Restaurants

**Daily Catch** ($$)
*323 Hanover Street, Boston*
*tel: 617/523–8567  Also at 261 Northern*
*Avenue*
An informal, cramped North End storefront with
seafood and pasta at reasonable prices.

**Dakota's** ($$–$$$)
*34 Summer Street, Lobby Level, Boston*
*tel: 617/737–1777*
Eclectic American fare, with seafood specialties;
classy and patronized by a well-heeled clientele.
Next to Filene's department store.

**Durgin Park** ($–$$)
*30 North Market Street, Faneuil Hall*
*Marketplace, Boston  tel: 617/227–2038*
This crowded historic spot, opened in the 1830s,
specializes in generous portions of chowder, baked
beans, pot roast, chunky prime ribs, and more.

**East Coast Grill and Raw Bar** ($$–$$$)
*1271 Cambridge Street, Cambridge*
*tel: 617/491–6568*
Spicy American and equatorial cuisine; specializes
in seafood, from simply grilled fish to more exotic
preparations. Expect to wait at peak times.

**Elephant Walk** ($–$$)
*900 Beacon Street, Boston*
*tel: 617/247–1500  Also at 2067*
*Massachusetts Avenue, Cambridge*
The concept behind this restaurant is a menu that
includes both Cambodian and French dishes, as
was common in the era of Cambodian colonialism.

**L'Espalier** ($$$)
*30 Gloucester Street, Boston*
*tel: 617/262–3023*
Sublime French and American cuisine and a long
wine list make this one of Boston's most
celebrated restaurants. In an 1886 townhouse;
elegant and romantic.

**Figs** ($)
*42 Charles Street, Boston  tel: 617/742–3447*
Choose from a wide array of excellent and creative
pastas and pizzas at reasonable prices. Also avail-
able are fresh, interesting antipasti and salads.

**Galleria Italiana** ($$–$$$)
*177 Tremont Street, Boston*
*tel: 617/423–2092*
Feel transported to Italy at this small, intimate
trattoria-style eatery. Fans rave about the home-
made pastas, seafood, and simple desserts. Also
enjoyable is a snack of antipasto at the wine bar
located in the front room of the restaurant.

**Gardner Museum Café** ($$)
*280 The Fenway, Isabella Stewart Gardner*
*Museum, Boston  tel: 617/566–1088*
A popular place to stop for lunch while taking in
the sights of the museums.

**Ginza** ($$)
*16 Hudson Street, Boston  tel: 617/338–2261*
Tucked away in Chinatown is one of Boston's best
sushi spots. Try the caterpillar maki. Also teriyaki,
tempura, and other Japanese standards.

**Grand Chau Chow** ($–$$)
*45 Beach Street, Boston  tel: 617/292–5166*
Well worth venturing into Chinatown to sample the
excellent seafood. Good noodle dishes, too.

**Hamersley's Bistro** ($$$)
*553 Tremont Street, Boston*
*tel: 617/423–2700*

The superb country French food is the draw at this
spare, yet cozy bistro. The food is hearty and the
pleasant staff exude an inviting warmth.

**Henrietta's Table** ($$)
*The Charles Hotel, 1 Bennett Street,*
*Cambridge  tel: 617/661–5005*
Set up like a farmer's market, the entry to this
restaurant sets the tone for the regional American
cuisine. Enjoy the fresh baked bread and the specialty items smoked to order in the open kitchen.

**Icarus** ($$–$$$)
*3 Appleton Street, Boston  tel: 617/426–1790*
The understated sophistication, the creative
American food, the well-selected wine list, and the
attentive staff keep regulars coming back to this
South End favorite.

**Jae's Cafe & Grill** ($–$$)
*520 Columbus Avenue, Boston*
*tel: 617/421–9405  Also at 212 Stuart Street,*
*Boston, and 1281 Cambridge Street, Cambridge*
This funky pan-Asian restaurant has a menu that
includes Korean, Japanese, and Thai specialties.
Expect a wait, as it is often crowded.

**Jimmy's Harborside** ($$–$$$)
*242 Northern Avenue, Boston*
*tel: 617/423–1000*
A favorite seafood restaurant in the Waterfront
district, complete with harbor views; chowder,
bouillabaisse, scampi, and daily specials.

**Joe's American Bar and Grill** ($$–$$$)
*279 Dartmouth Street, Boston*
*tel: 617/536–4200*
Grills and seafood are the popular choices at this
trendy hot spot in Back Bay.

**Julien** ($$$)
*Le Meridien Boston, 250 Franklin Street,*
*Boston  tel: 617/451–1900*
One of the most beautiful restaurants in the city;
fans also rave about the exciting and well-prepared
French-inspired menu.

**Lala Rokh** ($$)
*97 Mount Vernon Street, Boston*
*tel: 617/720–5511*
Excellent Persian food is served, interesting art-
work adorns the walls, and candlelight and Persian
music complete the experience.

**Legal Sea Foods** ($$)
*26 Park Plaza, Boston  tel: 617/426–4444*
*Also at 255 State Street, Prudential Center,*
*Copley Place, and 5 Cambridge Center, Kendall*
*Square, Cambridge*
This chain offers top-quality seafood: simply
presented and using very fresh ingredients.

**Lucia Ristorante** ($$–$$$)
*415 Hanover Street, Boston*
*tel: 617/523–9148*
Top-class, North End Italian restaurant with
specialties from the Abruzzi region.

**Maison Robert** ($$$)
*45 School Street, Boston  tel: 617/227–3370*
Located in the Old City Hall and opened in 1971,
Maison Robert is something of a Boston institution. The classic French cuisine has been updated
in recent years, but the whole experience is still
timeless and special.

**Marcuccio's** ($$–$$$)
*125 Salem Street, Boston  tel: 617/723–1807*
Modern Italian fare in a casually funky North End

storefront. The weekday tasting menu with wine is excellent value.

**Mistral ($$$)**
*223 Columbus Avenue, Boston*
*tel: 617/867–9300*
A great spot to people-watch, this fashionably hip restaurant boasts an eclectic menu.

**Il Panino ($$)**
*11 Parmenter Street, Boston*
*tel: 617/720–1336*
A plain setting, but accomplished Italian cooking. Located in the North End; often very busy.

**Pignoli ($$$)**
*79 Park Plaza, Boston  tel: 617/338–7500*
Superb New Italian cuisine in an unusual setting. The atmosphere is casually charged; a favorite in the city.

**Radius ($$$)**
*8 High Street, Boston  tel: 617/426–1234*
The high-style dining room, creative New American cuisine, and solicitous service make this financial district hot spot an excellent choice for a business dinner or special evening out.

**Rialto ($$$)**
*The Charles Hotel, 1 Bennett Street, Cambridge  tel: 617/661–5050*
Consistently rated one of the city's best restaurants, the Rialto is a top choice for a special occasion. The food is excellent, drawing inspiration from France, Italy, and the Mediterranean. The dining room is comfortable and sophisticated, the wine list extensive, and the staff helpful.

**Sonsie ($$)**
*327 Newbury Street, Boston*
*tel: 617/351–2500*
Opening onto fashionable Newbury Street, Sonsie has the feel of a chic Parisian café. Diners come as much to be seen as to enjoy the eclectic international menu that features brick-oven pizzas, as well as Asian- and Moroccan-accented entrees.

**Sultan's Kitchen ($)**
*72 Broad Street, Boston  tel: 617/728–2828*
Open only for lunch, this simple restaurant serves fresh and delicious Turkish cuisine at very budget prices. The taramasalata scores raves, as do the pitta sandwiches and shish kabobs.

**Tapeo ($$)**
*266 Newbury Street, Boston*
*tel: 617/267–4799*
Sit upstairs by the fireplace in this welcoming Spanish restaurant. Tapas are deservedly popular, as is the whole fish baked under a salt crust.

**Tremont 647 ($$–$$$)**
*647 Tremont Street, Boston*
*tel: 617/266–4600*
The bustling open kitchen is the focus of this small and stylish restaurant, located on the ground floor of a refurbished South End townhouse. The food is American bistro with international accents.

# Connecticut

## Connecticut River Valley
**Sage American Bar and Grill ($–$$$)**
*129 West Main Street at Route 9, Chester*
*tel: 860/526–9898*
Classic American grill fare—steak, prime rib, fresh seafood, as well as sandwiches and salads—in a converted Victorian brush factory overlooking a waterfall.

## Hartford
**Carbone's ($$–$$$)**
*558 Franklin Avenue, Hartford*
*tel: 860/296–9646*
Intimate and romantic; Italian-American food.

**Kashmir ($–$$)**
*481 Wethersfield Avenue, Hartford*
*tel: 860/296–9685*
Northern Indian cuisine.

**Max Downtown ($$–$$$)**
*185 Asylum Street, Hartford*
*tel: 860/522–2530*
Serves excellent contemporary American cuisine, with an imaginative blend of ingredients.

## Litchfield Hills
**Hopkins Inn ($$$)**
*22 Hopkins Road, New Preston*
*tel: 860/868–7295*
Celebrated restaurant in a Victorian summer house.

**Jessie's ($–$$)**
*142 Main Street, Winsted  tel: 860/379–0109*
A bastion of Italian cooking, known for its spicy clam soup.

**The Pub ($–$$)**
*1 Station Place, Route 44, Norfolk*
*tel: 860/542–5716*
An atmospheric pub, where pizzas and burgers jostle among more unusual and expensive options.

**West Street Grill ($$–$$$)**
*43 West Street, Litchfield  tel: 860/567–3885*
A view of the village green complements the imaginative menu.

## Mystic
**Randall's Ordinary ($$$)**
*Route 2, North Stonington  tel: 860/599–4540*
Everything is colonial: the menu, the building (which dates from 1685), and even the waiters' attire.

## New Haven
**Frank Pepe's ($)**
*157 Wooster Street, New Haven*
*tel: 203/865–5762*
Popular pizza-only establishment. The famous white clam pizza is not to be missed.

## Norwalk
**Avery's Little Kitchen ($)**
*49 South Main Street, South Norwalk*
*tel: 203/855–8515*
Jamaican specialties, including curried goat and coconut pastry.

# Maine

## Acadia and Bar Harbor
**Asticou Inn ($$$)**
*Route 3, Northeast Harbor*
*tel: 207/276–3344*
Formal fixed-price dinners in a stately setting; reservations essential.

**George's ($$–$$$)**
*7 Stephen's Lane, Bar Harbor*
*tel: 207/288–4505*

# Accommodations and Restaurants

Romantic, candlelit restaurant; the dinner-only menu has a distinct Mediterranean flavor.

## Bath
### Kristina's Restaurant and Bakery ($–$$)
*160 Center Street, Bath  tel: 207/442–8577*
The bakery's pies and cakes are renowned. Also exemplary is the New American cuisine, seafood, and grills.

## Bethel
### Mother's Restaurant ($–$$)
*Upper Main Street, Bethel  tel: 207/824–2589*
Cozy Victorian-style house. Eat on the porch in summer for a special treat.
### Sudbury Inn ($–$$)
*151 Lower Main Street, Bethel*
*tel: 207/824–2174*
Imaginative menu and excellent cooking; it also serves inexpensive sandwiches and pizzas. Accommodations available.
### Sunday River Brewing Company ($)
*Sunday River Road, Bethel  tel: 207/824–3541*
A popular hostelry near the ski resort, with its own brewed beers and light meals.

## Boothbay Harbor
### Andrew's Harborside ($$)
*12 Bridge Street, Boothbay Harbor*
*tel: 207/633–4074*
This typical New England seafood restaurant has a fine harbor view.

## Freeport
### Harraseeket Lunch and Lobster Co. ($)
*Main Street, South Freeport  tel: 207/865–4888*
An excellent-value, no-frills eatery serving fried seafood and lobster dinners.

## Penobscot Bay
### Cappy's Chowderhouse ($–$$)
*1 Main Street, Camden  tel: 207/236–2254*
A popular seafood diner with a quieter upstairs area overlooking the harbor. The food runs to chowder, seafood, sandwiches, burgers. There is also a bakery downstairs. No reservations.
### Fisherman's Friend ($–$$)
*School Street, Stonington  tel: 207/367–2442*
Seafood, meat, and poultry; and the specialty fried fish on Fridays.
### Village Restaurant ($–$$)
*7 Main Street, Camden  tel: 207/236–3232*
Unpretentious food and setting. Lovely view over the water.
### Waterfront Restaurant ($$)
*Bayview Street, Camden  tel: 207/236–3747*
Serves excellent seafood; there are also great views, especially from the outdoor deck.

## Portland
### Back Bay Grill ($$$)
*65 Portland Street, Portland  tel: 207/772–8833*
Serves a wide-ranging menu, with jazz supplying the background mood; jacket advised.
### J's Oyster Bar ($)
*5 Portland Pier, Portland  tel: 207/772–4828*
A no-frills shellfish and beer haunt, as popular with locals as with visitors.

### Street & Co. ($$–$$$)
*33 Wharf Street, Portland  tel: 207/775–0887*
Street & Co. is one of Maine's finest seafood establishments.

## York and Kennebunkport
### Arrows ($$$)
*Berwick Road, Ogunquit  tel: 207/361–1100*
Subtly flavored and well-presented offerings on a seasonally changing menu.
### Cape Arundel Inn ($$$)
*Ocean Avenue, Kennebunkport*
*tel: 207/967–2125*
Sophisticated dinner-only menu; and a view that overlooks the shore.
### Dockside Dining Room ($$)
*Harris Island Road, off Route 103, York Harbor*
*tel: 207/363–2722*
On its own island, this is an unbeatable place for views and seclusion. There's something for everyone on the varied menu.
### Hurricane ($$–$$$)
*Perkins Cove, Ogunquit  tel: 207/646–6348*
Good seafood entrees and desserts.
### The Impastable Dream ($$)
*105 Shore Road, Ogunquit*
*tel: 207/646–3011*
A cheerful, no-frills pasta place in an old house-turned-restaurant. No reservations.
### Mabel's Lobster Claw ($$)
*124 Ocean Avenue, Kennebunkport*
*tel: 207/967–2562*
This family-style eatery is a favorite haunt of George and Barbara Bush.
### Warren's Lobster House ($$)
*11 Water Street, Kittery  tel: 207/439–1630*
On the waterfront; a popular seafood venue with a large salad bar.

# Massachusetts

## The Berkshires
### Church St. Café ($$–$$$)
*65 Church Street, Lenox  tel: 413/637–2745*
Carefully considered style: classical music, art, greenery, and varied fare.
### Sophia's Restaurant and Pizza ($)
*490 Pittsfield Road, Lenox*
*tel: 413/499–1101*
There is nothing fancy about this eating place, but it serves good, honest fare, including Greek salads, pasta, pizzas, and grinders (filled rolls).
### 20 Railroad Street ($)
*20 Railroad Street, Great Barrington*
*tel: 413/528–9345*
A popular brisk-service bar/restaurant.

## Cape Ann
### Brackett's Ocean View ($$)
*27 Main Street, Rockport  tel: 978/546–2797*
On the harbor. Specializes in seafood.

## Cape Cod
### Captain Linnell House ($$–$$$)
*137 Skaket Beach Road, Orleans*
*tel: 508/255–3400*
This stylish mansion serves updated Continental cuisine. Dinner only.

**Chillingsworth** ($$$)
*2449 Main Street, Route 6A, Brewster*
*tel: 508/896–3640*
The finest French and nouvelle cuisine on Cape
Cod, and priced accordingly.

**Coonamessett Inn** ($$–$$$)
*311 Gifford Street, Falmouth*
*tel: 508/548–2300*
A period-style inn with regional fare. Some
accommodations are also available.

**The Flume** ($$)
*Lake Avenue, off Route 130, Mashpee*
*tel: 508/477–1456*
Run by a Wampanoag chief who serves unpretentious seafood, including superb chowder.

**High Brewster** ($$$)
*964 Satucket Road, Brewster*
*tel: 508/896–3636*
A charming former farmhouse with exposed beams
and paneling, making a memorable setting for
fixed four-course menus.

**Land Ho!** ($)
*Route 6A and Cove Road, Orleans*
*tel: 508/255–5165*
This informal eating place offers grilled fish,
chowder, sandwiches, and burgers.

**The Mews** ($–$$$)
*429 Commercial Street, Provincetown*
*tel: 508/487–1500*
A long-time favorite serving updated American fare,
plus lighter meals in the café.

**The Paddock** ($$–$$$)
*West End Rotary (next to Melody Tent), Hyannis*
*tel: 508/775–7677*
Formal sophistication sets off the Continental-
American cuisine.

**The Quarterdeck** ($$)
*164 Main Street, Falmouth tel: 508/548–9900*
Good food in a Colonial setting.

**Stir Crazy** ($–$$)
*626 MacArthur Boulevard, Pocasset*
*tel: 508/564–6464*
The Cambodian restaurateur here offers Southeast
Asian dishes with a spicy character, featuring
coconut milk, bean sprouts, peanut sauce, and lots
of chili. Tue–Sun dinner, plus Fri lunch. Closed Mon.

**Up the Creek** ($$)
*36 Old Colony Road, Hyannis*
*tel: 508/771–7866*
Informal and lively.

## Fall River
**L.A. Restaurant** ($–$$)
*108 South Main Street, Fall River*
*tel: 508/673–5890*
A modest dining room in a traditional Portuguese
enclave, which serves Portuguese-American fare,
including pork with clams.

**Waterstreet Café** ($–$$)
*36 Water Street, Fall River*
*tel: 508/672–8748*
Sandwiches, salads, and light meals take their
inspiration from the Mediterranean and Middle
East at this casually upscale café.

## Marblehead
**Driftwood** ($)
*63 Front Street, Marblehead*

*tel: 781/631–1145*
A popular local joint serving diner-style breakfasts
and lunches. Good fried seafood.

## Martha's Vineyard
**L'Etoile** ($$$)
*27 South Summer Street, Edgartown, Martha's
Vineyard tel: 508/627–5187*
An excellent traditional restaurant in the Charlotte
Inn. Updated classics are served in an exquisite
glass-enclosed dining room.

**Home Port** ($$–$$$)
*North Road, Menemsha, Martha's Vineyard*
*tel: 508/645–2679*
Offers unpretentious and wholesome fare such as
seafood and home-baked bread. Dinner only.

**Lambert's Cove Country Inn** ($$$)
*Off Lambert's Cove Road, West Tisbury,
Martha's Vineyard tel: 508/693–2298*
Good for a romantic dinner. Accommodations are
also available.

**Zapotec** ($$)
*14 Kennebec Avenue, Oak Bluffs, Martha's
Vineyard tel: 508/693–6800*
Innovative Mexican cooking.

## Nantucket
**Company of the Cauldron** ($$$)
*5 India Street, Nantucket tel: 508/228–4016*
A whitewashed interior, occasional harp-playing, and
a fixed-price menu. Two seatings for dinner only.

**Espresso Café** ($)
*40 Main Street, Nantucket tel: 508/228–6930*
Serves good-value lunches and light snacks.

**Topper's** ($$$)
*Wauwinet Road, Nantucket tel: 508/228–8768*
Elegant dining; New American cuisine.

## New Bedford
**Freestones** ($–$$)
*41 William Street, New Bedford*
*tel: 508/993–7477*
A former bank with mahogany panels and marble
floors. The menu features light meals as well as
more ambitious entrees.

## Newburyport
**Ciro's** ($–$$)
*1 Market Square, Newburyport*
*tel: 978/463–3335*
Located beside the park and river. It serves
excellent Italian food, with generous salads and
tempting desserts; good value.

**Scandia** ($$$)
*25 State Street, Newburyport*
*tel: 978/462–6271*
Seafood and meat dishes, well presented in a
lovely candlelit dining room.

## Plymouth
**Lobster Hut** ($)
*Town Wharf, Plymouth tel: 508/746–2270*
Serves excellent-value seafood, best eaten outside
overlooking the harbor.

## Salem
**Chase House** ($$)
*Pickering Wharf, Salem tel: 978/744–0000*

# Accommodations and Restaurants

This restaurant has lots of character, with low ceilings and exposed brick walls. Grills and seafood are the favored meals.

**Salem Beer Works** ($–$$)
*278 Derby Street, Salem  tel: 978/745–2337*
House-brewed beer and pub fare in a converted warehouse; convenient to the historic district.

## New Hampshire

### Canterbury
**Creamery Restaurant** ($$–$$$)
*Canterbury Shaker Village  tel: 603/783–9511*
Shaker-inspired cuisine, with lunches daily, four-course dinners on Fridays and Saturdays, and Sunday brunches.

### Concord
**Hermanos Cocina Mexicana** ($–$$)
*11 Hills Avenue, Concord  tel: 603/224–5669*
Ably concocted Mexican dishes; leave room for the desserts.

### Lake Winnipesaukee
**Le Chalet Rouge** ($$–$$$)
*385 West Main Street, Tilton*
*tel: 603/286–4035*
Good French cooking.

**Corner House Inn** ($$)
*22 Main Street at Route 113, Center Sandwich*
*tel: 603/284–6219*
A cozy, old-fashioned inn with traditional dishes such as crab cakes and veal Oscar.

**Hickory Stick Farm** ($$–$$$)
*66 Bean Hill Road, Belmont*
*tel: 603/524–3333*
Serves dinner and Sunday brunch. The menu has duck specialties; there is red meat, vegetarian cuisine, and seafood, too.

**Wolfeboro Inn: Tavern** ($)
*90 North Main Street, Wolfeboro*
*tel: 603/569–3016 or 800/451–2389*
An old-style tavern room; no frills but lots of history and often crowded. Serves good-value food and beers from around the world. It also has accommodations.

### Portsmouth
**B.G.'s Boathouse Restaurant** ($–$$)
*191 Wentworth Road, Portsmouth*
*tel: 603/431–1074*
A popular seafood venue, accessible by land or by boat. Reservations for large parties only.

**The Brewery** ($–$$)
*56 Market Street, Portsmouth*
*tel: 603/431–1115*
Ales are brewed on the premises, while the appetizing range of food includes stir-fries and spicy shrimp.

**Molly Malone's** ($$)
*177 State Street, Portsmouth*
*tel: 603/433–7233*
Steaks, seafood, and more are served in generous helpings.

### White Mountains region
**Margaritaville** ($)
*Route 302, Glen  tel: 603/383–6556*

A family-run establishment that offers genuine Mexican food.

**Olde Timbermill Restaurant and Pub** ($–$$)
*Millfront Marketplace, Main Street, Lincoln*
*tel: 603/745–3603*
On a former sawmill property. Reasonably priced Mexican, American, and European cuisine.

**Polly's Pancake Parlor** ($)
*Hildex Farm (I-93, exit 38), Route 117, Sugar Hill  tel: 603/823–5575*
Not only homemade pancakes, but also waffles, French toast, and quiches, all made using home-ground flour.

**Scottish Lion** ($$–$$$)
*Route 16, North Conway  tel: 603/356–6381 or 888/356–4945*
The fine views of the mountains from the dining room make this a popular spot for Sunday brunch and American-Scottish evening fare. There's also fine selection of Scotch whiskies.

**Snowvillage Inn** ($$–$$$)
*Stuart Road, Snowville  tel: 603/447–2818 or 800/447–4345*
A distinctive Austrian flavor to the cooking. Accommodations are also available.

## Rhode Island

### Block Island
**Finn's Seafood Bar** ($$)
*Water Street, Block Island  tel: 401/466–247*
Eat inside or outside.

### Bristol
**Lobster Pot** ($$–$$$)
*119 Hope Street, Bristol  tel: 401/253–9100*
A noted seafood haunt on the waterfront.

### Newport
**Brick Alley Pub** ($–$$)
*140 Thames Street, Newport*
*tel: 401/849–8291*
This cheerful, low-ceilinged restaurant serves American cuisine and pasta.

**Christie's** ($$)
*Off 351 Thames Street, Newport*
*tel: 401/847–5400*
Chrsitie's has a prime position, with a terrace right on the harbor: an apt setting for sampling seafood and Rhode Island wines.

**Gary's Handy Lunch** ($)
*462 Thames Street, Newport*
*tel: 401/847–9480*
A good stop-off for a sandwich and coffee (closed evenings).

**The Mooring** ($$–$$$)
*Sayers Wharf, Newport  tel: 401/846–2260*
Creatively prepared meats, glacial salads, and fresh local seafood. Overlooks the harbor.

**Newport Dinner Train** ($$–$$$)
*P.O. Box 1081, Newport, RI 02840*
*tel: 401/841–8700 or 800/398–7427*
*www.newportdinnertrain.com*
Train trips along Narragansett Bay include a Friday evening murder mystery tour, Saturday evening "Romancing the Rails" dinner, wine tastings, "Ra and Sail" (lunch on the train, followed by an after-noon sailing excursion), and a Saturday morning

magic show excursion. The excursions depart from
the depot at 19 America's Cup Avenue.
**Salas'** ($$)
345 Thames Street, Newport
tel: 401/846–8772
This bustling place is particularly popular with
families, who come to dig into the corn on the cob,
lobster, and clams.
**White Horse Tavern** ($$–$$$)
26 Marlborough Street, Newport
tel: 401/849–3600
America's oldest tavern (1673), complete with
beamed ceilings, whitewashed walls, and
small rooms. Champagne Sunday brunches,
lunches, dinners.
**Yesterdays** ($$)
28 Washington Square, Newport
tel: 401/847–0116
Serves a good range of food, wine, and beer.

## Providence
**Al Forno** ($$$)
577 South Main Street, Providence
tel: 401/273–9760
This contemporary Italian restaurant has a national
reputation. The wood-grilled pizzas, homemade
pastas, and other creations have won countless
accolades. No reservations.
**Geoff's** ($)
178 Angell Street, at Thayer Street, Providence
tel: 401/751–9214
A funky student hangout serving high-quality made-
to-order sandwiches. Also at 163 Benefit Street.
**Hemenway's** ($$$)
1 Providence Washington Plaza, Providence
tel: 401/351–8570
A top-notch seafood venue with a lively
atmosphere.
**Rue de L'Espoir** ($$–$$$)
99 Hope Street, Providence
tel: 401/751–8890
This long-established dining spot near the campus
of Brown University serves accomplished eclectic
American fare.

## South County
**Champlin's Seafood** ($$)
256 Great Island Road, Narragansett
tel: 401/783–3152
Scallops are the specialty here; also oysters and
lobsters. Sit outside on warm days.
**Nordic Lodge** ($$$)
178 East Pasquiset Trail, Charlestown
tel: 401/783–4515
The all-you-can-eat buffet features seafood, meats,
fresh fruits, and pastas.
**Spain Restaurant** ($$$)
1144 Ocean Road, Narragansett
tel: 401/783–9770
Authentic Spanish-Mediterranean cuisine;
delicious seafood.

## Tiverton
**Evelyn's Nannaquaket Drive-In** ($$)
2335 Main Road, Tiverton  tel: 401/624–3100
Just outside Fall River; diners come here to eat
generous portions of fried seafood while taking in
the view of Nannaquaket Pond.

# Vermont

## Bennington
**Alldays and Onions** ($$)
519 Main Street, Bennington
tel: 802/447–0043
A deli that opens as a restaurant in the evening.
The menu is innovative.
**Blue Benn Diner** ($)
102 Hunt Street (Route 7), Bennington
tel: 802/442–5140
A typical diner with excellent breakfasts served all
day, plus tortillas and burritos.

## Bristol
**Mary's** ($$)
1868 Route 116 North, Bristol
tel: 802/453–2432
Mary's has an unpretentious atmosphere, with an
interior hung with Vermont paintings. Beautifully
cooked food such as lamb and eggplant curry.

## Manchester
**Arlington Inn** ($$$)
Route 7A, Arlington  tel: 802/375–6532 or
800/443–9442
The inn's dining room draws admirers from afar for
its gourmet American cuisine. Accommodations
are also available.
**Bistro Henry** ($$)
Route 11/30, Manchester Center
tel: 802/362–4982
A small bistro serving intriguing Mediterranean
fare, good wines, and sinful desserts.
**Garlic John's** ($–$$)
Route 11 and Route 30, Manchester
tel: 802/362–9843
This Italian trattoria opens for dinner only.

## Newfane
**The Four Columns** ($$$)
21 West Street, Newfane  tel: 802/365–7713
An elegant setting for modern American cuisine.

## Stowe
**Partridge Inn** ($$–$$$)
Mountain Road, Stowe  tel: 802/253–8000
Excellent seafood restaurant across the road from
Ye Olde England Inne.
**Villa Tragara** ($$–$$$)
Route 100 south of Stowe  tel: 802/244–5288
A former farmhouse graced with an intimate
atmosphere for commendable fixed-price dinners.

## Woodstock and Quechee
**Bentleys** ($$)
3 Elm Street, Woodstock  tel: 802/457–3232
Graced with Victorian decor; the menu ranges from
the standard to the ambitious, and the desserts
are especially recommended.
**Firestones** ($–$$)
Waterman Place, Route 4, Quechee
tel: 802/295–1600
Serves interesting Mediterranean-inspired fare in
an upbeat setting.
**The Prince and the Pauper** ($$$)
24 Elm Street, Woodstock  tel: 802/457–1818
Nouvelle French food, served in a Colonial building.

# Index

## A

academia 22–23
Acadia National Park 109, 112–115, 229
Acadia Wild Garden 115
accommodations 268–277
  Boston 78, 268–269
  Connecticut 268, 269–270
  Maine 270–271
  Massachusetts 268, 272–273
  New Hampshire. 273–275
  Rhode Island 268, 275
  Vermont 268, 275–277
Adams 144
Adams, John 42, 182
Adams, John Quincy 42, 182
Adams, Samuel 42, 58
airports and air services 248, 259
Alcott, Louisa May 46, 64, 65, 166, 169
America's Stonehenge 192
American Museum of Fly Fishing 230
Amesbury, MA 173
*Amistad* 105, 182
Amherst, MA 175
  Emily Dickinson Homestead 175
  Mead Art Museum 175
Annalee Doll Museum 196
Ansonia 105
antiques information 264
Appalachian Trail 133, 144, 208
Aquinnah 160–161
architecture 12–13
  meeting houses and churches 73
Arlington, VT, Norman Rockwell Exhibition 231
artists 44–45
Ashley Falls 147
Atlantic Beach Park 221
ATMs 251
Augusta, ME 117
  Fort Western 117
  Maine State Museum 117
  State House 117
Ausable Chasm 227

## B

Bangor, ME 118
  Cole Land Transportation Museum 118
  Old Town Museum 118
Bar Harbor, ME 57, 112–113
Barre, VT 226
  Rock of Ages 226
Bartlett, NH 205
Bash Bish Falls 147
Basketball Hall of Fame 187
Bass Harbor Head Lighthouse 113
Bath, ME 118
  Maine Maritime Museum 118, 153
Baxter State Park 119
beaches 264
Bear's Den, MA 182
Beauport, MA 152

beavers 201
Becket, MA 25
Belfast & Moosehead Lake Railroad 131
Ben & Jerry's Ice Cream Factory 232, 234
Bennington, VT 226–227
  Park McCullough House 227
Berkshire Botanical Garden 147
Berkshire Hills 141, 143–147
Bethel, ME 120
Bethlehem, NH 205
biking 132, 256
Billings Farm and Museum 243
black bears 200, 201
Black Mountain 228–229
Blackstone River Valley 187, 220
Blithewold 218
Block Island 211, 213
Blowing Cave 136
Blue Hill 131
blueberries 110, 126
boating and sailing 257
bog and marsh life 164–165
Boothbay Harbor, ME 121
  Boothbay Railway Village 121
Boston 11, 48–85
  accommodations 78, 268–269
  Acorn Street 65
  African Meeting House 64
  airport 248
  Back Bay 13, 56, 62–63, 82
  bars and clubs 84–85
  Beacon Hill 56, 64–65, 82
  Black Heritage Trail 66
  Boston Athenaeum 66
  Boston Beer Museum 53
  Boston Common 50, 58
  Boston Harbor Islands 53
  Boston Garden 68
  Boston Marine Society 67
  Boston Pops 25, 79
  Boston Public Library 66
  Boston Symphony Orchestra 24–25, 79
  Boston Tea Party 33
  Boston Tea Party Ship and Museum 66
  Brahmins 56, 57
  Bunker Hill Monument 61
  Bunker Hill Pavilion 67
  Cambridge 51, 74–77, 83
  Charles Hayden Planetarium 71
  Charlesbank Park 62
  Charlestown 61
  Charlestown Navy Yard 67
  children's entertainment 245
  Children's Museum 68
  Chinatown 51, 83
  Christian Science Center and Mapparium 63
  Commonwealth Avenue 62
  Commonwealth Museum 69

Copley Square 63
Copps Hill Burying Ground 60–61
driving in 52
eating out 80, 84, 277
Ebenezer Hancock House 60
events 54
Faneuil Hall Marketplace 50, 59
Federal Reserve Bank 68
Fenway Park 68, 81
FleetCenter 68, 81
free sights and entertainment 78
Freedom Trail 50, 58–61
Gibson House 62
Granary Burying Ground 58
guided and self-guiding tours 53
Harrison Gray Otis House 68
Harvard University 74, 76–77
Institute of Contemporary Art 68–69
Isabella Stewart Gardner Museum 25, 69
John F. Kennedy Library and Museum 69
John Hancock Tower and Observatory 70
King's Chapel 58
Massachusetts Institute of Technology 74
Mount Vernon Street 65
Mugar Omni Theater 71
Museum of Afro-American History 64
Museum of Fine Arts 70–71
Museum of Science 71
music spots 85
New England Aquarium 72
New England Holocaust Memorial 68
New Old South Church 63
Nichols House Museum 65
nightlife 84–85
North End 50, 60, 83
North End Garage Park 61
Old Corner Book Store 58
Old North Church 60
Old South Meeting House 58, 73
Old State House 58–59
Park Street Church 58
Paul Revere House 60
Pinckney Street 64
Prudential Center Skywalk 62, 72–73
Public Garden 73
public transportation 53
research and technology 23, 56
river cruises 53, 71
St. Stephen's Church 38
shopping 82–83
South End 51
sport 81
Sports Museum of New England (FleetCenter) 68
State House 58, 73
traveling into 248

Trinity Church 63
Union Oyster House 60
USS *Cassin Young* 67
USS *Constitution* 67
USS *Constitution* Museum 67
walks 58–65
Waterfront 51
Bourne, MA, Aptucxet Trading Post Museum 154
Bowdoin College 122
Bradbury Mountain State Park 128
Brattleboro, VT 47, 241
Bread and Puppet Museum 236, 237
Bretton Woods, NH 41, 229
Brewster, MA 155
  Cape Cod Natural History Museum 155
Brick Store Museum 137
Bridgewater, VT 243
Bristol, CT 91
  American Clock and Watch Museum 91
Bromley ski area 240, 244
Brownington, VT 237
Brunswick, ME 122
  Art Museum 122
  Bowdoin College 122
  Joshua L. Chamberlain Museum 122
  Peary-MacMillan Arctic Museum 122
  Pejepscot Museum 122
  Skolfield-Whittier House 122
Bucksport, ME 122
  Fort Knox 122
Bulfinch, Charles 72
Burlington, VT 223, 227
bus services 258–259
Bush, George 43, 104, 137

## C

Cambridge, MA 51, 74–77
  Christ Church 77
  the Common 77
  Harvard Bridge 22
  Harvard University 22, 74–75, 76–77
  Longfellow House 75
  Massachusetts Institute of Technology (MIT) 22, 75
Camden, ME 128–129, 130
Camden Hills State Park 130
camping 264
Campobello Island, ME 122, 123
canoeing 120, 132, 242
Canterbury Shaker Village 192
Cape Ann 151–152
Cape Cod 154, 160, 16
Cape Cod Canal 154
Cape Cod and the Islands 140, 154–163
Cape Cod Light 158
Cape Cod National Seashore 132, 158
Cape Cod Scenic Railroa 155
Cape Poge Reservation 160

car rental 254–255
Casco Bay, ME 134
Castine, ME 130, 131
Castle in the Clouds 197
Cathedral Ledge 206
Cathedral of the Pines
  199
Cedar Tree Neck
  Sanctuary 160
Center Harbor, NH 197
Center Sandwich, NH
  197
Chester, CT 93–94
  Goodspeed Opera
    House 26, 94
Chester, VT 240
Chester-Hadlyme ferry
  93
children's entertainment
  244–246
Christa McAuliffe
  Planetarium 193
Christmas 194
Clark's Trading Post 205
climate and seasons
  250–251
Clinton, Bill and Hillary
  104, 160
coastal wildlife 164–165
colonial Pemaquid
  Restoration 121
Concord, MA 46, 167,
  168–169
  Concord Museum
    168–169
  Great Meadows 170
  Gropius House 170
  Old Manse 170
  Old North Bridge Battle
    Site 168
  Orchard House 169
  Ralph Waldo Emerson
    House 169
  Sleepy Hollow Cemetery
    170
  Walden Pond
    Reservation 170
  The Wayside 169
Concord, NH 192–193
  Christa McAuliffe
    Planetarium 193
  State House 193
Connecticut 86–107
  accommodations 268,
    269–270
  children's entertainment
    244–245
  events 90
  restaurants 277–278
  Connecticut River Valley
    92–95
consulates 262
Coolidge, Calvin 42–43,
  233
Copley, John Singleton 44
Coskata-Coatue Wildife
  Refuge 163
covered bridges 230
Craftsbury Common, VT
  236
cranberries 179
credit cards, lost 263
crime 262
Crockett Cove Woods
  Preserve 131
Cushing, ME, Olson
  House 130
Cutler, ME 126

D

Dalton, Crane Museum
  145

Deerfield, Historic, MA
  140–141, 175
Desert of Maine 128
Dickinson, Emily 47, 174,
  175, 176
Dinosaur Footprints
  Reservation 174
Dinosaur State Park 94
disabilities, visitors with
  228, 265
Dorset, VT 231
Dorset Mountain 235
drives
  Acadia's Park Loop Road
    114–145
  Litchfield Hills 98–99
  southern Vermont
    240–241
  White Mountains
    206–207
driving in New England
  254–256
Dublin, NH 199

E

early tourism 40–41
East Granby, CT, Old New-
  Gate Prison 94, 95
East Haddam, CT 94
East Haven, CT, Shore Line
  Trolley Museum 105
Eastport, ME 126
Echo Lake 113
economy 14–15
Edgartown, MA 161
Elizabeth Islands, MA
  161
Ellsworth, ME 127
emergencies 262–263
emergency telephone
  numbers 262
Emerson, Ralph Waldo 46,
  168–169, 170, 177
Essex, MA 152
European
  exploration 28–29
  settlement 30–31

F

fall 18–19
Fall River 166
  Battleship Cove 166
  Fall River Heritage State
    Park 166
  Marine Museum 166
Falmouth, MA 154–155
farm produce 264–265
farming 15
Farmington, CT 91
  Hill-Stead Museum 91
  Stanley-Whitman House
    91
Felix Neck Wildife
  Sanctuary 160
Ferrisburgh, Rokeby 231
ferry trips 159, 160, 161,
  162, 213
film and drama 26
First Night 194
fishing industry 15, 34,
  110, 116
fishing 132–133
Fitzwilliam, NH 199
Five Colleges Area 174
flora and fauna
  beavers 201
  black bears 200, 201
  Block Island 213
  bog and marsh life
    164–165

Cape Cod 154, 160,
  163
coastal wildlife
  164–165
  forest wildlife 200–201
  lobsters 164
  moose 200–201
  puffins 165
  whales and dolphins
    164, 165
Flume 207
folk arts and crafts
  238–239
  basketry 124,
    238–239
  Shaker crafts 149
  shopping for 17
food and drink 20–21
  see also restaurants
forest fires 263
forest wildlife 200–201
Fort Point, ME 153
Fort Ticonderoga, NY
  227
Foxwoods Casino 95,
  125
Franconia Notch road
  207
Freeport, ME 128
French, Daniel Chester
  45, 147
Frost Place 205
Frost, Robert 47, 198,
  205, 209, 226, 231
Fruitlands, MA
  166–167
Fryeburg, ME 120

G

Galilee, RI 221
Garden in the Woods
  170
Garrison, William Lloyd
  58, 64, 72
Gilbert Stuart Birthplace
  221
Gillette Castle 93
Glen, NH 205
  Story Land 205
Gloucester, MA 151
  Hammond Castle
    Museum 151
Glover, VT, Bread and
  Puppet Museum 236,
  237
Grafton, MA, Willard
  House and Clock
  Museum 187
Grafton, VT 241
Grafton Notch State Park
  120
Grand Isle, Hyde Log
  Cabin 227
Great Barrington, MA,
  Albert Schweitzer
  Center 147
Green Mountain National
  Forest 200, 231
Greensboro, VT 236
Gropius House 170
Groton, VT, USS Nautilus
  107
Gulf Hagas 119

H

Hail to the Sunrise
  Monument 143
Hairpin Turn 143
Halibut Point State Park
  152

Hamden, CT, Eli Whitney
  Museum 105
Hancock Shaker Village
  141, 145, 148
Hanover, NH 195
  Dartmouth College 23,
    195
Harrison, ME 120
Harrisville, NH 199
Hartford, CT 14, 95–97
  Billings Farm and
    Museum 243
  Harriet Beecher Stowe
    House 97
  Mark Twain House
    96
  Museum of Connecticut
    History 96
  Noah Webster House
    97
  Wadsworth Atheneum
    95
Harvard University 22,
  74–75, 76–77
  Arthur M. Sackler
    Museum 75
  Botanical Museum 75
  Busch-Reisinger
    Museum
    74–75
  Carpenter Center for
    Visual Arts 77
  Fogg Art Museum
    74–75
  Harry Elkins Widener
    Library 77
  Museum of Natural
    History 75
  Peabody Museum of
    Archaeology and
    Ethnology 75
Radcliffe College 77
Hawthorne, Nathaniel
  46, 64, 169, 170,
  185
health advice 262–263
Heritage Plantation 155
Higganum, Sundial
  Gardens 94
hiking 132, 133, 208,
  257
Hildene 230
Hill-Stead Museum 91
Hogback Mountain 241
Holyoke, MA 174
  Volleyball Hall of Fame
    174
Holyoke Range Park
  175
Horatio Colony House
  Museum 199
Housatonic Meadow
  State Park 98
Housatonic Valley 98
Hyannis, MA, J.F.
  Kennedy Museum 155
Hyde Log Cabin 227

I

Ice Glen 146
immigrants 38–39
industry and commerce
  14–15, 36–37
industrial growth 36–37
Isle au Haut 113, 153
Isles of Shoals,
  Appledore 40, 45
Islesboro, ME 129
Ives, Charles 24
Ivoryton Museum of Fife
  and Drum 93
Ivy League 22–23

# Index

## J

Jackson, NH 229
Jefferson, NH 205
Johnsonville, Historic, CT 94
Jonesport, ME 127

## K

Kancamagus Highway 206
Katahdin Iron Works 119
Keene, NH 199
  Children's Museum 199
  Horatio Colony House Museum 199
Kennebunkport, ME 137
Kennedy, J.F. 43, 69, 218
Kent 98
  Sloane-Stanley Museum 98
Kent Falls State Park 98
Killington, VT 228, 242, 243
King, Stephen 118
Kingfield, ME 120
Kipling, Rudyard 47
Kittery, MA 137

## L

Lake Champlain 132, 227
Lake Champlain Maritime Museum 227
Lake Dunmore 231
Lake Sunapee 196
Lake Waramaug 99
Lake Willoughby 236
Lake Winnipesaukee 190, 196–197
Lamoine State Park 127
language 260
leaf-peeping 18, 19, 250–251
Lenox, MA 46, 146
Lexington, MA 167
  Battle Road Visitor Center 168
  Buckman Tavern 167
  Fiske House 168
  Hancock-Clarke House 167
  Munroe Tavern 167
  Museum of Our National Heritage 168
  Paul Revere Capture Site 168
lighthouses 153
Lincoln, NH 204–205
Litchfield, CT 98–99
Litchfield Hills 98–99
Little Cranberry Island 113
L.L. Bean 128
lobsters 164
lobster fishing 116
Lockwood-Mathews Mansion 107
Long Point Wildlife Refuge 160
Longfellow, Henry Wadsworth 47, 75, 134, 135
Loon Mountain 206, 228
lost property 263
Lost River 207
Lowell, MA 37, 171
  Boott Cotton Mills Museum 171
  Lawrence Heritage State Park 171

Lowell National Historical Park Visitor Center 171
  Pawtucket Falls 171
  Working People Exhibit 171
Lower Shaker Village 195
Lubec, ME 123

## M

Machias, ME 126
Maine 14–15, 108–137
  accommodations 270–271
  children's entertainment 245
  events 111
  restaurants 278–280
Maine Maritime Museum 118, 153
Manchester, MA 151
Manchester, NH 198
  Currier Gallery of Art 198
  Robert Frost Homestead 198
Manchester, VT 230–231
  Hildene 230
maple syrup 234
Maple Grove Maple Museum and Factory 234, 236
Marblehead, MA 35, 186
Marconi Wireless Station 158
Marlboro College 241
Martha's Vineyard, MA 160
Mashantucket Pequot Museum and Research Center 95
Massachusetts 138–187
  accommodations 268, 271–273
  children's entertainment 245–246
  events 142
  restaurants 280–281
  see also Boston
Massachusetts Institute of Contemporary Art 144
Matinicus, ME 129
Melville, Herman 46, 145, 172
Menemsha, MA 161
Meredith Bay 197
Middlebury 231
Middletown, CT 39, 92
Miller State Park 199
Millinocket 119
Mohawk Trail 143
Monhegan Island 121
Monomoy Islands 153, 158
Monterey, MA 147
Montpelier, VT 223, 232
  Ben & Jerry's Ice Cream Factory 232, 234
  State House 232
  Vermont Historical Society Museum 232
Montshire Museum of Science 242
Monument Mountain Reservation 146
moose 200–201
Moosehorn National Wildlife Refuge 126
Moses, Anna "Grandma" 45, 226

Mount Cadillac 112, 114
Mount Desert Island 109, 112–115
Mount Equinox 230–231
Mount Everett State Forest 147
Mount Greylock 144
Mount Katahdin 119
Mount Kearsarge Indian Museum 196
Mount Mansfield 232, 233
Mount Monadnock region 190, 198–199
Mount Sugarloaf State Reservation 175
Mount Sunapee 196
Mount Tom 175
Mount Tom State Park 99
Mount Washington 205, 207, 208
Mount Washington Cog Railway 205
Mount Washington Valley 204
music 24–25
Mystic, CT 101
  Denison Homestead 101
Mystic Aquarium 101, 107
Mystic Seaport 101

## N

Nantucket, MA 162–163
  Hadwen House 162
  Jethro Coffin House 162–163
  Life Saving Museum 162
  Museum of Nantucket History 162
  Old Firecart House 162
  Old Gaol 162
  Quaker Meeting House 162
  Whaling Museum 162
Narragansett, RI, South County Museum 221
national forests 200, 204
Native Americans 28, 29, 30, 31, 124–125, 181
Natural Bridge State Park 143
Naumkeag, MA 147
New Bedford, MA 140, 172–173
  Fire Museum 172–173
  Glass Museum 172
  Whaling Museum 172
New Castle Island 203
New England Air Museum 95
New England Ski Museum 207
New England Winery 193
New Hampshire 188–209
  accommodations 273–274
  children's entertainment 246
  events 191
  restaurants 281–282
New Haven, CT 102–105
  Fort Nathan Hale 105
  Louis' Hamburgers 102
  Peabody Museum of Natural History 102
  Shubert Performing Arts Center 26, 103
  sporting events 104
  Yale Center for British Art 102–103

Yale Collection of Musical Instruments 103
Yale University 23, 102, 103–105
Yale University Art Gallery 103
New London, CT 106–10
New London Harbor Light 153
New Milford, CT 98
Newburyport, MA 173
  Cushing House Museum 173
  Custom House Maritime Museum 173
  Plum Island Beach 173
Newfane, VT 241
Newport, RI 214–218
  America's Cup Museum 218
  Astors' Beechwood 218
  Belcourt Castle 218
  Bellevue Avenue 216
  Breakers 217
  Château-sur-Mer 217
  Cliff Walk 214
  Doll Museum 216
  Elms 217
  Green Animals 218
  Hunter House 216
  International Tennis Hall of Fame 216
  Kingscote 217
  Marble House 218
  Museum of Newport History 216
  Newport Casino 216
  Ocean Drive 216, 218
  Rosecliff 217
  Touro Synagogue 215
  Trinity Church 215
  Wanton-Lyman-Hazard House 216
  White Horse Tavern 21
newspapers and journals 260
Niantic, CT 107
Noank, CT 101
North Adams, MA 144
  Massachusetts Institute of Contemporary Art 144
North Conway, NH 204
Northeast Historic Film 122
North Haven, ME 129
Northampton, MA 174, 17
Northeast Harbor 113, 115
Northeast Kingdom 133 224, 236–237
Norwalk, CT 107
  Billings Farm and Museum 243
  Maritime Aquarium 10

## O

Oak Bluffs 161
October Mountain State Forest 144
Odiorne Point State Park 203
Ogunquit, MA 137
Old Conway Homestead and Museum 129
Old Man of the Mountai 207
Old New-Gate Prison 94,

Old Saybrook, CT 92
  Connecticut River
    Museum 92
Old Sturbridge Village, MA
  140, 173
O'Neill, Eugene 26, 47,
  106
opening times 252
Orono, ME, Maine Logging
  Museum 118
Owls Head Transportation
  Museum 129

## P

Pairpoint Glass Works 155
Paper House 152
Passaconaway Historic
  Site 206
Passamaquoddy Bay, ME
  126
Patten, ME, Lumberman's
  Museum 119
Pawtucket, RI 36
  Slater Mill 36, 220
Pemaquid Point, ME 121,
  153
Penobscot Bay, ME
  128–131
Perkinsville, VT 242
Peterborough, NH 198–199
photography 264
Pico 228, 235
Pilgrim Fathers 180–181
Pioneer Valley 174–175
Pittsfield, MA 144–145
  Arrowhead 145
  Berkshire Museum
    144–145
Pittsford, VT, New England
  Maple Museum 234, 235
places of worship 264
Plymouth, MA 30, 140,
  177–179
  Antiquarian House 177
  Cranberry World 179
  Howland House 178
  Mayflower II 177
  Mayflower Society
    Museum 177
  National Monument to
    the Forefathers
    178–179
  Pilgrim Hall Museum 178
  Plimoth Plantation 179
  Plymouth Rock 177
Plymouth Notch, VT 233
  Coolidge Birthplace 233
police 262
politicians 42–43
Port Clyde, ME 129
Portland, ME 109, 134–135
  Children's Museum of
    Maine 134
  Fort Williams Park 135
  Portland Museum of Art
    134
  Portland Observatory
    134
  Victoria Mansion 134
  Wadsworth-Longfellow
    House 134
Portland Head Light 135,
  153
Portsmouth, NH 190,
  202–203
  Children's Museum of
    Portsmouth 203
  John Paul Jones House
    203
  Moffat-Ladd House
    202–203
  Strawbery Banke 202

USS Albacore 203
  Warner House 202
Proctor, VT 235
  Marble Exhibit 235
  Wilson Castle 235
Providence, RI 219–221
  Athenaeum 220
  Arcade 219–220
  Benefit Street 220
  Brown University 23, 220
  East Side 220
  Federal Hill 220
  First Baptist Church of
    America 219
  Haffenreffer Museum of
    Anthropology 220
  John Brown House 220
  RISD Museum of Art 220
  State Capitol 219
Provincetown, MA 158–159
  Pilgrim Monument
    158–159
public holidays 252
public transportation
  258–259
puffins 165
Puritans 30, 31, 180–181

## Q

Quabbin Reservoir 182
quarrying 15
Quechee, VT 243
Quechee Gorge 243
Quincy, MA 182
  Adams National
    Historical Site 182
Quoddy Head 123

## R

rail travel 258
Rangeley, ME 120
restaurants 276–283
  Boston 277
  Connecticut 277–278
  Maine 278–280
  Massachusetts
    280–281
  New Hampshire
    281–282
  Rhode Island 282–283
  Vermont 283
Revere, Paul 33, 55, 60
Reversing Falls 126, 127
Revolution 33
Rhode Island 31, 210–221
  accommodations 268,
    274–275
  children's entertainment
    246
  events 212
  restaurants 282–283
Rhododendron State Park
  199
Ripogenus Gorge 119
river and sea cruises
  Boston 53, 71
  Connecticut 94, 101,
    107
  Maine 121, 134, 135
  Massachusetts 155,
    159, 175
  New Hampshire 202
  Rhode Island 217
  whale watching 164
Rockland, ME 128, 129,
  130
  Farnsworth Art Museum
    and Homestead 130
  Shore Village Museum
    130, 153

Rockport, ME 130
Rockport, MA 152
Rockwell, Norman 45,
  146, 147, 150, 281
Rocky Hill–Glastonbury
  ferry 89
Rocky Neck State Park 107
Roosevelt, Franklin D. 123
Rose Island Lighthouse 153
Ruggles House 127
Ruggles Mine 195
Rumford, ME 120
Russell-Colbath House 206

## S

Sabbaday Falls 206
Sabbathday Lake, MA 149
Saco 137
Saint-Gaudens National
  Historic Site 195
St. Johnsbury, VT 236
  Fairbanks Museum and
    Planetarium 236
Salem, MA 35, 140,
  184–185
  Chestnut Street 185
  History Alive! Cry
    Innocent 184
  House of the Seven
    Gables 185
  Peabody Essex
    Museum 185
  Salem Maritime National
    Historic Site 185
  Salem 1630: Pioneer
    Village 185
  Salem Witch Museum
    184
  Salem witches 183
  Witch Dungeon Museum
    184
  Witch House 184
sales tax 252
Salt Pond Visitor Center 158
Sandwich, MA 155
Scarborough Marsh
  Nature Center 165
Scargo Hill Tower 155
Schoodic Point, ME 113
seafaring 34–35
Searsport, ME 131
  Penobscot Marine
    Museum 131
Seashore Trolley Museum
  137
Sebago Lake, ME 120
Selden Neck State Park 93
Shakers 148–149, 192,
  195, 238–239
Shelburne, VT 237
Shelburne Falls, MA 143
shopping 16–17, 82–83,
  128, 137, 204
Siasconset, MA 163
Silver Lake, VT 231
skiing 228–229
Skinner State Park 175
sleigh rides 229
Sloane-Stanley Museum 98
Smugglers' Notch, VT
  228, 233
Smith College 174, 175
snowboarding 228
snowmobiling 229
snowshoeing 229
Somes Sound, ME 113
South County, RI 221
South Hadley, MA 174
Sports Museum of New
  England
  FleetCenter, Boston 68
  Lowell 171

Springfield, MA 187
Springfield, VT, Eureka
  Schoolhouse 243
Squam Lake, NH 197
Squam Lake Natural
  Science Center 197
Squanto 181
Stanley Museum 120
Sterling and Francine
  Clark Art Institute 144
Stockbridge, MA 146–147
  Chesterwood 147
  Merwin House 147
  Mission House
    146–147
  Norman Rockwell
    Museum 147, 150
Stonington, CT 101
Stonington, ME 131
Storyland 205
Stoughton Pond 242
Stowe 228, 233
Stowe, Harriet Beecher
  46–47, 97
Stratton, VT 228
Sunday River, ME 132,
  229
Sunday River Bridge 120

## T

Tamworth, NH 197
Tanglewood, MA 25, 146
telephones 261
television and radio 261
Tenants Harbor, ME 129
Terryville, CT, Lock
  Museum 91
Thanksgiving Day 182
Thimble Islands 94
Thoreau, Henry David 46,
  170
timber industry 14–15,
  109, 110, 118
tourism 14, 40–41
tourist offices 266
tours and packages 253
Townshend State Park 241
traveler's checks, lost
  263
traveling
  around New England
    254, 258–259
  to New England 248
Twain, Mark 46, 96

## U

Union, ME 117
UVM Morgan Horse Farm
  231

## V

Valley Railroad 93
Vergennes, VT 231
Vermont 15, 222–223
  accommodations 268,
    275–276
  children's
    entertainment 246
  events 225
  restaurants 283
Vermont Teddy Bear Co.
  237
Vermont Wildflower Farm
  237
Victory Bog 236
villages 100
Vinalhaven, ME 129
Vineyard Haven, MA 161

# Index/Acknowledgments

## W

Wakefield, NH, 
Washington County
Jail 221
Wapack Trail 199
Washington, CT, Institute
for American Indian
Studies 99
Washington, George 33, 97
Watch Hill 221
Water Country 203
Water Wizz 221
Waterford, ME
Eugene O'Neill Theater
Center 26, 106
water sports 133
Waterville Valley 228
weather information 261
Webhannet River Marsh
137
Weirs Beach, NH 196–197
Wellfleet, MA 158
Wells National Estuarine
Sanctuary 164–165
West Cornwall, CT 98
West Rindge, NH 199
Western Gateway Heritage
State Park 144

Western Lakes 120
Weston, CT 240
Vermont Country Store
17, 240
Wethersfield, CT 97
Webb-Deane-Stevens
Museum 97
whales and dolphins 164,
165
Whale's Tail 205
whaling 34, 162, 172
Wharton, Edith 46, 146
Whistler, James McNeill
45
White Lake State Park 197
White Mountains 132,
190, 204–208
White River Junction, VT
242
whitewater rafting 121, 133
Wickford, RI 221
Williams, Roger 31, 211
Williamstown, MA 144
Hopkins Observatory 144
Sterling and Francine
Clark Art Institute 144
Williams College
Museum of Art 144
Wilmington, VT 241
windjammer trips 131

Windsor, CT 94–95
Trolley Museum 94–95
Windsor, VT 242
American Precision
Museum 242
Old Constitution House
242
winter sports 228–229
Wiscasset, ME 135
Fort Edgecomb 135
Wolf Neck Woods State
Park 128
Wolfeboro, NH 197
Woods Hole, MA 155
National Marine
Fisheries Aquarium
155
Woods Hole
Oceanographic
Institution 155, 164
Woodstock, NH
204–205
Woodstock, VT 242–243
Billings Farm and
Museum 243
Vermont Raptor Center
243
Worcester, MA 187
Higgins Armory Museum
187

Worcester Art Museum
187
Worcester Common 16
writers and thinkers
46–47

## Y

Yale University 23, 102,
103–105
Beinecke Rare Book
and Manuscript
Library 104–105, 23
Sculpture Garden 105
Sterling Memorial
Library 104
York, ME 136–137
Elizabeth Perkins House
136, 137
Emerson-Wilcox House
136
John Hancock
Warehouse and Wharf
136–137
Nubble Lighthouse 136
Old Gaol 136
Wells Auto Museum
137
Wild Kingdom 137

## Picture Credits

The Automobile Association would like to thank the following photographers, libraries, and associations for the assistance in the preparation of this book.

ALLSPORT UK LTD. 81a Boston Celtics Basketball, 81b Boston Celtics Robert Parish. APPALACHIAN MOUNTAIN CLUB 208 (Robert J. Kozlow). BOSTON ATHENAEUM 32b *The Bloody Massacre perpetrated in King St.* BOSTONIA SOCIETY 34a Shipbuilding, 35a 1392 Sailing Card, 35b Boston Wharf, 36a Macullar Parker Co., 38b John Fitzgerald, 38 Hugh O'Brien. BOSTON SYMPHONY ORCHESTRA 24b, 79a, 79b Boston Symphony Orchestra. BRISTOL COUNT CONVENTION & VISITORS BUREAU 166 Fall River, 172 New Bedford. TELFAIR H BROWN 106 CGC CORBIS from cover silouette (Peter Guttman). "EAGLE." DEPARTMENT OF ECONOMIC DEVELOPMENT CONNECTICUT 91b New England Aquarium. JOHN EATON PHOTOGRAPHY 250 Horse & cart. MARY EVANS PICTURE LIBRARY 27 Landing of Pilgrim Fathers, 28/9 Indians attacking settlers, 28 John Cabot, 29 Pilgrim Fathers, 30/1 Pilgrim Fathers visited by Massacoit, 30 Metacomet, 31 John Winthrop, 32a Americans drilling soldiers, 33a Boston Tea Party, 42b John Quincy Adams, 42c Samuel Adams, 46/7 Tom Sawyer's band of robbers, 46 Topsy, 47b Louisa Mary Alcott, 55b Paul Revere, 148/9 Shaker women at work, 176 Emily Dickinson, 180/1 Miles Standish, 180 Mayflower, 181 Pilgrim Fathers, 183 Salem witches, 183b Salem witches Title page, 183c Salem witch's arrest. FARNSWORTH ART MUSEUM 44 *Shipping in Down Fleet Waters* (F.H. Lane), 130 *Romance of Autumn* (George Bellows). B. GRANT 204 Echo Lake. RONAL GRANT ARCHIVES 26a *The Whales of August*, 26b *The Bostonians*, 26c *On Golden Pond.* D. HAMILTON 40a Menu, Profile House, 40b Profile & Franconia Notch RR. HARVARD UNIVERSITY ART MUSEUMS 74 Matsumoto Koshiro. IMPERIAL WAR MUSEUM 150 *Freedom from Want* (Norman Rockwell). J. LYNCH 9b Sweetgum leaf, 15a Waitsfield Farm, 145a Sterling & Francine Clark Inst., 151a Cape Ann, 151b Gloucester Memorial, 167 Fruitlands, 168 Alcott sign, 169 Concord Bridge, 174 Amherst College Campus, 175 Deerfield Dwight House, 185b Masthead Salem Peabody Mus 186 Marblehead, 187 Worcester Armory, 199 Mt. Monadnock. T. LYNCH 16c Shelburne General Store, 232 Montpelier State House. MANCHESTER AND THE MOUNTAINS CHAMBER 228, 229 (Robert Bossi), 230 (Hubert Schriebl) MAS SACHUSETTS OFFICE OF TRAVEL & TOURISM 194a Faneuil Hall. J. McELHOLM 144 Oxford, 214 Newport Bridge. MUSEUM OF FINE ARTS BOSTON 45 *Boston Common at Twilight.* NATURE PHOTOGRAPHERS LTD. 119 Baxter State Park (A.J. Cleeve), 164/5 Common dolphin, 165a Great blue heron, 165b Cape Cod saltmarsh (P.R. Sterry), 200 Labrador tea (R. Burbidge). VIRGIN ATLANTIC AIRWAYS 248 Plane. BART A. PISCITELLO 38a Blessing the Fleet PLIMOUTH PLANTATION 178 Plymouth. PORTLAND MUSEUM OF ART 44/5 *Boy in a Boatyard* (Winslow Homer. PRESERVATION SOCIETY OF NEWPORT COUNTY 216 The Breakers, 217 Rosecliff. MDC QUABBIN 182 Quabbin Dam. REX FEATURES LTD. 43b George Bush. SCRIMSHAW WHALING MUSEUM 239a Bone pie crimper. STRAW BERY BANKE MUSEUM 13b Goodwin Mansion. THE MANSELL COLLECTION LTD. 55a Paul Revere. GARY THIBEAULT 124/5 Foxwoods Casino. TOPHAM PICTURE SOURCE 209b Robert Frost. VERMONT DEPARTMENT C TRAVEL & TOURISM 237 Shelburne Boat, 253a Burlington Jazz Festival, 253b Maple Festival St. Albans. WADSWORTH ATHENAEUM 33b *Battle of Bunker Hill* (Col. John Trumbull), 42a, 43a Rauchenburg Robert Retroactive, 94/5 American XIXC Quilt. WORLD PICTURES 135 Portland Head. WORLD PICTURES 74/5 B. YARVIN 99 Litchfield. ZEFA PICTURE (UK) LTD. 70 Boston at night, 80 Café. S. ZIGLAR 25 Tanglewood Lawn.

The remaining photographs are held in the Automobile Association's own photo library (AA PHOTO LIBRARY) and were taken by M. Lynch with the exception of pages 53, 197, 207, 218 taken by C. Coe; the spine, back flap, and pages 3, 5b, 6, 9a, 10a, 12b, 18, 22a, 23, 34c, 36b, 40/1, 50, 51b, 54, 55c, 59a, 60a, 63a, 63b, 65, 68, 69, 71, 75, 76a, 76b, 82b, 86, 87, 89, 90, 92, 94, 95b, 101b, 103b, 108, 109, 110a, 110b, 111, 114a, 116a, 125, 133, 138, 140b, 141, 142, 143, 145b, 146, 147, 148, 149, 158/9, 161, 162, 163a, 163b, 170, 184, 188, 189, 190a, 190b, 191, 196b, 203a, 205, 225, 236, 245, 249, 255a, 256, 257b, 258a, 258b, 260, 261, 265b, 267 taken by R. Holmes and 8 taken by C. Sawyer.

## Acknowledgments

The authors would like to thank Sarah Mann at Discover New England, and the staff of all the state and regional offices of travel and tourism, chambers of commerce, and visitor bureaus who gave such valuable assistance in the planning, researching, and checking of this book. Thanks also go to DestINNations, Virgin Holidays Virgin Atlantic Airlines, and Northwest Airlines.

## Contributors

Original copy editor: Eric Inglefield
Revision editor: OutHouse Publishing Services    Revision verifiers: Colin Follett, Carolyn Heller